Debating Biology

Relations between the biological and social sciences have been hotly contested and debated over the years. The uses and abuses of biology, not least to legitimate or naturalize social inequalities and to limit freedoms, have rightly been condemned. All too often, however, the style of debate has been reductionist and ultimately unfruitful. As we enter an age in which ultra-Darwinian forms of explanation gather momentum and the bio-tech revolution threatens a 'Brave New World' of possibilities, there is an urgent need to re-open the dialogue and rethink these issues in more productive ways.

Debating Biology takes a fresh look at the relationship between biology and society as it is played out in the arena of health and medicine. Bringing together contributions from both biologists and sociologists, the book is divided into five themed sections:

- *Theorizing Biology* draws on a range of critical perspectives to discuss the case for 'bringing the biological back'.
- *Structuring Biology* focuses on the interplay between biological and social factors in the 'patterning' of health and illness.
- *Embodying Biology* examines the relationship between the lived body and the biological body.
- *Technologizing Biology* takes up the multiple relations between biology, science and technology.
- *Reclaiming Biology* looks at the broader ethical and political issues these agendas raise.

Written in an accessible and engaging style, this timely volume will appeal to a wide audience within and beyond the social sciences, including students, lecturers and researchers in health and related domains.

Simon J. Williams is Reader in Sociology and Co-Founder of the Centre for Research in Health, Medicine and Society, University of Warwick. **Lynda Birke** was previously Senior Lecturer, Centre for the Study of Women and Gender, University of Warwick and is now retired. **Gillian A. Bendelow** is Senior Lecturer in Sociology, University of Warwick.

Debating Biology

Sociological reflections on health, medicine and society

Edited by

Simon J. Williams, Lynda Birke and Gillian A. Bendelow

Routledge
Taylor & Francis Group

LONDON AND NEW YORK

First published 2003
by Routledge
11 New Fetter Lane, London EC4P 4EE

Simultaneously published in the USA and Canada
by Routledge
29 West 35th Street, New York, NY 10001

Routledge is an imprint of the Taylor & Francis Group

Typeset in 10/12pt Sabon by Graphicraft Limited, Hong Kong
Printed and bound in Great Britain by MPG Books Ltd,
Bodmin, Cornwall

British Library Cataloguing in Publication Data
A catalogue record for this book is available from
the British Library

Library of Congress Cataloging in Publication Data
Debating biology : sociological reflections on health, medicine,
  and society / edited by Simon J. Williams, Lynda Birke, and
  Gillian A. Bendelow.
      p. cm.
   Includes bibliographical references and index.
   1. Social medicine. 2. Biology—Social aspects. I. Williams,
Simon J. (Simon Johnson), 1961– II. Birke, Lynda I. A. III.
Bendelow, Gillian, A. 1956–

RA418.D384 2003
306.4′61—dc21

                                        2002037178

ISBN 0-415-27902-X (hbk)   0-415-27903-8 (pbk)

Contents

Contributors

Ellen Annandale is Senior Lecturer in Sociology at the University of Leicester.

Gillian A. Bendelow is Senior Lecture in the Department of Sociology, University of Warwick, and Co-Director of the Centre for Research in Health, Medicine and Society.

Ted Benton is Professor of Sociology at the University of Essex.

Lynda Birke is a feminist biologist and a freelance writer in North Wales, formerly of the Centre for the Study of Women and Gender, University of Warwick.

Mildred Blaxter is Honorary Professor of Medical Sociology in the School of Medicine, Health Policy and Practice, University of East Anglia.

Mike Bury is Professor of Sociology at Royal Holloway, University of London.

Peter Conrad is the Harry Coplan Professor of Social Sciences in the Department of Sociology at Brandeis University, USA.

Nick Crossley is Senior Lecturer in the Department of Sociology at the University of Manchester.

Basiro Davey is Senior Lecturer in Health Studies in the Department of Biological Sciences at the Open University.

Anne Fausto-Sterling is Professor of Biology and Gender Studies at Brown University in Providence, Rhode Island, USA.

Renée C. Fox is the Annenberg Professor Emerita of Social Sciences, and a Senior Fellow of the Centre for Bioethics at the University of Pennsylvania, USA. She is also a Research Associate at Queen Elizabeth House, the International Development Centre at the University of Oxford.

Arthur W. Frank is Professor of Sociology at the University of Calgary, Canada.

Eileen Green is Professor of Sociology and Director of the Centre for Social and Policy Research at the University of Teesside.

Frances Griffiths is Senior Clinical Lecturer at the Centre for Primary Health Care Studies, University of Warwick.

Brian Hall is Principal Lecturer in the Department of Applied Social Studies at London Metropolitan University (previously London Guildhall University).

Marsha Henry is Lecturer in the Centre for Health and Social Care, School for Policy Studies, University of Bristol.

Paul Higgs is Senior Lecturer in Sociology at University College London.

Heather T. Jacobson is a PhD candidate in sociology at Brandeis University, USA.

Ian Rees Jones is Professor of Sociology of Health and Illness at St George's Hospital Medical School, London.

David Kelleher is Reader Emeritus at London Metropolitan University (previously London Guildhall University).

Michael P. Kelly is Director of Research and Information at the Health Development Agency. He also holds an honorary chair in the Department of Public Health and Policy at the London School of Hygiene and Tropical Medicine, University of London.

Louise M. Millward is a Research and Development Specialist at the Health Development Agency.

Lee F. Monaghan is Lecturer in Sociology at the University of Newcastle upon Tyne.

Graham Scambler is Professor of Medical Sociology and Director of the Centre for Medical Sociology, Social Theory and Health at University College London.

Sasha Scambler is a Lecturer in Medical Sociology and Policy at the University of Surrey, Roehampton.

Anne Scott is a Lecturer in Sociology at the University of Canterbury, Christchurch, New Zealand.

Tom Shakespeare is Director of Outreach at the Policy, Ethics and Life Sciences Research Institute, Newcastle.

Bryan Turner is Professor of Sociology at the University of Cambridge and a Fellow of Fitzwilliam College.

Mike Wadsworth is Professor in the Department of Epidemiology and Public Health, University of London, and Director of the MRC National Survey of Health and Development.

Simon J. Williams is Reader in the Department of Sociology, University of Warwick, and co-founder of the Centre for Research in Health, Medicine and Society.

Introduction

Debating biology

Simon J. Williams, Lynda Birke and Gillian A. Bendelow

Why debate biology? Has biology been 'neglected' or downplayed in past/present sociological theory – as the title of this book implies? Does this matter? Can new non-reductionist positions be recovered or developed here, for instance? And what issues does this raise for contemporary debates on health, medicine and society and the challenges of the twenty-first century? These are some of the questions which contributors to this volume have addressed, starting from the premise that bridging the gap between sociology and biology does indeed matter.

'Biology' may be viewed as both a subject of scientific study and set of living processes and animating principles, with complex relations between the two.[1] As a body of knowledge, clearly demarcated from the 'human sciences', biology emerged late in the nineteenth century. For various reasons, those boundaries have since been carefully maintained, leading to schisms that bedevil any attempt to think through them. So, 'biology' has come to mean the study of processes largely internal to bodies, while 'human sciences' have focused on behaviour and practices of humans. Nonhumans, however, remain in the sphere of the biological. These divisions, which reinforce cultural separations of (human) culture from nature, and mind from body, are thus maintained by the disciplinary boundaries themselves. As a result, the living processes called 'biologica' do not seem to have a place in the study of human societies, or are seen only in terms of discursive construction. Where, then, does (the/a) sociology of health or a sociology of the body stand? And where, too, lies lived experience of those living processes, especially when they are going awry in disease?

Just as 'biology' is problematic, so too are appeals to 'nature'. It is quite possible nonetheless, as Soper rightly argues, to recognize that there is 'no reference to that which is independent of discourse', yet to 'dissent from any position which appeals to this truth as a basis for denying the extra-discursive reality of nature' (Soper 1995: 8). Nature, from this latter (realist) standpoint, refers to the 'structures, processes and causal powers that are constantly operative within the physical world, that provide the objects of study of the natural sciences, and condition the possible forms of human intervention in biology or interaction with the environment. It is the nature to whose laws we are always subject even as we harness them to human purpose, and whose processes we can neither escape nor destroy' (1995: 155–6).[2]

Sociology has not entirely neglected these questions, of course. Biological considerations, for example, can be found in classical scholarship and debate. From Marx's deliberations on man as a 'natural animal',[3] to Parsons's theorizing of relations between biological, personality, social and cultural systems, and from Spencer's (in)famous 'organic analogies',[4] to Elias's theory of 'symbol emancipation' and the 'civilizing process', the lines of these debates can be traced. To this we may add Foucault's own critical observation that sociology, or more specifically medical sociology, had its origins in nineteenth-century social medicine (Turner 1992: 152). Yet invoking the biological is far from bringing it directly into theory; on the contrary, the biological has at best served as a foil for the sociological imagination, and at worst been dismissed or denounced altogether. Either way, the biological has remained under-theorized: a problem worsened today, in many respects, given the current tendency (as touched on above) to reduce the world to our social constructions of it.

There are, to be sure, many (good) reasons for past/present sociological distrust or scepticism of the biological, in whatever guise. The *biologisms* of the recent past, for instance, including Social Darwinism, eugenics and (Nazi) racial science, could all be roundly condemned on a number of counts: 'philosophically, because they violated the logical distinction between facts and values; scientifically, because genetic differences on the distribution of mental and moral traits among individuals and races appeared insignificant; and morally, because of the cruelties committed in their name' (Kaye 1986: 2). Recourse to the biological, it seems, has too often served dubious ends: called upon to legitimate inequalities and to limit freedoms. So why invoke the biological, we might ask? Surely social and cultural change outstrips biological evolution by far?[5]

Perhaps, but that in itself does not challenge the belief proposed by many advocates of neo-Darwinism, that any processes of social evolution are nonetheless constrained by earlier processes of biological evolution. Our ancient hunting and gathering past, in this story, is the foundation of what we are today, and no amount of cultural change can wipe that away. Linked to a growing fascination with genetics, this belief has resurfaced in the guise of evolutionary psychology (EP). The dangers of a 'gene's eye' view of the world – which in the hands of EP effectively reduces us to lumbering, dispensable machines in-the-service-of our 'selfish-genes' via the 'modularized' architecture of our minds – has rightly engendered much heated discussion and debate here, particularly when accompanied by erroneous claims of a victory over a misplaced notion of the 'Standard Social Science Model' (SSSM).

What is needed then, is not a retreat into former dualisms, nor a slide into any assimilation of sociology to biology or vice versa, but (re)newed dialogue. We need to recover or develop (new) non-reductionist ways of envisaging these relations in an attempt to go beyond any such dualisms. Fortunately, there are a number of more or less promising signs here. Some biologists, for example, have sought to move beyond simple biologisms, to find other ways of speaking about living organisms and about human existence (e.g. Rose 1997). Meanwhile, challenges come from outside academia, from several of the new social movements: environmentalist and animal rights activists, for example, call into question the profound divisions between nature/culture and animal/human which underlie so much academic debate. And within sociological theory there are new challenges which expose the limits of reductionism, and which draw upon a variety of non-reductionist positions in doing so.

First, and perhaps most obviously, there have been several explicit calls to re-conceptualize the relationship between biology and the social sciences, and hence to reconstruct the established division of labour. Benton (1991), for example, over a decade ago, raised just these issues, highlighting both the urgency and desirability of a new alignment of the social with the (other) life sciences.[6] Networks of categorical oppositions of the mind/body, nature/culture, biology/society, meaning/cause, human/animal variety, he noted, were intellectual obstacles in the way of meeting many contemporary challenges, from the politics of health to ecological agendas. The task of any proposed realignment, from this viewpoint, can now be seen as one of

> providing conceptual room for organic bodily and environmental aspects and dimensions of social life to be assigned their proper place without, at the same time, abandoning the very real intellectual achievements of the 'founding figures' of the modern social sciences in defence of the autonomy and specificity of those disciplines vis-à-vis the life-science specialisms.
>
> (1991: 25)

Dickens (2000) too, whilst mindful of the historical problems of social Darwinism, seeks new ways in which evolutionary thought and social theory can be combined, bringing together historical materialism and aspects of contemporary biology to create a 'Social Darwinism' which is 'fit' for the twenty-first century. (Critical) realist agendas mesh closely with these arguments, themselves coming to the fore in social theory today as a viable if not vital alternative to the worst excesses of reductionism, be it social or biological.[7] As Sayer succinctly puts it:

> Biological, chemical and physical powers are necessary conditions for the existence of the social world but the latter has properties – particularly or 'essentially', communicative interaction and discourse, which are irreducible to or emergent from these ontological strata. If we couple this stratified ontology with a critical realist analysis of causation, in

which ... the existence of a causal power is not uniquely and deterministically linked to a particular outcome, then it becomes possible to see that the acknowledgement of a biological (and other physical) substratum of social life need not be seen as denying variety and agency at the social level. (2000: 100)

Rose and Rose's (2000) appositely entitled volume *Alas Poor Darwin: Arguments Against Evolutionary Psychology* gives further voice to these debates – from biologists, anthropologists, sociologists, cultural critics and philosophers – challenging any such reductionism whilst providing the basis for a richer understanding of the biosocial nature of the human condition.[8] Steven Rose emphasises how all organisms are engaged in evolutionary becoming; for humans particularly, that becoming has created societies, and invented technologies and cultures – and it is a becoming that enables future change rather than tying us into the past. 'We ... are profoundly shaped by [our cultures and technologies] in ways that make our futures as individuals, societies and species radically unpredictable', Rose argues; human becoming thus 'enables us to create individual lives and collective societies whose future lies at least in part in our own hands' (2000: 263).

These debates in turn link to broader concerns with the body and society. If recent sociological theory has renewed interest in the body, then we must be mindful of the need to challenge prevailing dualisms – for example, through lived notions such as *embodiment*, which helps to overcome past (sociological) problems associated with the disembodied rational actor. Bodies *become*, both as biological entities and – simultaneously – (as) socially engaged actors.

The emotions, too, in parallel fashion, have enjoyed a reversal of fortunes in recent years given centuries of neglect. Dismissing emotion (as 'irrational'), from this latter embodied perspective, is itself unreasonable and unnecessary. On the one hand, postmodern and post-structuralist critiques have proved useful here, as a source of challenge to ossified dualisms. On the other hand, this has often come at too high a price, bringing with it a form of discourse determinism, perhaps a postmodern 'free-for-all', in which the matter of bodies, to put it bluntly, is no real matter at all.[9] The sociology of the body and emotions, nevertheless, given its eclectic theoretical base and the move toward a more integrated phase of theorizing, remains a key domain and a vibrant arena in which these debates are unfolding, including some more or less promising attempts to go beyond the biological without leaving it out altogether (Hochschild 1983; Turner 1992; Williams and Bendelow 1998).

Debates within various strands of feminism echo and deepen these arguments; themselves in many ways serving to problematize (malestream) claims that the sociology of the body, let alone a 'return' to the biological, is 'new' at all. Feminists, to be sure, have experienced a somewhat ambivalent relationship to their 'biological bodies', given centuries of oppression based upon them; yet at the same time, feminist activism has necessarily drawn on concepts of biological bodies in areas such as women's health. Recent theoretical debates, nonetheless, have helped bring the biological body (back) in, in important ways – from Haraway's (1991) deliberations on the immune system and the biopolitics of postmodern bodies, to Fausto-Sterling's (2000) critical reflections on 'Sexing the body', and from Grosz's (1994) corporeal feminism, to Birke's (1999) call to bring biological science and feminist theory together in newly enmattered ways which include rather than deny our fleshy bodies. These authors seek to engage biology with feminist theory in new ways.

Men's bodies, too, have been the subject of much discussion and debate in recent years, particularly through a growing corpus of literature on masculinities (Connell 1995). The politics of gender relations, in this respect, has itself become more complex and contested, including greater attention to *differences within* as well as *similarities between* genders, and the need to think of gender as more than a social or biological dichotomy (Annandale 1998: 154).

From here it is but a short step to a series of agendas in health, in which the limits of reductionist thinking, if not the search for viable alternatives, are increasingly apparent. A number of examples may given here, from on-going research into health inequalities – particularly work on the 'socio-biological translation' and the tracking of biological and social risks across the lifecourse – through the (biological) body in chronic illness and the disability debate, to the growing popularity of so-called 'holistic health' and 'natural healing'. The 'bio-tech revolution' too, of course, with its reductionist solutions to complex problems, poses a series of important challenges in health as elsewhere. Key questions here, include the following: Is the new genetics a 'backdoor' to eugenics (Duster 1990)? How do we ensure that the benefits of these new technologies outweigh the risks? Is this the beginning of a new global phase of bio-capitalism, bio-colonialism, bio-prospective, bio-patenting, or even bio-piracy, call it what you will (Lock 2001)? Are we moreover, as some claim, on the verge of a new 'posthuman' future (Fukuyama 2002)? And what of our rights as well as our responsibilities?

Answers to these questions remain unclear. The dangers, however, should not be underestimated. Triumphalist accounts of scientific progress and the conquest of disease, and the merits of individual choice, for example, mask how genetic technologies can undermine people's freedom by intensifying genetic determinism and discrimination, individualizing responsibility for health and welfare, and fanning the flames of intolerance toward diversity (Kerr and Shakespeare 2002): eugenics by outcome, that is to say, rather than policy intent. Regulation, moreover, is largely ineffective, not least because it is all too often guided by goals of perfect health and commercial profit (Kerr and Shakespeare 2002). What is needed instead, Kerr and Shakespeare argue, is to listen to people directly affected by the new genetics, particularly disabled people and women, and to challenge the values and practices that shape genetics, thereby helping to ensure that the mistakes of the past are not repeated in the present or that problems are currently being grown for the future. 'Genomics', they conclude, 'demands both global and local monitoring and controls through democratic means. Otherwise global eugenics will flourish' (2002: 189).

The need for a critical sociology is vital here, as this suggests; one which not simply champions deliberative democracy in the public sphere, but works towards viable, non-reductionist positions to draw upon in so doing. Ecological politics and animal welfare/rights agendas, in their many forms, add further urgency and potency to these debates whilst reminding us, at one and the same time, of our place in the world and the dangers of anthropocentric self conceit (read deceit). Denying our evolutionary kinship and commonalities with other species, and/or our ecological interdependencies with living and non-living forces and process, from this latter viewpoint, is indeed unwarranted and unnecessary.

What this amounts to, then, are a series of key agendas and challenges which necessitate, nay demand, a rethinking of biology/society relations. On the one hand, as we have noted, these developments are already (well) underway. On the other hand, much remains to be done, given renewed dangers of reductionism in a new global era of bio-capitalism. Whether this spells a 'posthuman' future is of course an open question, though caution is clearly need here in any such claims. What it most certainly does spell, however, to repeat, is the need for a re-engagement or rapprochement of the biological and social sciences in a non-reductionist spirit which: (i) lays to rest the false starts and problems of the past whilst (ii) respecting the discrete analytical potential and autonomy of both in an ontologically stratified and epistemologically diverse world.

It is against this backdrop of growing concerns and emerging debates that the present volume is located. Taking critical issues and cutting-edge developments in health, medicine and society as a focal point, the emphasis here is on *debating* the salience and significance of biology/society relations as played out in these interrelated arenas and substantive domains of inquiry. Health, as noted earlier, is a key site from which to fashion these (evolving) debates given a range of pertinent topics, from the limits of biomedicine to inequalities in health, chronic illness and disability to the impact of innovative health technologies. The word *debating* is critical here. There is no policing of a distinct party line, in other words, but a commitment instead to open discussion and debate from a variety of angles and viewpoints. What does emerge very clearly, nonetheless, in keeping with the foregoing concerns, are a series of arguments which seek to recover or develop anew a series of non-reductionist positions of the *both/and* rather than the either/or variety; positions which help us meet the above challenges, in health and beyond, in a constructive and informed fashion as part and parcel of on-going dialogue and debate.

The aims of the book then, to summarize, are as follows:

(i) To *debate* critically the merits of the case for bringing 'biology' and the 'biological' 'back' into sociology (terms themselves under critical investigation);
(ii) To *expose* critically the limits of reductionist thinking, biological or social, through a range of alternative (non-reductionist) positions and (non-dualist) viewpoints;
(iii) To *explore* these issues in relation to key challenges, developments and debates regarding health, medicine and society.

Whilst our emphasis is on debating these issues sociologically, however, we have tried to draw on a variety of voices. The book, therefore, includes contributions both from sociologists (of health and illness) and (feminist) biologists, as well as those with other disciplinary backgrounds, interests and involvements (in addition to sociology) in areas such as medicine, nursing, ecology and wildlife photography. It also includes many key international figures in the field with a wealth of expertise to draw upon. A properly informed debate, we argue, demands no less.

Structure and content of the book: outlining the debates

The book is divided into five themed sections concerning various dimension of the biology/society debate, themselves cross cutting and inter-related, which in turn relate to key agendas in health, medicine and society.

The first theme, *Theorizing biology,* involves a preliminary discussion of the case for bringing the biological 'back' in, drawing on a range of critical perspectives in so doing. Key issues here include: (i) the case for an evolutionary approach to human disease which brings biological and cultural (read broadly) processes together, thereby 'bridging the gap' (Basiro Davey: Chapter 1), (ii) the limits of Ultra-Darwinism/evolutionary psychology (EP) (Paul Higgs and Ian Rees Jones: Chapter 2); (iii) feminist debates on biology, (non-human) animals and science (Lynda Birke: Chapter 3) and; (iv) critical realist attempts to theorize biology–society relations, taking Juvenile Batten disease as a case study (Graham Scambler and Sasha Scambler: Chapter 4). During the course of their contributions, the authors return to, and reassess, former dichotomized modes of Western thought and practice in an attempt to rethink biology/society relations, in ways which take us beyond the Scylla of 'biology-as-bedrock' and the Charybdis of social or cultural constructionism. The chapters, in this respect, set the stage for the contributions which follow.

The second key theme, *Structuring biology,* focuses specifically on the interplay between biological and social factors in the 'patterning' of health and illness according to factors such as class (Mildred Blaxter: Chapter 5), gender (Ellen Annandale: Chapter 6), ethnicity (David Kelleher and Brian Hall: Chapter 7) and ageing (Mike Bury and Mike Wadsworth: Chapter 8). How, for example, does society affect health deep within the recesses of the human body? What is meant by the 'socio-biological translation'? To what extent are these relations reciprocal and mutually reinforcing over time? Are developmental perspectives and life-course approaches useful here? Can the notion of 'capital' provide some sort of synthesis of these concerns? And to what extent does recourse to the biological provide the basis for a critique rather than a legitimation of existing social arrangements: a process in which the latter negates and distorts the former? These are some of the questions taken up and addressed by contributors in this section of the volume. What emerges here are a complex series of interactions and relations between biological and social factors, themselves variable at any point in time, which may indeed be more or less profitably approached through *dynamic* notions such as 'health capital' across the lifecourse.

Building on these issues, the third key theme, *Embodying biology*, focuses on the interweaving of biological and social factors in and through a series of corporeal agendas and health-related matters concerning: the problematic sex/gender and nature/nurture distinctions (Anne Fausto-Sterling: Chapter 9); childhood bodies and the limits of social constructionism (Simon Williams and Gillian Bendelow: Chapter 10); body-building, steroids and health (Lee Mongahan: Chapter 11); the biological and social dimensions of chronic illness, identity and the body (Louise Millward and Mike Kelly: Chapter 12); and the liminal qualities of sleep, death and dying (Simon Williams: Chapter 13). Key questions addressed here include the following: What do these issues reveal about the nature and status of our physical being and material existence? To what extent does an adequate sociological engagement with the body, in sickness and in health, force us to confront and incorporate the biological in social explanation? And what implications does this have for existing notions of selfhood and identity? The underlying message emerging from these diverse contributions is clear. Relations between the biological and the social are *lived*, *experienced* and *expressed* in and through our *embodied* being-in-the-world, with all the *contingency* and *uncertainty* this entails, from birth to death. The lived body and the biological body are themselves, in other words, inextricably intertwined in a mutually informing fashion: the former incorporating the latter. The ethereal body of social constructionism is thereby both problematized and more fully materialized.

The fourth section, *Technologizing biology*, takes up the multiple relations and mediations between biology, science and technology, within and beyond medicine, including debates surrounding (selective) childbirth and human reproduction in India (Marsha Henry: Chapter 14); the new genetics and disabled people (Tom Shakespeare: Chapter 15); the bio-statistical and biosocial dilemmas of hormone replacement therapy (HRT) (Frances Griffiths and Eileen Green: Chapter 16); cosmetic surgery/breast enhancement (Peter Conrad and Heather Jacobson: Chapter 17); (xeno)transplants (Renée Fox: Chapter 18); and the bio-chemical self in the era of Prozac (Nick Crossley: Chapter 19). What challenges do these developments raise? How should they be theorized and understood? What rights, risks and responsibilities are at stake here? To what extent are the very boundaries between human, animal and machine being reconfigured in the process? And what role should sociology play in these developments and debates? On the one hand, these contributions underline the bewildering array of possibilities which stretch before us: possibilities which take us from *control* to *transformation, enhancement* to *modification, replacement* to *replication.* On the other hand they remind us, in doing so, of the risks inherent in these very developments, not least the possibilities of new forms of reductionism, by default or design, intent or outcome, in this Brave New, if not 'Posthuman', World.

These foregoing debates, in turn key into a broader series of bioethical/ biopolitical agendas, themselves touched on throughout the volume but more fully addressed in this fifth and final section: *Reclaiming biology.* Key issues here include: thinking through the boundaries of bioethics in a (post)human world (Arthur Frank: Chapter 20); (realist) reflections on the relationship between biology, vulnerability and politics (Bryan Turner: Chapter 21); the red and green agendas of ecology and health (Ted Benton: Chapter 22), and finally; the search for an 'alternative' metaphysics of relations and translations between the biological and social world (Anne Scott: Chapter 23). A mobilization around the (bio)politics and (bio)ethics of health, as these chapters amply testify, has never been more vital, not least through a defence of human rights, a reaffirmation of our ecological relations and responsibilities to the world around us, and a commitment to 'alternative' visions which take us beyond the limits of reductionism and dualism alike. One outcome of rethinking issues this way, as Benton elegantly puts it, is 'to theorise social relations not simply as relations between social actors, . . . but also as relations between human social actors and elements or aspects of non-human nature: physical objects and forces, artefacts, chemical substances, populations of cultivated, domesticated and wild varieties and species of non-human animals and plants, spatial envelopes, land and ecosystems, both modified and unmodified by past human activity, and so on'. It also, of course, provides a potent rallying call to action, both inside and outside the academy, with a series of promising new alliances forged en route.

This volume, then, provides various ways of bringing biology 'back' in, both to sociology in general and to medical sociology in particular, drawing on a range of different perspectives, viewpoints and topics in so doing. These are part and parcel of an on-going (and long over-due) debate, if not collective struggle. We need to find ways of overcoming our heritage of deeply entrenched dualisms, to find ways of acknowledging ourselves as social and biological actors. The task is urgent, as new (global) threats to health and to bodily and species integrity emerge. The stakes are high: they implicate us all.

Notes

1 Critics no doubt will gleefully pounce at this point, particularly those of a strong constructionist persuasion, countering any such pronouncements themselves as socially constructed. This may well be so, but pushed to an extreme, an important insight is traded for an untenable position.
2 See also Franklin (2001) on *Nature and Social Theory*.
3 For debates as to Marx's views on these and related matters, see Geras (1983) and Benton (1989, 1993), for example.
4 It was Spencer indeed, as Dickens (2000: 19) reminds us, who coined the term 'survival of the fittest', some ten years in fact before Darwin's *Origin of the Species*. See also Benton (1991, 2000) on the Darwin–Wallace debate.
5 This flags a long-running debate as to whether we are talking here, in any such theories of social evolution, of *analogies* and *parallels* struck with the natural world, or of human society as *part* of nature (see for example Dickens 2000: 19–25).
6 Hirst and Woolley's (1986) book *Social Relations and Human Attributes* provides another important reference point here in the recent past: a book which attempts to overcome a number of divisions within sociology, including a detailed exposition and exploration of relations between biology and culture.
7 The sociology of *translation*, developed by Latour (1993) and others, is another more or less promising development here, given its refusal to countenance the notion that society is constructed through human action and meaning alone, stressing instead a variety of human and non-human relations in a hybrid world.
8 The target of these criticism includes the likes of distinguished sociologists such as Runciman (1999) who, in *The Social Animal*, draws on many of these assumptions, including Dawkins' (1976) notion of 'memes'. For a compelling critique of this 'granular' approach to culture, see Benton's (2000) chapter in the Rose and Rose volume.
9 Writers such as Haraway (1991), of course, steer a more considered path here, as one might expect from a feminist biologist and historian of science.

References

Annandale, E. (1998) *The Sociology of Health and Medicine*, Cambridge: Polity.
Baldi, P. (2001) *The Shattered Self: The End of Natural Evolution*, Cambridge, MA: MIT Press.
Benton, T. (1989) 'Marxism and natural limits: an ecological critique and reconstruction', *New Left Review*, 178, 51–86.
Benton, T. (1991) 'Biology and social science: why the return of the repressed should be given a (cautious) welcome', *Sociology*, 25, 1: 1–29.
Benton, T. (1996) 'Marxism and natural limits: an ecological critique and reconstruction', in T. Benton (ed.) *The Greening of Marxism*, New York: Guilford Press.
Benton, T. (1993) *Natural Relations: Ecology, Animal Rights and Social Justice*, London: Verso.
Benton, T. (2000) 'Social causes and natural relations', in H. Rose and S. Rose (eds) *Alas Poor Darwin: Arguments Against Evolutionary Psychology*, London: Jonathan Cape.

Birke, L. (1999) *Feminism and the Biological Body*, Edinburgh: Edinburgh University Press.

Connell, R.W. (1995) *Masculinities*, Cambridge: Polity.

Dawkins, R. (1976) *The Selfish Gene*, Oxford: Oxford University Press.

Dickens, P. (2000) *Social Darwinism*, Buckingham: Open University Press.

Duster, T. (1990) *Backdoor to Eugenics*, New York: Routledge.

Fausto-Sterling, A. (2000) *Sexing the Body*, New York: Basic Books.

Franklin, A. (2001) *Nature and Social Theory*, London: Sage.

Fukuyama, F. (2002) *Our Posthuman Future*, London: Profile Books.

Geras, N. (1983) *Marxism and Human Nature: Refutation of a Legend*, London: Verso.

Grosz, E. (1994) *Volatile Bodies: Toward a Corporeal Feminism*, Bloomington and Indianapolis: Indiana University Press.

Haraway, D. (1991) *Simians, Cyborgs and Women*, London: Free Association Press.

Hirst, P. and Woolley, P. (1986) *Social Relations and Human Attributes*, London: Tavistock.

Hochschild, A.R. (1983) *The Managed Heart: The Commercialization of Human Feeling*, Berkeley CA: University of California Press.

Kaye, H.L. (1986) *The Social Meaning of Modern Biology: From Social Darwinism to Sociobiology*, New Haven/London: Yale University Press.

Kerr, A. and Shakespeare, T. (2002) *Genetic Politics: From Eugenics to Genome*, Cheltenham: New Clarion Press.

Latour, B. (1993) *We Have Never Been Modern*, Hemel Hempstead: Harvester Wheatsheaf.

Lock, M. (2001) 'The alienation of body tissue and the biopolitics of immortalized cell lines', *Body and Society*, 7, 2–3: 63–91.

Rose, H. and Rose, S. (eds) (2000) *Alas Poor Darwin: Arguments Against Evolutionary Psychology*, London: Jonathan Cape.

Rose, S. (1997) *Lifelines: Biology, Freedom, Determinism*, Harmondsworth: Penguin.

Rose, S. (2000) 'Escaping evolutionary psychology', in H. Rose and S. Rose (eds) *Alas Poor Darwin: Arguments Against Evolutionary Psychology*, London: Jonathan Cape.

Runciman, G.W. (1999) *The Social Animal*, London: Fontana Press.

Sayer, A. (2000) *Realism and Social Science*, London: Sage.

Soper, K. (1995) *What is Nature?*, Oxford: Blackwell.

Spelman, E. (1988) *Inessential Woman: Problems of Exclusion in Feminist Thought*, Boston, MA: Beacon Books.

Turner, B.S. (1992) *Regulating Bodies: Essays in Medical Sociology*, London: Routledge.

Williams, S.J. and Bendelow, G. (1998) *The Lived Body: Sociological Themes, Embodied Issues*, London: Routledge.

Part I

Theorizing biology

Critical perspectives

1 Evolution and human disease
Bridging the biology/culture gap

Basiro Davey

The starting point for this chapter is a desire to 'clear the decks' of some old cargo concerning the antipathy between sociology and biology in the hope of not tripping over it later. Without this baggage, it becomes easier to make the case in what follows that an evolutionary perspective helps to integrate biological and sociological perspectives on human disease. The proposition that human culture (used here as a shorthand for human social interactions, structures and the products of social organization) cannot be split off from biological processes, except as a temporary act of mind, is supported by examples of interactions between biological and cultural evolution which have profoundly influenced patterns of human disease. The chapter ends with some reflections on how a biological perspective might inspire sociological interest in human evolution.

Biological determinism versus the anthropocentric universe?

One of the most impenetrable barriers to communication between sociology and biology continues to be the unflinching reductionism that characterizes many molecular biologists, summed up in a remark attributed to James Watson, co-discoverer of the molecular structure of DNA, that 'there are only atoms. Everything else is merely social work' (quoted in Rose 1988: 161). In the last two decades, molecular biology has come to dominate biological thinking about human disease, but the molecular revolution has reached evolutionary biology too. Nineteenth-century taxonomists classified organisms on the basis of similarities and differences in their physical structures, but in the twenty-first century evolutionary relationships are being reconstructed on the basis of similarities and differences in their DNA. This technology has also shed light on the origins of infectious diseases in humans and other animals – a subject discussed later.

In similar vein, Darwin's recognition of the driving force of evolution as competition between variant *organisms* for the resources that support their reproductive success, has been challenged by the proposition that the *gene* is the agent of evolutionary change. Since *The Selfish Gene* (1976), Richard Dawkins has argued that organisms are complex 'survival machines' controlled by their genes to behave in ways that maximize the propagation of those genes in subsequent generations. Influential critics of Dawkins' version of evolutionary theory (Brian Goodwin, Steven Jay Gould, Richard Lewontin, Steven Rose, among others) have stepped forward from within biology to fight what has become known as the 'Darwin wars'. But the gene remains the dominant biological motif at the start of the new millennium. Dawkins' gene-dominated vision chimes with the sentiment expressed by Watson that everything beyond the molecular is *subsidiary* to the action of genes and that human culture is a *consequence* of genetic evolution. The main objective of this chapter is to present biological and cultural evolution as a two-way street.

The deterministic language with which biologists generally describe the body and 'disease' has come under much critical scrutiny from within sociology (for example, Martin 1987; Birke 2002; and Section III, this volume). Sociologists have sought to reclaim 'illness' or 'dis-ease' as the felt experience of an individual with a personal history unfolding in a dynamic social context. The body is envisioned as a socially constructed place under siege from a biomedical description that threatens to obliterate other perspectives. The focus on individual genes as the prime determinants of disease is refuted by social research revealing patterns of distribution along gradients of material circumstances. Comparative studies within and between societies consistently find evidence that health and illness are associated with cultural variables, for example in gender relations, self-esteem or social value, which cannot be explained by biological processes.

Yet biologists generally ignore the social perspective and focus solely on *proximal* causes of disease, i.e. those operating on, within or between material bodies (of other species as well as ourselves). The *distal* causes are situated further back in a web of undifferentiated 'factors' willingly conceded to the social sciences and thereafter disregarded. Most sociologists have accepted this mutually convenient arrangement, inhabiting an anthropocentric universe in which biological influences do not intrude on analyses of disease patterns based on material deprivation or the failure of entitlement to goods and services. The impact on human societies of other life forms as sources of food, transport, traction, clothing and shelter has, until recently, been conceded to anthropology.

However, biological perspectives have begun to be welcomed into the social arena, as this book demonstrates. Biologists and sociologists have united to oppose the 'armchair theorizing' of evolutionary psychologists who deduce that human acts such as rape and infidelity evolved in our hunter-gatherer ancestors as adaptations to ensure species survival (Rose and Rose 2000; Higgs and Rees Jones, Section I, this volume). The disciplines have joined forces to research the interaction of stress and nutrition during pregnancy on foetal 'programming', and to begin unravelling how low social value or lack of control in the workplace might lead to degenerative diseases in later life (Section II, this volume). The conviction that human disease cannot be divided into biological and cultural components forms the jumping off point for the next section of this chapter.

Biology/culture interactions and the evolution of infectious disease

Language that suggests 'intentionality' often contaminates discussions of evolutionary theory, particularly where infectious disease is involved. Bacteria and viruses are described as though they had foresight and could work out which adaptations of form or function would be a 'good bet' and worth the effort of evolving. This error obscures the *random* generation of variation between individuals, regardless of species, which is one of the necessary conditions for biological evolution. Without it, nothing more complex than a single cell could have evolved and every cell would be a member of an identical clone.

Evolutionary theory counsels that modern humans and their pathogens (a collective term for all kinds of infectious agents) are only the *current* versions of life forms that remain subject to random variation among their members, and on which natural selection continues to act, as it has done since the first cells evolved 4,000 million years ago. There is no progress towards perfection. HIV is not the 'cleverest' virus ever to infect us, but only the current and *temporarily* the best-adapted version of billions of less successful variants, any of which might become dominant in the future if altered environmental conditions increase their reproductive success. This proposition can be most powerfully illustrated by examining the origins of most human infectious diseases.

Agriculture, pastoralism and human disease

The agricultural revolution began around 8,000 BC in a few scattered places in present-day Iraq, Iran, China, Mexico, the Andes and coastal West Africa. The replacement of nomadic hunter-gatherer populations by largely settled communities subsisting on locally-grown crops and the products of herded livestock (pastoralism) occurred so slowly that 4,000 years later it had not reached most of Western Europe (including the UK), South-East Asia, the Americas or Africa south of the equator. Even at the end of the fifteenth century AD, when agricultural wealth funded the start of European colonization of other continents, the indigenous peoples whose lands were appropriated still lived mainly as hunter-gatherers.

The reason for emphasizing the slow pace at which agriculture and pastoralism spread from its origins is that this cultural shift had the necessary *time* to impact on the gradual evolution of humans and their pathogens for reasons outlined below. The domestication of poultry and large mammals for food and clothing, the building of shelters from skins and thatch, and the storage of surplus provisions in defended settlements, stoked the population explosion that followed the agricultural revolution wherever it spread. However, it also brought humans into contact for the first time with the microbes, parasites and vermin that were an inevitable consequence of fixed habitation and close proximity with domesticated livestock (for an unrivalled account, see Diamond 1998). Even as the fertility rate increased due to improved food security, the upsurge in infectious and parasitic diseases drove infant mortality rates to unprecedented heights and reduced the expectation of life at birth – a position that barely changed in Europe until the middle of the eighteenth century. The impact of infection can also be traced in the decline in average adult height that followed the adoption of agriculture, and which has still not been entirely recovered in European populations despite post-war improvements in nutrition.

At first sight it may appear obvious why settled communities are more subject than nomadic peoples to infectious disease. In the absence of modern sanitation systems, waste accumulates and makes food-borne diseases inevitable; it leaks into streams and spreads water-borne infections such as cholera and typhoid. The fleas of vermin attracted to stored food bring plague and typhus; flies that also take blood from livestock transmit sleeping sickness. Malaria and schistosomiasis extend their range because the mosquitos and snails that transmit them breed in irrigation ditches.

Yet this analysis ignores one important factor: some major pathogens that cause human infectious diseases originated in *animals* brought into domestication during the agricultural revolution. Genetic comparison of human pathogens and their counterparts in domestic species reveal that tuberculosis, diphtheria, smallpox and measles originated in cattle. Pathogens of pigs, ducks, dogs and horses adapted to give rise to several other human infections, including influenza, pertussis (whooping cough), polio and the common cold. Worms and flukes that infest humans depend on pastoralism because they complete their lifecycles by circulating between people and their cattle, pigs and sheep. Of the 1,415 species of infectious and parasitic organisms currently known to cause human diseases, over 60 per cent have already been identified as originating in other animals (Taylor *et al.* 2001).

For 10,000 years pastoral communities have been continuously exposed to pastoral pathogens as people milked, slaughtered, skinned and ate their livestock and fertilized crops with animal manure. They also acquired pathogens from non-domesticated species, including primates, as forests were cleared for agriculture and grazing land. An evolutionary perspective explains how a system of cooperative social organisation (agriculture and pastoralism) enabled pathogens from domesticated species to adapt to life in human hosts. The speed with which pathogens reproduce holds the key to this first 'epidemiological exchange' and to our inability to prevent it.

Bacteria take as little as twenty minutes to replicate by cell division, viruses can reproduce billions of times in a few hours, and parasites reproduce in a few days. When any organism replicates, small random changes occur in its genes, which are passed on to its progeny, creating endless variation in the fine details of physical structure and biochemistry between individuals. Genetic variation is created when humans (and all other organisms) reproduce, but pathogens replicate so much faster than humans that they can generate vastly more variants than we can. Additionally, bacteria can transfer genetic material 'horizontally' between neighbouring cells; and when two different strains of virus infect the same host their genes can sometimes combine, creating a virus with novel properties. If a variant of a 'pastoral' pathogen is generated that can survive long enough to reproduce in a human, the disease it causes can cross the species barrier. In the new host, natural selection winnows out the least-adapted pathogens, leaving the best-adapted to expand their numbers. Over thousands of years, some become totally adapted to infecting people.

However, the evolution of new pathogens also acts as a selection pressure on human populations. Although there have only been around 400 human generations since the agricultural revolution began, a degree of resistance to animal-derived pathogens evolved in human populations where pastoralism was established at an early date. The European continent was swept by infectious diseases derived from other species, for example, losing 25 per cent of its population to plague in the fourteenth century as rats spread along trade routes from China to the English fens. The 'more resistant' individuals survived to produce more children than the 'susceptibles', passing on the genetic trait for infection resistance, so the proportion who could survive these epidemics increased in each generation. These complex evolutionary relationships exerted a profound influence on the globalization of infectious diseases in human populations.

European colonialism and the second epidemiological exchange

The accumulation of wealth from trading the products of agriculture and livestock enabled hierarchies of ownership to develop across Eurasia. There is no 'social gradient' in entitlement among hunter-gatherers, but material inequality is an insidious feature of settled cultures, evident in the current social patterning of disease and disability. Agricultural wealth created the social stratification and the distribution of political power in the ancient civilisations of Egypt, Greece and Rome. It supported the rise of medieval European societies and fuelled their colonial ambitions, which have shaped the global political economy of the modern world.

Biological influences on the current ethnic distribution of populations has received little attention compared with the impact of socioeconomic, cultural and political forces. Yet it is significant that more than 5,000 years of co-existence had already taken place between Europeans and their domestic livestock before they attempted to colonize the Americas. The first voyage of Columbus in 1492 began what the American historian Alfred Crosby has termed the 'Columbian exchange' (Crosby 1986). Within 100 years of Columbus landing in Hispaniola, the indigenous population of

North America had fallen from an estimated eighteen million to under two million, wiped out by 'European' diseases. The tiny expeditionary forces begun by Cortès (1519) and Pizarro (1531) destroyed the Aztec and Inca civilisations of Mexico and Peru, in large measure due to the import of smallpox and measles.

Death rates from 'European' infections among the colonists were relatively low because their populations had evolved some resistance after 5,000 years of living with domestic species, but the indigenous people of the Americas had rarely kept animals. It is a curious geophysical accident that so few of the native mammals and birds of the American continents had proved amenable to domestication: in parts of the Andes, wild llamas and alpacas were herded on unfenced ranges, and guinea pigs, turkeys and ducks were kept in some places. But before the colonists arrived, indigenous populations had never encountered cattle, sheep, pigs and horses, and had very little by way of 'novel' infections to exchange for the smallpox, measles, influenza, diphtheria and the rest, which destroyed them. Perhaps only syphilis made the return journey.

In the seventeenth and eighteenth centuries, a similar 'epidemiological exchange' led to the extinction of native peoples during the colonisation of other predominantly hunter-gatherer territories in Australasia, Southern Africa and the Pacific islands. The colonization of the Indian sub-continent introduced the same infections that had swept through the Americas, and the irrigated colonial plantations spread malaria and cholera from small pockets of endemic disease throughout the region and across Europe. Cholera reached London in 1832, killing 7,000 people. Only in tropical Africa, the 'white man's grave', were the colonists held back until the nineteenth century by infections to which they had evolved no immunity: yellow fever derived from monkeys, sleeping sickness caused by a parasite endemic in the vast herds of 'big game' animals, and the ever-present malaria. But the capture of twenty million slaves from these regions completed the second epidemiological exchange by transporting African pathogens to the Americas.

Present-day echoes of past epidemiological exchanges

European colonial expansion affected not only the global distribution of human infectious diseases, but also the evolution of some non-contagious conditions. For example, the genetic variants associated with cystic fibrosis occur in one person in twenty in populations of European origin – much higher than the expected ratio. People who inherit two copies of the CF gene (one from each parent) develop cystic fibrosis and, until modern advances in treatment, usually died without passing on the CF genes, which ought therefore to have declined over time in population prevalence. Evolutionary theory offers a possible explanation for the persistence of CF genes in European (but not other) populations. They would only be sustained at such a high level if a reproductive *advantage* resulted from inheritance of *one* copy of a CF gene, relative to individuals who lacked it altogether. The CF genes interfere with salt (and hence fluid) transport across cell membranes, particularly in the gut, and it is possible that inheritance of a single CF gene may reduce the loss of salts and water during diarrhoeal diseases such as cholera. CF genes may therefore be *adaptations* that increased survival and hence reproductive success in the European populations where cholera first became endemic – the population gain outweighing the deaths from cystic fibrosis.

The same process sustains a high prevalence of sickle-cell genes in African peoples, and thalassaemia in populations bordering the Mediterranean, in both cases because inheritance of a single 'disease' gene confers some protection against malaria. Most recently, a genetic variant has been identified in up to one in fourteen Caucasians, which offers some resistance to HIV infection in individuals who inherit two copies. Genetic 'archaeology' suggests it arose in Europe about 700 years ago and spread so rapidly through the population that it must have given a significant reproductive advantage to individuals who inherited it then (Stephens *et al.* 1998). The implication is that some resistance to the great medieval epidemics of plague or perhaps smallpox may have been conferred by this gene, which subsequently protected the colonists who exported European infections around the world. It may now hold the key to a genetic vaccine against HIV.

Evolution and present-day disease patterns

It could be argued that even if evolutionary processes unfolding over thousands of years can be detected in present-day disease patterns, their influence is now only a faint echo of a distant past, submerged under sociocultural forces of far greater contemporary importance. No attempt will be made here to argue otherwise, but some examples of *continuing* interactions between biological and cultural evolution at least demonstrate the importance of keeping both in view.

A third epidemiological exchange is already underway, as the globalization of air travel, tourism and the food industry transports infectious diseases to new locations, and the exploitation of pristine habitats exposes settlers to previously unknown pathogens. The impact on human evolution of AIDS can already be discerned in the rapidly falling expectation of life in Sub-Saharan Africa. The emergence of HIV and dozens of other new or transported pathogens reminds us that cultural changes alter the course of biological evolution, and that the evolutionary clock has not stopped ticking for us any more than it has for other species.

The evolution of drug resistance

The pace of change in the evolving relationships between humans and their pathogens is sometimes swift enough to be visible within the space of a few years. The rapid evolution of multiple drug-resistant (MDR) strains of pathogenic bacteria since the 1980s is an example of biological evolution being driven by cultural changes – in this case the excessive prescription of antibiotics, and the tendency to stop taking the drug before the bottle is empty. This situation has exerted a dangerous selection pressure on bacterial populations. The bacteria that survive the first few doses of antibiotic are those most resistant to the drug's action; if treatment is stopped 'early' they will repopulate their host with their more drug-resistant progeny. Antibiotic resistance in the bacterial population is driven upwards at each repetition of this cycle, until the drug becomes useless. The dosing of livestock with antibiotics and the anti-bacterial agents in household products exacerbate the problem.

Western hospitals are now breeding grounds for MDR-pathogens, including the 'flesh-eating' bacteria of tabloid headlines. They are a major cause of hospital-acquired infections (HAIs), which affected an estimated 100,000 people and contributed to over 1,000 deaths in English hospitals in 2000, at a cost to the National Health Service of £1 billion (National Audit Office 2000). In Scotland more people died as a result of HAIs than were killed in road accidents. Cultural factors driving the evolution of drug-resistant pathogens in hospitals are the over-prescription of antibiotics, poor antiseptic measures and ineffective sterilization of equipment. Paradoxically, technological and medical progress has also played a part, by increasing the number of patients who survive but stay longer in high infection-risk areas such as intensive therapy units.

A different complex of cultural factors underpins the evolution of MDR-strains of tuberculosis, which have increased significantly in many parts of the world. In the worst affected region, Estonia, over 40 per cent of all TB cases surveyed in 1999 were multiple-drug resistant (World Health Organisation 2000). The selection pressures underlying the evolution of MDR-TB are the socioeconomic conditions that promote TB itself: poverty, homelessness, unemployment and population displacement. People in these conditions cannot easily keep to a strict daily drug regimen that must be maintained for up to six months to be effective. Treatment that gets underway and stops or becomes erratic creates the optimum conditions for drug-resistant pathogens to evolve. The rapid emergence of MDR-strains of HIV in the wake of the initially successful combination therapies is already causing concern.

The asthma epidemic and the 'hygiene hypothesis'

The increasing prevalence of childhood asthma in the twentieth century, particularly in Europe and English-speaking countries, offers another example of interactions between biology and culture. The widespread belief that the asthma epidemic is due to rising atmospheric pollution is challenged by evidence from countries such as the former East Germany, which has much lower asthma rates than West German cities, despite far greater industrial pollution. Comparative studies point to a complex relationship between social conditions and the evolution of certain genes involved in the immune response against respiratory infections. The so-called 'hygiene hypothesis' (Strachan 2000) points out that asthma rates have risen as family sizes have fallen and personal and household hygiene have increased. As a result, the opportunities for 'unhygienic' contact between older and younger children in industrialized nations have steadily reduced, except in societies such as former East Germany where employment rates among women were consistently high and most children attended nurseries from early infancy.

Biological research has uncovered mechanisms that could promote asthma in 'hygienic' environments (reviewed by Holt *et al.* 1997). The immune system in babies appears to be 'educated' by early and repeated exposure to common respiratory bacteria, prompting the development of lifelong immune-response mechanisms that preferentially recognize bacterial components. In the absence of this exposure, the immune system is less able to distinguish between pathogens and other organic material entering the body in infancy, and it tends to react to harmless domestic allergens such as pet fur and the droppings of house dust mites. These allergens have increased in domestic environments as affluence has brought pets into the home, at the same time as central heating and wall-to-wall carpets have boosted mite infestation.

Thus, the asthma epidemic may be a consequence of a protective biological adaptation to infection being subverted by the effects of domestic and wider social changes. This example further illustrates the point that as cultures undergo evolutionary change, they simultaneously affect the biological universe of which they are an intrinsic part, and vice versa. The compartmentalization of biology 'outside' culture inserts an artificial barrier into what is a continuous dynamic exchange.

Taking the long view

'Biological time' simultaneously spans the 4,000 million years since the first life forms evolved, and the infinitesimal fractions of seconds in which billions of molecular interactions occur within every living cell. Multiply the two together and it becomes clear that the number of molecular interactions that have taken place within (and between) living cells during this vast expanse of evolutionary time is so huge as to be beyond estimation. Then factor in the interactions between more than 30 million species believed to be alive on earth today, and all their predecessors back through 4,000 million years, and the potential for biological change to occur over such a timescale is at once evident. The final section of this chapter offers some reflections on the 'long view' of biological evolution, which might inspire sociological imaginations.

The Red Queen hypothesis and the evolution of sex

The gradual evolution of resistance to specific pathogens in human populations has been occurring in only the last 10,000 years. It builds upon a far
more fundamental adaptation to infection evolved at least a billion years
earlier. The generation of new defences against infection in host species
cannot keep pace with the much faster reproductive rate of their pathogens.
As the Red Queen says to Alice in *Through the Looking Glass* (Carroll
1871): 'here, you see, it takes all the running you can do, to keep in the
same place'. Pathogens can cram many generations into each of their host's
reproductive cycles, continuously evolving new adaptations that counteract
the host's defences. The potential for pathogen evolution to 'outrun' the
evolution of their hosts is so apparent, that one might predict that pathogens should by now have become resistant to all host defence mechanisms.
The Red Queen hypothesis suggests that the evolution of *sex* was a key step
in preventing this catastrophe (Van Valen 1973).

The offspring of sexual reproduction make a quantum leap in terms of
their genetic difference from the previous generation, because half their
genes are derived from each of two genetically unique parents. Pathogens
that evolve more effective mechanisms for surviving in one generation of
their host are faced with a new combination of genes in the progeny of
sexual matings – and hence encounter altered host defences to which they
are less resistant. From an evolutionary perspective, sex may be an *adaptation* to infection, a product of natural selection that tipped the balance of
survival back in the host's favour. This perspective offers an interesting
backdrop to sociological discourses on gender, which take biological sex
as a 'given' rather than an evolved characteristic.

The 'us and them' problem

The anthropocentric tendency mentioned earlier constructs humans as
essentially 'different' from other organisms. A boundary is drawn around
'us' as a species, which allows all other organic matter to be viewed as
'foreign'. But turn the evolutionary clock back far enough and the inappro-
priateness of distinguishing between 'us' and 'them' is revealed.

To take one example, minute structures called mitochondria in all animal
cells, and chloroplasts (their counterparts in plants), are believed to be the
evolutionary descendants of the first single-celled organisms – primitive
algae. A theory of the origins of life proposes that these algae were incorporated into the sheltering world of later and larger cells as they evolved, and
over millennia became adapted as the mitochondria and chloroplasts we
see today. This act of incorporation of 'them' into 'us' was a defining step,
presaging the diversification of life on earth. The algae and their descendants
have trapped and released the energy that drives the moment-to-moment
molecular interactions within and between cells throughout 4,000 million

years of evolution. Viewed from this perspective, humans (and all other organisms) owe their existence to this ancient fusion between species. Additionally, some of the genes controlling human embryonic development have been acquired from the DNA of viruses; moreover, we cannot digest plants without the symbiotic bacteria in our guts.

The division of 'us' from 'them' is most eloquently demolished by the Italian philosopher-chemist Primo Levi. In *The Periodic Table* he tracks a single carbon atom arriving on earth in a meteor from a distant star. After billions of years it is fused into the skeletons of primitive sea creatures, sedimented as limestone and released into the atmosphere by the blow of a pickaxe, inhaled by a falcon, exhaled to fall in rain onto a grape vine and passes into a man as he drinks a glass of wine. It arrives at last in a human cell.

> This cell belongs to a brain, and it is my brain, the brain of *me* who is writing; and the cell in question, and within it the atom in question, is in charge of my writing, in a gigantic minuscule game which nobody has yet described.
>
> (Levi 1986: 232)

Since all matter is cycling and recycling endlessly between cells and atmospheres and the inorganic world of rocks and minerals, it makes little sense to think of human bodies as the 'products' of either our genes or our cultures, but rather as a meta-phenomenon emerging from the interaction between these two. Evolutionary theory proposes that we are, like all other life forms, 'works in progress', constantly exchanging matter with and altering our environments in endlessly perturbable relationships, which are themselves shaped by cultural forces. It is as true for biological as for sociological theory that nothing stays the same – 'matter' as much as 'meaning' is subject to continual change – and on this ground the disciplines might find common cause.

References

Birke, L. (2002) 'Anchoring the head: the disappearing (biological) body', in G. Bendelow, M. Carpenter, C. Vautier and S. Williams (eds) *Gender, Health and Healing*, London: Routledge, pp. 34–48.

Crosby, A.W. (1986) *Ecological Imperialism: The Biological Expansion of Europe 900–1900*, Cambridge: Cambridge University Press.

Dawkins, R. (1976) *The Selfish Gene*, Oxford: Oxford University Press.

Diamond, J. (1998) *Guns, Germs and Steel*, London: Vintage.

Holt, P.G., Sly, P.D. and Böjrkstén, B. (1997) 'Atopic versus infectious diseases in childhood: a question of balance', *Pediatric Allergy and Immunology*, 8: 53–8.

Levi, P. (1986) *The Periodic Table* (paperback edition), London: Abacus, Sphere Books Ltd.

Martin, E. (1987) *The Woman in the Body*, Milton Keynes, Bucks: Open University Press.

National Audit Office (2000) *The Management and Control of Hospital Acquired Infections in Acute NHS Trusts in England*, London: HMSO.

Rose, S.P.R. (1988) 'Reflections on reductionism', *Trends in Biological Science*, May: 161–2.

Rose, H. and Rose, S. (eds) (2000) *Alas Poor Darwin: Arguments Against Evolutionary Psychology*, London: Jonathan Cape.

Stephens, J.C., Reich, D.E., Goldstein, D.B. *et al.* (1998) 'Dating the origin of the CCR5-32 AIDS-resistance allele by the coalescence of haplotypes', *American Journal of Human Genetics*, 62: 1507–15.

Strachan, D.P. (2000) 'Family size, infection and atopy: the first decade of the "hygiene hypothesis"', *Thorax*, 55 (Suppl. 1): S2–S10.

Taylor, L.H., Latham, S.M. and Woolhouse, M.E.J. (2001) 'Risk factors for human disease emergence', *Philosophical Transactions of the Royal Society of London*, 356: 983–9.

Van Valen, L.M. (1973) 'A new evolutionary law', *Evolutionary Theory*, 1: 1–30.

World Health Organisation (2000) *Anti-Tuberculosis Drug Resistance in the World: Report No. 2, Prevalence and Trends*, Geneva: WHO.

2 Ultra-Darwinism and health

The limits to evolutionary psychology

Paul Higgs and Ian Rees Jones

Introduction

In Ian McEwan's best-selling novel *Enduring Love* (1998) one of the main characters, Joe, gives a glowing description of the 'intellectual revolution' brought on by Darwinian-influenced forms of thought such as evolutionary psychology. He goes on to suggest that this revolution shattered the post-war consensus of a malleable human nature. Instead, humans have a 'nature', part of which is fixed and part of which is developmental. The fact that a novel such as *Enduring Love* can deal with, and to a considerable degree, sympathize with evolutionary psychology demonstrates the impact of what Steven Jay Gould has called 'Ultra-Darwinism'. There have been many battles as to the intellectual respectability and coherence of Ultra-Darwinism and its earlier incarnation of sociobiology, and it is clear that they will continue for the reasons McEwan's protagonist suggests. Our task in this chapter is to comment on evolutionary psychology as the most recent form of Ultra-Darwinist argument presented to the social sciences and to show how it seeks to change the relationship between biology and social science. Using examples from the sociology of health we demonstrate that evolutionary psychology ultimately reduces the social to the biological in ways that generally preclude further analysis of the complexity of social relations.

Why have Ultra-Darwinist accounts of social processes become dominant in recent years? It could be argued that their growing strength is related to advances in biology, genetics and game theory. Another reason may be that these accounts have successfully distanced themselves from what is now seen as the discredited discipline of sociobiology. These new accounts stress that they cannot be used to justify racist conclusions by arguing that all humans share a common biological and adaptive root. Others have tried to argue that there is also no necessary connection between these views and the conservative right. Ultra-Darwinist thought has also successfully colonized public discourse through the popularizing of 'evolutionary psychology' in many different media particularly through the vehicle of popular science books aimed at a mass market. This chapter will begin therefore by addressing the assumptions of this 'new' approach to the relationship between biology and social science.

Evolutionary psychology: the new sociobiology?

In 1998, E.O. Wilson wrote 'that all tangible phenomena from the birth of stars to the workings of social institutions . . . are ultimately reducible . . . to the laws of physics' (Wilson 1998: 297). Few contemporary writers would probably go as far as Wilson who is best known as the founder of the discipline of sociobiology. In recent years, the hard line position that all social understanding will be based on biology has been superseded by a softer more flexible approach that recognises some limits to biology. Indeed, many of the more recent writers go out of their way to distinguish themselves from earlier sociobiology, claiming that the approach of evolutionary psychology for instance is not sociobiology by another name.

The new 'softer' approach places a greater emphasis on the 'brain' as a depository for a complexity of evolved dispositions that interact with the social environment. Genetic survival and reproduction is still at the heart of all animate life but in humans at least, there are evolved psychologies also at work. The route from gene to behaviour goes via a 'big brain' that has some flexibility in determining the outcome of the link between genes and behaviour. This added sophistication, many evolutionary psychologists believe, moves them away from genetic determinism towards a radical and important new discipline capable of explaining many aspects of individual and social behaviour.

In its essentials, evolutionary psychology applies our grasp of evolutionary processes acting by selection over thousands of generations to our historical understanding of human societies. Humans have evolved over millions of years but the evolution of modern humans has occurred in the most part in the context of nomadic hunter-gatherer societies. The environment in which these hunter-gatherer societies existed is characterised as one of physical, social and cultural consistency. The time that humans have spent in hunter-gatherer communities is long enough for behaviours to be selected for and adaptation to occur. This social context is referred to by some evolutionary psychologists as the Environment of Evolutionary Adaptedness (EEA). Following from this it is argued that modern humans have been 'selected' for a specific environment which no longer generally exists. The move away from EEA began about 12,000 years ago with the introduction of agriculture. A further radical shift occurred with the development of industrial societies approximately 200 years ago which moved humans even further away from the realities of a hunter-gatherer existence. The introduction of industrialization involved rapid social and cultural change and created instability. This occurred over an insufficient period for any selection processes to have a major effect. Thus, for evolutionary psychology, human physiology, psychology and behaviour are adapted to function in a specific hunter-gatherer environment rather than in agriculture or industrialization. In facing the environmental, physical, cultural and social demands of the twenty-first century we are like square pegs in round holes. Much of our behaviour and physical and mental illness as well as variations between groups and between generations, genders, parents and siblings can therefore be explained by reference to our evolutionary past.

However, this elegant and seductive account hides a multitude of sins. Sociobiology and evolutionary psychology attempt to use science to explain the meaning of our existence (Kaye 1997). This is the metaphysical baggage at the core of these positions. This core transforms the science into myth despite its reductionist roots. Moreover, there is a tendency to move beyond explanations of 'natural' phenomena to justify and validate behaviour. Thus, human actions are given a 'cosmic sanction' by reference to their being adaptive. The sexual fickleness of males is an oft-cited example. Ultra-Darwinist thought also tends to anthropomorphize evolutionary processes. The selfish gene is the most well-known example of this (Dawkins 1976). Through the construction of metaphor to explain the 'gene's eye' view of the world, selfish genes become 'deified' and myths are created. Equally, the notion of a stable evolutionary environment (EEA) has been criticized. Work by Creaven (2000) illustrates the gross assumptions underlying the undifferentiated nature of hunter-gatherer society by contrasting them with more pluralist accounts of the anthropological record. These criticisms however fail to acknowledge the shift in evolutionary thought from selfish individuals to notions of altruism. Despite many claims to the contrary, evolutionary psychology is still open to the charge of reductionism. Genes are segments of DNA that code for the construction of protein molecules. The purpose of genes is to produce more genes and natural selection occurs at the level of the gene. Evolutionary psychologists argue that the brain is hard-wired to serve this purpose. This does not, however, make the problem of reductionism disappear. For here it is the mind that is reduced to the genetically determined neuronal machinery of the big brain. In other words, however large a role given to the brain by the evolutionary psychologist, it is still based on hard-wired genetic programming. Human culture is still ultimately bound to biology and where human reason diverges from the need for genetic success it is potentially maladaptive. Finally, by privileging adaptive qualities and taking a gene's eye view of things, evolutionary psychology is potentially dehumanizing as it leaves little room for reflexivity or consciousness. For example, Badcock argues that we are not designed to understand the idea of evolution because it mitigates against individual survival and reproductive success. For humans to understand their very limited role in the order of things would not be good.

The result is that human beings suffer from a psychological myopia where their own existence and importance in the grand scheme of things is concerned. They see themselves and their immediate environments clearly, but their minds cannot grasp the vast expanses of other humans and evolutionary time that surround them.

(Badcock 2000: 36)

Sociology and evolutionary thought

W.G. Runciman, in recent work (Runciman 1998) argues that it is possible to apply evolutionary theory sociologically. In the past, there has been a considerable amount of evolutionary thought in sociology from Comte, Spencer, Marx, Weber to Michael Mann. However, Runciman has explicitly tried to use a neo-Darwinian approach. He posits a non-teleological theory of qualitative change, where there is no necessary progress towards a pre-determined end state. Accepting that there is genetic transmission over successive generations, culture also has similar properties. Using Richard Dawkins' idea of 'memes' (Dawkins 1976) as the appropriate unit of transmission, culture is information that has been successfully transmitted over time by the process of 'descent with modification'. In depicting processes of information transfer as the mode of activity, the charge of seeing evolution as metaphor is avoided. Runciman draws a distinction between his anti-reductionist view of evolutionism and the reductionism of sociobiology. Accusations of genetic reductionism, he argues, are incorrect because evolutionary psychology implies flexible and conscious decision-making in response to environmental change. He claims ideological neutrality for his evolutionist perspective and emphasizes the scientific basis for his approach claiming that testable hypotheses are derivable from positing a causal mechanism for information transfer thus avoiding the 'just so' stories of sociobiology. However, Runciman has been criticised for applying analogies for 'natural selection' to human institutions. Benton (2000) goes further in arguing that Runciman has a 'machine view' of human agency and draws too heavily on the circular reasoning of evolutionary psychology. He argues that the problem for sociologists is that we believe that 'societies, unlike species do have designers'.

> So there is a place for unintended consequences, contingency and impersonal forces in historical explanation: but these are the results of institutional structures, power relations, social conflicts, mistaken assumptions, betrayals, communicative failures, and so on of intentional agents not of 'machines' for the 'replication of practices'.
>
> (Benton 2000: 216)

Consequently, evolutionary psychology adds little to sociology that is not either already there or erroneous in its reductionism. Bringing an Ultra-Darwinist approach into sociology leads, as Benton points out, to a view that society is just the outcome of mental processing on the part of individual people who make it up. This becomes apparent if we consider some examples of evolutionary approaches to research addressing social issues in health.

Applications to health and welfare

Much of the evidence for evolutionary explanations in health is dependent on the statistical relationships between variables produced by so-called 'black box' epidemiology and an acceptance of medical and social data as natural facts. For example, data on crime and disease rates are presented without reference to the cultural and social contexts in which they are produced and re-produced. These 'facts' are then used to buttress explanations that are rooted in notions of biologically determined 'fixed' behaviour. While evolution is a process, much evolutionary psychology research postulates hypotheses linking evolution and modern human behaviour. For example, explanations for the differential rates of AIDS globally have concluded that populations of African ancestry are 'inclined to greater frequency of uninhibited disorders such as rape and unintended pregnancy' (Rushton and Bogaert 1989). As 'proof' of this they argue that people of Asian ancestry have a greater frequency of inhibitory disorders and therefore a lower rate of sexually transmitted disease. Ironically, rates of HIV infection are increasing in Asia regardless of such 'inhibitory' characteristics. Christopher Badcock, on the other hand, seeks to explain anorexia nervosa in terms of evolutionary adaptive behaviour of women's need for reproductive success. Anorexia is triggered in young women as a way of suppressing fertility as a way of postponing their reproductive lives (Badcock 2000: 164). There are, however, elements of the evolutionary psychology canon that present a more sophisticated 'take' on the approach and in so doing represent an important challenge to our understandings of social aspects of health and illness.

Health inequalities

Bruce Charlton, in developing evolutionary based accounts of inequalities in health (Charlton 1996), argues that the causes of economic stratification and the correlation between social location and health can be traced to evolved universal human psychological processes. According to him, we are designed for the EEA but live in post-industrial societies. He states: 'it is this mismatch which leads, ultimately to health inequalities' (Charlton 1996: 3).

Charlton focuses on three adaptive behaviours: nepotism, reciprocal social exchange and the drive to seek higher social rank manifest in strategies of sexual selection. He argues that the 'status-seeking instinct' is the ultimate cause of the association between class and health. Causation is however indirect because health is affected by access to resources. To support his argument he cites evidence from archaeological studies showing necessary association between status and life expectancy in hunter-gatherers where status was not linked to resources and contrasts this with agricultural societies where there is evidence of substantial differences in life expectancy. He goes further to cite arguments for an instinct for egalitarianism and sharing in hunter-gatherers as a way of avoiding conflict and maintaining stability – called counter dominant instincts. This is where many critics of evolutionary psychology make a fundamental mistake, assuming that there is a necessary correspondence with selfish behaviour. Charlton argues that within all of us therefore there are drives to dominate and drives to share – the result he argues, is 'equal but vigilant sharing'. Changes to society that involve an over-emphasis on competition could therefore be seen as damaging because they go against our instincts and drives. He argues that the research agenda for inequalities in health should focus on these mechanisms, particularly those that might be maladaptive to our present day environment. He postulates that the drive to increase status may be damaging to health and relates this to risky behaviour among young men and the link between stress, status and coronary heart disease. Charlton extends his argument to the notion of long-termism and status-dependent abilities to invest in the future. He argues that the marked class gradient in smoking and non-smoking behaviour patterns is influenced by a working-class propensity to short-termism. The biological foundations of social inequalities postulated here are also present in the work of Wilkinson on the importance of social hierarchy.

> When facing imminent physical danger and risk of wounding, it is important that the blood should clot quickly in order to minimize blood loss. This is achieved by increases in the clotting factor, fibrinogen, in response to increased adrenaline produced during stress. In monkeys the most common attacks are by dominant animals on subordinates. But higher fibrinogen levels are also more common in junior office staff, as if their subordinate positions put them at risk of physical attack from their superiors. Increased fibrinogen levels seem to be one of the contributors to the much higher rates of heart attack in junior staff than in senior staff.
>
> (Wilkinson 2000: 48)

Focusing on the psychosocial impact of hierarchy often minimizes discussion of the social structures that give rise to inequality (Coburn 2000). Dealing with effects rather than causes has been criticized from the Black Report onwards. To understand the global nature of health inequalities it is clearly not productive to rely on the importance of evolved dispositions.

Step-parents

Daley and Wilson's work on murder in families is one of the most frequently cited works in the evolutionary psychology canon (Daly and Wilson 1988).

They hypothesized that parents care less for children where they have no genetic link than for children where they do have a genetic link. The cited evidence to support this hypothesis is higher rates of child murder among step-parents in Canada. However, work on Swedish data reverses these findings and raises doubts about the claims (Temrin *et al.* 2000). Daly and Wilson are criticized for glossing over statistical problems with small numbers of events. They also lump together many different and diverse family situations. Definitional differences between lovers, and step-fathers, recent partnership and long-standing relationships are ignored. Daly and Wilson's own data do not necessarily support their original hypothesis given that many step-fathers are 'good' parents. Crucially, the Swedish data point to the fact that genetically related children in step-families were more likely to be killed by the genetic parent than the non-genetically related one. Social conditions in Sweden and Canada such as ease of abortion and the existence of criminal records also influence such homicides. Overall, parental investment strategies play a limited role in explaining patterns of child homicide, the social context in which families exist being much more important.

These examples have been chosen because they represent two of the most influential applications of evolutionary causality in the field of health and welfare. While they certainly can provide 'food for thought', the narrowness of their reading of the link between the biological and the social inhibits further research. The problem, as Rose points out (Rose 1997), is in the tendency towards totalizing genetic explanations. Dynamic social phenomena are transformed into fixed measurable characteristics for the purpose of analysis (often of a limited form). Complexity is ignored in the rush to localize the causes of social phenomena in the brain. Moreover, by claiming scientific neutrality, the immersion of these approaches in political positions is often unacknowledged.

Politics of evolutionary psychology

Social Darwinism has had a long and tainted history. The furious arguments around sociobiology are merely the latest episode. Evolutionary psychology claims to have no political line, to be free of ideology and only interested in promoting a scientific view of who human beings 'really are'. However, the naturalistic fallacy is an ever-present feature of Ultra-Darwinist thought. Socio-political judgements are made by taking a leap from *is* (i.e. it is natural) to '*ought*' (i.e. then it must be right and good). The danger is that the basic approach can be used to validate and justify the status quo. For example, arguments that social inequalities are bad because they are unnatural, may appear a challenge to right-wing free-market individualism. However, the challenge is flawed because it only questions that which disturbs notions of what is good by reference to evolution. For instance, if it can be shown that certain types of child-rearing practices have evolutionary explanations and justifications then other types of child-rearing practices must be suspect. Glass ceilings exist because women choose low incomes because that is their biological reality (Browne 1998). Women are not natural risk takers, they care less about money, status and power, their talents lie elsewhere. The implicit conservatism and anti-feminism is obvious. Furthermore, we would argue along with Kaye (1997) that evolutionary psychology goes beyond the naturalistic fallacy. The description of what *is* is guided by the myths, metaphors and metaphysics of the discipline and this in turn influences the drive to speculate on the leap from is to ought. A reification occurs where what is considered 'natural' is judged so by reference to evolutionary psychology's criteria and these in turn support the development of the criteria by which judgements are made.

Whereas to reform Darwinists (e.g. Huxley) human culture could free us from natural selection, now in the early twenty-first century, post-industrial societies are our oppressors because they suppress our biological needs and drives. So modern disease patterns, manifest in the epidemiological transition, are symptomatic of our biological evolution being out of synch with modern social, cultural and economic environments in which our bodies function. The moral task therefore is to master modern culture. Such thinking appears to be informed by a sense of crisis in modern culture. But, as we have noted earlier, evolutionary psychology does not necessarily support the conservative capitalist ideology. Rather it is a form of 'Romanticism' (Kaye 1997) a mythical Ur-harmony between nature and human culture. It has been noted in the past that reductionism and associated scientific moralities become attractive in times of social and cultural confusion. Clearly as wider social processes collapse, evolutionary psychology fits easily with an atomized society in which social change is off the agenda. The importance of evolutionary psychology in these times is as much in what it excludes as what it promotes. The possibility of multiple levels in evolution as expounded by Gould, Lewontin and others is dismissed as politically inspired. Rose's idea of lifelines (Rose 1997) and the complexity of the relations that the human-biological organism experiences are similarly ruled out.

Evolutionary psychology is a new name for sociobiology and at the same time it is something new in itself. It is susceptible to the same critiques as those levelled against sociobiology, because it shares the same reductionism. However, because of its notions of adaptive altruism and within-group and without-group conflict, it captures people's imagination. In essence it is part of the political zeitgeist. As we have argued elsewhere (Higgs and Jones 1999) evolutionary accounts may lack *validity* but by offering simple and plausible explanations they have a *viability*. This viability connects with post-modern pragmatism and through it evolutionary psychology could increasingly dominate thinking.

Ultra-Darwinism and a note of caution

After fierce debates within sociology, social constructionism has risen to pre-eminence over the last twenty years and indeed has become somewhat institutionalized. Social constructionism gained its momentum from developments in the sociology of knowledge, from social and cultural anthropology and from politicized reactions to scientific medical power, perhaps most notably feminist critiques of medicine and medical technology. The standard view that science is seen to have a privileged access to 'nature' is one very clearly espoused by evolutionary psychology. Sociologists have pointed to the flaws in this claimed objectivity which in reality is saturated in relations of power. The 'knowledge' claims of medicine and science cannot be separated from its practices and institutions. The practices and concerns of evolutionary psychology, such as the use of social 'facts' to buttress moral arguments or a reliance on the 'objective' and 'amoral' gene, are easily subjected to a host of different criticisms and interpretations. Foucaldian analyses point to there being many discourses of the human body, the bio-medical being merely one. Here there is no such thing as an 'authentic' human body existing outside medical discourse. There are no essential features to the body, its evolution or indeed its evolved psychology. In effect the body is historically and culturally located. From this viewpoint, attempts to paste our understandings of biology on to ethnocentric understandings of nomadic society, and then re-import the result to develop explanations to support our historically and culturally contingent understandings of modern illnesses, are an enormous conceit.

Social constructionist approaches to the body promulgate over-socialized and over-politicized accounts. In so doing, they may be neglecting experiential dimensions of the body and effectively ignoring the effects of biological processes and their medical manipulation on people's lives. Contributions to this volume, in contrast, attempt to incorporate social and biological facts into accounts of the body. The chapter by Scambler and Scambler on juvenile Batten disease, for example, draws attention to the need for realist accounts of the body located in its physicality. In drawing together the biology and sociology of people with disabilities and chronic illnesses we need to go beyond experiences and give some role to biological processes that lie underneath the phenomenological level. This means that we have to engage with the ontology of human embodiment and here some of the debate connected to evolutionary psychology can be helpful.

What features of the connection between the body and society does evolutionary psychology make us address? First and foremost is an acceptance that the biological body is a product of evolutionary processes. The fact that we stand up gives rise to back pain, it also means that people who cannot use their legs are differently-abled. In both cases the biological has different consequences for the social. Back pain causes time off work and is therefore an economic issue while the lack of opportunity for wheelchair users is a component in their oppression. There are many other examples of the biological basis to human existence. What is important is not to reduce one to the other as evolutionary psychology often does. There are proximal and distal effects and causes for both biological and social processes. Sociology should attempt to integrate rather than explain away these interconnections.

Acknowledging our biological influences creates opportunities as well as limits and consequently has considerable implications for our understanding of perceptions of the self, identity, risk and the body. There is a tension in the sociological literature of the body, between the importance given to the body in post-modern culture as a focus for our identities, one that has no firm foundations, and attempts to reintroduce biological elements into theories of social action. The discourse of the biological is at individual, social and political levels. If there is no sociological understanding of these discourses at these levels, there can be no appropriate sociological intervention. The ground is surrendered to those for whom the biological is more fixed and the social merely reflective. What this means is that sociologists will have to confront some of their own weaknesses regarding biological foundations of topics such as language acquisition, strength and endurance of biological ties, and gender differences in health.

A second point that needs addressing is what could be termed the biological consequences of social processes. Evolutionary psychology places considerable importance on how the biological is influenced by psychological processes. The social sciences are already there but in an uncritical way. A considerable amount of social epidemiology is concerned with demonstrating how social position or social processes have short- and long-term effects on biological processes, whether this be black lung amongst miners or high cortisol levels among stressed office workers. A major thesis for social inequalities in health relates directly to diet amongst mothers during pregnancy leading to damage of the neural tubes of foetuses. Very few social constructionist writers would dispute these facts (though they might question the organization of them). For these reasons it is important to see that avoiding arguments that start with the biological leads, ultimately, to ineffective social science.

Whilst there has been much discussion about our biological origins and genetic determination, what increasingly seems to be the case is the transcendence of the biological and any direct relation to evolutionary processes. For example in the field of ageing, not only can people live longer, because of medical interventions, but some of the fundamentals of life itself seem to be challenged. The reality of IVF overcoming infertility is only matched by post-menopausal women conceiving and having children. A new set of issues may have been brought into being by these developments, but they are more the arena of ethics than biology. This suggests that the idea of biological fixity should be tempered by our capacity to change the environment.

If, as we have identified, there is a need for us to engage with these ideas then we must do so with a proper notion of grounded behaviour if we are to construct oppositions. It is possible to see limits to the application of these ideas. What form should society take? What preventive strategies are involved. Do these include: selective abortion, education, policing, imprisonment or sterilization? How are maladaptive behaviours to be identified in this nightmare world? We need to take some ideas seriously and engage with these accounts. We should not be afraid to examine the impact of these ideas on people's experiences of health and illness, on the implications for population medicine and the ways these ideas are channelled and expressed through the mass media.

Conclusion

The claims evolutionary psychology makes to be different to sociobiology do not free it from many of the criticisms levelled at earlier proponents of evolutionary explanations for human behaviour. Much of evolutionary psychology relies on thin concepts of society and flawed understandings of social processes. The utilization by evolutionary psychologists of a stereotypical standard social science model (SSSM) which sees all social thinking as starting with the mind as a *tabula rasa* infinitely capable of adaptation is clearly wrong. Social constructionists, on the other hand, too easily fall into expressing this categorization. They do not engage with these problems but rather by-pass them by reference to the contingency of scientific facts and the culturally dependent nature of scientific discourse. In contrast, we would argue, human beings need to be seen as having evolved. But, the importance of this fact is far overweighed by the last 12,000 years of human history. From the development of agriculture onwards we, as a species, create ourselves and now even have the capacity to destroy ourselves. Sociology is about understanding social processes and social institutions, but we need to have an adequate understanding of how human subjects are constituted human in the first place. From a classically Marxist perspective Norman Geras writing about Marx's conception of human nature writes:

> if human beings have a history which gives rise to the most fabulous variety of social shapes and forms, it is because of the kind of beings they, all of them, are; human nature . . . plays a part in explaining the historical specificities of the nature of man.
>
> (Geras 1983: 108)

In conclusion, as concept-bearing agents, we have the capacity to objectify biology. Evolutionary psychologists make this mistake by focusing on the selfish gene. On the other hand social constructionists view any engagement with biological accounts of our species with suspicion. They are equally guilty of objectification. Neither response is necessary or logical. We argue that the objectification of nature does not allow us to see the proper relationship that we have with nature. Bio-social accounts of humans remain underdeveloped because the field remains cluttered with the 'straw men' produced by these two camps. Realist sociology can play a role in clearing the field by engaging constructively with the biological.

References

Badcock, C. (2000) *Evolutionary Psychology: A Critical Introduction*, Cambridge: Polity.

Benton, T. (2000) 'Social causes and natural relations', in H. Rose and S. Rose (eds) *Alas Poor Darwin: Arguments Against Evolutionary Psychology*, London: Jonathan Cape.

Browne, K. (1998) *Divided Labours: An Evolutionary View of Women at Work*, London: Weidenfeld and Nicholson.

Charlton, B. (1996) 'What is the ultimate cause of socio-economic inequalities in health? An explanation in terms of evolutionary psychology', *Journal of the Royal Society of Medicine*, 89: 3–8.

Coburn, D. (2000) 'Income inequality, social cohesion and the health status of populations: the role of neo-liberalism', *Social Science and Medicine*, 51: 135–46.

Creaven, S. (2000) *Marxism and Realism*, London: Routledge.

Daly, M. and Wilson, M. (1988) *Homicide*, New York: Aldine de Gruyter.

Dawkins, R. (1976) *The Selfish Gene*, Oxford: Oxford University Press.

Geras, N. (1983) *Marx and Human Nature: Refutation of a Legend*, London: Verso.

Higgs, P. and Jones, I.R. (1999) 'Evolutionary psychology and health: confronting an evolving paradigm', *Journal of Health Services Research and Policy*, 4, 3: 187–90.

Kaye, H. (1997) *The Social Meaning of Modern Biology: From Social Darwinism to Sociobiology*, Newhaven: Yale University Press.

McEwan, I. (1998) *Enduring Love*, London: Vintage.

Rose, S. (1997) *Lifelines: Biology, Freedom, Determinism*, London: Penguin.

Runciman, W.G. (1998) 'The selectionist paradigm and its implications for sociology', *Sociology*, 32: 163–88.

Rushton, J.P. and Bogaert, A.F. (1989) 'Population differences in susceptibility to AIDS: an evolutionary analysis', *Social Science and Medicine*, 28, 12: 1211–20.

Temrin, H., Buchmayer, S. and Enquist, M. (2000) 'Step-parents and infanticide: new data contradict evolutionary predictions', *Proceedings of the Royal Society of London*, 267: 943–5.

Wilkinson, R.G. (2000) *Mind the Gap: Hierarchies, Health and Human Evolution*, London: Weidenfeld & Nicolson.

Wilson, E.O. (1998) *Consilience: The Unity of Knowledge*, London: Little, Brown & Co.

3 Shaping biology

Feminism and the idea of 'the biological'

Lynda Birke

What does the call to 'bring back' the biological mean? Was biology ever in the social sciences in the first place? Being a biologist working on feminist theory has always been a tricky path for me to tread, not least because academic feminism has so long played down the biological. And within feminism, there has been another slippery path: for while the biological processes of the body are largely absent from theory, they are always there – if problematically – in much feminist activism, particularly around women's health.[1] So, if I speak as a biologist or as an activist, I tend to use the language of empirical science, with its reliance on facts and probabilities; but if I move to theory, I must be familiar with the fashionable rhetoric of 'discourses' and 'representation' of the body. Bringing them together, bringing the biological and bodily health, into how we theorize the body, is not an easy task.

Moreover, if we are to debate how (or if) we want to 'bring biology back', then we need to know what it is that we do *not* want (crude genetic determinism, for example). And, importantly, we need to identify *what kind* of biology we want to readmit. 'Biology' is both a subject of study, and a term used to describe set(s) of processes by which organisms work (as in 'human biology'). Some areas of biology-as-practice get a great deal of attention (such as biotechnology and modern genetics), both in scientific literature and in social criticism. Feminist critics of science have focused, for example, on claims made about the power of particular genes to affect human characteristics (and particularly behaviour), as well as the potential harms that might result from genetic manipulation. Another area receiving critical focus is evolution, especially in the form of evolutionary psychology, with its implications that many aspects of our behaviour are hard-wired into us through natural selection.

Yet the study of biology is much more than that. In this chapter, I want to use two areas of inquiry as starting points in order to frame my question about what kind of biology we want to allow back in. One of these is feminist work on the body, and, to a lesser extent, I draw also on ideas about how we think about nonhuman animals. Our ideas about what biology is relies heavily on particular ideas about animals; moreover, how we think about bodies and their processes derives much from experimental procedures involving the bodies of animals. For these reasons we need to bring animals into sociology as much as 'the biological'.

Both of these sources call into question the divisions between biology and the social. Clearly, if feminists are to explore 'the biological', then we do not want that to mean new ways of speaking about biological underpinnings of gender: it is precisely such determinism that we have fought strenuously for so many years. But that struggle cannot deny the biological body altogether – the domain of so much excellent feminist activism throughout the world in women's health (see for example, Shodhini 1997). Nor should it deny the ways in which our knowledge of bodies is derived. So, exploring 'the biological' must also question how and why nonhuman animals always fall into that category, while human behaviour does not – a division which itself reinforces biological determinism (Birke 1994). So, my main focus here is to indicate, first, the meaning(s) of biology that we might want to reject, then, second, to indicate some kinds of biology that might be more acceptable.

Separating ourselves from biology: better things to do with our lives?

Western feminism, like several other of the new social movements, has had an ambivalent relationship with biology.[2] Feminism shares with the social sciences in general a history of rejecting (or at least ignoring) the biological: yet this rejection has added poignancy, for women are so often culturally associated with the messy, abject, body and its biological functions. In that sense, biology poses *particular* problems to feminism over and above the problems it poses to sociology. As Elizabeth Spelman has noted, attending to bodily needs has fallen on women throughout Western history: 'Superior groups, we have been told from Plato on down', she notes, 'have better things to do with their lives' (1988: 127). 'Inferior' groups have tended to become associated with bodily functions, with nature, with animality: small wonder that feminists have sought to avoid the biological – if by 'biological' we imply something fixed, essential and bestial.

In part, this rejection of the biological stems from a politically necessary opposition to crude biological determinism. Women, we have had to assert, are not simply born into the role of housewife. But that rejection assumes a model of the body as somehow fixed and presocial. This assumption in turn is fuelled by the growing power of genetic narratives which, in their most extreme forms, posit bodies as epiphenomena, mere carriers of the genes.

It is hardly surprising, then, that Western feminists of the 1970s and 1980s critiqued crude biological determinism – which is so contrary to the possibilities of social change – and advocated that gender and sexuality were socially constructed. Strategically necessary though that move was, it relied on rather simplistic (and dualistic) notions of gender, separated out from 'sex' as a kind of biological substrate. Later, with the increasing prevalence of postmodernism, a new wave of feminist theory emerged in the 1990s which questioned ideas of sex as substrate, and which prioritized flux and the discursive construction of our ideas about gender/sexuality.

Yet the problems of biological/social dualism remain. The biological body is still treated differently from human behaviour. Feminists tend to object strongly (and with good reason) to claims that, say, women's hormones predispose them to like ironing (see Birke 1999). Yet few of us, I assume, would want to contest that oestrogens affect the uterus, or that evolutionary processes have helped to shape our opposable thumbs. So, the objections to determinism applied only to human behaviour and not to the biological body – a tricky distinction.

Nor did the objections apply to animals. Rather, animals become categorized as belonging to 'biology' in ways that we do not; their behaviour is thus, by default, biologically determined, hard-wired, instinctive, while ours is adaptable and the proper focus of sociological inquiry. But if all animals' behaviour is thus determined, then – unless humans are made of completely different stuff and were dumped on earth by aliens rather than evolving here – it would follow that some of our behaviour must be similarly hard-wired. So, if we want to challenge that claim for humans it means that we have to look again at the claim regarding nonhumans. The two feed off each other. I have argued elsewhere that, if feminists want to challenge biological determinism on all fronts, then one route must be to take on board the growing calls to recognize at least some kinds of nonhuman animals as clever, adaptable, aware, and cultural – just like us (Bekoff 2002). If we do accept that, then it makes it much more difficult to make claims about simple hard-wiring in our own species.

Another reason why dualism persists is that emerging theory about embodiment – important though that has been – tends to treat the body as an inscribable surface, on which culture acts. For some phenomena – such as body piercing, that may be a valid approach. But it leaves the biological body and its inner processes apart, left in the rag-bag category of 'the biological'. Even if some recent theory seems to dissolve boundaries between bodies and their representations, the *biological* body does not enter social theory. As such, that inner body remains presocial, foundational, while its surface becomes endlessly malleable (Shilling and Mellor 1996). As several critics have noted, however, this focus is problematic, for it marginalizes experience, particularly how the body is *lived* – and particularly in illness. Furthermore, leaving the inner body out leaves little room for understanding the complex ways in which illness is generated across and between social divisions such as class. Can pain, emotion, sexual excitement, ill-health or disability, or the relationships between cardiovascular disease and social histories be understood only in terms of cultural inscription?

Yet messy biological processes do not go away. Just because of hyperbole from some advocates of genetics, can we really deny that genes affect our bodily functions, and hence our health and how we are in the world? Or that we are, indeed, animals, belonging to the primate order? Or – relatedly – that we are products of processes of evolution? In common with many others, I have problems with the rejection of 'biology' that seems to underlie so much feminist theory, for not only does it deny my own bodily experiences (pain and bleeding for instance), but it also puts me in a tricky position with respect to the science that I spent years learning. Like Meera Nanda (1996), I have not found science always abhorrent (critical of it though I may be): it can also be useful, even liberating. And it is in the context of women's health where it can, in principle, become so, when women find ways to challenge medical assumptions and power.[3]

Women and health: 'deviations from the norm'

Even if feminist theory has tended to play down any discussion of the biological, the processes of biology matter to many activists. What kind of biology enters into these debates? For those working on environmental politics, or on health activism, knowing what biology has to say about eco-systems or reproductive health, say, is a crucial part of the political action – even if that knowledge is simultaneously being challenged for its sexism. A substantial part of feminist engagement with issues of health, for example, has addressed the ways in which biomedicine – both as practice and discourse – excludes or marginalizes women. In study after study, women's health needs have been largely defined with respect to male bodies – as well as assumptions made about race and class.[4] As a result, women's bodily processes become the deviations from a norm. The significant exception is reproduction, where it is women's role as reproducers rather than men's that is foregrounded; women thus become defined in terms of reproductive systems.

Although there have been significant changes in the ways that these arguments have run, they remain key concerns. However much we might debate differences among 'women', there is still a substantial literature detailing aspects of *women's* health (women and smoking, for example).

There is a real dilemma here for feminists, however: on the one hand, we must take issues of women's health seriously. We need to know, for example, if a particular environmental hazard is likely to affect the health of women differentially, or to threaten reproductive capacity. We need to understand how changes in gender and class play out in their impacts on women's health. Yet on the other hand, the 'body' that is at the centre of discussions of health remains quite passive, seeming to be acted upon by these various external agents. So, women's health literature may focus on the impact of (say) environmental toxins *on* fertility. Fertility here (and the organ structures associated with it, such as the uterus) is the substrate, while the biological processes themselves lack agency.

Feminist activism in health starts from women's exclusion from medical knowledge and practice. Activists have pointed to ways in which such exclusion disempowers women, and have therefore sought to promote women's knowledge of how their bodies work as an act of empowerment. Wresting power from the doctors was (and is) central to this kind of politics. In that sense, the self at least has agency in her refusal to accede passively to medical demands.

However, it is not always clear that advocating women's greater knowledge leads to a less passive or negative understanding of the body, not least because the source of much of our understanding about 'how bodies work' comes inevitably from biomedicine itself (Birke 1999), which has been notoriously negative in its descriptions of women's biological processes. Thus one member of the Boston Women's Health Collective lamented that, in writing for *Our Bodies, Ourselves*, she had uncritically repeated the biomedical story of menstruation and menopause as deficiencies – hardly an empowering description, as she later acknowledged (Bell 1994).

So, while feminist theory tends to eschew the biological, biology does enter the debate in some areas of feminist activism, such as environmentalism and health. But that engagement is often ambivalent, moving uneasily between outright rejection and a need to take on board what science says. However much we may, at times, need to accept the science, we can also recognise that the stories science tells are limited, that they recreate the passive body and hard-wired organisms that we want to disavow.

What kind of biology?

The acted-upon body, then, is a product of a biomedicine and related study of biology that has typically seen the individual – human or nonhuman – as separated out from the environment in which s/he lives. That tendency is exacerbated by the way in which physiological data are acquired, often from laboratory studies of highly standardized animals kept under tightly controlled and unvarying conditions. In controlling the laboratory environment, scientific studies thereby separate out the physiology from the more varying environment in which most organisms actually live.

And then, if there are changes in the individual organism and/or its behaviour, biologists routinely seek causes within. Only much later might external causes be added into the picture – if at all. Yet no organism, anywhere on earth, is so isolated: all are deeply embedded in, and part of, multiple environments. Biologists know this in principle, yet all too often treat the organism (or its constituent parts) as existing in a vacuum.

Looking within for causes goes hand in hand with biological determinism. Even if the scientific report tells of genes, hormones, or whatever, influencing some outcome (the development of sexuality, say), it is just a small step to infer that the biological factor(s) cause sexuality to develop in that way. Moreover, many such studies are done first in nonhuman species: these studies, however, *begin* from the premise that the causes of behaviours lie within. For example, most scientific knowledge about how the sex hormones influence behaviour comes from animal studies, which in turn presume that sex differences in behaviour derive from biological causes. That such differences are also influenced by social factors – even in rats – does not usually enter the equation. Determinism is thus built into the theories in the first place.

Yet what about the kind of biology that we might want to bring into social theory? Clearly we do not want to renew deterministic accounts, however covertly. We need to find ways of acknowledging that internal biology is a factor in our becoming, while at the same time recognizing that there are many other factors too, that influence our becoming who we are, especially in relation to behaviour[5] (see Fausto-Sterling, this volume). Furthermore, we can draw on much wider areas of biological enquiry than the usual Genes 'R' Us story to situate ourselves biologically (ourselves as part of ecosystems for instance). It's not biology that we need to reject wholesale; rather, it is simplistic assumptions that certain biological processes are primary, and that it's the biology of the isolated individual that matters.

An underlying part of the problems facing anyone who wants to conceptualize biology differently is that modern biology seems to be obsessed with genes and molecules. There simply is not a well-developed science of the whole organism (Tauber 1994). So it is frustratingly difficult to find ways of thinking about either biological bodies or animal awareness that do not fall into the abyss of reductionism. But there are ways, and we need to follow them to explore how our biological bodies are both situated in, and part of, a multitude of environments and simultaneously act upon those environments. Only then can we relate our biological bodies to the concerns of feminist politics and sociological theory.

Within recent feminist theory, there have been several recent calls to recognize the materiality of the body – an important step in bringing biology back in. This was, for instance, a feature of Elizabeth Grosz's 1994 book, *Volatile Bodies*. Others have emphasized phenomenological accounts to foreground the lived experience of the body – for example, in relation to pregnancy (see Marshall 1996). Another approach to bodily materiality within recent sociological work draws on Bourdieu's notion of habitus – that is, we learn through social engagement to comport ourselves, to exert control over our bodies (Bourdieu 1984; Lovell 2000). So, social class can influence bodily habitus (through foods eaten, or learning ways of being/ moving in the world), and thus the acquisition of cultural capital. Such processes, moreover, could influence our experiencing of our bodies and hence our health.[6]

The idea of habitus is certainly useful, in that such concepts begin to acknowledge bodily materiality. Moreover, culture impacts upon bodily habitus in ways that might in turn affect biological processes. Nonetheless, much of this theory – however sensitive to materiality – seems to me still to ignore the inner workings of the body, which therefore must remain within the purview of biomedicine. So, in order to ponder how habitus might affect what happens inside our bodies, we must necessarily turn to the discourses of natural science: there are few others (although 'alternative' medicine provides less reductionist means of describing the inner body: see Scott, this volume). The concept of habitus does not say much about how habitus is manifest *within* the body: how, for instance, might differences in how we move through the world reflect in differences in bodily functions? In health?[7] And might these differences in being-in-the-world also contribute to different ways of behaving among other species that we like to call hard-wired – to turn the usual logic on its head?

Just as sociologists seeking to theorize the lived body have sought out particular theories that best fit the demand to move beyond the presocial body, so too have some biologists, who have tried to resist the hegemonic stories of powerful genes.[8] We are not just outcomes of genetic dictates, these authors insist; on the contrary, we are bodily located in particular contexts. They seek to draw on other ways of thinking about biological processes which are less determinist than the story of all-powerful genes and which are potentially more fruitful for thinking about the engagement of sociology and biology.

Thinking about wider contexts is clearly crucial to thinking about the kind of biology on which we want to draw. But a starting point for that development has to be a cross-disciplinary effort to challenge our culture's investment in ideas of discontinuity – that is, the notion that humans are fundamentally and qualitatively different from other species. Both biology and sociology contribute to this belief, despite biology's adherence to evolutionary theory. That is, whenever biologists paint a picture of nonhumans as puppets of their genes or evolutionary heritage, it permits a reading of that picture implying either that humans, too, are puppets of their genes or that humans are different. To bridge the divide, we need to acknowledge and develop further emerging ideas of animal consciousness, emotionality and cultural difference (Bekoff 2002). That is surely a better way of acknowledging evolutionary continuity than the determinist route.

To move towards a more suitable model of biology, we can draw on models of biological systems that emphasise dynamic, rather than static, processes, and that prioritize agency. Steven Rose is one exponent of such a view, insisting that we understand the developmental trajectories of organisms – what he calls their 'lifelines' – as a way of emphasizing the ongoing process of engagement of the organism in its own life history. The organism – any organism, from human to moss to amoeba – thus is not simply *being*, but *becoming* (Rose 1997). It is always in the process of becoming and always making over its environment. So, to understand the sociology of health, we must simultaneously take on board how our bodily health and functions themselves structure the very sociological processes that influence health. What is more, these two-way processes interact throughout our lives, creating different life histories.

This kind of thinking fits with recent feminist scholarship on the body, which has sought to transcend concepts of the bounded body and self by insistence on corporeal fluidity and flow (Grosz 1994). While such approaches seem to play down the biological processes of the body's insides, they share with the biologists' challenges a desire to think about the body as *process(es)* rather than fixed. However, much of this writing emphasizes flows of information (such as genetic or electrical information) in ways that ignore bodily boundaries; like Dawkins's selfish genes, the information is at centre stage and the body becomes epiphenomenal (Birke 1999). Yet we can, as Rose (1997) has argued, think of these processes happening at more than one level simultaneously: genes *and* the body rather than genes instead of the body. Wholeness matters, too.

We can think about 'the body' as existing in, and part of, a nexus of forces, moving through the world and co-creating it. To take that stance de-emphasizes the factors which might 'act upon' the body and prioritizes engagement with the world in which we move. Part of that co-creation is of course how social and cultural forces do indeed write upon the body as surface – but part, too, is how they communicate with the body's inside.

Feminist biologists have been among the voices demanding a more nuanced view of 'the biological' in social theory, seeking to prioritize the engagement of a developing organism with the world in which it lives. We are, these authors insist, not simply emerging out of some blueprint in the DNA; rather a developing embryo is itself part of a process of creation. That co-creation is just as true of an amoeba or a snake or a lion as it is of us. To take the example of how sex differences develop, temperature matters more than genetic dictates for many reptiles.[9] And if you are a newborn rat, how your mother treats you matters as well as hormones in how you exhibit 'gendered' behaviour in later life.

It is that complex engagement throughout life – with biological matter, with the inanimate world, with other social actors – that act together to create (for example) the structures of gender with which we are familiar. To draw on recent feminist insights, we must be aware of the multiple ways in which 'gender' and 'sex' are culturally constructed (including the anthropocentric – or mammalocentric – assumptions that the human way of developing sex is the best one!). Yet we must also be aware of constraints in development, and how those constraints are in turn constructed. Some of these may be the product of social decisions (such as the decision to allocate newborns with phalluses of 'intermediate' length to one or the other sex); others may be products of complex structural processes in embryonic life.[10] But constraints there are.

That call for a new approach to the biological is, however, rather an abstract one and we need to take it further, to avoid ending up with theory that still does not adequately match up the biological and the social. To begin with, sociologists need to engage more overtly with ideas in biology (as this volume attests), and to think through how biological processes might be involved in social ones without assuming that biology equals determinism. So, too, do biologists need to take seriously the complexities of human (and nonhuman) social life without reducing it to simple rules; they need also to recognize the assumptions they make about the causes of behaviour in nonhuman organisms. But the task is not easy. It is one thing to emphasize what kind of biology we want: it is another to take that further and to figure out how we can develop or use it.

Part of the problem, it seems to me, is that in advocating a more dynamic approach to biology we have not spelled it out enough, so the 'dynamic approach' becomes a kind of magic word. How is that played out in the world of living bodies? What does it mean in relation to the human behaviour that is the foundation of sociological interest? These are important questions which we must address (as other chapters of this book argue).

To spell it out a little more, I will take two concrete examples. These illustrate the complex interactions between social/environmental structures and our biological bodily selves; and they also illustrate, in slightly different ways, how scientific knowledge is generated. The first example is from studies of the immune system. We are now familiar with concepts of 'stress' and how that (whatever it is) can compromise the body's defences. Emily Martin's fascinating study (1994) of concepts of immunity indicates, too, that ideas have changed dramatically over the last thirty years. Where once they relied on analogies of bodies as fortresses, mounting defences, now that has largely given way to discourses of immune systems capable of reacting to their environment – that can be 'tuned up'. These, Martin argues, parallel discursive shifts in the wider culture, particularly in corporate culture.

Now a view of the body's functions that emphasizes its engagement with its environment is (uses by management apart) an improvement. To draw on biology, however, requires making distinctions between conflicting and controversial theories. Weasel (2001), for example, explores major theories of how immune systems work in relation to different feminist epistemologies. In particular, she focuses on the predominant view, which posits a self–other dichotomy and notes how that model, while useful, fails to explain an observation of considerable importance to women, namely, that the foetus ('other' to the mother, biologically) is not normally rejected by maternal physiology. An alternative, and contested, view is the 'danger' theory, whereby the immune system responds to danger signals rather than other-recognition. Weasel considers this theory to be one on which feminist thinking could more usefully draw. Among her reasons for making this claim are that the danger theory better explains the data (including maternal–foetal interactions) and that it is less reductionist in that it acknowledges the situatedness of the immune system.

For some time, it has been widely accepted that the nervous system can influence immunity (the 'stress' argument); more recently, biologists have begun to recognize how the immune system in turn can affect the brain.

Thus, Maier and Watkins (1999) for example argue that the immune system can function as a diffuse sense organ, informing the brain about potentially harmful events in the body. But crucially how the organism itself behaves then becomes part of the host's defences (an obvious example is lying down when you have a fever, or changing the diet). So, rather than thinking mainly in terms of how social factors influence long-term health, we could also consider how we as social and biological actors affect the process. Exposure to harm, of any sort, can change the body and so change behaviour. For instance, an infection can trigger release in a vertebrate body of chemicals called cytokines; some of these affect the brain and hence behaviour – the cytokine interleukin-1 for example reduces sexual behaviour in female laboratory rats.

Now I would not wish to imply any simple jump from laboratory findings to the complexities of human behaviour at the social level. I use this rather to underscore (a) how specific examples might illustrate how biology can be 'brought back in', in the sense that biology can pose questions about *how* social engagement impacts upon bodies and health; (b) how some theories might work better for us in connecting to social theory than others; and (c) how tricky it is to talk about biology without falling into the abyss of determinism (just as it's tricky to speak of social processes without falling into the abyss of relativism)! But here, nonetheless, there seems to be fertile ground for exploring ways in which our biological processes are indeed situated within and part of our social world. The functioning of the immune system, particularly, reminds us that we are not, as we sometimes fancy, living in splendid biological isolation – as Basiro Davey aptly reminds us in her chapter.

A second example of the interaction between social engagement and biological processes comes from the recent literature on endocrine disrupters. Until the 1990s, most of the concern about environmental hazards focused on direct risks to health (e.g. from chemicals that might cause cancer). However, it now seems clear that many chemicals to which we are exposed can also adversely affect reproduction without necessarily compromising individual health, even in tiny amounts. They do this by mimicking the effects in the body of the body's own hormones – hence, endocrine disrupters. Media accounts have emphasized how, for example, male Florida alligators have developed tiny penises, and fish in Britain have been reported as changing sex. Chemical spills and sewage effluent were, it seems, the respective culprits in promoting what newspaper reports promptly entitled 'gender bending'; meanwhile, other headlines referred to effects in humans, particularly an alleged decline in male sperm count. Needless to say, these data and their interpretations have also been the subject of much controversy, not only between scientists but also in the public domain (see Birke 2000). Some scientists, for instance, dispute the 'safe' levels of exposure, arguing that we have always been exposed to exogenous hormones (through plant foods for instance).

To other scientists, 'disrupters' is a somewhat misleading term, for it can be read as implying that there was a previous constancy that has been disrupted. This ignores the ways in which every species's physiology (including hormones) has co-evolved with those of other organisms, with the ecosystems of which it is part. There have certainly been hormones around in the water, and in the food we eat, for millennia. To an extent, our endocrine systems have evolved in relation to these – in a fluid and constant interchange, since we excrete steroids into the environment. So, the presence of additional chemicals necessarily shifts that balance, with potential consequences for reproduction.

Indeed, so entwined are these processes, that effects on animal bodies may become cumulative. Arguments about the threshold, or 'safe' level, may be futile for chemicals that mimic molecules occurring normally within bodies; in that case, thresholds are automatically exceeded with exposure (and we are exposed to a multiplicative cocktail of such molecules). Defining 'safe' levels has little meaning in this case. Moreover, effects of disrupters can accumulate over generations, altering hormones in foetuses or eggs, which then grow into adults with altered hormonal sensitivities and reproductive function. Here, again, is an area of biological inquiry with considerable significance for how humans engage with the social world, and for their future health. It is also a salutary lesson in how human activities are changing the world – with consequences for all species, and their futures on this earth.

Now, the examples of such complex interactions I have chosen to discuss are rather arbitrary. My point, however, is to use them to encourage us to think beyond any notions of the biological body as presocial, or primary, and to think about it as engaged, as part of its milieu. These specific details may seem a far cry from rarified social theory about, say, corporeal flows and gender. Yet if we are truly going to bring biology into our thinking about social theory and the body, then I think we are going to have to bother with some of those biological details, to try to understand how those processes operate in (and change) the context of our social engagement. What this means is not only trying to understand how social factors influence bodies (health), but also how bodies and their biology influence social processes. But we must understand these as constantly engaging processes, not as determinants. Endocrine disrupters thus provide an example less of how A affects B (though it is that also) but of how human biology is a dynamic set of processes, nested in among other dynamic sets of processes or systems (and, in this case, the politics of global capitalism and industrial production). To understand health/bodily outcomes of these processes requires a quite different approach to understanding biology than the reductionist one.

Among other things, to emphasize the dynamic agency of biological processes is to acknowledge their own role in their organization. Several theorists now emphasize the significance of self-organization within systems in nature (see discussion in Rose 1997). That is, organization within a system (such as an organism) emerges out of the prior state(s) of that organism. That, it seems to me, offers a compromise between the excesses of genetic determinism and the notion that the body can be understood only discursively or as flows/fluidities. Self-organized systems are fluid and constantly in exchange with their worlds; yet they often appear to be constrained, and highly stable. They are neither fixed nor completely open-ended, they are both/and.

With examples like that of endocrine disrupters, we can begin to see how bodily processes comprise systems fluidly connected to our social and physical environments. More specifically, we can begin to understand better how the impact of social divisions on health can exert effects over generations. As Peter Dickens (2001) notes, there is growing evidence that children from poorer backgrounds are affected biologically before they are even born. These effects (which include those from endocrine disrupting chemicals) in turn influence physiological function, bodily habitus, and future health. Not only does this have nothing to do with genetics (as some determinists would claim), but it is, Dickens argues, an instance of how capitalism may, in the long term, be 'shaping human biology in its own image' (ibid.: 106).

And not only human biology, of course, for other kinds of animals are quite literally and intentionally being reshaped in the service of biotechnology, while others are influenced, just as we are, by the environmental changes to which our bodies are exposed. There are another set of issues here to be concerned about – such as how much the planet's biodiversity is threatened by these processes of reshaping biology, and how much the welfare of individual animals is compromised by new biotechnological creations.

For women, struggles over reproductive rights and issues of control over their own bodies become more acute in a world of growing medical/technological intervention. And reproductive health is further threatened by what some critics see as a barrage of oestrogenic compounds in the environment. In this context, it is crucial that we challenge the biology-as-bedrock arguments, and work towards understanding our biology as part and parcel of our socially engaged selves. We urgently need to 'bring back' *this* kind of biology to the social sciences and to feminism – not only to further our understanding of bodily health but also to counter the seemingly endless claims of biological determinism. This is not only a political or academic challenge, but it is also fundamentally about recognizing the multiple levels of 'our bodies, ourselves'.

Notes

1 This is not to say that such biological processes can necessarily be known without its embeddedness in social and cultural processes. It is just that, while we can acknowledge that intertwining, the literature almost exclusively focuses on those social processes.

2 Yearley (1991) notes how the environmental movement is both hostile to science and technology (which help to create environmental problems) and must call upon scientific knowledge at times to arbitrate environmental disputes. To some extent, this ambivalence applies also to other social movements. Animal rights, for instance, is hostile to the science that uses laboratory animals, yet must refer to scientific arguments about evolutionary similarities to make their arguments.

3 I don't wish to imply that knowing a bit of science can permit women to take on the medical establishment (would that it were so!). However, women working in women's self-help health groups often do find it emancipatory to take control over access to medical knowledge: my own experience in such groups bears this out.

4 For a general overview, see Whittle and Inhorn 2001. This raises the problem of essentialism, in that all women, irrespective of differences, are subsumed under the term 'women'. There are, however, commonalities, since most women, globally, reproduce. On the impact of difference in relation to women's health research, see Whittle and Inhorn, ibid.

5 Many biologists would accept this, even suggesting that the critics are making mountains out of molehills. However, while biological writing often pays lip service to the interactions between genes and environment, all too often it uses phrases which lend themselves to deterministic interpretations. This is particularly clear when the same research is reported in the media. In the end, the culturally relevant face of biology that emerges from such research is indeed the determinist one. I would also suggest that the enormous interest in genetics and biotechnology among critical scholars working in science studies also helps to fuel the hegemony of genetic discourses. Other areas of biological inquiry are sadly neglected by critics.

6 Social and cultural variation in experience of menarche and menstruation is one example; or the ways in which gender and race can influence how ill health is experienced; see Whittle and Inhorn 2001. Bourdieu did discuss the acquisition of gender in early life, but has been criticized by feminists for binding sex and gender too tightly, of making them over-determined socially (Lovell 2000).

7 And if differences in how we move through the world might become manifest in individual bodies, what does that say about the conclusions drawn from highly standardized studies of very inbred laboratory animals?

8 Among others, these include Rose 1997, Birke 1999 and Fausto-Sterling, this volume.

9 Higher incubation temperatures for many species of turtles and lizards can favour males or females, depending upon the species.

10 In embryonic development, the emergence of structures typically affects – and thereby constrains – the development of further structures. Examples in vertebrates include the pentadactyl limb (with five digits) and the eye.

References

Bekoff, M. (2002) *Minding Animals: Awareness, Emotions and Heart*, Oxford: Oxford University Press.

Bell, S.E. (1994) 'Translating science to the people: Updating *The New Our Bodies, Ourselves*', *Women's Studies International Forum*, 17: 9–18.

Birke, L. (1999) *Feminism and the Biological Body*, Edinburgh: Edinburgh University Press.

Birke, L. (2000) 'Sitting on the fence: biology, feminism, and gender-bending environments', *Women's Studies International Forum*, 23: 587–99.

Bourdieu, P. (1984) *Distinction: A Social Critique of the Judgement of Taste*, London: Routledge.

Dickens, P. (2001) 'Linking the social and the natural sciences: is capital modifying human biology in its own image?' *Sociology*, 35: 93–110.

Grosz, E. (1994) *Volatile Bodies: Toward a Corporeal Feminism*, Bloomington and Indianapolis: Indiana University Press.

Lovell, T. (2000) 'Thinking feminism with and against Bourdieu', *Feminist Theory*, 1: 11–32.

Maier, S.F. and Watkins, L.R. (1999) 'Bidirectional communication between the brain and the immune system: implications for behaviour', *Animal Behaviour*, 57: 741–51.

Marshall, H. (1996) 'Our bodies ourselves: why we should add old fashioned empirical phenomenonology to the new theories of the body', *Women's Studies International Forum*, 19: 253–65.

Martin, E. (1994) *Flexible Bodies: Tracking Immunity in American Culture from the Days of Polio the the Days of AIDS*, Boston: Beacon Press.

Nanda, M. (1996) 'The science quesion in post-colonial feminism', *Economic and Political Weekly*, **April 20–7**, WS2–WS7.

Rose, S. (1997) *Lifelines: Biology, Freedom, Determinism*, Harmondsworth: Penguin.

Shilling, C. and Mellor, P.A. (1996) 'Embodiment, structuration theory and modernity: mind/body dualism and the repression of sensuality', *Body and Society*, 2: 1–15.

Shodhini Collective (1997) *Touch Me, Touch Me Not: Women, Plants and Healing*, New Delhi: Kali for Women.

Spelman, E. (1988) *Inessential Woman: Problems of Exclusion in Feminist Thought*, Boston: Beacon Press.

Tauber, A.I. (1994) *The Immune Self: Theory or Metaphor?*, Cambridge: Cambridge University Press.

Weasel, L. (2001) 'Dismantling the self/other dichotomy in science: towards a feminist model of the immune system', *Hypatia*, 16: 27–44.

Whittle, K.L. and Inhorn, M.C. (2001) 'Rethinking difference: a feminist reframing of gender/race/class for the improvement of women's health research', *International Journal of Health Services*, 31: 147–65.

Yearly, S. (1991) *The Green Case: A Sociology of Environmental Issues, Arguments and Politics*, London: HarperCollins.

4 Realist agendas on biology, health and medicine

Some thoughts and reflections

Graham Scambler and Sasha Scambler

It is undeniably the case, at least to this point of human history, that the objects of healers' attentions have been as variable over time and space as have the qualities and praxis of healers themselves. It is evident, for example, that the general foundationalist premises of mind–body dualism and the particular 'expert' theories and models of disease with which we in Britain are familiar, together with the healers who sign up to and utilize them, are characteristic of Western modernity; and we can reasonably assume that these premises, theories/models and healers will one day, and perhaps sooner rather than later, be reformed, displaced or superseded. Our present expert 'knowledgeabilities', in other words, are required to be seen as *conventional* rather than *arbitrary*. These knowledgeabilities might indeed, and easily, have been different from how they are – that is, they have been touched, sometimes even assaulted, by contingency – but they could *not* have adopted *any* form and content. One way of appreciating why this is so is through a consideration of what Bhaskar (1978) calls the 'epistemic fallacy'. This results from a conflation of epistemological and ontological matters. It is committed when *our knowledge of what exists* is not distinguished from *what exists*, allowing for the reduction of ontology to epistemology; and it is committed often, with abandon and by sociologists and practitioners of the life and medical sciences alike. This chapter is about ontology as much as epistemology and it espouses and commends a broadly critical realist approach to the biological and social sciences alike.

In the opening section we offer a straightforward, attenuated case-study, comprising an orthodox western *biomedical* account of a rare condition termed 'juvenile Batten disease', extending to its aetiology, course, clinical management and prognosis. The second section outlines the central tenets of Bhaskar's critical realism, incorporating a number of credible and useful elaborations ventured by sympathetic commentators and critics. Attention is briefly paid to the concept of *ontological stratification*; the *transformational model of social activity* and the *relational model of society*; the modes of inference, *retroduction* and *abduction*, especially associated with critical realism; and what we shall call the concept of *ontological differentiation*;

as well as to critical realism's potential ramifications for the understanding of juvenile Batten disease. The third and final section focuses on the interface between biology and sociology, again with reference to juvenile Batten disease. At this point some suggestions and conjectures drawing on critical realism and the unfolding arguments of this chapter are mooted which, we believe, carry the potential to undermine or side-step many of the problems sociologists have identified in their relations with both biology and medicine.

Juvenile Batten disease: a rare problem

The group of metabolic diseases known as the neuronal ceroid lipofuscinoses (NCLs), or, more familiarly, by the generic term *Batten disease* (after the British neurologist Frederick Batten), are inherited genetic disorders which are potentially fatal because the chemical imbalances said to give rise to them are resistant to treatment, that is, given the current state of knowledge within the life and medical sciences. All of the childhood variants of NCL/Batten disease are passed on through autosomal recessive inheritance (i.e. for transmission, both parents must have at least one copy of the 'faulty' gene). For all its rarity, *juvenile Batten disease* is the most common neurodegenerative disorder of childhood. In the absence of epidemiological studies its prevalence can only be estimated through the number of diagnoses recorded at large hospitals and on Charity databases. These enquiries suggest that between 50 and 100 children in the UK are affected by juvenile Batten disease at any one time, although this may well be an underestimate (Goebbel *et al.* 1999).

Research suggests an average age of symptom onset for juvenile Batten disease of about 6 years, with an average age of diagnosis of about 8 years (Goebbel *et al.* 1999). The clinical profile is harsh. Visual failure is a common initial symptom, succeeded by increasing clumsiness and – often discernible through problems with schoolwork – speech difficulties, short-term memory loss, a decreasing attention span and deteriorating cognitive skills. Adams and colleagues (1997) identify five stages in an unrelenting clinical trajectory:

a)   visual impairment, sometimes preceding retinal changes by a matter of months;
b)   after approximately two years, the onset of generalized seizures and myoclonus, often accompanied by irritability, lack of control of emotions and stuttering or jerky speech;
c)   gradual intellectual deterioration, affecting attentiveness, memory and mental activity . . . movements are usually slow and tremulous . . . to which are added elements of cerebral ataxia and intention tremor;
d)   severe dementia, with movement becoming extremely difficult and speech all but impossible . . . screaming may occur when disturbed or forced

to move . . . muscles are wasted, although tendon reflexes remain lively and the plantar reflexes are extensor;

e) lying, curled up in bed, blind and speechless . . . strong extensor plantar reflexes . . . occasionally adopting dystonic postures . . . ending in death ten to fifteen years after onset.

This trajectory remains typical, although the speed of transition between stages is variable; treatment/care is increasingly directed at keeping the child/adult active and involved for as long as possible; and life expectancy is extending, with some now living as long as twenty-five years after onset.

Early diagnosis is important since there is a 25 per cent chance that each subsequent child will develop the condition, although because of its rarity testing is only carried out as a matter of course when siblings have already been diagnosed. Testing and diagnosis are in fact often delayed for the first child until the child has shown symptoms for several months, even years, because the disease progresses slowly. Frequently, because sight is affected early, it is opticians or ophthalmologists who first detect an underlying problem, triggering medical testing. Basic research on aetiology, testing and therapy continues, but there is currently no cure or treatment capable of arresting or reversing the course of juvenile Batten disease, so management remains focused on controlling its symptoms. As well as doctors, ophthalmologists, nurses, physiotherapists, speech therapists, occupational therapists, rehabilitation workers and counsellors may be involved in management and in the increasingly multifaceted and consuming task of caring for the child and his or her family (Scambler 1999). Episodic hospitalization may be occasioned by such 'crises' as uncontrolled epilepsy and the need to insert a peg for feeding in the event of the loss of the swallowing reflex.

Before this brief account of the biomedical narrative of juvenile Batten disease is subject to analysis, it will be necessary to say something about the philosophical perspective on which the analysis rests, namely, *critical realism*.

Key tenets of critical realism

Ontological stratification

Bhaskar (1978, 1989a) may have cashed in a number of debts to his predecessors in philosophy, most recently to Harre, but his early arguments on the philosophies of the natural and social sciences are genuinely innovative. His thesis, initially addressing the study of the natural world, may be expediently interpreted for present purposes as emerging from a critique of Hume's empiricism in general, and his regularity theory of causation in particular. Bhaskar's rebuttal of Hume's (and other empiricists') arguments cannot be examined or debated in depth or detail here (see especially Archer *et al.* 1998). Suffice to say that he deploys a Kantian (transcendental) argument to assert that, given the developments in human knowledge that have *in fact* occurred, there *must* exist real, that is, mind-independent, 'objects' of that knowledge, possessed of certain properties and emergent powers, which argument leads to a postulate of ontological stratification. He maintains that if, as Humean empiricism insists, human knowledge were restricted to atomistic events given in experience, then something like the regularity theory of causation would obtain. However, the world is, and must be, stratified: it is *not* comprised merely of events (the *actual*) and experience (the *empirical*), but also of underlying mechanisms (the *real*). These mechanisms are *intransitive*, that is, they exist whether or not they are detected; they are *transfactual*, that is, they are enduring, not transitory; and they *govern or facilitate events*. This is as true for knowledge of the social as for knowledge of the natural world.

In the social world in particular, events are typically (a) 'unsynchronized with the mechanisms that govern them', and (b) 'conjointly determined by various, perhaps countervailing influences so that the governing causes, though necessarily "appearing" through, or in, events can rarely be read straight off' (Lawson 1997: 22). The governing causes, or *generative mechanisms*, can rarely be 'read straight off' because they only manifest themselves in *open systems*, that is, in circumstances where numerous mechanisms are simultaneously active and there is therefore limited potential for experimental *closures*.

In both the natural (life/biomedical) and the social sciences the objects of enquiry are necessarily 'theoretical' in the sense that they are necessarily unperceivable: they cannot be empirically identified independently of their effects. Social sciences like sociology differ from the natural sciences, however, in that the objects of their enquiries not only cannot be identified independently of their effects, but they do not *exist* independently of their effects. Moreover, sociology, in pursuit of generative mechanisms through their effects in open systems, must accept an absence of spontaneously occurring, and the impossibility of creating (for example, through laboratory experiments), closures. This denies sociologists, 'in principle', decisive test situations for their theories. Since the criterion for the rational confirmation and rejection of theories in sociology cannot be 'predictive', it must be 'exclusively explanatory' (Bhaskar 1989a). Thus explanation displaces prediction; and to *explain* a phenomenon is to provide an account of what might be termed its *causal history*.

Transformational model of social activity and relational model of society

Distancing himself from Durkheimian 'reification' and Weberian 'voluntarism', Bhaskar argues that society does not exist independently of human activity, but it is not the product of the latter. Joseph (2002: 32) puts it well:

social structures are both the necessary conditions for and the reproduced outcomes of human action. Structures pre-exist and hence shape
and determine human action, but at the same time, the continued
existence of these structures depends upon the activities of the agents
they govern.

A real ontological difference, if also a mutual ontological dependence,
exists between *people* and *society*, society being defined in terms of a 'network of relations' (hence the 'relational model of society'): 'people are not
relations, societies are not conscious agents' (Collier 1994: 147). In Bhaskar's
own familiar words,

> society is both the ever-present *condition* (material cause) and the
> continually reproduced *outcome* of human agency. And praxis is both
> work, that is, conscious *production*, and (normally unconscious) *repro-
> duction* of the conditions of production, that is society. One could refer
> to the former as the *duality of structure*, and the latter as the *duality of
> praxis*.
>
> (1989a: 34–5)

People do not work, Bhaskar elaborates, to reproduce the capitalist economy
any more than they marry to sustain the nuclear family,

> yet it is nevertheless the unintended consequence (and inexorable result)
> of, as it is also a necessary condition for, their activity. Moreover,
> when social forms change, the explanation will not normally lie in the
> desires of agents to change them that way, though as a very important
> theoretical and political limit, it *may* do.
>
> (1989a: 35)

The connection between the transformational model of social activity and
the relational model of society has been summarized by Bhaskar as follows:

> the relational conception does not of course deny that factories and
> books are social forms. But it maintains that there being *social*, as
> distinct from (or rather in addition to) material, objects, consists only
> in the relationships between persons or between such relationships
> and nature that such objects causally presuppose or entail. The *social*
> conditions for the structures that govern the substantive activities of
> transformation in which human beings engage (and which constitute
> the immediate explanation of these activities) can thus only be relations
> of various kinds: between people and each other, their products, their
> activities, nature and themselves. If social activity is to be given a social
> explanation it is in this nexus that it must be found. *It is thus in
> the enduring relations presupposed by, rather than the actual complex*

> *motley of, particular social forms, that on this conception, sociology's theoretical interest lies.*

(1989b: 81; emphasis added)

Retroductive and abductive inference

The modes of inference associated with the critical realist search for explanations are retroduction and abduction. In his text on critical realism and economics, Lawson (1997) refers to retroduction in terms of 'as if' reasoning:

> it consists of the movement, on the basis of analogy and metaphor amongst other things, from a conception of some phenomenon of interest to a conception of some totally different type of thing, mechanism, structure or condition that, at least in part, is responsible for the given phenomenon.

(1997: 24)

So a retroductive inference moves from a knowledge of events to a knowledge of mechanisms, at a deeper level or strata of reality, which contributed to the generation of those events. Abduction is likewise geared to the discernment of mechanisms, but involves a process of inference from lay, or first-order, accounts to sociological, or second-order, accounts of the social world.

'Constant' event patterns or 'invariant' regularities may not obtain in open systems, but 'partial' regularities do. Lawson (1997) calls these *demi-regularities* or *demi-regs*. A demi-reg is

> a partial event regularity which *prima facie* indicates the occasional, but less than universal, actualization of a mechanism or tendency, over a definite region of time-space. The patterning observed will not be strict if countervailing factors sometimes dominate or frequently co-determine the outcomes in a variable manner. But where demi-regs are observed there is evidence of relatively enduring and identifiable tendencies at play.

(1997: 204)

Demi-regs, and especially contrastive demi-regs, can inform and guide sociological research by 'providing evidence that, and where, certain relatively enduring and potentially identifiable mechanisms have been in play' (1997: 207).

Ontological differentiation

Ontological differentiation here acknowledges that the objects of enquiry of the natural (life/biomedical) sciences and social sciences like sociology are both *real* and *different*. This is a matter broached somewhat tangentially by Creaven (2000) as part of his attempt to achieve a synthesis of critical realism and Marxian materialism. Drawing on the work of Archer (1995), he argues that a 'strong explanatory account of human nature, and of the non-social subject' is indispensable in providing 'micro-foundations' for the theory of social structure and human agency. He offers another transcendental argument at this point: human nature and the non-social subject denote 'an ensemble of species powers, capacities, dispositions and psycho-organic needs and interests' which 'logically must be held to exist in order to account for the existence of human society and culture' (2000: 139). Moreover, the concept of human nature, he continues, albeit more controversially, affords 'a means of explaining the handful of constants which can be found in most societies past and present', as well as enabling social scientists 'to furnish social theory with an ethical and political yardstick for measuring the degree to which empirical societies are respectively constraining or enabling of real human needs or interests ("evaluative realism" and the concept of human "well-being")' (2000: 140) (See also Turner, this volume).

None of this, Creaven insists, is tantamount to perpetrating the 'naturalistic fallacy', that is, of collapsing society and culture into human biology, human nature or human subjects. He is worth quoting at some length here in light of our discussion in the next section:

> at the same time as humanity's species-being and attendant powers and capacities are transmitted 'upstream' into social interaction and socio-cultural relations (supplying the power which energizes the social system, constraining and enabling socio-cultural production and reproduction, and providing a certain impetus towards the universal articulation of particular kinds of cultural norms or principles), structural–cultural and agential conditioning are transmitted 'downstream' to human persons (investing in them specific social interests and capacities, shaping unconsciously much of their psychological and spiritual makeup, and furnishing them with the cultural resources to construct personal and social identities for themselves). At the 'micro' level, the result of this complex dialectical interaction between these *distinct layers of human and social reality* is precisely the individual as the bearer or embodiment of a complex articulation of psycho-organic and socio-cultural properties. That is to say, human persons are simultaneously constituted as the concrete bearers of the specific social relations, agential collectivities and institutional roles of which they are a part (social being), of the capacities, powers, needs and interests inherent in them as members of a particular biological species (species-being), and of the process which welds these human and social elements together in the life of the individual (personal biography mediated by social and non-social experience).
>
> (2000: 140–1; emphasis added)

Creaven utilizes Geras's (1983) distinction between 'human nature', as defined above, and 'humanity', referring to those ephemeral cultural characteristics which humans acquire as a consequence of their immersion in historically specific social relations, to stress that the 'nature of humanity' in any given epoch is 'always moulded by the interface between species-being and social being in the life-process of human individuals' (Creaven 2000: 141).

Biology and the social in juvenile Batten disease

Like Creaven, Williams makes use of the works of Bhaskar and Archer to advocate and elaborate a straightforwardly critical realist perspective, in his case in relation to the theorization of chronic illness and the disability debate. He underlines the risks of committing the epistemic fallacy:

> the body, in short, diseased or otherwise, is a real entity, no matter what we call it or how we observe it. It also, like all other social and natural domains, has its own mind-independent generative structures and causal mechanisms. As such it has an ontological depth independent of epistemological claims, right or wrong, as to its existence.
>
> (1999: 806)

'Disease labels', for Williams (1999: 806), are 'merely *descriptive*, not *constitutive* of disease itself' (ibid.).

Setting out to proffer a credible critical realist account of disease and disability, he introduces a 'temporal model' reminiscent of Bhaskar's analysis summarized earlier, but expressed in Archer's (1995) morphogenetic terms, namely, a model comprising *structural conditioning*, which necessarily *pre-dates* the actions which transform it, and about which we may or may not be consciously aware; *socio-cultural interaction*; and either *structural elaboration* (morphogenesis) or *structural reproduction* (morphostasis). He argues that such a model is superior both to postmodernist representations of 'structures' as mere constructs, subject only to 'discursive negotiation', and to disability theorists' exaggerated picture of the social as a 'one-way determinative structure'.

Disability, he argues, is the sole product of neither the impaired body nor a socially oppressive society. Rather, it is an emergent property, located, temporally speaking, in terms of the *interplay* between the biological reality of physiological impairment, structural conditioning and socio-cultural interaction leading to structural elaboration/reproduction. Within this model, he continues: 'structures may be faithfully reproduced or transformed through the conscious awareness and critical praxis of social agents, both individually and collectively: a factor of considerable importance to the disability movement as a whole. The social, in short, is more satisfactorily addressed (i.e. no mere linguistic contrivance), and the body/society relationship, in turn, more adequately worked through (i.e. *both* structural conditioning and degrees of agential freedom) from this critical realist position' (1999: 810). In the case of juvenile Batten disease, such a position permits acknowledgement both of the unyielding physicality of those multiple disabilities which are its issue and which invade all aspects of the lives of affected children and their families, and also of the social ramifications of living with uncertainty, *angst*, family adjustment, felt, enacted and courtesy stigma, and the like.

But how, in the light of our visitations of both the general critical realist contributions of commentators like Bhaskar, Archer and Creaven and the more specific and germane treatment of chronic illness/disability by Williams, might our earlier biomedical synopsis of juvenile Batten disease be analysed further? It will be apparent that we are more than sympathetic to the approaches we have summarized, although all have their points of vulnerability. The four theses we wish to outline and briefly defend in this chapter are very much at one with these approaches. They can be advanced under the following rubrics:

1) the *ontological differentiation* thesis, asserting that the theoretical (and unperceivable) objects of the various natural (life/biomedical) and social sciences are *real* and *different*;
2) the *rationality* thesis, asserting, in critical realist terminology, that the social, changing and fallibilistic properties of knowledgeabilities do not require the acceptance of judgemental relativism;
3) the *social structures* thesis, asserting that the principal contribution of sociology to the explanation of processes of disease/disability lies in its elucidation of the ways in which real relations not only inform perceptions and behaviour but mitigate against *purposive change*.
4) the *division of mental labour* thesis, asserting that the most *effective* way of enhancing knowledge of processes of disease/disability may well be to forsake (premature) inter-disciplinary integration.

The ontological differentiation thesis

The concept of ontological differentiation has already been explicated. Its purchase in the context of phenomena like juvenile Batten disease should be self-evident. The real objects of biomedical and clinical enquiry, yielding through retroduction/abduction generative mechanisms purporting to account for the 'signs' and 'symptoms' associated with the disease label of juvenile Batten disease, are clearly *different* from the real objects of social scientific/sociological enquiry, yielding through similar processes of inference mechanisms to account for the contemporary modes of study and labelling of disease and its treatment, together with its impact, untreated as well as treated, on personal biography and the wider society. The objects of enquiry are real for the biologist/clinician and the sociologist alike, but they are, indeed *must* be, possessed of quite different properties and powers. For example, research into the nature of the CLN3 gene associated with juvenile Batten disease in general (and into a dysfunctional membrane protein identified in CLN3 some five years ago in particular), or research into haplotype analysis as a way of making carrier detection and prenatal diagnosis more accurate, or research into gene therapy and cell stem transplants, are suggestive of generative mechanisms which have little in common with generative mechanisms like class, gender and ethnicity which feature in sociological research.

Archer, Creaven and Williams are in their diverse ways right to insist that sociology must acknowledge not only ontological stratification but also ontological differentiation; and that it must accept, too, concepts like Creaven's 'human nature' and the 'non-social subject' and Archer's 'sense of self', as well as that of Williams's 'real impaired bodies'. Neither the former acknowledgement nor the latter acceptance carries any entailment of biological reductionism, let alone lends credibility to the dogmatic excesses of programmes like sociobiology or evolutionary psychology.

The rationality thesis

Archer and her colleagues (1998: xi) write: 'critical realism claims to be able to combine and reconcile ontological realism, epistemological relativism and judgemental rationality'. Sayer (2000: 47) defines epistemological relativism in this sense as the view that the world can only be known in terms of available descriptions or discourses. What critical realists reject is judgemental relativism, that is, the view that one cannot judge between different discourses and decide that some accounts are better than others. After all, if all knowledge is transitive and fallible, it does not follow that all knowledge is equally fallible; and if all facts are theory-dependent, it does not follow that they are theory-determined (Danermark *et al.* 2002).

One of us has argued elsewhere in favour of a universal (formal or procedural) concept of rationality grounded (but not 'founded') in Habermas' theory of communicative action and discourse ethics (Scambler 1996, 2002). We would add to this a defence of the so-called 'principle of charity', which recognizes that, although the substantive theories and pragmatic thrust and outcomes of knowledgeabilities concerning the body have varied sufficiently across time and place as to suggest, *prima facie*, Kuhnian incommensurability, it is *in fact* generally possible for us both to empathize with and to make sense of how and why past and geographically distant thinkers and healers have differed and do differ from their Western counterparts in high modernity. Arguably, the rationality thesis would not be plausible, and the principle of charity could not apply, in the absence of a universal biological substrate to human affairs.

The social structures thesis

As Williams insists, it is important to acknowledge the reality of bodies, impaired or otherwise. In this context he offers a rare, explicitly critical realist word in support of the WHO's International Classification of Impairment, Disability and Handicap, 'one which places it on both a firmer (i.e. ontological) and sociological (i.e. morphogenetic) footing' (1999: 813). Juvenile Batten disease wounds and destroys the faculties of the young who are affected and prematurely takes away their lives: the biomedical narrative sketched earlier is compelling. To articulate this in terms of the dominant discourse of era and place, that is, in relation to the 'territorialization' of the 'body-with-organs' as organism (Fox 1993), amounts either to yet another reiteration of the trivial truth that all knowledge is social, or to a falling foul of the epistemic fallacy.

As Williams notes, however, this is not at all to deny the salience of 'identity reconstruction', the more so given the 'variety of negative imagery surrounding disability, both past and present' (1999: 811). He approvingly quotes Hughes and Paterson, who state:

> the extent to which impairment can be re-presented (displaced from its association with the grotesque and its role as the other relative to the aesthetic ideals about the body) and reconstructed (in terms of pride and positivity as opposed to a site for the existential fears of the non-disabled community) could be a matter of considerable importance for the development of a cultural politics of identity.
>
> (1997: 332)

The importance of social structures in this context (understood as sets of internally related objects of sociological enquiry (Danermark *et al.* 2002)) is axiomatic. The social structures thesis maintains that an understanding of social structures is crucial for explaining extant categorizations, attributions and behaviours of life-scientists, doctors, patients and carers. However, as Bhaskar accepts in his transformational model of social activity, it also maintains that social structures can generally be expected to nullify or frustrate intentional efforts to secure change, at least in the short- and medium-term. This is not to say, of course, that activists and their allies *cannot* secure change, merely that it is much rarer for them to do so than is frequently assumed.

The division of mental labour thesis

Creaven (2000) points out that there are distinct 'layers of human and social reality'; and that at one and the same time, as previously noted (1) 'humanity's species-being and attendant powers and capacities are transmitted "upstream" into social interaction and socio-cultural relations', and (2) 'structural–cultural and agential conditioning are transmitted "downstream" to human persons'. The individual, in other words, is a complex (dynamic, dialectical) mix of psycho-organic and socio-cultural properties. It is clear, in accordance with the ontological differentiation thesis, that natural/life-scientists, clinicians and social scientists attend to different 'layers of human and social reality'. Each, from the geneticist to the sociologist or anthropologist, has potential relevance to understanding the lot and circumstances of the person with juvenile Batten disease. The division of mental labour thesis suggests that, although the lot and circumstances of the person with juvenile Batten disease cannot be explained by members of any single 'discipline', it may nevertheless hasten the processes of scientific discovery, that is, be optimally effective, to assume otherwise. Rather than pursue interdisciplinary *integration*, in the face of ontological differentiation and in ways that remain cloudy, even foggy, due to epistemological difference in relation to socially constructed discipline-based knowledgeabilities, it may pay to (continue to) work within disciplinary boundaries, expanding or contracting one's contribution *only when compelled to do so* (i.e. as a result of, say, genetic or sociological advance). It is the thesis about which we have most doubts, but one which seems to us worthy of consideration.

To conclude this brief series of reflections, the case for a realist – even, as we have argued in this chapter, a *critical* realist – perspective in biological and social research alike is compelling; and most notably in the face of strong versions of social constructionism and judgemental relativism on the one hand, and doctrinaire forms of biological reductionism on the other, it is also a matter of some urgency. It is a matter, incidentally, which calls for a painful rethink of research methods that has barely begun (Byrne 2002). Turning to juvenile Batten disease once more, we would contend that the objects or generative mechanisms of interest to geneticists, biologists and other life scientists, clinicians and sociologists are equally *real* but *different*; that it remains possible, although often easier in principal than in practice, to reach a rational judgement of the epistemic merits or otherwise of rival discourses and accounts of the genesis, course, treatment, impact on the individual and social 'handicaps' associated with juvenile Batten disease; that it is easy to exaggerate our capacity to intervene *socially* to alleviate the disability and handicap accompanying this unrelenting and as yet lethal condition (which is not of course to proscribe vigorous activism to these ends); and that we have hardly started to think through the epistemological issues raised by multi-disciplinary research on juvenile Batten disease, especially concerning ontological differentiation, let alone prepared the ground for effective inter-disciplinary integration.

References

Adams, R., Victor, M. and Roper, A. (1997) *Principles of Neurology*, 6th edn, New York: McGraw-Hill.

Archer, M. (1995) *Realist Social Theory: the Morphogenetic Approach*, Cambridge: Cambridge University Press.

Archer, M., Bhaskar, R., Collier, A., Lawson, T. and Norrie, A. (eds) (1998) *Critical Realism: Essential Readings*, London: Routledge.

Bhaskar, R. (1978) *A Realist Theory of Science* (2nd edn), Brighton: Harvester.

Bhaskar, R. (1989a) *The Possibility of Naturalism* (2nd edn), Hemel Hempstead: Harvester Wheatsheaf.

Bhaskar, R. (1989b) *Reclaiming Reality: A Critical Introduction to Contemporary Philosophy*, London: Verso.

Byrne, D. (2002) *Interpreting Quantitative Data*, London: Sage.

Collier, A. (1994) *Critical Realism: An Introduction to Roy Bhaskar's Philosophy*, London: Verso.

Creaven, S. (2000) *Marxism and Realism: A Materialist Application of Realism in the Social Sciences*, London: Routledge.

Danermark, B., Ekstrom, M., Jakobsen, L. and Karlsson, J. (2002) *Explaining Society: Critical Realism in the Social Sciences*, London: Routledge.

Fox, N. (1993) *Postmodernism, Sociology and Health*, Milton Keynes: Open University Press.

Geras, N. (1983) *Marx and Human Nature: Refutation of a Legend*, London: Verso.

Goebbel, H., Mole, S. and Lake, B. (1999) *The Neuronal Ceroid Lipofuscinoses (Batten Disease)*, Amsterdam: IOS Press.

Hughes, B. and Paterson, K. (1997) 'The social model of disability and the disappearing body: towards a sociology of impairment', *Disability and Society*, 12: 325–40.

Joseph, J. (2002) 'Five ways in which critical realism can help Marxism', in A. Brown, S. Fleetwood and J. Roberts (eds) *Critical Realism and Marxism*, London: Routledge.

Lawson, T. (1997) *Economics and Reality*, London: Routledge.

Sayer, A. (2000) *Realism and Social Science*, London: Sage.

Scambler, G. (1996) 'The "project of modernity" and the parameters for a critical sociology: an argument with illustrations from medical sociology', *Sociology*, 30: 567–81.

Scambler, G. (2002) *Health and Social Change: A Critical Theory*, Buckingham: Open University Press.

Scambler, S. (1999) *Juvenile Batten Disease: An Overview*, Leatherhead: SeeAbility.

Williams, S. (1999) 'Is anybody there? Critical realism, chronic illness and the disability debate', *Sociology of Health and Illness*, 21: 797–819.

Part II

Structuring biology

Inequalities in health

5 Biology, social class and inequalities in health
Their synthesis in 'health capital'

Mildred Blaxter

The biological is an awkward topic in inequality studies, largely avoided. In part this is because of the demonization in medical sociology of heredity, the spectre of eugenics and its excesses. Ever since the Black Report in 1979, research on class inequality in health, faced with the biological, has defensively been intent on emphasizing the materialist view. The tension between medical sociology and its sister disciplines of epidemiology and public health, equally about sick or healthy bodies, is perhaps illustrative. Epidemiologists have been somewhat reluctant to use social class as a variable, partly because of the risk of implied eugenics. Straightforward genetics can of course be part of epidemiological science, as can straightforward environmental causes of disease. Combining them is dangerous. 'Class', since it cannot be seen or measured except by proxy, is treated warily and often simply as a confounder.

Problems of class and biology also depend to some extent on how inequality is defined, whether in terms of the difference between the top and bottom of the social scale or, crudely, the middle and the working class, or in terms of a fine-grained gradient of health inequality. The latter has been much more fashionable of recent decades, in part because of the extremely influential work of Marmot and colleagues, but also because the dichotomous view smacks of old-fashioned and discredited 'under-class' analysis. It has to be admitted that the contemporary model of inequality creates a paradox for examining the cause of social class differences in health. It is easy to conceive of health-damaging or health-advantaging material differences between social classes I and V: there is no need to invoke genetic differences, for the mechanisms are clear. Elaborations of materialist explanations are required for fine-grained differences as conventionally measured in occupational terms.

In a somewhat similar fashion, the supremacy of materialist explanations for differences between societies has been challenged by the work of Wilkinson (1996) and others. A large body of both cross-sectional and longitudinal research over recent decades has found statistical or ecological associations between measures of income inequality and health status at the population level, both between and within countries, and in both low-income and high-income countries. An individual's health appears to be affected by the *distribution* rather than (or as well as) the absolute level of wealth in their society. Again, this has required some elaboration of the simple equation between poverty and its physical dangers to health.

Another reason for the unease about the biological in inequalities research is that the biological can be seen as too redolent of the medical model. Medical sociology has traditionally distanced itself from the body by the disease/illness distinction: disease and mortality rates, studied in the epidemiology of health inequalities, belong to the medical model; illness, while still located in the body, is somewhat less clearly associated with social class and is more likely to be considered in terms of constructions and perceptions. Even though the medical model may be something of a sociological caricature, teaching that it is an antithesis to the social model of health has tended to remove the physicality of the body.

Williams's (1999) view of disability studies is illuminating in offering a parallel case to class. It is pointed out that the disability movement has tried to 'write the body out' of the biological/social equation, and disability, from this viewpoint, has 'nothing to do with the body and its ailments but everything to do with society, its prejudices and barriers'. If even the impaired body can be seen in this way as conceded to medicine, then this may apply even more clearly to the class-identified body, since social class is even more obviously a social product.

The influence in sociology of constructionism has obviously been crucial in a separation of social epidemiology and sociological interpretivism. If the sociological task is only to analyse how the body is experienced and interpreted by actors, then what is not perceived is not of interest. An 'overprivileging of agency' can easily slide into an epistemological relativism, where the setting, including the context of social class, is defined by the views of the individual, ignoring any broader social forces beyond their consciousness (Wainwright and Forbes 2000: 267). As Bhaskar (1979) pointed out in the seminal realist response to interpretivism, there is an 'epistemic fallacy' in collapsing ontology into epistemology.

These are suggested as some of the reasons why both the 'facts' of social epidemiology and the theoretical approaches of sociology have created an unease about the biological in inequalities research. Some of the different ways in which the biology of class *has* been discussed will be considered in this chapter, together with some of the reasons why none, alone, has proved entirely adequate, before finally attempting a synthesis in terms of the concept of 'health capital'.

Cultural consumption

Several contemporary movements in sociology can be seen as ways of avoiding the most obvious aspects of biology, while still acknowledging the embodiment of social class. One of these concerns cultural consumption and the body. Goffman had noted that symbols of class status are anchored in the body, that dress, deportment, gesture, speech and so on are constituents of 'social style'. Following Bourdieu, this has been elaborated into a popular theme, analysing the structuring forms of stratification, or the way in which lifestyle, shape, diet, or activities such as sport, are used to indicate social distinction. Class-related bodies are formed within habitus and taste, bodily forms become more or less prestigious, and class culture which is turned into nature (that is, embodied) helps to shape the class body (Bourdieu 1984: 190).

The commodification of this process, emphasizing the range of dietary, exercise, slimming, body maintenance and decoration products available, is a popular theme. It is interesting to speculate, though beyond the scope of this chapter, why this became so prominent a topic in the latter decades of the twentieth century. Was it not equally true of the 1920s, or the 1890s? Magazines of these periods illustrate it no less clearly than the contemporary women's magazines so often analysed. However, the point about the commodified body (no less now than then) is that it becomes 'sign-wearing, sign-bearing' (Williams 1995), with a premium placed on youth, beauty and fitness.

The cultural view of embodied class emphasizes the differences which have been said to exist between the attitudes of the working class and the middle class to their own bodies: a working-class emphasis on function, lesser importance given to fitness for its own sake, a more ready acceptance of the inevitability of decline, a greater tendency among those who are more socially deprived to define health simply in terms of the absence of disease. These differences have indeed been demonstrated in many studies, though it can be questioned how great or fundamental a class difference they represent, and how much their expression is an artefact of research situations.

In the health promotion field there is, however, some suggestion that culture is not relevant simply to the appearance or experience of inequality, but also to its creation: more middle-class concepts of positive fitness, beliefs about caring for the body, are actually a contributory cause of better health. While there is no doubt that class-related material resources must enable those aspects of health-consumption which do in fact improve health (not all, of course, do), there has been some resistance to the suggestion that working-class people are necessarily rooted in a health-damaging culturally bound setting from which they cannot escape. The emphasis on consumerism – with the associated globalization – might in fact suggest the likelihood of change. Class-related bodily forms are unlikely to remain static, as, indeed, Bourdieu noted. By their nature, they are continually changing.

Theorists of reflexive modernity such as Beck have taken this further, to argue that class structures are breaking down: identity is referenced to consumer culture rather than class. This is especially so for youth cultures – style, appearance, leisure activity – which are becoming classless, formed in peer group relationships rather than class cultures. Several studies through-out developed countries have demonstrated that social class differences in health in youth are almost non-existent, with an emergent pattern of inequality in early adulthood, with the shift to the young person's own occupational class. Equalization in youth is not uniform for all dimensions. Major impairments arising from birth or early childhood are still class-related, but others – acute illness, accidents, mental health – are more clearly age-based experiences cutting across the influence of social class (West 1997).

Various explanations for this are offered. It has been suggested that any lack of inequality is specific to this one time of life: adolescence is a 'healthy' period, with less room for variation, with the effects of work environments or long-term unhealthy lifestyle habits yet to come. It may be that even if the lifestyles of young people are indeed becoming less differentiated, today's teenagers will become more class-differentiated in cultural consumption relevant to health when they are middle-aged. On the other hand, we have no way of judging the possibility that they will be less so than previous generations: this is not something much discussed, because it is not congruent with the current orthodoxy, driven to look for inequalities, not convergences.

That young bodies, at least, may be becoming culturally less class-differentiated, does not of course imply that the same is currently true of adult or ageing bodies. It is obvious that resources, both monetary and non-monetary, are differentially available as life goes on. Bodies can be abused in any social class, but can be more readily serviced by those with money, time and information. The 'cultural' body will remain, though its useful-ness for the explanation of class inequality in health is not altogether clear.

The web of lifecourse influences on the class-related body

These explanations are more often sought in a different paradigm. Much of the tremendous upsurge of research in social epidemiology of recent decades has been devoted to the attempt to trace out the web of causal influences throughout life. Longitudinal research, and in particular the birth or childhood cohorts in Britain and elsewhere, has been particularly fruitful. One example of this, for instance, is the study of Hertzman *et al.* (2001) of the influences from birth to age 33 in the 1958 British birth cohort, using an interactive framework of society and lifecourse to explain self-rated health. In this perspective, there are three processes acting between early life and adult life: latent effects, independent of intervening experience; pathway effects, whereby the early environment sets individuals on life trajectories that affect health over time; and cumulative effects. Latency effects, that is, specific biological or developmental factors at sensitive periods of early life, have lifelong effects. Hertzman *et al.* note that these may be difficult to distinguish from pathway effects, where, for instance, the social class of parents determines the child's environment, and eventually their life chances through such mechanisms as education and social networks. Cumulative effects refer to the building up of advantaging and disadvantaging factors, and the duration and intensity of physiological or psychosocial damages.

There are also contemporary circumstances which clearly affect adult health, which are at the simplest level those things which have traditionally been studied cross-sectionally such as income or factors of the physical environment, and at the most complex concepts such as the 'social capital' of civil society. The analysis of Hertzman *et al.* conceives of the individual lifecourse as an arrow running from gestation to old age, subsuming latent pathways at the beginning of life, and with pathway and cumulative factors unfolding throughout. Using a wide range of variables at different levels of social aggregation, the analysis found that the effects of childhood factors (e.g. birthweight, height, parental behaviour, education) were not removed by including contemporary factors (e.g. work, material circumstances, social support). But conversely, contemporary factors contributed to the prediction of self-rated health over and above lifecourse factors. Each dimension was distinct from the others.

This particular study relates to the health outcome of self-rated health, and it has to be noted that (however clearly relationships to other measures, including mortality, have been shown) this is not the same as disease or mortality: it is demonstrable that different measures of health, whether as state or status, process or capital, may be affected in different ways. Self-rated health may be an indication of current well-being, while objective measures of morbidity and mortality represent the combined impact of lifecourse experiences on the body.

'Trace-back' studies can also be illuminating. That of Berney *et al.* (2000), of a cohort in 1997–8 who were first studied in 1937–9, examining largely occupational and residential hazards, showed the relationship between childhood disadvantage and cumulative exposure throughout life. Disadvantage in childhood, in terms of both health and social position, is linked to subsequent levels of disadvantage: material and environmental damage accumulate, in ways related to social class.

These are simply examples of the complexity of the lifecourse socio-biological web, and the sophistication of the immense current research effort devoted to tracing it. It is generally agreed that social mobility, though it adds a complicating factor, does not *explain* class inequalities as they are measured in adult life Obviously, early life experiences do not have the same effect for everyone. There are downward spirals, and there are escape routes, depending on the individual and the resources available.

The social/biological mechanisms

All this does not explain *how*, in terms of biological mechanisms, social class or social disadvantage actually affect health. The fact has to be accommodated that dysfunction, disease and death are bodily mechanisms which must have physiological causes.

It is agreed that the mechanisms are not, largely, genetic. For instance, Tarlov (1996) estimates that straightforward genetic inheritance may account for between 1 and 5 per cent of the total disease burden, and indirect evidence such as blood grouping provides evidence of genetic homogeneity across social classes.

At the beginning of life mechanisms are involved which are clearly biological: events during gestation as indicated by birth-weight, and in infancy, have been related to several chronic diseases in later life, such as cardiovascular disease, diabetes or obstructive lung disease (Barker 1992). It may be that this is early programming in utero or in earliest infancy, or directly-caused long-term damage. The achieved height of populations, associated with early life experience including nutrition, correlates with life expectancy. It is also thought that adequate quality of nutrition is important during particular developmental periods for the development of the brain as well as other organ systems.

It may be, however, that such things as low birth-weight and infant growth act as markers for other causal factors such as the social circumstances of the family of birth, with some influence on the likelihood of a disadvantaged life trajectory. Throughout life, it is easy to see how the most obvious material insults will affect the body – hygiene, diet, pollution, accidents, harmful work – but it is difficult to see them as more than a partial explanation for inequality at both the top and bottom of the class scale. Other evidence is adduced to show the necessity for explanations which, while keeping material disadvantage central to social class inequalities in health, allow for more than the direct physiological effects.

Thus a need is felt to find what Tarlov (1996: 71) calls the sociobiologic translation: the way in which social characteristics are perceived, processed into biological signals, and converted into disease:

> how human beings receive messages regarding their social conditions, convert the information into perceptions, and then translate the perceptions into biological signals that are antecedents to diseases which may take decades before becoming clinically apparent.

It has long been known that distress, grief, and other damaging emotions can harm physical health. That psychological stress can contribute to mental illness and affect health-damaging behaviour is generally agreed, but the search has been for specific mechanisms by which stress can be transformed into specific disease or general susceptibility. The biological systems known to be concerned are common to most mammals. On perceiving threat or danger, the body is prepared for fight or flight through the nervous and endocrine systems, and adverse consequences for health result if arousal is sustained or constantly recurring. Brunner (1996), for instance, suggests the plausibility of pathways by which an adverse psychosocial environment produces an excess of coronary heart disease: direct psychoendocrine mechanisms disturb normal physiological functioning, distinct from, though cumulative with, indirect mechanisms of relevant health behaviours. A unified explanation is proposed, linking psychosocial factors with increased risk of metabolic syndrome type abnormalities. Tarlov (1996) offers a schema beginning at the start of life which involves the perception of inequality, with a clash between expectations and reality eventually creating a chronic dissonance which triggers biological signals that are the antecedents of disease.

The concepts which are invoked to provide the link to social circumstances are those such as feelings of control, self-efficacy and social cohesion. Low social status engenders psychological distress as expressed in feelings such as shame, lack of self-esteem, lack of dignity and respect. The recently very active 'social capital' movement argues that community processes such as social cohesion and mutual trust are buffers against the effect of stress and poor living conditions, though problems about aligning this social capital theory with class remain, perhaps, to be addressed.

Faced with the paradox of such regular inequalities with seemingly so complex a web of social causes, the temptation must always be to look for single causes. Social stress research, in biological, psychological and social fields, has provided plausible accounts of how social inequalities in health arise. Stressors, particularly if they are long-term, are unevenly distributed in society: to a large extent parallel with, and cumulative with, material resources. Coping and buffering resources in response to stress are similarly differentially distributed by social class.

There has, however, been some reaction against too great an emphasis on psychological responses to social stress, or their sociobiologic translation to disease. As Muntaner and Lynch (1999) have noted, the problem of over-privileging internal dynamics is that it can result in individual or community-blaming, an approach which may yield anti-egalitarian public health policies.

The relative income hypothesis

The 'relative income' hypothesis, that an individual's health is affected by the distribution of wealth in their society, was mentioned as one of the reasons why class-related bodies, seen in terms of economic disadvantage and material deprivations, have been found somewhat awkward as a concept in inequality studies. Class structure and income distribution are not necessarily the same, of course. It is possible to have unequal income distributions in very differently structured societies. That absolute poverty affects health is not in question, but queries arise about why health inequality persists or even widens in richer western societies. As Wilkinson (2000: 65) notes, 'social and economic systems are constantly changing, and it is becoming increasingly important to distinguish between the effects of class and the effects of inequality'.

However, as Wilkinson goes on to argue, the 'sociobiologic translation' offers explanations for the observed relationships. Psychosocial pathways provide the link between socioeconomic circumstances and health. The biology of chronic stress provides knowledge of the risk factors for adverse physiological changes. These include low status, lack of control, stressful life events, insecurity in work, housing, or income – all things over which the individual has little control, in an unequal society. Income inequality undermines social cohesion and harms psychosocial health at the individual level. Hierarchies of dominance in an unequal society create behavioural responses which include discrimination and prejudice, conflict and social tension.

There has been some debate about this thesis. Gravelle *et al.* (2002) for instance, among others, argue that there are conceptual difficulties in using aggregate cross-sectional data as a means of testing hypotheses about the effect of income and its distribution on the health of individuals, because of artefactual effects of non-linearity in the individual health–income relationship. On the other hand, Ellison (2002) notes that the curvilinear relationship might simply be a reflection of the mechanism of the relative income hypothesis, if income inequality does in fact have an independent effect on individual health. Discussion continues, but the theory remains as one of the most interesting ways of considering contemporary class-related bodies. In particular, it emphasizes the importance of thinking about what affects the body's defences, rather than regarding health simply in terms of exposure to infections or other external hazards (Wilkinson 2000: 37).

Social Darwinism

Reaction to the crude forms of sociobiology and social Darwinism has been one of the reasons why mainstream sociology has been wary of considering class-related bodies. Some of the work which has been mentioned has, however, been incorporated into a modified social Darwinism, taking account of, for instance, Barker's work on perinatal health, together with the relative income hypothesis.

Dickens (2000), for instance, notes that since health deteriorates in societies where the differences in power relations are most extreme, there are possible long-term relations between capitalism, ontology and human evolution (p. 98). Ill health is passed on through families because 'A pregnant woman gives an unwitting "weather forecast" to her unborn child, signalling the kind of world into which he or she will be born'. This can be passed on from one generation to the next, so that 'we can therefore begin to envisage a biological mechanism contributing to the continued reproduction of an "unfit" underclass' (p. 109).

This obviously remains highly controversial. More intriguing is the suggestion that 'a way in which evolutionary thought and social theory can be combined' can be found in considering the potential of the new genetics. Human biology is itself evolving, not by pure accident but by its manipulation: the exercise of social power could thus be having long-term effects on evolution. This is 'perhaps just part of a more general and long-term process of "real subsumption", one in which capital is modifying human biological structure in its own image' (p. 116). This is achieved not only by the possibility of deliberate genetic manipulation, but by a more subtle process – a 'gradual embedding' of a division between abstract and concrete thinking in the biological structure of the population, since the power relations of modern society mean that conceptual work is highly prized and practical work downgraded. What is being suggested is Darwinian selection by aptitude.

Such an argument is somewhat different to Davey's (this volume) that a new evolutionary theory (avoiding intentionality, incorporating randomness, and taking proper time-scales into account) must be included as an integral part of understanding human social processes. It is also probably less generally acceptable, though all attempts to incorporate the advances of biological science into understanding inequality must remain the most exciting contemporary undertakings.

General susceptibility or disease-specific inequality?

One of the most important arguments from the 1970s concerned the possible identification of a *general* susceptibility to ill health related to social class inequalities. Other influences than polluted atmospheres, poor diets, smoking, dangerous work, which might account for particular forms of ill health must be sought for the regular pattern of mortality by social class. Part of the rationale behind the extensive work identifying factors such as stress, lack of control, and other psychosocial explanations, was the search for general causes which might map on to these general patterns. The work of the Whitehall Study among others was influential in suggesting a social class difference in susceptibility to a variety of specific insults. While the effect of specific causes such as smoking was undoubted, the regular difference in health between social grades seemed to be related to generalized differences in susceptibility to pathogens. This work was crucial in turning attention away from single health-harming behaviours, or a crude emphasis on specific material factors, to a wider concept of social class relationships.

Biology has been brought back in, as already described, by asking what the precise physiological mechanisms might be. However, another clearly biological approach is more recently being introduced by the suggestion that attention should return to disease-specific morbidity and mortality. Davey Smith *et al.* (2001), for instance, review life-time approaches to class inequality and suggest that the mechanisms of general susceptibility, within the stress paradigm, may conceal the true complexity of inequality. The relative importance of socially patterned exposures at different stages of life differs between particular causes of ill health. Different conditions are influenced in different ways – some especially by early-life causes which decrease in importance, and some by adulthood or lifecourse determinants which become of increasing importance throughout life.

These authors point out that class inequalities in objective measures of mortality and morbidity result from a tendency for a few important causes of ill health (CHD, stroke, lung cancer and respiratory disease) to show large socioeconomic differentials. In the course of this century, these causes of death have become the most important and their social gradient has become steeper. The concentration of risk factors for these diseases in disadvantaged groups underlies the inequality in overall health status.

This emphasis on the importance of specific diseases, rather than imply-ing a return to biological reductionism, can contribute to more complex and satisfactory models of social class inequality in health. These are dis-eases which usually manifest themselves clinically only after relatively long periods of exposure to combined and persistent risk factors. Tarlov notes that the transduction of signals into specific disease may well receive its specificity from polygenic inheritance, but the distribution of predisposing combinations of genes does not differ greatly by social strata. The social gradients in the prevalence of disease are due to the social characteristics within which lives are played out. Social structure leads to clustering, over time and cross-sectionally, of multiple risk factors in the same individuals: 'Human bodies in different social locations become crystallised reflections of the social experiences within which they have developed' (Tarlov 1996: 84).

Lay perceptions of embodied health

The 'psychobiologic translation' which has been discussed suggests that subjective perceptions of inequality cannot be irrelevant, if inequality in health derives in any large part from psychosocial processes of reaction to stress. To suggest that the translation from experience to processes of the immune or other systems proceeds mechanically and unperceived by the individuals involved is to reinstate a mind/body dualism which would present an irreconcilable paradox. In the field of chronic illness it has been suggested that understanding requires a sociology which integrates the physicality of the body, for the obvious reason that illness is experienced in the body. Class-related health is perceived in the body, too. Whether people themselves identify class-related inequalities is another way of attempting to study embodied health.

Several studies exploring lay concepts have shown that, in practical terms and as lay accounts, people often do identify class-related inequalities. In their own lives they commonly identify environmental or work-related causes of disease. They can, however – and this is particularly true of those who have disadvantaged lives – resist general ideas of class-related inequality specific to health: health 'is the one area in which we are all equal', for we all have to die. Lay reports may claim that the 'rich' may have particularly unhealthy lifestyles; sedentary and indoor work is less conducive to fitness than manual and outdoor work; people of all classes can be exposed to stress; health is to a great degree in one's own hands; absolute poverty and deprivation (including of medical care) are a thing of the past, so 'of course we are all healthier now'.

Bourdieu's practical logic and logic of practice, or Giddens' discursive consciousness and practical consciousness, are relevant (Williams 1995). As it is too much to ask informants to explain principles of actions largely taken for granted, so it is too much to ask them to place themselves in a class structure, especially when asking about an embodied life. George Brown among others speaks of 'distal' causation, which it is incumbent on researchers to establish, not lay people to know. Asked about a one-off health event respondents often say in effect 'this happened because of an exploitative job', or 'this happened because of material deprivation at the time'. But asked for general accounts of health, they are hardly likely to invoke the class structure. There are too many interweaving influences and events, too complex from the close viewpoint of the individual, to be ascribed to such an abstract 'cause'.

However, even if this sort of regular variation is not discernible in lay presentations, the probabilities of disease and death, constructed out of actual events into Standardized Mortality Ratios by social class, are still real. Any absence of such models is not folly or ignorance on the part of informants, but simply that epidemiological reality and personal experience have complicated relationships with each other. The perceived complexity is particularly obvious if the dimension of time is included (Blaxter 2000).

Health capital

What lay accounts do demonstrate clearly is an idea of health capital. This simple metaphor clearly associates class with the body, the central repository of this capital. As economic capital is represented by the waxing and waning of monetary value, so health capital consists of bodily currency – strength fitness, immune status, inherited tendencies, developmental spurts and hiccups, physical damage, vulnerability. Like economic capital, it can be 'measured' at one point of time, but represents a process of accumulated gain and loss. It can, like economic capital, be lost or gained in more or less completely accidental ways, unconnected with the lifecourse and not predictable. But, again like economic capital, it is not normally random but part of a cumulative and recognisable pattern. A genetic stock of health capital is laid down at conception: in utero, at birth and in early infancy it is elaborated and the basis is provided for health in later life. Opportunities exist throughout life for the augmentation or depletion of this capital, through education, family life and occupation. Wadsworth (1997) offers a summary of how the childhood cohorts have shown in particular detail how health capital is accumulated or dispersed throughout childhood. A poor start in life, associated with poorer parental socioeconomic class and vulnerability to illness, can be reinforced by lower levels of parental concern about education, lower achievement, and subsequent lower occupational class and poorer health.

Throughout life, this health capital is depleted – by behaviours such as smoking or unwise eating, by work dangers and stresses, by childbearing among women, by the strains of social and family life, by environmental damage, by accidental infection and trauma and by simple degradations of time. It can also be augmented, by 'healthy' behaviour or the deliberate search for 'fitness', or by positive, life-enhancing circumstances. Eventually, of course, all health capital must be spent, but the whole of 'inequalities' research demonstrates how the timing and nature of this loss is socially-patterned. The depletion of health capital is most obvious at the ages when chronic or degenerative disease is beginning to strike. Thus social class effects press most heavily in middle age. A notable finding of the Health and Lifestyle surveys (Cox *et al.* 1993) was that there were not only clear differences by social class in the proportion of people in middle and old age who said, re-interviewed after seven years, that their health had deteriorated, but also class differences in age-related deterioration in some measured bodily characteristics such as lung function, with smoking history controlled for.

As Bury and Wadsworth note (this volume), there has been a preoccuption with premature mortality. Descriptive statistics of the nation's health, considering social class, have tended to stop at formal retirement age, if only because it is then less easy to categorize people. With an ageing population, this preoccupation should give way to more sensitive data, examining disruption and continuity across the entire life course.

Health capital is obviously not *only* the physiological condition of the body's organs, nor heredity, nor the effects of age, nor the state of the immune system, and we find its complexity difficult to measure. This does not mean, however, that individuals themselves do not have some clear perception of it and talk of it at length. They express this as in quite large part inherited, in part influenced by chance, in part the consequence of social circumstances, and in part in the individual's own hands to dissipate or increase. Clearly-expressed lay ideas of health capital involve many of the biological pathways and relationships of social-epidemiological research – the apparent power of pre- and post-natal circumstances in shaping the limits for future health; the importance of childhood environment; the effects of working environments. People themselves are clear that loss and gain can be very gradual, or can be sudden. They are also clear that part of this is in their own hands, but much is not.

Individual trajectories cannot of course be seen in isolation. The individual lifecourse is part of social time. Class-related bodies may be associated with economic conditions in particular historical periods, or with changing behavioural patterns. Social factors operate in the light of wider forces which leave their mark on each generation (Wadsworth 1991). There are period effects of living through epidemics, economic depression, or traumatic eras of history, and long-term consequences of general changes in social conditions and lifestyles which do not have causes specific to the individual though they affect individual bodies. Thus the determinants of health capital are cohort-specific and not entirely individual: the concept links the individual lifetime with the temporal movement of social history.

Conclusion

An attempt has been made to consider the reasons why biology has been found so difficult to deal with in the study of class-defined inequalities in health, and how the various ways of trying to incorporate it have remained somewhat separate from each other and – though each is interesting and important in its own right – none, individually, wholly convincing.

Both the 'cultural' and the epidemiological body provide descriptions, rather than complete explanations, for the difficult question of class-based inequalities. Materialist explanations are obviously important, and the psychosocial 'translations' of them add to the understanding of the varying mechanisms involved. However, as Forbes and Wainwright (2001) note, any debate about whether social status is psychologically referenced through stress, self-esteem, social dysfunction or distress, or socially referenced through income, occupation, housing, the physical environment, or work dangers, is unprofitable. Of course, the answer is through both, and the body is the link and the boundary between them.

A health capital model is a simple way of combining social-epidemiological, cultural and constructivist approaches into a realist framework. Even genetics can be given a modest place. Health capital is essentially a metaphor, but it is perhaps more than that. As a heuristic, it may serve to direct research towards ways of dealing with the complexity of class-related patterns of health, and at the same time anchoring explanations firmly in the body.

The model admits the impact of power and exploitation, gives structure and agency equal weighting, and accommodates both the cultural and economic aspects of the 'market' in which the capital is gained and lost. It does not necessarily exclude that which is outside individual consciousness, and while it accepts the constructed nature of social facts it does not deny physical facts. While noting the importance of psychosocial pathology, it admits other sorts of class-related damage.

Above all, as a model it accommodates processes of time, both individual and societal, and both 'real' or biological, or constructed by the individual. Its gain and loss is intimately connected with the mutual interplay of agency and structure across time. Health capital connects the different stages of life together, and the varying influences that bear upon health status at any point of time.

This is not to deny the importance of class in the understanding of health inequalities. To note that an individual life moves between classes as defined by the Registrar General's schema, that groups of people may have more or less continuity, greater or less security, longer or shorter acceleration and deceleration in status and rewards, is not to dismiss class as an explanatory variable but to elaborate it. Class and time are intimately related, for in a very real sense class represents the resources for the control of time: ability to plan health capital as one might economic capital; ability to exercise choice over the future; ability to connect the different stages of the lifecourse.

Class is embodied to the extent that bodily attributes and events – inheritance from the beginning of life, fitness, energy – can influence the trajectory of the lifecourse. However, acceptance that the biological is, ultimately, the currency of health capital is, similarly, not to remove the social from the explanation of inequalities in health.

References

Barker, D.J.P. (ed.) (1992) *Fetal and Infant Origins of Adult Disease*, London: British Medical Journal.

Berney, L., Blane, D., Davey Smith, G. and Holland, P. (2000) 'Lifecourse influences on health in early old age', *in* H. Graham, (ed.) *Understanding Health Inequalities*, Buckingham: Open University Press, pp. 79–95.

Bhaskar, R. (1979) *A Realist Philosophy of Science*, Brighton: Harvester.

Blaxter, M. (2000) 'Class, time and biography', *in* S.J. Williams, J. Gabe and M. Calnan (eds) *Health, Medicine and Society: Key Theories, Future Agendas*, London: Routledge, pp. 27–50.

Bourdieu, P. (1984) *Distinction: a Social Critique of the Judgement of Taste*, London: Routledge.

Brunner, E. (1996) 'The social and biological basis of cardiovascular disease', *in* D. Blane, E. Brunner and R. Wilkinson (eds) *Health and Social Organisation*, London: Routledge, pp. 272–303.

Cox, B.D., Huppert, F.A. and Whichelow, M.J. (1993) *The Health and Lifestyle Survey: Seven Years On*, Aldershot: Dartmouth Publishing.

Davey Smith, G., Gunnell, D. and Ben Schlomo, Y. (2001) 'Lifecourse approaches to socio-economic differentials in cause-specific adult mortality', *in* D.A. Leon and G. Walt (eds) *Poverty Inequality and Health*, Oxford: University Press, pp. 88–124.

Dickens, P. (2000) *Social Darwinism*, Buckingham: Open University Press.

Ellison, G.T.H. (2002) 'Letting the Gini out of the bottle? Challenges facing the relative income hypothesis', *Social Science and Medicine*, 54, 4: 561–76.

Forbes, A. and Wainwright, S.P. (2001) 'On the methodological, theoretical and philosophical context of health inequalities research: a critique', *Social Science and Medicine*, 53, 6: 801–16.

Gravelle, H., Wildman, J. and Sutton, M. (2002) 'Income inequality and health: what can we learn from aggregate data?', *Social Science and Medicine*, 54, 4: 577–90.

Hertzman, C., Power, C., Matthews, S. and Manor, O. (2001) 'Using an interactive framework of society and lifecourse to explain self-rated health in early adulthood', *Social Science and Medicine*, 53, 12: 1575–85.

Muntaner, C. and Lynch, J. (1999) 'Income inequality, social cohesion and class relations', *International Journal of Health Services*, 29: 59–81.

Tarlov, A.R. (1996) 'Social determinants of health: the sociobiological translation', *in* D. Blane, E. Brunner and R. Wilkinson (eds) *Health and Social Organisation*, London: Routledge, pp. 71–93.

Turner, B.S. (1992) *Regulating Bodies: Essays in Medical Sociology*, London: Routledge.

Wadsworth, M. (1991) *The Imprint of Time: Childhood History and Adult Life*, Oxford: Oxford University Press.

Wadsworth, M. (1997) 'Health inequalities in a lifetime perspective', *Social Science and Medicine*, 44, 6: 859–70.

Wainwright, S.P. and Forbes, A. (2000) 'Philosophical problems with social research on health inequalites', *Health Care Analysis*, 8: 259–77.

West, P. (1997) 'Health and inequalities in the early years: is there equalisation in youth?', *Social Science and Medicine*, 44, 6: 833–58.

Wilkinson, R.G. (1996) *Unhealthy Societies: the Afflictions of Inequality*, London: Routledge.

Wilkinson, R.G. (2000) *Mind the Gap: Hierarchies, Health and Human Evolution*, London: Weidenfeld & Nicolson.

Williams, S.J. (1995) 'Theorizing class, health and lifestyles: can Bourdieu help us?' *Sociology of Health and Illness*, 17, 5: 577–604.

Williams, S.J. (1999) 'Is anybody there? Critical realism, chronic illness and the disability debate', *Sociology of Health and Illness*, 21, 6: 797–819.

6 Gender and health status
Does biology matter?

Ellen Annandale

On the question of whether biology matters for gender and health, the response must definitely be 'yes'. There is no straightforward answer to the quandary of 'who is sicker' in a universal sense, but women and men do have different life spans and often experience health and illness in different ways. Despite several decades of intensive research, the reasons for the social patterning of health by gender remain enigmatic.

Although both biological and social factors have always been a component part of social scientific research on gender and health status, the role of biology has typically been downplayed in favour of social explanations. This is a legacy of the distinction between the biological (sex) and the social (gender) drawn by second wave feminists to challenge biological determinism. These distinctions and the heavy emphasis upon the *social* production of women's ill health have cast a very long shadow over research on gender and health status. Despite increased interest in the role of biology at present, we are still struggling to specify the interaction of biological and social factors and what the health consequences are. All too often empirical research focuses only on a cluster of proximate causes and gender and health lose their social structural moorings. Without these moorings we are left with findings – similarities and differences on various measures of health by gender – for which we have no explanation. This is evident in the current shift in research away from the driving assumption that 'women are sicker, but men die quicker' towards an appreciation of the more complex pattern of similarities and differences in morbidity and mortality by gender. This shift is important, but there is a danger that documenting complexity becomes an end in itself, leaving the question of why still largely untouched. It is therefore important to develop a theoretical base from which to address both the general question of why patterns of similarity and difference in morbidity and mortality exist and the more specific question of the role of biology. This chapter aims to contribute to this development.

The chapter begins from the simple standpoint that the answer to the question of how social and biological factors interact to produce health in relation to gender lies within the specific social and historical circumstances of people's lives. It is these circumstances that need to be articulated as a theoretical basis for research. The biological and the social have been drawn into a new symphysis by recent changes in the social relations of production and consumption and by new ways of thinking within the social and biological sciences. At the same time that social scientists and some biologists began to stress that biology is open and transformable, rather than fixed, late capitalism has made a virtue of the mutability of the gendered (social and biological) body as it is positioned and re-positioned within new consumption practices. Not only traditional gender roles ('the social'), but also distinctions between sexed ('biological') bodies are diminishing through what Hennessy (2000) terms the continual tooling and retooling of the desirous subject. Importantly for this discussion, active engagement of the 'lived body' in new and changing patterns of consumption can be linked in a preliminary way to changing patterns of health and illness by gender. The chapter begins by briefly considering ways of thinking about the biological and the social within the social and biological sciences. It then reflects upon the connection between these new ways of thinking and new more fluid forms of sex(biology)- and gender(social)-related practices within contemporary capitalism. Recent shifts in mortality patterns and a case study of melanoma (skin cancer) are used to illustrate the contention that the social and the biological are drawn together into a new system within late capitalism and that articulating this system may be a way forward for understanding the relationship between gender and health status.

The biological and the social

The distinction between *sex* as biological difference and *gender* as social or cultural difference between men and women has been subject to much critical debate in recent years. As noted earlier, the distinction had, and still has, an important political function for feminists working on gender and health status. Traditionally patriarchy has treated biological sex and social gender as one and the same: gender follows directly on from sex, and women's inferiority is a natural product of her (inferior) biological make-up. This is what I will call the traditional or 'old single system' of patriarchy. By breaking the tight connection between sex and gender feminists were able to argue that women's relatively poor health is the result of social oppression, not biological inferiority.[1] However many problems followed in the wake of this new perception. Notably, as Moi (1999: 4) puts it, when social gender becomes the variable, biological sex becomes the essence; 'immobile, stable, coherent, fixed, prediscursive, natural and ahistorical: the mere surface on which the script of gender is written'. As biology was cast aside it became unknowable, standing as little more than that which is not social (Birke 1999). Of course biology has not been ignored completely. Feminist critics of science, for example, have mounted forceful critiques of overdetermined scientific, including medical, representations of differences between the male and female body. But here the aim is not so much to engage with biology than to demonstrate that what passes as scientific objectivity is riddled with social and political assumptions. A kind of cultural reductionism is in play as social gender becomes 'a barricade thrown up against the insidious persuasiveness of [biological] sex' (Moi 1999: 15). This tendency, which I will call the 'social difference approach', has been marked in empirical research on gender and health status. If it gets a mention biology is typically a residual factor which plays an unarticulated background role to a cluster of more important social factors, such as socioeconomic, employment-related, educational and social attitudinal differences between men, women and their health.

But things are beginning to change. Theoretically, it is increasingly stressed that the social and the biological, sex and gender are bound together, but in a different way to the 'old single system'. The common concept drawing these oppositions together across the sciences is 'openness'. For example, in post-structuralist work and beyond (e.g. Butler 1993) biology has to be conceived as open, rather than closed or fixed, in order for the discursive construction of sex to take place. Social scientists as well as some biologists, stress openness as a counter to biological determinism. Birke (1999), for example, envisages organisms as self-actualizing agents. Here bodies have agency in relation to their environment as they constantly interact to change, both inside and out. Dickens (2000) similarly stresses that the human organism does not blindly respond to the environment, but is actively involved in making that environment. This is seen in ontogenesis, human development from embryo to young adult. Here 'development is not simply encoded by genes', 'the social and physical environment plays a key role in terms of affecting how basic, genetically-based, processes are formed during an individual's development as that individual responds to and indeed changes her or his external environment' (Dickens 2000: 61). The development of the infant brain and of consciousness, for example, take place through engagement with the world. These changes extend beyond the academy. As Martin (1999: 106) discusses through the example of the immune system, in society at large people are moving away from a mechanical view towards a conceptualization of the body as fluid, flexible, and ever-changing.

But such thinking is still in its infancy. As Birke (1999) relates, to date we know very little empirically about how social engagement impacts on the body. One reason for this may be that, stimulating though they are, many of the points about the openness of the biological body and its formation in relation to the social and physical world fail actually to locate the body in *any particular time and space*. The interaction of the social and the biological is curiously de-contextualized. It often seems to bear little direct relation to what is happening to people in the everyday world in which they live. This grounding is crucial for understanding the relationship between gender and health status. In moving from the traditional framework of 'gendered difference' in health towards complex cross-cutting patterns of similarity and difference among women and men, researchers are engaging – albeit often implicitly – with the massive and diverse changes that are taking place in men's and women's lives in western developed capitalist economies. It is therefore important for research on gender and health status, that new ways of thinking about the relationship between the biological and the social, sex and gender are embedded in this particular social and historical context.

The biological and the social, sex and gender in patriarchal capitalism

Capitalism, as Dickens (2000) explains, shapes human biology in its own image. It also shapes the way that we think about relationships between the biological and the social, sex and gender. For example, during industrial capitalism, sex (as biology) and (social)gender were dimorphic with biological sex determining social gender. Men earned the family wage, while women, when not drawn into the work force as a reserve army of labour, worked unpaid in the home. Since there was no need to pay the cook and cleaner, servicing men for free reduced the cost of men's labour power i.e. the level of subsistence wages and boosted employers' profits. But this dichotomy does not make economic sense for late capitalism which relies heavily upon fluid and malleable identities which are formed equally, if not more, in the sphere of consumption as production.

The steadfast roles of male breadwinner, female homemaker and all that accompanied them in attitudinal and behavioural terms, are being torn apart by far-reaching changes in employment, education, family and house-hold structure, leisure and consumption. Limitations of space mean that these changes can only be sketched here. Changes in the gender composition of the workforce have been especially dramatic. This is linked to industrial restructuring through the decline of manufacturing and the emergence of an economy dominated by the service industries and 'people work'.[2] The growing participation of married women has been particularly marked. Most of the increase in women's jobs has been in part-time work (itself a feature of the service sector). Even so, the level of commitment to employment appears to vary little by gender (Gallie 2000). Changes within education have been equally striking, with girls now outpacing boys in achievement at both GCSE and 'A' level in the UK. The 'dual burden' of paid and unpaid work for women remains, but the male–female gap has been narrowing (Gershuny and Fisher 2000: 634–5). These changes have been accompanied by a falling birth rate, a rise in one-parent and lone households and an increase in divorce. This is the backdrop for quite revolutionary – but very complex – changes in the lives of men and women. There do seem to have been 'gains' for women. However, protestations such as Coward's (1999: 14) 'tidal wave of social emancipation' for women are certainly premature, as is her castigation of feminists for the sorrows of men, such as insecurity in the workplace and loss of self-esteem. This gives too much weight to gender when other social divisions such as social class, age and ethnicity are also important. For example, although age prescriptions are weakening, age is still a major marker of difference, with older women being far less likely to have 'caught up with men' in areas like employment opportunities, education, income and so on than their younger counterparts. Moreover, the 'gains' among younger women in areas such as education need to be read alongside worrying trends such as the rise in criminal convictions among juvenile women.[3] Walby's (1997: 1) conclusion that contemporary lives are changing in complex ways, not simply for better or worse, for either men or women is therefore an apt summary of the present situation.

The opening up of the biological body (as described by social and natural scientists) and the opening up of the social body, as described above, means that sex (biology) is no longer tied so directly in traditional ways to gender i.e. to what I have called the *'old single system'*. The mapping of what is traditionally thought of as male sex onto male gender, and female sex onto female gender, has begun to give way to a more flexible, or open, system. This is not to say that we have begun to experience sex and gender as a free choice. Indeed the more flexible character of sex(biology) and (social)gender has a strong and systematic guiding hand from contemporary patriarchal capitalism which profits from the new markets that an increasingly diversified 'gender economy' generates. So I am not suggesting that social gender and biological sex are no longer connected – it is still not possible to think about sex without thinking about gender, and vice versa – but rather that they are being drawn into a new, more complex and shifting relationship. A *'new single system'* is born in which social(gender) and biological(sex) depend on each other for understanding just as much as before, but where the meaning of biological sex and the meaning of social gender, as well as the connections between them, are more fluid.

The commodification of sex and gender

Individualization is the defining feature of much current thinking about the relationship between the individual and society in the west. Beck and Beck-Gernsheim (2002: 30, 31) argue that 'there has been a social impetus toward individualization of unprecedented scale and dynamism' which 'forces people – for the sake of their survival – to make themselves the centre of their own life plans and conduct'. This 'self-culture' is a fertile ground for the commodification of sex and gender. Sex and gender are positioned and re-positioned as capitalism has extended commodity marketing 'further than ever into the body and the unconsciousness, and heightened the manipulation of human needs and desires for corporate profit' (Hennessy 2000: 4–5). It is important then to consider the empirical nature of these new relations of biological sex and social gender.

Table 6.1 Relations of sex and gender

	Biology	Gender
Old single system	Male (sex)	Male (gender)
	Female (sex)	Female (gender)
New single system	Male (sex)	Female (gender)
	Female (sex)	Male (gender)

Table 6.1 depicts the 'old single system' where sex and gender map onto each other and the 'new single system' where gender identities, attitudes and behaviours are no longer tied so directly to biologically defined sex. Approbation and censure of 'men behaving like women' and perhaps more often, 'women behaving like men', feature so frequently in media headlines that it is easy to view the gender-related changes of the 'new single system' as commonplace. But they are actually revolutionary effects of commodity capitalism which is breaking down 'oppressive and at times brutally constraining traditional structures and ways of life' (Hennessy 2000: 29). But academic commentators have been troubled by the culture of individualization which surrounds new gender identities. Discussion has mostly been about young women, especially from feminist writers who have expressed their concern that the de-traditionalization of their lives has been accompanied by a new 'free-market feminism', vitalized by the seductions of individual success, the lure of female empowerment and the love of money' (McRobbie 2000: 213). Consider, for example, Whelehan's (2000: 37) depiction of the new girl icon: 'she is active rather than passive, and ruthlessly self-seeking in her own pleasures. Outspoken and sometimes aggressive, the new girl has no truck with feminine wiles, yet she looks deceptively like a pin-up'. A cluster of images come together in the woman who accentuates her 'biological sex', yet acts like a 'traditional man' with all of the negative implications for her health, such as the well documented rises in cigarette smoking and in excessive alcohol consumption. As noted earlier, where 'men acting like women' is concerned, attention is typically on the 'emasculation' that has purportedly followed in the wake of 'women's emancipation'. Pope *et al.* (2000: 48), for example, associate this change with men's growing interest in body image, arguing that women's parity in many areas of life has left men with 'primarily their bodies as a defining source of masculinity'. Popular debate in particular seems to be lapsing into a zero-sum game, when the real need is to recognise that the kinds of gender-shifts that we have been referring to are the natural product of a new system of sex/gender which actively encourages more fluid gender identities and behaviours. Body image, for example, is a multibillion dollar industry which now not only capitalizes on male as well as female insecurities, but also actively fosters them. The tobacco industry now

targets women as the single largest product marketing group in the world.

But changes under the rubric of 'female sex/male gender' and 'male sex/female gender' (Table 6.1) are only the visible front of the 'new single system' of sex/gender. The changes actually go deeper and are much more complex. The experience of being male or female is multiple and often laced with contradictions as people in their everyday lives are drawn into complex relations of apparent complicity with and resistance to commodity capitalism. Hyper-masculinity and hyper-femininity (among 'biological men' and 'biological women' as well as in 'cross-gendering' e.g. transvestites), for example, can be conceived of as a form of resistance which stretches, and therefore challenges, the 'old single system' of sex/gender while also engaging with the 'new single system'. Counter identities become ensnared in the net of the new system that they are trying to escape from. Naomi Klein captures this well in *No Logo*. Protesting the oppressive images of brand advertising, Klein and her contemporaries found that

> once we'd embarked on a search for new wells of cutting-edge imagery, our insistence on extreme sexual and racial identities made for great brand-content and niche-marketing strategies. If diversity is what is wanted, the brands seemed to be saying, then diversity was exactly what we would get. And with that, the marketers and media makers swooped down, airbrushes in hand, to touch up the colours and images in our culture.
>
> (Klein 2001: 111)

To date discussion of these shifts has concentrated upon the fluidity of gender, leaving sex as a fixed property. Social gender is still foregrounded to the neglect of biological sex. As we saw earlier 'openness' is beginning to concern the biological, as much as it does the social body within the 'new single system' of sex/gender. When the biological body is discussed, the focus is usually on reproduction. Immutable in the 'old single system', the reproductive body is no longer unequivocally sexed. Sex re-assignment surgery is the self-evident example of this. But of course biology is about more than reproduction and other less dramatic bodily changes follow from what Dickens (2000) terms the 'biological embedding' of social experience in capitalist society. *New gender identities, attitudes and behaviours reach deeply into the body's interior and alter its traditional health profile.* As health problems that were once largely the province of men begin to increasingly affect women (e.g. lung cancer), and vice versa (e.g. melanoma), the materiality of the biological body is modified and takes on character-istics more typical of the 'opposite sex' (the damaged lung, skin lesions). At the population level patterns of morbidity and mortality begin to shift as marked differences attenuate due to the continual re-making of sex/gender. This, then, is an example of how social engagement affects us bodily as,

Table 6.2 Changing mortality

Time	Mortality patterns	Relationship of Sex(biology)/ Gender(social)	Social changes
First era up to late 1800s	Equal Male advantage		Social and economic improvements for women
Second era until late 1970s	Female advantage 'women are sicker, but men die quicker'	'Old single system'	'Openness'
Third era 1980s–present	Closing gap? (improvements for men?)	'New single system'	

to extend Dickens' (2000) line of argument, patriarchal capitalism shapes biology in its own image and with it our experience of health and illness.

Health status

Changes in mortality differentials are a good illustration of the biological embedding of gendered social experience. For the purpose of this discussion we can divide history into three rough eras (Table 6.2). The *first era* covers modern history up to the late 1800s. Although it over-simplifies matters considerably, this period was characterized by either greater longevity among men or more or less equal life spans for men and women in the west. That is, the greater female life expectancy we are now accustomed to generally did not exist. The turn around to female advantage/male disadvantage began in the late 1800s and is generally attributed to improvements in women's social and economic circumstances (although there is still an unresolved question of whether it is an effect of an innate biological advantage for women which emerges under favourable conditions). In the *second era* (late 1800s–1970s) widening mortality differentials strongly favoured women. In England and Wales up to the 1950s, women had about a four-year advantage in life expectancy at birth. This grew to peak at around six years by the late 1960s (a trend mirrored in most western countries). Ironically, the construction of women as biologically and socially inferior appears to have conferred a mortality advantage. At the population level, being kept further away from dangerous employment (risks of serious injury and industrial disease), from motor vehicle driver mortality (being less likely to own or drive a car), and from risks to health like cigarette smoking, alcohol and dangerous sports (social sanctions, lack of time and money), may have protected women from early death, while hegemonic masculinity made men vulnerable.

However, the 'old single system' does not seem to have protected women across the board, since the female advantage in life expectancy appears to have occurred alongside a higher burden of ill-health during life.[4] However, as discussed earlier, the 'social difference approach' set in train in the 1970s laid a heavy political emphasis on *social*(gender) rather than biological(sex) and on gender *differences* rather than similarities. Illness has a subjective quality and, while death itself is clear-cut, its social and biological causes may not be. This indeterminancy means that the underlying assumptions of the 'social difference approach' could easily have led researchers to over-look similarities between men and women (for e.g. building research on the expectation of difference, failure to report similarities – see Macintyre *et al.* 1996). So while the second era seems to be characterized by distinctions, with respect to morbidity in particular they may actually be less marked.

The *third era* is characterized by less clear cut differences in patterns of illness and a closing mortality gap which, in the UK, began in the 1970s and became a recognised trend by the 1980s. Actual life expectancy figures show that although there were gradual improvements for men and women over the period 1981–8, the male gain was larger (3.9 years gained by men, 2.9 years by women). The life expectancy gap narrowed significantly, from 6.0 years in 1981 to 4.9 years in 1998, with a 4.1 year gap predicated for 2021 (ONS 2000). 'If the present trend of a reduction in the difference of about one and a half years per generation continues, in one hundred years' time men . . . will be living as long as women' (Connolly 2002: 1014). The third era is therefore characterized by a gradual chipping away of the female mortality advantage (largely due to improvements in male death rates) and increasing recognition that patterns of morbidity by gender are not as distinctive as they once were (or were thought to be).

I suggest that the driving force behind this shift to the third era is the 'openness' of the social and the biological within the 'new single system' of sex/gender. At the population level, the explanation often given is that men and women are becoming more similar. Vallin *et al.* (2001: 165), for example, refer to a convergence of behaviour patterns where men are not only cutting back on 'harmful habits, which were previously markedly male' such as smoking and drinking, but also 'beginning to copy women in their attitude to health' e.g. better attuned to health issues and making greater use of health services. Women on the contrary, are taking up more health-damaging behaviours. Cigarette smoking is a case in point. In OECD countries, smoking-attributable deaths changed from one female death for every sixty-eight men in 1955, to one for every thirty-four in 1995 (Ernster 2001). New gender identities reach deep into the interior of the body, re-fashioning traditional patterns of health and, ultimately, the timing of death. This is equally apparent when we turn from all-cause mortality to specific causes of death, here taking the example of melanoma.

The incidence of malignant melanoma (skin cancer) rose steadily during the second half of the twentieth-century. Although incidence is still higher among women, increases during the 1990s are almost entirely attributed to a rise among men (alongside a levelling off among women). Over the six years to 1998 in England and Wales, male rates increased by 12 per cent and female rates by just 2.1 per cent. The gap between men's and women's rates of melanoma is now the narrowest it has been for the last twenty-five years. However, mortality is, and always has been, higher amongst men (Cancer Research UK 2002; ONS 2001).

Why is male incidence rising (while female incidence is declining)? And, why are men more likely to die from skin cancer than women? A limited biological explanation is unlikely given that the melanocytes (pigment cells) of the skin which can become malignant are present in approximately equal numbers and are similarly distributed over the body in both sexes. In the majority of cases skin cancer is caused by exposure to the sun's ultraviolet radiation. While having a suntan may still be valued rather more by women, there is evidence that it is increasingly important to men. But although there is a similar level of awareness among men and women about the risks of sun exposure, men are less likely to protect themselves by the use of sunscreens, protective clothing, etc. and are more likely to get burnt than women (see e.g. ONS 1997). New expectations of the desirable tanned/healthy looking male body therefore co-exist with traditional male attitudes to risk. Higher male mortality has also been linked historically to the site of the disease. The main melanoma site for men is the trunk (mid back) (35 per cent men, 14 per cent women) and for women, the lower limbs (posterior calves) (50 per cent women, 18 per cent men) (data for England and Wales, ONS 2001). Here again biological and social factors interact: different male/female clothing styles expose different parts of the body to risk and mid-back lesions have a much worse prognosis (Wizemann and Pardue 2001).

I suggest that the health-related changes that have been briefly discussed here should be understood as more than simply the social experience of women and men becoming more similar. They reach deeply into the interior of the body altering traditional health profiles. The 'new single system' of sex(biology)/(social)gender is part of what Ebert (1995: 353) terms 'an economy of differences'. Capitalism shapes biology in its own image (Dickens 2000) and that image is one of an increasingly flexible body ever attuned to the consumption needs of patriarchal capitalism. In this context changing patterns of morbidity and mortality are themselves moments in time. For example, the rise in lung cancer in women and skin cancer in men may continue for some time, but not without social stricture and calls for changes in gender-related behaviour. The social (gender) and the biological (sex) are therefore drawn together into a new symphysis within contemporary patriarchal capitalism.

Notes

1 Until around the mid-1990s, the predominant focus was on *women's* health. Gender comparative research and research on men's health in its own right is therefore quite recent. For a historical review of research on gender and health status, see Annandale and Hunt (2000).
2 In the early 1900s there was a 58 percentage-point difference in the labour force participation rates of men and women, by the end of the twentieth century, this had dropped to only 18 percentage points (Gallie 2000).
3 For example, the rate of ratio of males to females aged 10–14 found guilty or cautioned per 100,000 of the population changed from eighteen males for every female in 1937, to just four males for every female in 1997 (Hood and Roddam 2000).
4 The apparent paradox 'women are sicker, but men die quicker' is usually explained in terms of an excess of minor and/or chronic, but not life threatening, illnesses among women.

References

Annandale, E. and Clark, J. (2000) 'Gender, postmodernism and health', in S. Williams, J. Gabe and M. Calnan (eds) *Health, Medicine and Society*, London: Routledge.

Annandale, E. and Hunt, K. (2000) 'Gender inequalities in health: research at the crossroads', in E. Annandale and K. Hunt (eds) *Gender Inequalities in Health*, Buckingham: Open University Press.

Beck, U. and Beck-Gernsheim, E. (2002) *Individualization*, London: Sage.

Birke, L. (1999) *Feminism and the Biological Body*, Edinburgh: Edinburgh University Press.

Butler, J. (1993) *Body Matters*, London: Routledge.

Cancer Research UK (2002) 'Experts warn of skin cancer "time bomb" as cases continue to rise', http://www.cancerresearchuk.org/press/pressreleases/sunsmart Accessed 15 July 2002.

Connolly, C.K. (2002) Letter, *British Medical Journal*, 323, 7320: 1014–15.

Coward, R. (1999) *Sacred Cows*, London: HarperCollins.

Dickens, P. (2000) *Social Darwinism*, Buckingham: Open University Press.

Ebert, T. (1995) 'Writing the political: resistance (post)modernism', in J. Leonard (ed.) *Legal Studies as Cultural Studies*, NY: State University of Albany Press.

Ernster, V. (2001) 'Impact of tobacco use on women's health', in J. Samet and S. Yoon (eds) *Women and the Tobacco Epidemic*, Geneva: WHO.

Gallie, D. (2000) 'The labour force', in A.H. Halsey and J. Webb (eds) *Twentieth-century British Social Trends*, Basingstoke: Macmillan.

Gershuny, J. and Fisher, K. (2000) 'Leisure', in A.H. Halsey and J. Webb (eds) *Twentieth-century British Social Trends*, Basingstoke: Macmillan.

Hennessy, R. (2000) *Profit and Pleasure: Sexual Identities in Late Capitalism*, London: Routledge.

Hood, R. and Roddam, A. (2000) 'Crime, sentencing and punishment', in A.H. Halsey and J. Webb (eds) *Twentieth-century British Social Trends*, Basingstoke: Macmillan.

Klein, N. (2001) *No Logo*, London: Flamingo.

Macintrye, S., Hunt, K. and Sweeting, H. (1996) 'Gender differences in health: are things as simple as they seem?', *Social Science and Medicine*, 42: 617–24.

McRobbie, A. (2000) *Feminism and Youth Culture* (2nd edn), London: Macmillan.

Martin, E. (1999) 'The woman in the flexible body', in A. Clarke and V. Olesen (eds) *Revisioning Women, Health, and Healing*, London: Routledge.

Moi, T. (1999) *What is a Woman?*, Oxford: Oxford University Press.

Office of National Statistics (ONS) (1997) *Health in England 1996*, London: HMSO.

Office of National Statistics (ONS) (2000) *National Population Projections*, London: HMSO.

Office of National Statistics (ONS) (2001) *Cancer Trends in England and Wales 1950–1999*, London: HMSO.

Pope, H., Phillips, K. and Olivardia, R. (2000) *The Adonis Complex*, New York: The Free Press.

Vallin, J., Meslé, F. and Valkonen, T. (2001) *Trends in Mortality and Differential Mortality*, Strasbourg: Council of Europe Publishing.

Walby, S. (1997) *Gender Transformations*, London: Routledge.

Whelehan, I. (2000) *Overloaded*, London: The Women's Press.

Wizemann, T. and Pardue, M. (2001) *Exploring the Biological Contributions to Human Health: Does Sex Matter?*, Washington DC: National Academy Press.

7 Ethnicity and health

Biological and social inheritance

David Kelleher and Brian Hall

Introduction

This chapter will be concerned with exploring the problems and possibilities in making links between the biological and social determinants of health. Rather than posing these as separate and alternative ontological positions, it will be argued that there is a need to understand the interdependence of the biological and social as part of both a causative and cultural order. Furthermore, the way health is experienced, e.g. by different ethnic groups, requires a rethinking of how communication is determinative of our symbolic social life-world.

From as far back as there are records, it seems that we have known that our health is affected by forces, natural and spiritual. The Hippocratic tradition taught the significance of the natural environment as well as the need for the body's 'humours' and 'passions' to be in equilibrium. This could be achieved through the 'healing forces inherent in living organisms' which provided the basis for 'therapy' (Capra 1983: 341).

Healers, whether augurers, witch-doctors, shamans, herbalists or physicians, through their special knowledge and rituals, variously laid claim to special authority and status. As Chaucer described in the fourteenth century

> With us ther was a Doctour of Physik . . .
> he was grounded in astronomye.
> He kepte his pacient a ful greet deel
> In houres by his magyk natureel.
>   (Chaucer 'General Prologue' to
>   *The Canterbury Tales*, lines 411–16)

As his account tells us, the diagnosis of illness was, in medieval times, as much a matter of astronomical divination (houres being the astrological hours relating to the zodiac) as of the essential body forces or humours. Consequent treatment using medication required knowledge of appropriate extraction from nature whether based on mineral, plant or animal. Such knowledge was part of natural history, often requiring the recognition of the signification of certain plant structures and their representation of particular parts of the body (e.g. the wild pansy, *viola tricolor*, known as 'heartsease'). The attention to form and structure then became an end in itself through the work of Linnaeus. As Foucault comments,

> This, no doubt, is why natural history, in the Classical period, cannot be established as biology. Up to the end of the eighteenth century, in fact, life does not exist: only living beings. These beings form one class, or rather several classes, in the series of all the things in the world.
> (Foucault 1970: 160)

It was perhaps not till the 1850s and the work of Louis Pasteur, initially a crystallographer and chemist, that modern biology achieved its theoretical and empirical defining moment, its epistemological break. Through his experiments he demonstrated that the existence of micro-organisms in decaying material was not the result of what the 'vitalists' believed was 'spontaneous generation', but due to already existing micro-organisms in the air. We owe the subsequent 'germ theory' of disease to Pasteur and others, such as Robert Koch, whose 'postulates' are the basis for determining which microbe causes which disease. This view of the causes of health provided a crucial basis for rejecting not only earlier 'spiritual' conceptions of the body and healing but also contemporary versions of 'internal balance' as advocated by Claude Bernard, who is now recognized as the founder of physiology.

A further impetus to 'non-vitalist' thinking came with the evolutionary theory of life-forms by Charles Darwin in 1859. His was not the only version of 'natural selection' at the time. A similar conception was formulated by Alfred Wallace but he 'identified a number of distinctively human powers or "faculties" whose preservation in human or pre-human populations was inexplicable in terms of natural selection' (Benton 1991: 10).

Wallace's version with its continuing emphasis on spiritual 'essences' (ibid.) was to succumb to the Darwinian account. In part this may be seen as the result of the 'solution' which was provided by Gregor Mendel with his 'units of heredity'. Alternatively it may be that the acceptance of scientific ideas was less to do with solely rational or empirical reasoning than the wider societal interests and ideas. Darwin's appeal to the then patriarchical society is illustrated by his view that: 'Man is more courageous, pugnacious, and energetic than woman, and has more inventive genius' (quoted in Capra, 1982: 106).

Mendel's work was ignored till the turn of the century, so it is only then that we can speak of the development of 'genetics'. Following this particular biological model, health, both morbidity and mortality, can be traced back to the moment of conception: the physical process of fertilization and the mix of two sets of chromosomes, one from each of the biological parents, to form an individual's genotype.

This genetic inheritance is seen as shaping the body, height, sex, intelligence and even social and cultural identity. Indeed health is increasingly seen as pre-ordained on the basis of the genetic blue-print, more than environmental factors or according to God's plan as some cultural groups believe.

There have been other 'biologies', notably underlying complementary and non-western homeopathies. However the bio-medical version of biology, which is predicated on chemical and genetic explanations and hence cures, based commonly on drugs and maybe genetic engineering, is effectively the dominant way of thinking. As already indicated there are clearly cultural and economic reasons for this, including the obvious fact that drugs and even now parts of the genome can be patented and sold, 'commodified'.

The significance of such developments is not just that health has been appropriated increasingly by scientific thinking but in the mode of its appropriation. One sociological reaction has been to take on this biological (increasingly genetic) model by disputing the significance of purely biological causes of disease. Such writing, though offering different explanatory factors, e.g. environmental and social determinants of ill-health, is nevertheless similar in that the type of explanation is still essentially positivist and reductionist.

In the realm of biology, though, there have continued to be some non-reductionist, more holistic disciplinary developments, notably in neuroscience and developmental psychology. Understanding the potential contribution of these approaches to the discourse of biology has been opened up by writers such as Benton (1991), but will not be developed here. Instead the main opposition to the predominantly reductionist biology will be considered in terms of an alternative 'non-positivist' sociology. Health is herein conceptualized as dependent not on internal or external causes but on individuals' own behaviours, and understood through the interpretation of social meanings and cultures.

This constructionist version is thought to be fundamentally opposed to the earlier positivist paradigms. Both positions, however, may be understood in terms of the Cartesian separation between 'body' and 'mind'. As such they share the same ultimate aim of explanation, but do so within different sides of the body/mind playing-field. The positivist domain has led on to the medicalization of the body (including mental states) and health. In the 'idealist' domain, the interpretivist views have concentrated on social and cultural processes. By emphasizing the 'real' mental consequences of socially constructed identities and symbolic communications, such a position has itself substantively historicized the 'mind', rejecting a path in search of a universal 'logos'.

The next two sections will elaborate these two views by showing how understanding the 'well-known' ethnic differences in health might be possible from within either framework. This leads on to an attempt at integrating the 'split' ontological playing-field by the reconceptualization of the relationships between the biological (bio-medical/genetic) and the social (cultural) through a communicative model of the social life-world.

Positivist explanations: external and internal causes

There have been ever-expanding medical and sociological literatures identifying the external, social determinants of health: work, housing, marital status, social class, pollution, food production and preparation methods, education and health behaviour.

Epidemiologically it has been recognized that the prevalence of many conditions has been different for different ethnic groups, e.g. cancer, diabetes, hearing impairment, heart disease, infant mortality and mental health. It is widely recognized that the rate of schizophrenia is high amongst Black African and Caribbean immigrants, Bangladeshi children have high levels of hearing impairment, and the Irish experience high rates of mental illness, lung cancer and accidents. In some cases the ethnic differences are subtle, e.g. higher incidence of breast cancer amongst Ashkenazim (Northern European) Jewish women than Sephardim (Southern) Jewish women.

Explanations of such difference include environmental conditions (ethnic minorities often live in more deprived areas and suffer from poorer housing and overcrowding) and selective processes (e.g. migrating people or refugees may become less healthy because of becoming isolated). Explanatory factors also include cultural attitudes and behaviours. The Irish, for instance, are said to be more stoical and tend not to visit a GP until their complaint has worsened.

There are other non-social, internal explanations of differences based in inherited predispositions. Sickle cell disease which affects mainly African people and the particularly high rate of non-insulin dependent diabetes of Bangladeshi families are examples.

Many of the most powerful claims, recently based on discoveries from the work on the Human Genome Project, are that many diseases and conditions are caused by genetic (chromosomal) mutations, thus playing down the effects of physical and social environments as reported by sociologists such as Tarlov (1996), Wilkinson (2000), Holtzman and Marteau (2000). These writers have continued to stress the 'fact' that health is likely to continue to be much more influenced by poverty-related factors such as diet, housing and working conditions than by genetic ones. Tarlov (1996) argues that it is important to differentiate between conditions such as cystic fibrosis, Huntington's chorea and others caused by the inheritance of a single 'gene' (allele), and those more numerous conditions brought about by polygene inheritance which make people susceptible to diseases or conditions such as diabetes. Holtzman and Marteau (2000: 143) make the point: 'The complexity of the genetics of common diseases casts doubt on whether accurate prediction will ever be possible'.

Although Tarlov (1996) goes on to say that estimates are that single genes are likely to be responsible for no more than 5 per cent of the total disease burden, the links between biological and sociological analysis can be seen when we try to make sense of the epidemiological variations of diabetes, one of the common conditions referred to above. The variations are greatest in the non-insulin dependent form of diabetes mellitus (NIDDM), which is experienced by about 80 per cent of people with diabetes. Although it is called NIDDM or Type 2 diabetes it is accepted that some of these sufferers will go on to require insulin treatment, which even in the case of genetically engineered insulin is expensive, and may therefore not be available in developing countries. This form of diabetes usually starts in middle-age but onset tends to be earlier in some groups such as people from South Asia or the Pima Indians in the USA, and this means that prevalence rates are particularly high in these groups. Why this is so is one of the links between biology and environment which have to be unravelled.

Among other groups which have puzzlingly high rates of diabetes are the native people of the Pacific island of Nauru and the Indian population of South Africa. The high rate of the people of Nauru is often explained as being a result of their change of lifestyle when they ceased to be manual workers producing their own food and became wealthier people living a sedentary lifestyle. To explain diabetes as a disease of affluence is not a completely satisfactory explanation however; not all wealthy countries have high prevalence rates, and further, no single item of diet can be shown to be the cause of diabetes. The amount of exercise taken is also important, as is the degree of obesity.

This is where there appears to be a genetic element involved, in the propensity to become obese, particularly in the waist–hip region of the body. This is shown in studies of South Asian people living in England. They have a prevalence rate four times that of people who are described in medical literature as being Caucasian (one of four 'racial' categories still used in medicine). One explanation offered is that they have a genetic resistance to making use of their bodies' insulin as a result of having what is called a 'thrifty' gene. The presence of this is explained as being one which enabled them to survive in climates where there were frequent periods of drought and famine. It is also the case, however, that many middle-aged people in this group who are now living in situations where famine is not one of the hazards they face, do not take much exercise, particularly in a climate which does not encourage them to do so. In addition their children want to eat western fast foods and, in many cases, these are simply added to their traditional diet of two meals with rice every day. While evidence from 'thrifty gene' studies do make a case for genetic predisposition in relation to NIDDM, it also suggests the need for studies of the role played by culturally determined eating patterns. A study of two groups of ethnically different migrants to Fiji, for example, shows that the Melanesian migrants had low prevalence rates for both rural and urban dwellers while those from India had high rates for both groups, which at first appears to indicate a genetic explanation. We do not know, however, the extent to which the two groups maintained their cultural eating patterns.

Here, then, are two conceptually distinct forms of explanation. An incomplete biological explanation, which even if augmented by evidence from the Human Genome Project, would appear still to be dependent on the sociological. Such biological and sociological explanations are essentially part of the same 'positivist' endeavour to explain (and to be able to deal with) causes of ill-health. Whether they develop in a more oppositional or complementary manner, they will inevitably remain within this version of the human/social body and mind.

Constructionist accounts: ethnicity as culture and identity

Sociological work on identity, whilst aware of the important effects of the physical environment is more directly concerned with the social relationships of people, the gendering of biological sexual differences, the factors structuring those relationships, and their effect on identity. It may be therefore that while genetic factors create our physical identity, sociological theory offers a more complex view of what identity is.

Stuart Hall writing about the identities of black people from the Caribbean explains that:

> We cannot speak for very long, with any exactness, about one experience, one identity without acknowledging its other side – the ruptures and discontinuities. . . . Cultural identity, in this second sense, is a matter of becoming as well as of being. . . . Cultural identities come from somewhere, have histories. But like everything which is historical they undergo constant transformation.
>
> (Hall 1997: 112)

Hall, taking a constructionist view, indicates that the changes in identity are not occurring simply by changes individuals make for themselves; they are subject also to the power and position of the other in society. So as well as the self-construction work on identity which goes on, there are also structural factors which are less easily escaped from, which link individual agents to the constraints of society. Ang (2000), addressing Hall's view of identity, suggests that it is as much about the future as the past and notes how identity becomes important politically in some contexts. He observes how in Australia identity politics are used in a reactionary way to resist the inflow of Asian immigrants, abandoning political multiculturalism and appealing to an essential biological notion of what it is to be Australian, which would keep Australia white. In this kind of cultural politics the biological bases of identities and the constructed identities of people are subject to the power of external political pressures. Evidence which shows therefore the importance of the historical/economic political contexts in understanding the prevalence of biological and sociological ideas.

Culture in a constructionist approach to identity is, then, one of the factors linking biology and sociology. Such sociologists may either ignore or presume the biological (genetic) construction of the physical body as the basis of identity. Their main intention though is to show how culture constructs differences to produce the identities with which people live. Fanon (1967) sees national cultures as collectively shared ways of expressing feelings and attitudes to life, something suppressed sometimes for long periods by colonialist regimes wanting to impose their ideas. Feelings lying dormant during colonialism come to be important as a vital part of national identity in countries which have thrown off colonial regimes.

For Bourdieu, and many other sociologists, social classes are important as they have sub-cultures, or a habitus; groupings of people who share a way of life largely determined by their access to wealth. Whether it is with people of the same class or people from the same country or ethnic group with the same genetic inheritance that we identify, this identification with others helps individuals create a sense of subjective security. Tarlov notes the wealth-related form of culture and identity as important in shaping a person's future. 'Identity is a trait that informs an individual who he [*sic*] is and where he belongs within the social structure. . . . Who am I and with whom should I associate? It helps youth formulate their expectations, both the possibilities and limitations' (Tarlov 1996: 84).

He goes on to say that plans made by developing identities may clash with reality when individuals become aware of inequalities in education, job opportunities and life chances. Within this concept of culture therefore ethnic origins or class origins may be important to the individual in the self-construction of identity; but when ethnic origin is apparent to others, through the biological effects on people's physical appearance, as it is particularly for black or Asian people in the UK or USA, this also affects how they are perceived and the place they are able to gain in society. The differences they perceive between themselves and others may be given much greater significance by others than the genetic differences on which they are based, leading to the creation of ideas of superiority and inferiority between ethnic groups.

What Tarlov (ibid.) does not mention is how gender development and identity are also influenced by social structures and individuals themselves. The way in which gendering of small biological sexual differences between men and women varies from one culture to another is noted by Risman (2001) in a critical review of Biological Limits of Gender Construction (Udry 2000). Udry, in his summing up of the interesting correspondence relating to his article, agrees with Risman, but also makes the point that: 'each culture has its own version of gender . . . gender is not randomly created across cultures . . . hormones constrain gender but environments create gender' (Udry 2000: 618).

This dual way in which identity as part of culture operates with the biological is particularly important for most immigrant peoples as instanced above. But as well as having an effect on their relationships with white people, ethnic origin may also be something which people living in the UK or the USA, may find a positive side to their difference, seeing it as an important part of their identity. Through being aware of their 'routes' as Hall (1996) calls it, maintaining their religion, language, diet, all parts of their culture, they not only sustain links with their homeland but gain a sense of who they are (Taylor 1989) and from where they have subjectively as well as objectively come.

Irish men and women in England are an example of a group who in appearance may look like people in the 'host' community but who nevertheless experience a sense of *differance* (Derrida) when their way of talking is remarked on, when they resent being called 'Paddy' or 'Biddy' and object to 'Irish' jokes which make all Irish people appear stupid. The sense of difference makes them aware of their Irishness, whereas before at home in Ireland it was something they did not think about. The culture which they attempt to sustain and, with it their identity, undergoes changes however as they respond to the changed situations they experience at work, when buying food, when taking a drink in a pub or when challenged by police.

Anthias (2001) in a rethinking of culture and ethnicity has started with the concept of hybridities, a term, which has biological associations, and has been suggested as useful in explaining the intermingling of people in a diaspora. She then goes on to develop her own suggested replacement for this, translocational positionality. She looks at the argument of Hall (1998) which suggests that increased migrations have led to the breakdown of the certainties of 'old' cultures and the development of new ethnicities through a process of interculturality. 'The terms hybridity and diaspora [in a revived form] open up spaces hitherto foreclosed by traditional approaches to ethnicity and migration, and involve anti-essentialist projects and critiques of static notions of ethnicity and culture' (Anthias 2001: 620).

Anthias goes on to argue that although use of the terms hybridity and diaspora are an advance on essentialist ideas of ethnicity, culture and identity, they also present problems. One of the problems she identifies is that hybridity entails 'cultural syncretism', the implied fusion of the migrant culture into the dominant one. In a multicultural society however the immigrants' culture is to some extent sustained, even amongst the second generation, and remains a source of collective and individual identity.

Although for many Irish people living in England the cultural practices that they draw on in their everyday lives change, their ethnic sense of belonging remains. It is sustained not least by others in the dominant group who cannot accept their difference and refer to them as Paddy or even 'Fenian bastards' assuming they share the politics of the IRA. This is not an argument for continuing, essentialist notions of culture and ethnicity, nor for an essentially biological view of identity. For all immigrant groups their developing culture reflects the experience of life and work in England or elsewhere, and their ethnicity is related to the nation from which they came. Both of these will be reflected on and interrogated as they become contributory parts of their developing identities. Their identity will be continually made and re-made.

As Anthias says, many new British Muslims base their identity on this hybrid culture. Kelleher and Islam (1996), in their study of Bangladeshi people with Type 2 diabetes for which, as already noted, there is a high prevalence rate and no satisfactory explanation, comment on how the elements of ethnicity, culture and identity came together in the way they managed their diabetes:

> Their culture and in particular their religion gave them a sense of identity and of belonging to a community in an environment which was strange, unfriendly and sometimes hostile. . . . They saw themselves as Bangladeshis and, to varying degrees, Muslims, and frequently talked about 'our people'.
>
> (Kelleher and Islam 1996: 232)

Anthias makes another valid critical point in saying that differences between ethnic groups are often 'racialized' when they are placed in an hierarchical position. Brah (1992) is critical of what she calls 'ethnicization', that is defining people by their ethnic background as though this was of an essentialist, biological nature. Ahmed (1996) is critical of the use of an essentialist notion of culture. He argues that in playing down the material basis of society, it has not been a helpful concept in directing medical and other resources to those ethnic groups most in need. He concludes however, by welcoming 'a re-appropriation of a much more politicised and contextual notion of "culture"'(Ahmed 1996: 215).

As we argued earlier, the biological and sociological might come together in a complex, multi-disciplinary causal model, but it must remain partial. Likewise even if biology can be augmented by a sophisticated culturally informed understanding of changing social identities, the prospect for this is similarly to remain in an 'interpretivist' paradigm. This will not achieve the sought for political and empowering understanding which Ahmed and others seek. For the realization of such a prospect, we must turn elsewhere.

Beyond the Cartesian legacy: culture and biology in the Lifeworld

Currently links between biological work and sociology have been developing, and in recent years there has been a sociological focus on 'bringing the body back into sociology' (Frank 1990; Williams and Bendelow 1998; Howson and Inglis 2001). This has been done in a number of ways, one of the most powerful has been through using the philosophy of Merleau-Ponty. He has suggested that it has been the theoretical separation of mind and body following Descartes' work, which led to a sociological concentration on mind and reason, and how the mind makes sense of the body. The developing embodiment work in sociology has suggested that mind and body constitute one organism which works together to make sense of, and manage, the experience of the person in the world in sickness and in health. (See Part III, this volume.)

How can such a synthesis of body and mind be accomplished without reverting to one or other of the firmly established, positivist or constructionist, traditions? A major figure in sociology and social philosophy who draws on the interpretivists Mead and Schutz is Habermas. He sees culture as part of the Lifeworld, a resource, 'a stock of knowledge' on which people draw in their interpretations of the world and which thus influences how they act.

> Language and culture and assumptions of what is appropriate in particular contexts are shown to be part of the background of the Lifeworld in which people communicatively interact and these provide speakers and listeners with common background convictions which they use in reaching understandings but which also allow them to negotiate new understandings in changing situations.
>
> (Habermas 1987: 129)

In his view of culture it is important therefore to note that it is not something which is static, but something on which people reflect and is renegotiated as situations change.

Important in this conception of the Lifeworld, which extends the ideas of Schutz and Mead, is the central role of language in communicative action. Language, as Darwin in the nineteenth century suspected, Chomsky in the twentieth century asserted, and recent genetic work appears to confirm, is a basic human ability. Equally important however, is the extension of Weber's notion of rationality. Habermas argues that the language of communicative action, which is the language occurring in those non-coercive situations in everyday life where the form of argumentation is used, is a style of argument employing a particular form of rationality. For Habermas, the cognitive–instrumental, purposive rationality used in positivist science is not the only form of rationality. In his view, in the Lifeworld in post-traditional society, there is a 'freeing' of values from institutions and reflection on the moral expectations from the mores of culture. There is therefore, a greater need to identify the ways in which cultural changes become legitimated through processes of argumentation in the Lifeworld.

The Lifeworld operates through communicative action on the everyday practices of people, but it also connects to the System, via expert systems and the steering mechanisms of money and power to the external world of economic power blocs. In these areas of life, the dominating part of society, the rationality operating is of the cognitive–instrumental form, different from the rationality Habermas sees as part of the interactional mechanism used by people in groups in the public sphere. Science is one of the expert systems in the Modern world separated from the sphere of morality, but strongly connected to the System; it is one of the forces colonizing the everyday affairs of the Lifeworld.

The discoveries of the Human Genome Project are being broadcast through the media into the Lifeworld. Biology, part of an expert system, is being introduced into the public sphere, not in contexts where the Human Genome discoveries can be discussed and made sense of through communicative action, but in pre-digested bulletins in which conclusions are already drawn and applications to medical practice clearly stated: 'the genome for Alzheimer's has been identified and treatments will be developed within X years . . .'. Two small but recently published ways of resisting this particular colonization of the Lifeworld are instanced in Scambler (2001). One (Scambler and Britten 2001) is the discussion of how the expert 'voice of medicine' revealed in doctor–patient consultations can be seen to be part of the wider domination of the Lifeworld by the System as a whole. The other example (Kelleher 2001), takes up from there by suggesting how in self-help groups the talk sometimes may be of the communicative action kind of exchange. This allows members to discuss, for example, their lay experiences of genetically derived insulin in the treatment of their diabetes and to develop an alternative voice to the voice of medicine.

Habermas has also suggested how some of the modern forms of protest group, are based in 'the grammar of the forms of life'. By this he means that rather than challenging the distribution of wealth, they are generating discussion in the Lifeworld, discussion in which experts' views on a wide range of issues are challenged; some of them linking science and morality to debate ecological issues, animal rights, the position of women in society, all making links with new arguments in biology (see Part V, this volume). Such groups also provide the possibility of their members using group membership as a basis of identity, thus contributing to sociological ideas.

Taylor (1989) argues that Habermas is concerned with 'mapping the connections between identity and the Good', a phrase redolent of the way scientists describe their work on the Human Genome Project. He is also readdressing the 'mind and body' division, which has been largely lost to us since the time of Descartes. Habermas is therefore one social philosopher who stands against an unquestioning acceptance of an essentialist nature of biological identity. But, crucially, the knowledge of biology – and its socially constructed discourse – is not to be disregarded. Instead, it must be re-appropriated.

Conclusion

The promise of improving health as a result of the discovery of DNA and the greater knowledge of disease processes developing with the work of the

Human Genome Project are important advances. The central focus of this chapter however has been to suggest that the developing links between sociology and biology are important and can be continued. From the moment of conception the biological and the environmental are interacting, worked on by cultures and social experience and by the self-constructing of identities through the groups with which people choose to identify. Socio-cultural differences must be specified and linked with the more detailed polygenetic knowledge relating to, for example, non-insulin dependent diabetes coming from work on the Human Genome Project as discussed earlier.

Sociology must operate as a critical discipline in the public sphere, using environmental and constructionist concepts such as culture and identity to show how biology and the discoveries of the Human Genome Project can be linked to them. The powerful mass media style of messages about the discoveries coming from the Human Genome Project must be resisted and discussion joined in Lifeworld settings where communicative action takes place.

References

Ahmed, W. (1996) 'The trouble with culture', in D. Kelleher and S. Hillier (eds) *Researching Cultural Differences in Health*, London: Routledge.

Ang, I. (2000) 'Identity blues', in P. Gilroy, L. Grossberg and A. McRobbie (eds) *Without Guarantees*, London: Verso.

Anthias, F. (2001) 'New hybridities, old concepts: the limits of culture', *Ethnic and Racial Studies*, **24**, 4: 619–641.

Benton, T. (1991) 'Biology and social science: why the return of the repressed should be given a (cautious) welcome', *Sociology*, **25**, 1: 1–29.

Brah, A. (1992) 'Difference, diversity and differentiation', in J. Donald and A. Rattansi (eds) *Race, Culture and Difference*, London: Sage.

Capra, F. (1983) *The Turning Point: Science, Society and the Rising Culture*, London: Fontana.

Chaucer, G. (1957) *The Canterbury Tales*, 'The General Prologue', Oxford, Oxford University Press.

Fanon, F. (1967) *The Wretched of the Earth*, London: Penguin.

Foucault, M. (1970) *The Order of Things: An Archaeology of the Human Sciences*, London: Tavistock.

Frank, A. (1990) 'Bringing bodies back in: a decade review', *Theory, Culture and Society* 7: 131–62.

Giddens, A. (1991) *Modernity and Self-Identity*, Cambridge: Polity.

Habermas, J. (1987) *The Theory of Communicative Action*, Vol. 2, Cambridge: Polity.

Hall, S. (1996) 'Who needs identity?', in S. Hall and P. du Gay (eds) *Questions of Cultural Identity*, London: Sage.

Hall, S. (1997) 'Cultural identity and diaspora', in P. Mongia (ed.) *Contemporary Postcolonial Theory*, London: Arnold.

Hall, S. (1998) 'New ethnicities', in Kobena Mercer (ed.) *Black Film/British Cinema*, London: I.C.A. Document 7.

Holtzman, N.A. and Marteau, T.M. (2000) 'Will genetics revolutionize medicine?', *New England Journal of Medicine*, **343**, 2: 141–4.

Howson, A. and Inglis, D. (2001) 'The body in sociology: tensions inside and outside sociological thought', *Sociological Review Monograph*, Oxford: Blackwell.

Kelleher, D. (2001) 'New social movements in the health domain', in G. Scambler (ed.) *Habermas, Critical Theory and Health*, London: Routledge.

Kelleher, D. and Islam, S. (1996) 'How should I live?', in D. Kelleher and S. Hillier (eds) *Researching Cultural Differences in Health*, London: Routledge.

Risman, B. (2001) 'Calling the bluff of value free science', *American Sociological Review*, **66**, 4: 605–11.

Scambler, G. (2001) *Habermas, Critical Theory and Health*, London: Routledge.

Scambler, G. and Britten, N. (2001) 'System, lifeworld and doctor–patient interaction: issues of trust in a changing world', in G. Scambler (ed.) *Habermas, Critical Theory and Health*, London: Routledge.

Tarlov, A.R. (1996) 'Social determinants of health', in D. Blane, E. Brunner and R. Wilkinson (eds), *Health and Social Organisation*, London: Routledge.

Taylor, C. (1989) *Sources of the Self*, Cambridge: Cambridge University Press.

Udry, J. (2000) 'Feminist critics uncover determinism, positivism and antiquated theory', *American Sociological Review*, **66**, 4: 611–18.

Wilkinson, R. (2000) *Mind the Gap: Hierarchies, Health and Human Evolution*, London: Weidenfeld and Nicholson.

Williams, S.J. and Bendelow, G. (1998) *The Lived Body: Sociological Themes, Embodied Issues*, London: Routledge.

8 The 'biological clock'?

Ageing, health and the body across the lifecourse

Mike Bury and Mike Wadsworth

Introduction

The social and biological processes of ageing and the lifecourse demonstrate the intimate connections between the body, self and society. The argument of this chapter will be that these connections can be seen at both the individual and societal levels. An obvious example might be that of changes in longevity. As average longevity improves – the result of declining mortality in infancy and across the lifecourse – so more individuals experience the processes associated with growing old, and the more society itself 'ages'. Today in western societies the majority of individuals can expect to live into old age. The ageing of populations is the cumulative expression of changes in the experience of health and illness for groups of individuals passing through the lifecourse in a particular historical period. In addition to reductions in early mortality, low fertility produces a secular change towards fewer children and thus a greater number of older people, themselves living longer on average than in the past. Thus, changes in longevity and the lifecourse shape society itself, in terms of its age structure and social composition.

In many ways the ageing population in the West, and increasingly in many other parts of the world, is the successful outcome of attempts to prevent disease and early death, and thus to prolong life: the long-standing aims of public health. An ageing population can therefore be seen as a success story for modern society. Nonetheless this produces the 'paradox of survival' (Bury and Holme 1991) where the valued goal of avoiding pain, suffering and death in early life is accompanied by fears of poor health and dependency often associated with growing old, especially very old age. The expansion of human freedom in postponing death and the problems associated with later life thus express the tensions which the connections between health, ageing and the lifecourse inevitably create.

From this viewpoint concerns about 'dualism' in our thinking on ageing, or about the need to 'bring the body or biology back in' to social analysis may be exaggerated. Any satisfactory account of ageing and the lifecourse is bound to touch on the complex interactions between the social and the biological. As Riley *et al.* (1988) point out, the sociology of age and ageing has to take into account both the way society is stratified by age, involving the 'flow' of ageing of specific cohorts, and the way ageing occurs as a lifelong process of 'growing older from birth to death' comprising biological, psychological and social processes (Riley *et al.* 1988: 247). As we shall see, ageing for individuals is a dynamic process involving interactions between inheritance, early biological developmental processes, and social influences. That ageing is socially patterned suggests that individual experience (including that of the body) and human agency are influenced by cultural and material conditions.

Different disciplines will approach these interactions in different ways. This sometimes provides grounds for the fear of too great a separation of the biological and the social. Biologists may concentrate on smaller and smaller physiological, chemical or genetic processes, seemingly divorced from immediate human relevance or social context. They may also approach ageing as if it were a series of fixed mechanisms in the common 'biological clock' of the human body, especially those concerned with reproduction. Descriptions of 'normal ageing' can highlight examples of bodily change such as in the efficiency of the immune system in later life, in the musculoskeletal system, or in sensory systems such as vision – all of which decline with advancing years (Hipkiss and Bittles 1989: 6–7). Yet the biology of ageing is increasingly dealing with processes that are the result of changes in the health profiles of ageing populations – most notably that of a greater preponderance of chronic disorders. And these are part of the social development of society. The examples used by Hipkiss and Bittles make the point: musculo-skeletal problems such as arthritis and problems with vision and hearing increase in incidence as people age, and they have greater social salience as society 'ages'. Knowledge of biological changes across the lifecourse therefore ties scientific discourses on the body to structural features of a changing society.

Nevertheless, there are cogent arguments in the social sciences that stress the analytically separate character of the social from biological or 'natural' processes. And for good reason. John Searle, for example, has argued persuasively that 'brute facts' are different from 'institutional facts'. Trees, diseases and genes all exist separately from knowledge about them in ways that 'money', 'marriage' or 'universities' do not (Searle 1995: 35). Unlike natural phenomena, Searle argues, descriptions of social objects enter into the very constitution of what they are. The paper, metal or computer signals that 'make up' money cannot be sufficient to define it; only its usage and meaning makes this happen. Thus social facts are in key respects not open to scientific enquiry, in that, compared with natural objects, they are not predictable. Revolutions and voting in elections are not of the same order as spheres descending a sloping plane. The latter obey natural laws, the former do not.

However, this separation is neither complete nor radical. Searle himself is keen to trace the 'hierarchy' on which 'institutional' or social facts rest.

This is particularly evident if we consider the body, health and ageing from a social viewpoint. It is clear that none of the processes at work can occur or continue without underlying physiological and biological processes. If we do not eat and replace the energy and proteins that the body needs, we will go into a decline and eventually die. Biology sets real, we might say 'brute' limits to human endeavours. These can sometimes be strongly determining as in the case of a genetic abnormality in an individual or the effects of famine on a whole population. Nevertheless, health and ageing take on distinct features that cannot readily be reduced to biology. These features concern the intentions and meanings which individuals hold about their health (governing the health related risks they take, for example) and the collective forms which they take, reflected in the social patterning of both health and risk: for example, smoking and obesity are now strongly associated with deprivation.

Riley *et al.* (1988) make the point that there is a plasticity in the individual human ageing process, as social and psychological factors interact with biological processes. Such an interactive view of ageing works in both directions, with biological parameters shaping and limiting social behaviour, and social conditions influencing the development of the human body. Moreover, 'ageing and social change' as an 'institutional' process take on meanings of their own, as is currently the case with public policy debates concerning the 'ageing population' and future plans for pensions, health and social care. Thus society shapes ageing at the individual level, and changes in health and ageing of populations shape the changing structure and culture of society. Our starting point, therefore, is that biology and the body do not have to be 'brought in' to the sociological analysis of ageing and the lifecourse, though they have not always been explicitly recognized in the sociological treatment of the subject, partly for reasons that Blaxter (this volume) discusses in the context of inequalities. They are at the centre of studies of ageing, however, just as changes in human ageing and the lifecourse shape the societies in which they occur. This interactional view informs our discussion below.

The biological clock

Although, as intimated, the 'biological clock' usually refers to time passing in the period of fertility, new thinking about processes of ageing and health shows that it is appropriate now to use it with reference to much longer periods of life. Health and psychological studies concerned with the long-term, demonstrate that essential aspects of ageing begin well before the onset of later life (Brunner 2000). Ingenious methods have been used, including studies of migration, follow-up of cohorts throughout life (Wadsworth 1999), and catch-up in later life with cohorts studied in childhood (Barker 1998). This work has shown that, just as height growth has to take place during a window of opportunity that closes in the late teenage years, so also almost all essential aspects of organ development are completed before birth or soon afterwards. This is known as biological programming (Barker 1998), and the degree of growth and development attained may be called biological capital (see also Blaxter on 'health capital', this volume). Although it is sometimes implied that biological programming determines health opportunities for all in later life, this is no more or less true than it is that compulsory education, which is completed soon after growth stops, determines socio-economic and other opportunities throughout adulthood. Clearly these influences can be profound, but to regard them as solely determining is to misunderstand the dynamic character of the developmental processes at work. An overdetermined model – be it biological or social – will fail to account for key features of experience, for example, within group variations and differential rates of social mobility.

Social context is the key element in both development and use of the individual's health capital. For example, prenatal development is strongly associated with maternal physique, health, and health associated behaviour, and each of these elements relates to the social environment, not only in its immediate effect but also for its effect in the much longer term. Illsley and Kincaid (1963) noted that maternal physique, shown in the national perinatal mortality study to be an important aspect of risk, had been determined in the childhood of mothers in that study during the economic depression. They argued that the effect of the depression on their growth might account for the wide socio-economic and geographical differences in early-life deaths in their children. However, Illsley (1986) also showed how such factors could interact with forms of 'social selection' over time to produce change, for example in social position (as measured by occupational social class) between birth and marriage.

Processes of long-term risk to health are similarly socially driven over long periods of the lifecourse. For example, adult overweight and obesity are known risks for raised blood pressure, and the interaction of that adult risk with risk developed in early life illustrates how risk may accumulate throughout life (Table 8.1).

The table shows that early life and adult sources of risk each had an effect, and that the combination of high risk in both periods was associated with greatest risk of raised blood pressure: 24 per cent of women in the group that had the high risk in childhood and the high risk of adult overweight or obesity had raised/treated blood pressure, and so did 29 per cent of men in the group defined the same way. In this example both types of risk are driven by social factors. The childhood risks also increase the likelihood of the adult risk; poor social circumstances in childhood increase the risk of occupying an adult manual social class position which is a risk for obesity, and adult overweight and obesity are associated with low social class in father's and own generation, as well as with adult exercise and eating habits (Prentice and Jebb 1995).

Explanations are sought for how the major risks to health presented by poverty, chronic stress and adverse health related behaviour (diet, alcohol

Table 8.1 Infant social circumstances, prenatal and postnatal growth in relation to body mass index and raised blood pressure at age 43 years (percentages in each cell are the proportion of that population who have raised blood pressure)

	Body mass index at age 43 years	
Aggregate score, in thirds, of father's social class, infant crowding, birth weight, height at 2 years (highest thirds are best circumstances, lowest thirds are worst circumstances)	*Not overweight or obese*	*Overweight or obese*
Men	(*n* = 585)	(*n* = 661)
Highest third	13.1%	12.2%
Middle third	14.0%	19.2%
Lowest third	15.9%	29.1%
	(NS)	(*p* <0.001)
Women	(*n* = 715)	(*n* = 435)
Highest third	8.0%	8.0%
Middle third	9.7%	15.9%
Lowest third	17.2%	24.1%
	(*p* = 0.020)	(*p* <0.001)

consumption, exercise, smoking) have their biological effect. Each of these risks affects health and development in childhood as well as adult health. Chronic stress, for example, is associated with poor growth in childhood and with increased risk of cardiovascular disease, and is hypothesized to be translated into health damage via a brain–hormonal pathway. Poverty, similarly, has an adverse effect on both growth, and on childhood and adult health; Brunner (2000) suggests biologically plausible pathways to explain how poverty induces poor health. The effects of smoking, little exercise and alcohol abuse are also known to affect adversely development before birth and growth in childhood, as well as adult health. Thus for individuals, social and biological adversity may interact and accumulate from childhood to produce current and/or future risk to health (Wadsworth *et al.* 1999).

The social processes associated with health are all subject to change with time. As the social context changes, the nature of some effects will also change (e.g. stress), and others, such as poverty, and adverse health related habits will change in prevalence and in population distribution. Differences may be seen within and between generations, and that has a value for testing hypothesized effects. For example, by using the concept of agency, signalling the 'intentions and meanings' with respect to their health and other valued aspects of their life, a recent study goes beyond current explanations for the uneven social distribution of health related behaviour. It shows that the individual's presentation of self (in terms for example of conformity, gender identity) is associated with health related behaviour and how it changes over time in response to changes in health education advice (Schooling 2001).

In summary, it may be argued that the biological clock starts at conception, and possibly in some respects in the childhood of the previous generation. At the same time the biological clock is driven by a series of interactions with social processes including those of human agency.

Why biology is of importance to sociology

The roots of biological risk, then, are found in the social circumstances of individuals and of societies. For the individual that has already been discussed, these are expressed in terms of the development of health capital in early life and the interaction of health capital with social processes and influences throughout life.

At the societal level recent evidence shows a relationship between social organization and health. The health indicators used in most social and epidemiological research have been mostly limited to death in the first year of life, and premature adult death before the age of 60 years. That is because these are available for most countries and most areas, and are also sensitive to social circumstances. Studies using these indicators have shown associations with health that raise important questions about the possible processes of cause and effect. For example, in India the infant death rate is lowest in the one state that, at the time of the study, provided educational opportunities and rights of inheritance for women (Wadsworth 1999). In the USA premature death from heart disease was strikingly low in the town of Roseto before the Second World War, but as high as elsewhere in the same state in more recent times. Bruhn and Wolf (1979) attributed this to diminishing 'social cohesion'. In the old USSR infant death rates rose as the post-communist changes brought increasing uncertainty of socio-economic circumstances of everyday life and rising family disruption. And international comparative studies of wealth distribution show that the most equitable economies are associated with the lowest infant death rates (Wilkinson 1996).

Biology is also important to a sociology of the lifecourse as one of the powerful factors associated with social change. The application of effective biological knowledge through public health, nutrition, and the control of infection and fertility brought great increases in the life expectation of people in developed countries. Expected length of life for those born in 1901 was 52 years in women and 48 years in men, but women who lived to be 40 years old (i.e. until 1941) could then expect a further 17 years of life, and men in similar circumstances could expect a further 19 years. For the generation born in 1951 the expected years of life were 72 for women and 66 for men. Fertility control has also changed employment patterns and aspirations for employment (Halsey and Webb 2000), and all aspects of gender relations. Furthermore, biological knowledge brought great improvements in health and safety in the work place, and developed measures of health against which to set standards of work environment and entitlement to benefit and compensation.

As medical care has become increasingly effective the demands for its availability have been tempered by new expectations of how the 'responsible citizen' should reduce health risks by taking exercise, not smoking, and moderating other areas of personal behaviour. Although such responsibility is sometimes legislated (e.g. car seat belts), it is largely a seemingly increasing expectation and a source of quasi-moral debate. Similarly questions of responsibility, both individual and collective, are raised by the new genetic knowledge (see Shakespeare's chapter, this volume).

Sociology and ageing

It seems clear, therefore, that sociology has much to learn from and much to contribute to the biological study of the body, health and ageing. Biology, society and human agency can be seen to interact powerfully, especially in periods of rapid social change. There seems little prospect of such change – economic, technical, scientific and cultural change – slowing in the foreseeable future.

That such dynamics should influence the process of ageing – across the lifecourse – is thus hardly surprising, though their neglect by mainstream sociology is more so. At the least, these interactions indicate that key biological aspects of the human body and their relationship to health are neither static nor fully understood outside their social context, and that in developing a full account of the body sociology needs to address both health and ageing.

As we have noted in considering changes in longevity, growing old is not a new phenomenon for those who could survive the hazards of early exposure to health risks, historically posed by life-threatening infections. Thane (2000) has commented that even in the early modern era, once the individual had survived the early part of life – or, rather, if they did – a long life was a distinct possibility. She estimates that in seventeenth century England those aged 60 and over comprised 9 per cent of the population, in the eighteenth and nineteenth century 7 per cent. In the last half of the twentieth century the figure rose rapidly to 18 per cent (Thane 2000: 20), and today stands at 21 per cent according to the 2001 census.

What is historically new is that the majority of individuals at birth can now expect to live into old age. It is clear we hope, even from the short analysis offered here, that changes in social context, individual behaviour and biology across the lifecourse have combined to produce this altered situation, and the variations and inequalities by which it is characterised. That such change has occurred suggests that both biology and sociology need to reorientate themselves to regard health and ageing as core issues.

Space permits only a brief indication of possible items on the sociological research agenda.

The first issue is of course, the patterning of health and the influence of early development on adult and later life. Biographical approaches to health and illness are now combining with the collection of data on birth cohorts and from other sources to provide a more nuanced picture of health and the lifecourse. These data increasingly examine the outcome of early influences in older populations. The earlier preoccupation of public health and sociology with 'premature mortality' and early adult health is therefore being supplemented with more sensitive data related to an ageing population. Biographical approaches in particular can examine disruption and continuity across the lifecourse, and the interaction of agency and structure in their occurrence. Such an approach also offers the prospect of overcoming tendencies towards early 'biological programming' of the kind suggested by Barker. As Vagero and Illsley have noted, and as we have attempted to illustrate here, 'biological and social influences are not mutually exclusive' (Vagero and Illsley 1995: 232). It seems clear, however, in assessing the contribution of these influences as the lifecourse unfolds that 'social capital' becomes relatively more important (Wadsworth 1991: 150–1) as individuals move into adulthood and their middle and later years.

However, as individuals progress through old age, it can often be the case that biological parameters begin once more to assert themselves. Though we have stressed the 'plasticity' of ageing, and some of the many changes which have influenced this over the twentieth century, it is still the case that many health problems are strongly associated with biological age. Any study of the body and health in later life is thus bound to confront the question of chronic illness and disability. National surveys of disability have frequently underlined the links between age and health status.

In the largest British survey on the subject, 70 per cent of the six million people found to be disabled in Britain (using a relatively low threshold in defining disability) were aged 60 and over, and nearly a half were aged 70 and over. The very old emerged as the most affected by disability, and this is likely to be the focus of continuing interest in the future. In that survey 63 per cent of women and 53 per cent of men aged 75 and over were disabled (Martin *et al.* 1988: 127). The gender imbalance is noteworthy in these figures, in part the result of biological differences; for example, women suffer more from arthritis, one of the leading causes of disability. Despite these data, and many others that tell a similar story, few sociologists, even those concerned with disability, have focused on ageing and the lifecourse. For example, a number of recent collections of essays in the sociology of disability, published in the UK, make little or no mention of the issue.

Most importantly, such an analysis clearly needs to recognize the place of gender in disability, health and the lifecourse (Arber and Ginn 1991; Bury 1995). As new data emerge from cohort studies and other sources that deal with later life there will be a need to bring together approaches which combine the study of health, ageing and gender (Bury 2000: 102; Annandale, this volume). Arber and Ginn's work is of value here in that it explores both sex differences, in the sense of those aspects of health that are biologically given, and the interactions of these with gender roles.

Finally, there is the issue of assessing health trends with change over time. Much has been written about the possibility of the 'compression of morbidity' – the process in which poor health and disability may be relegated to the very last years of life (Fries 1989). If such changes are underway they hold out the prospect of healthier old age as new cohorts bring higher levels of 'health capital' and 'social capital' into later life. Laslett, for example, based his whole approach to the development of the 'Theory of the Third Age' on such a presumption (Laslett 1989). Laslett argued for a re-thinking of the lifecourse to take into account the implications of the ageing population. He suggested that transitions from the 'second age', essentially that of paid employment, to the 'third age' of retirement will be highly variable. Indeed 'retirement' is an increasingly fluid category with larger proportions of both men and women exiting the labour market before official retirement age. For Laslett this opens up a new and potentially extended period of the lifecourse, the 'third age', in which to pursue valued goals.

This approach is normative as well as analytical in that it emphasizes the need to reject earlier patterns of behaviour – withdrawal and disengagement particularly associated historically with widowhood – in favour of an active and engaged later life. Such a prospect depends in large measure on good health and a high level of bodily and psychological fitness. If morbidity is compressed into the very last years of life (designated by Laslett as the final 'fourth age') then such a view seems warranted. Part of the problem with this argument lies in the fact that evidence for such morbidity compression is difficult to gather and difficult to assess. Recent data from the UK General Household Survey, for example, show an increase in self-reported long-standing illness at all ages, over the age of 60 (Office of National Statistics 2001). Thus healthier profiles among many individuals in later life may belie considerable morbidity levels in the elderly population as a whole.

Some 'postmodern' approaches to ageing have echoed this contradictory situation by suggesting that the ageing body is increasingly experienced as a 'mask', behind which a more youthful outlook is maintained. This, it is suggested, means that markers and boundaries surrounding ageing, whether of a 'biological clock' variety or of fixed social transitions such as retirement, are weakening (Featherstone and Hepworth 1991). A clearer picture of trends in health status, disability and thus of the ageing body are central to testing such ideas. One of the difficulties with postmodern writing on ageing, as on other subjects, is that, suggestive though they often are, they tend to be 'data free'. Optimistic views of the changing lifecourse, where age related boundaries are blurred and new forms of agency rather than the constraints of material hardship prevail, may point towards a future trend. However, good quality empirical evidence, both qualitative and quantitative, is necessary in order to evaluate how far such optimism is warranted. As we have shown here, material hardship continues to play a significant role in health and well-being across the lifecourse – set in train at birth and reinforced by continuing difficulties – at least for a significant minority. Whether this is the result of persisting deprivation for some or the result of more general inequalities across the whole social structure is a matter of continuing debate. Whatever one's view, assessing the balance between optimistic and more pessimistic views of ageing and the lifecourse remains an important focus of research (Bury 2000).

Whilst sociology alone cannot hope to resolve such matters it can bring new ideas and empirical evidence to bear on them. At the least these considerations suggest that the body and the lifecourse will remain at the centre of the sociology of health and ageing. In doing so it also provides sociology with important windows on the changing nature of society itself.

References

Arber, S. and Ginn, J. (1991) *Gender and Later Life: A Sociological Analysis of Resources and Constraints*, London: Sage.

Barker, D.J.P. (1998) *Mothers, Babies, and Disease in Later Life* (2nd edn), Edinburgh: Churchill Livingstone.

Bruhn, J.G. and Wolf, S. (1979) *The Roseto Story*, Norman: University of Oklahoma Press.

Brunner, E. (2000) 'Toward a new social biology', in L.F. Berkman and I. Kawachi (eds) *Social Epidemiology*, Oxford: Oxford University Press, pp. 306–31.

Bury, M. (1995) 'Ageing, gender and sociological theory', in S. Arber and J. Ginn (eds) *Connecting Gender and Ageing: A Sociological Approach*, Buckingham: Open University Press.

Bury, M. (2000) 'Health, ageing and the lifecourse' in S.J. Williams, J. Gabe and M. Calnan (eds) *Health Medicine and Society: Key Theories, Future Agendas*, London: Routledge.

Bury, M. and Holme, A. (1991) *Life After Ninety*, London: Routledge.

Featherstone, M. and Hepworth, M. (1991) 'The mask of ageing and the postmodern life course', in M. Featherstone, M. Hepworth and B.S. Turner (eds) *The Body: Social Processes and Cultural Theory*, London: Sage.

Fries, J. (1989) 'The compression of morbidity: near or far?', *The Milbank Quarterly*, 67, 2: 208–32.

Halsey, A.H. and Webb, J. (2000) *Twentieth Century British Social Trends*, London: Macmillan.

Hipkiss, A. and Bittles, A. (1989) 'Basic biological aspects of ageing', in A. Warnes (ed.) *Human Ageing and Later Life: Multidisciplinary Perspectives*, London: Edward Arnold.

Illsely, R. (1986) 'Occupational class, selection and the production of inequalities in health', *Quarterly Journal of Social Affairs*, 2: 151–65.

Illsley, R. and Kincaid, J.C. (1963) 'Social correlations of perinatal mortality', in N.R. Butler and D.G. Bonham (eds) *Perinatal Mortality*, Edinburgh: Churchill Livingstone, pp. 270–86.

Langenberg, C., Hardy, R.J., Kuh, D.J.L., Brunner, E. and Wadsworth, M.E.J. (forthcoming) 'Central and total obesity in middle aged men in relation to lifetime socioeconomic status', *Journal of Epidemiology and Community Health*.

Laslett, P. (1989) *A Fresh Map of Life: The Emergence of the Third Age*, London: Weidenfeld & Nicolson.

Martin, J., Meltzer, H. and Elliott, D. (1988) *The Prevalence of Disability Among Adults*, London: HMSO.

Office of National Statistics (2001) *Social Trends*, London: HMSO.

Prentice, A.M. and Jebb, S.A. (1995) 'Obesity in Britain: gluttony or sloth?', *British Medical Journal*, **311**: 437–9.

Riley, M.W., Foner, A. and Waring, J. (1988) 'Sociology of age', in N.J. Smelser (ed.) *Handbook of Sociology*, London and Newbury Park, CA: Sage.

Schooling, C.M. (2001) *Health and Behaviour in a Social and Temporal Context*, PhD thesis, University College, London.

Searle, J.R. (1995) *The Construction of Social Reality*, London: Penguin Books.

Thane, P. (2000) *Old Age in English History*, Oxford: Oxford: University Press.

Vagero, D. and Illsley, R. (1995) 'Explaining health inequalities, beyond Black and Barker', *European Sociological Review* **11**, 3: 219–41.

Wadsworth, M. (1991) *The Imprint of Time: Childhood, History and Adult Life*, Oxford: Oxford University Press.

Wadsworth, M.E.J. (1999) 'Early life', in M.G. Marmot and R.G. Wilkinson (eds) *Social Determinants of Health*, Oxford: Oxford University Press, pp. 44–63.

Wadsworth, M.E.J., Bartley, M.J. and Montgomery, S.M. (1999) 'The persisting effect of unemployment in early working life on health and social well-being', *Social Science and Medicine*, **48**: 1491–9.

Wilkinson, R.G. (1996) *Unhealthy Societies: the Afflictions of Inequality*, London: Routledge.

Part III

Embodying biology

Corporeal matters

9 The problem with sex/gender and nature/nurture

Anne Fausto-Sterling

For a good century and a half, scientists, social scientists and politicians have appealed to biological difference to explain social inequality between men and women, people of African descent and Caucasians, members of different economic classes and people of different religions. In turn, a wide variety of scholars writing over a long period of time have critiqued these scientific claims (Russett 1989; Fausto-Sterling 2000). In the mid-1980s, I drew a composite picture gleaned from the writings of contemporary biological and social scientists: these writers claimed that women are naturally better mothers, while men are genetically predisposed to be aggressive, hasty and fickle. They may rape to pass on their genes. Women's lack of aggressive drive and native ability ensures that they will always earn less, thus guaranteeing equal pay discriminates against men (Fausto-Sterling 1992).

At the time, I critically examined the underlying scientific evidence, demonstrating its procedural and interpretive weaknesses. I also suggested that instead of setting nature against nurture we reject the search for root causes and substitute a more complex analysis in which an individual's capacities emerge from a web of mutual interactions between the biological being and the social environment. Although I had the right idea, the moment was not right to express it in terms that might unify biological scientists, sociologists, developmental psychologists, and feminists. I believe that now that moment of unification is upon us.

In the 1970s, feminist social scientists proposed a theory that created two categories: *sex*, the supposed biological essence that underlay gender and *gender* the social overlay that produced two different categories of being – men and women, through an ill-defined process of socialization. This theoretical approach had many virtues. It permitted the examination of differential treatment of boys and girls in school and men and women in the workplace. It opened the door to a virtual growth industry of cultural analysis examining the construction of gender ideology in the media and on the streets. But it also had a big drawback. Leaving 'sex' in the realm of scientifically verifiable fact left feminism vulnerable to a new tide of biological difference. Indeed, that new tide is very much with us (see for example: Udry 2000; Wizemann and Pardue 2001).

For some, sex encroaches deep into the territory of social difference, while for others it is a minimal entity. If there is something that we could call 'naked sex' (Kraus 2000) – that which is left when all gender is stripped away – we have to argue about for how much of gender difference it can account. If we leave naked sex to biologists and biologically oriented social scientists, we will find that the territory allotted to it is growing apace while the explanatory power of socially produced gender shrinks in proportion. In the sex versus gender model, biological sex is opposed to social sex. Nature is opposed to culture, the body becomes the recipient of culture, and gender becomes the content of culture. Worst of all, for those interested in social change, naked sex is often – albeit incorrectly – seen as immutable, while gender, is often, albeit incorrectly, seen as malleable. To the extent that the sex/gender analysis of social difference reinforces our view of the material body as a natural given, our feminist debate influences the structure of other struggles. Indeed, the biological debates about race and about sex have intersected and mutually constructed one another for a good two centuries (Russett 1989).

In *Sexing the Body: Gender Politics and the Construction of Sexuality* (Fausto-Sterling 2000), I detail several examples of how the biology–culture debate about the body plays out. Let me briefly pick one of these – an alleged sex difference in the structure of a part of the brain called the corpus callosum. Scientists have argued about whether or not there is a sex difference in the corpus callosum for a more than 100 years. Some think that the (real) difference might explain sex/gender variation in verbal and spatial ability and that the knowledge of such difference should be used to shape educational policy. Others believe there is no difference. I use this scientific debate to think about how social arguments sustain scientific disputes, concluding that we will not resolve the *science* at issue until we have reached some form of consensus over the *social policy* at hand.

While the above insight is important, however, I want here to emphasize a different aspect of the problem. Suppose, hypothetically, someone proved beyond a doubt that a sex difference in the corpus callosum was clearly linked to verbal and spatial abilities. Would that mean that feminists adhering to the sex/gender distinction would have to agree that educators need to treat boys and girls differently when they teach maths and English? Would that force us to accept the argument that we cannot expect there to be more women engineers than the 9.2 per cent employed in the US workforce in 1997? At its worst, too strict an adherence to the sex/gender dualism puts us in just such a position. At its best, it leaves feminists in a position of constant defensiveness, with all of our energy focused on refuting or mitigating the latest findings of sex differences produced by biomedical researchers. Psychologist Susan Oyama refers to this as hauling 'phenomena back and forth across the biological border' (Oyama 2000: 190). I, for one, am tired of being in this position, and this weariness has pushed me – and other theorists – to think differently about biology, culture, sex, and gender (see, for example, the chapters by Birke and Annandale, this volume). In making new theory, we reclaim a defining position in the social debate about gender and we can direct our creativity towards breaking new pathways rather than fighting off the dogs that nip constantly at our heels.

I find especially helpful a set of approaches that I have gathered under the flag of Developmental Systems Theory, or DST for short. From the point of view of DST, neither naked sex nor naked culture exist. Findings of so-called biological difference do not imply a claim of immutability or inevitability. Consider once again the corpus callosum. Some scientists believe that this brain structure differs in men and women; others that it differs in left- and right-handers and yet others believe that it differs in gay and straight men (where it is really a stand-in for a gendered account of homosexuality). Elsewhere I write about the uncertain nature of these conclusions (Fausto-Sterling 1992; Fausto-Sterling 2000), but here I want to think about what it might mean if these claims were scientifically uncontestable. In bringing a DST approach to the claim of brain differences in adult men and women, the assertion of difference becomes a starting point. The interesting question is how the differences developed in the first place. For example, this possible difference in the adult corpus callosum is not present in the brains of small children. A DST researcher will want to design experiments to test hypotheses about how different experience leads to a divergence in brain development. Instead of asking how anatomy limits function, one asks how function shapes anatomy. To claim a biological difference is not to claim immutability.

New research questions become apparent when we turn matters around in this way. What childhood experiences and behaviours contribute to the developing anatomy of the brain? Are there particular developmental periods when a child's brain is more or less responsive to functional stimuli? How do nerve cells translate externally generated information into specific growth patterns and neural circuits? Answering these latter questions will require the skills of molecular biologists and cell biologists as well as psychologists, sociologists and cultural theorists. DST will not put basic biologists out of business, but will set their research in a different intellectual framework.

Just as a claim of biological difference does not imply immutability, a claim of socially induced difference does not necessarily imply malleability. For example, if differential social experience produces differences in brain anatomy and thus in brain function, later experiences would then be interpreted and integrated by a differently functioning brain. Change to a predifferentiated state would be improbable. Many people consider it extremely difficult to change from being hetero- to homosexual or vice versa. But the fact that a particular form of sexual desire is hard to change does not mean that it hasn't been socially caused.

How, more specifically, can DST help to form a new research agenda which depends upon the mutual construction of sex and gender? Psychologists Esther Thelen and Linda Smith list some of the basic goals of developmental systems theory (Thelen and Smith 1994). The first is to understand the origins of novelty. Thelen and Smith discuss behavioural novelty – starting to crawl and then to walk for example, but I would like to use DST to elucidate the emergence by the age of two-and-a-half of gender differences in play and the ability to categorize self and others by gender. Infants are not born with these behaviours. Rather, the behaviours emerge during the first two to three years of life. We have a sketchy idea of the timing of such emergence but little in the way of coherent theory to explain our observations (Ruble and Martin 1998).

A second goal of DST is to reconcile global regularities with local variability. In the case of gender, this means understanding the emergence of general features recognizable as something we call gender, while at the same time incorporating into our story the enormous within-group variability.

A third goal of systems theory is to integrate developmental data at many levels of explanation. Consider Judith Butler's controversial and frequently misunderstood assertion that 'gender ought not to be construed as a stable identity . . . rather, gender is an identity tenuously constituted in time, instituted in an exterior space through a *stylized repetition of acts*' (Butler 1990: 140; emphasis in the original). Butler was not thinking specifically about physiological mechanisms by which the body might materially incorporate gender. Nevertheless, a systems approach to the body insists that relatively stable states of being emerge from a process of repetitive trial and error. Thus Butler's notion of repeated performance, designed to describe gender development at the psychoanalytic level, could become a starting point to design studies aimed at understanding the material basis of gender. 'Material basis' is here understood as a set of physiological and social expressions which emerge as individuals learn about social gender, practice it, and make it their own. That brain anatomy might itself develop in particular ways in response to such practice and repetition seems likely to me, but is a hypothesis that requires specification and testing.

Such an application of DST to Butler's ideas of performance also provide an answer to Pheng Cheah's critique of Butler (Cheah 1996). Cheah argues that Butler's account of gender development is philosophically wanting because it only applies to humans, a fact that leaves human gender critically unconnected to the rest of biology. Most biologists, however (myself included) view human biology – including sex/gender development – as falling along a continuum. DST can provide accounts of how gender materializes in the body that will work for all animals, not just humans. Granted there are some big discussions about consciousness and intentionality in non-human primates that must be held along the way. But stretching claims such as Butler's about repetitive performance to develop a systems account of the biological materialization of gender in humans, will open the door to understanding biological development more broadly, and confront untenable claims that human materiality differs fundamentally from that of other animals.

A fourth goal of developmental systems theory is to provide a biologically plausible yet non-determinist account of the development of behaviour. As

Thelen and Smith write, 'the boundaries between what is innate and what is acquired become so blurred as to be at the very least uninteresting compared to the powerful questions of developmental process' (Thelen and Smith 1994). A fifth goal is to understand how local processes, that is, what happens in a particular family or to a particular child or a particular random experience, can lead to global outcomes. For example, most children learn to walk. But the individual paths they take to that accomplishment can vary quite a lot.

A final goal for DST is to establish a theoretical basis for generating and interpreting empirical research that breaks out of the idea of adding up so much nature and so much nurture to create a final outcome. This means learning how to apply statistical systems that do not partition variance. (For critiques of the Analysis of Variance approach to the study of human difference see: Wahlsten 1990.)

Psychologists have most successfully applied DST to phenomena that have little to do with gender. Studying such applications, however, can help us to construct a research agenda aimed at explicating the emergence of gender in early childhood and its subsequent development throughout the life cycle. Consider how Thelen and her colleagues investigate the question of how we learn to walk. In the 1940s and 1950s, psychologists described the stages of learning to walk – up on all fours, crawling, standing, walking holding on, etc. They reasoned that each new stage directly reflected changes in the brain. But how can the millions of neurons, the wide variety of muscle contraction patterns, and the complex patterns of neuronal activity, ever result in a highly specific movement such as putting one leg in front of another? During development, individuals go through periods of instability as they incorporate new tasks – be they motor, cognitive or emotional. In an infant, seemingly random motor activity, for instance, eventually emerges into new and fairly stable forms of movement, first crawling, then walking.

A recent example illustrates why developmental systems theory has begun to replace more rigid accounts of stages of neuromuscular development. In 1992 pediatricians recommended that to minimize the danger of sudden infant death, infants be place on their back (supine) or side to sleep rather than on their bellies (prone). Since the recommendation and a public education campaign, the percentage of US infants sleeping in the prone position has decreased from 70 per cent to 27 per cent. With that change has come another – a dramatic shift in the age at which infants reach motor milestones such as pulling to stand up, crawling, creeping and rolling from a prone to supine position (Davis *et al.* 1998). The observation that sleep position affects the timing of motor development makes perfect sense to a systems theorist, since neuromuscular development is an *effect* of use and experience. That both supine and prone sleepers learn to walk at about the same time may reflect the fact that by one year of age they have all developed the strength needed to sustain independent walking. But supine and prone sleepers don't attain that strength in exactly the same way or according to the same time schedule.

As long as the basic conditions – the force of gravity, the firmness of the ground, neuromuscular responses (indeed these are all part of the system of walking), remain stable, the ability to walk remains stable as well. But the stability is what DST theorists call 'softly assembled'. Walking, for example, is a flexible ability. We don't use exactly the same neuromuscular responses when walking on different substrates, yet we walk. Walking can take on different strides – ambling, strolling, fast-walking. It can adjust to an injury in a knee joint, etc. Softly assembled states can dissolve into new periods of instability and new types of stability can emerge from these seemingly chaotic events – learning to walk again following muscle atrophy or traumatic injury would be one such example.

Consider as another example, the development of the retina and the ability to see. The axons of nerve cells from the retina of each eye connect to a part of the brain known as the lateral geniculate nucleus. Some of the retinal axons from the right eye connect to the lateral geniculate nucleus of the left hemisphere while others connect to the right hemisphere, while the opposite is true for axons from the left eye. Within the lateral geniculate nucleus, axons from the two eyes terminate in separate alternating layers. There is also an additional level of organization in these projections called ocular dominance columns. Initially, neither the layering of these lateral geniculate nucleus axons from left to right nor the dominance columns are present, but via an active process of axon retraction and elaboration, eventually the adult connections emerge.

These events do not occur seamlessly in response to some internal logic of genes acting spontaneously inside cells. Rather, visual experience plays a key role. The firing of certain neurons strengthens their connections. Neuroscientists say 'cells that fire together wire together, those that don't won't.' The fact that light, entering the eye after birth is necessary for a completely functional set of eye–brain connections explains why it is so important to remove congenital cataracts no later than six months after birth (Le Grand *et al.* 2001).

In the development of vision, key features of developmental systems theory emerge. First, specific connections are not *programmed* by some genetic blueprint. Genetic activity, rather, guides development by responding to external signals reaching specific cells at specific times. Early in development these signals come from other cells while at a later time signals include spontaneous electrical activity generated by developing nervous tissue and, still later, light entering through the newborn and infant eye. A functional system emerges from a context-bound system in which seemingly random activity – that is spontaneous nerve firings and visual input – evolve into more highly structured form and function. Often these connections must happen during a critical window of development. One general point to be made is that different kinds of connections have different degrees of plasticity. Some critical windows reside only in one stage of the life cycle because that is the only time when (so far as we currently know) the entire system is constructed in a particular way. In some cases an end state can be produced by more than one initial starting point while in others only one initial starting point can produce an end state. Other systems, though, may be open to change more than once in a life cycle or may even be continuously modifiable during the life cycle. Thus a key notion of developmental systems theory is that there are periods of relative stability and other moments of great instability. During unstable moments important changes can occur which in turn resolve into new and stable form and function. An important future task for biologists and social scientists, working together, is to apply these concepts to gender formation during the life cycle.

How might DST apply to the analysis of sex and gender? Consider the uproar over biologist Simon LeVay's 1991 article reporting differences in the microanatomy of both male and female brains and in the brains of gay and straight men (LeVay 1991). The initial response from many of us was to point out the technical shortcomings of the study, but in a recent study some of these have been overcome. Neuroanatomist William Byne could not replicate the gay/straight differences that LeVay reported. But as had LeVay, Byne found measurable differences between men's and women's hypothalamuses (Byne *et al.* 2001). Given that his is the third independent report of this anatomical brain difference, I think we would be hard-pressed to deny the finding. But accepting the difference need not push us into a bio-determinist corner. Instead, we need to insist that scientists ask developmental and functional questions about the difference. Most importantly, we need to hammer home the point that differences found in adults arise during development.

This insistence opens the door for a theory and practice of what contemporary theorists call embodiment. Recall the DST concept of softly-assembled states. Although relatively stable, such states can dissolve into chaotic periods out of which new types of stability can emerge. Consider the conflict between the idea that homosexuality is inborn versus the thought that it is somehow learned after birth. Sometimes this argument resolves into a debate about whether the trait is unchangeable or whether it can be altered by force of will. There is bad thinking on both sides of this argument. For many homosexuals, same-sex attraction is a stable state of desire. If we think of that stability as being softly assembled, however, it becomes less surprising that it can sometimes become destabilized and after a period of disarray, some new quasi-stable form of desire can emerge.

Recent work on the nature of memory in rats can help us conceptualize my argument. Consider rats that have been fear-conditioned to associate a tone with an electric shock. At first, the conditioned response is unstable. It requires about six hours and some protein synthesis to consolidate. The memory associating a tone with shock, however, can be pushed out of what I will call its softly assembled state by preventing more protein synthesis at the time that memory is again evoked by playing the tone (Nader 2000).

The conclusion from this experiment is that when a memory is drawn upon and then stored again, new memory proteins are made. In these experiments, memories become destabilized and open to revision for a brief period before a new period of stability begins.

The concept that memory can be revised during episodes of retrieval can be useful in thinking about homosexuality. Consider the statement by a gay person that they always remember being different. Perhaps they remember liking dolls instead of trucks (or for lesbians, liking trucks instead of dolls). If, during the evocation of memory, it is possible to edit and incorporate contemporary information, then memory itself becomes part of a system that produces the sexual preference or gender identity. The memories are perfectly real, but they become progressively adjusted, presumably throughout childhood and into adulthood, to take into account new experiences and newly available information. Surely it is possible for social and neuro-scientists to collaborate in applying the study of memory processing and revision to the acquisition of gender identity and sexual orientation. Such applications have the potential to provide a dynamic account of embodiment rather than the less plausible view that some people are born with a homosexual homunculus which merely unfolds over a lifetime.

In light of my discussion of DST I propose a new research agenda for the study of sex and gender differences. First, we need to think more about individual differences than group averages. This means studying individual development and accepting the idea that there are many different individual paths to a global outcome. Feminist social theory contains rich work on the emergence of sex and gender differences, much of which examines mid- and late child development or adulthood. But we know little about the early emergence of difference. And it's the early emergence of difference that is often used as evidence for a biological cause for difference.

We can, however, say a few things about early development. At seven months, on average, infants respond differently to male and female voices. By nine months, they can tell the sexes apart largely on the basis of hair length. But other contributions to an infant's ability to discriminate sexes such as height and smell have not been well studied. Children can differentially label the sexes by about thirty months but they are better at labelling adults than they are at labelling other children. Children take quite a while before they use genitalia as clues to sex and before they are able to do this they rely heavily on hair cues. In the United States small children believe that figures with blond curly hair are female. Adolescents, but not younger children, use dynamic clues, such as running or sitting to identify gender (Ruble and Martin 1998).

The racial specificity of such findings make future, culturally specific studies imperative. Most studies of early development of gender perception have been done on white middle-class children in America and the entire question of constructing culturally neutral accounts of gender difference continues to vex feminist theory. Indeed, a central component of a feminist social science research agenda must be to examine the early development of gender constructs and behaviours in different cultures and in different socio-economic groups and within different ethnic and racially-defined communities (see also part II, this volume). If we develop process-based theories of human development rather than relying on averages and statistical norms, we will have fewer problems including human variation in our accounts of gender development.

After children learn to identify gender they then develop a separate concept – that gender is constant and stable. At first children don't necessarily believe that 'once a girl always a girl'. It takes a while for young children to develop the notion that, first, genitalia provide a reliable way of distinguishing between boys and girls and second that one of the implications of knowing about genital difference is that gender is fixed. The ages at which these two ideas develop – although certainly older than three years – have yet to be clearly resolved.

By about two-and-a-half years of age (white, middle-class American) children begin to show knowledge of gender stereotypes, about objects (dresses versus trousers, trucks versus flowers) and activities (active playing, passive playing, playing in the home-making corner, throwing a ball, playing with trucks). Although they know about these gendered stereotypes, social scientists have yet to assess which ones children learn first. I offer the above, abbreviated description of the development of gender awareness in children not as an account of how gender emerges, but rather as an invitation. I ask developmental systems theorists who have produced fascinating but non-gendered accounts of motor and cognitive development to use DST to think about gender. Similarly, I request social scientists who study gender to break away from the traditional biological, psychoanalytic, cognitive social learning or gender schema approaches. Instead, I encourage them to look at the trajectory that I've sketched above, fill in important gaps, and begin to use developmental systems theory to understand the process by which gender emerges at very young ages. How does it stabilize? What might contribute to its destabilization, and how does it restabilize and change during the process of an entire life cycle?

At the same time I invite feminist theorists in the humanities to revisit the social sciences with a new developmental systems theory vision. This is the impulse of the current vogue of the term embodiment among feminist theorists. Embodiment suggests a process by which we *acquire* a body rather than a passive unfolding of some preformed blueprint. Beginning to understand that the world works via systems will enable us to specify more clearly the links between culture and the body and to understand how nature and nurture, sex and gender are indivisible concepts. Finally, the political fallout from these ideas remains to be addressed. We – and here I mean feminist political theorists – need to think harder about how engaging with the world of sex and gender from a DST point of view will affect our strategies for social change.

References

Butler, J. (1990) *Gender Trouble: Feminism and the Subversion of Identity*, New York: Routledge.

Byne, W., Tobet, S. and Mattiace, Linda, A. *et al.* (2001) 'The interstitial nuclei of the human anterior hypothalamus: an investigation of variation with sex, sexual orientation and HIV status', *Hormones and Behavior*, **40**: 86–92.

Cheah, P. (1996) 'Mattering', *Diacritics*, **26**, 1: 108–39.

Davis, B.E., Moon, R.Y., Sachs, H.C. and Ottolini, M.C. (1998) 'Effects of sleep position on infant motor development', *Pediatrics*, **102**, 5: 1135–40.

Fausto-Sterling, A. (1992) *Myths of Gender: Biological Theories about Women and Men*, New York: Basic Books.

Fausto-Sterling, A. (2000) *Sexing the Body: Gender Politics and the Construction of Sexuality*, New York: Basic Books.

Kraus, C. (2000) 'Naked sex in exile: on the paradox of the "sex question" in feminism and science', *National Women's Studies Association Journal*, **12**, 3: 151–77.

Le Grand, R., Mondloch, C.J., Maurer, D. and Brent, H.P. (2001) 'Early visual experience and face processing', *Nature*, **410**: 890.

LeVay, S. (1991) 'A difference in hypothalamic structure between heterosexual and homosexual men', *Science*, **253**: 1034–7.

Nader, K., Schafe, G.E. and Le Doux, J. E. (2000). 'Fear memories require protein synthesis in the amygdala for reconsolidation after retrieval', *Nature*, **406**: 722–6.

Oyama, S. (2000) *Evolution's Eye: A System's View of the Biology–Culture Divide*, Durham: Duke University Press.

Ruble, D. and Martin, C.L. (1998) 'Gender development', in N. Eisenberg (ed.) *Social, Emotional and Personality Development*, New York: Wiley, pp. 933–1016.

Russett, C.E. (1989) *Sexual Science: The Victorian Construction of Womanhood*, Cambridge: Harvard University Press.

Thelen, E. and Smith, L.B. (1994) *A Dynamic Systems Approach to the Development of Cognition and Action*, Cambridge: MIT Press.

Udry, J.R. (2000) 'Biological limits of gender construction', *American Sociological Review*, **65**, 3: 443–57.

Wahlsten, D. (1990) 'Insensitivity of the analysis of variance to heredity–environment interaction', *Behavior and Brain Sciences*, **13**: 109–61.

Wizemann, T.M. and Pardue, M.-L. (eds) (2001) *Exploring the Biological Contributions to Human Health: Does Sex Matter?* Washington, DC: National Academy Press.

10 Childhood bodies

Constructionism and beyond

Simon J. Williams and Gillian A. Bendelow

Introduction

One area where relations between the biological and social are sure to get the proper airing they deserve, you might think, is in relation to that crucial first phase of our lives called 'growing up' or 'childhood' as it has now come to be known. Reductionist pitfalls and dualist legacies, nonetheless, are as apparent here as any other domain; more so perhaps given the dominant conceptualization of children as 'incomplete' beings in the process of becoming 'complete' adults. The sociology of childhood, in this respect, has made important strides forward in recent years, challenging many of these former assumptions along the way. Problems remain however, not least through the dominance of social constructionism within and beyond the sociology of childhood; itself yet another form of reductionist thinking when expressed in 'strong' terms, this time albeit draped in sociological rather than biological garb.

Our aim in this chapter therefore is simple, namely to chart some of these debates, as played out within the sociology of childhood, with particular reference to those (recent) attempts to overcome any such divisions and reductionist pitfalls, thereby bringing the biological and the social together in profitable (new) ways. The first section, fittingly enough, provides some critical comments on the social construction of childhood assessing both its pros and cons in relation to other so-called 'presociological' viewpoints. This in turn paves the way, in the remainder of the chapter, for a consideration of various other sociological positions regarding children and childhood bodies, which, successfully or otherwise, bring the biological and the social into a (somewhat) closer alignment, with particular reference to issues of embodiment and emotion. The chapter, in this respect, provides yet another timely and topical reminder of the need to bring the biological back in, in childhood as elsewhere, problematizing a series of former divisions and dichotomous forms of thinking along the way. What then of these social constructionist approaches to childhood? How far do they take us and where do we go from there? It is to these very questions that we now turn, as a clue to the themes that follow.

Social constructionism 'versus' . . . ?

To fully appreciate the salience and significance of social constructionist approaches to children and childhood, we need to take a step back, albeit briefly, to what some have dubbed 'presociological' views of the child (James *et al.* 1998). These, in James and colleagues' elegant terms, comprise a variety of viewpoints, from the so-called 'evil child' (the philosophical antecedents of which can be traced back to Hobbes), through Rousseau's 'innocent' child, Locke's 'immanent' child, to Freud's 'unconscious' child. Perhaps most relevant for our purposes however, is the notion of the 'naturally developing child', which as James *et al.* put it (uncharitably perhaps), involves an 'unholy alliance' between the human sciences and human nature in the guise of 'developmental psychology': a discipline which has effectively 'colonized' childhood in a 'pact' with medicine, education and government agencies alike. Developmental psychology in this respect, they note, capitalises on two everyday assumptions:

> First, that children are natural rather than social phenomena; and secondly, that part of this naturalness extends to the inevitable process of their maturation. The belief in children's naturalness derives from the universal experience of being a child and the persistence and commonplace experience of having and relating to children; the belief in the inevitability and even 'good' of their maturation emanates from a combination of post-Darwinian developmental cultural aspirations and, conflated with these, the post-Enlightenment confusion of growth with progress.
>
> (James *et al.* 1998: 17)

A key figure here, of course, is the Swiss biologist and psychologist Piaget (1955), whose 'cognitive-developmental theory' or 'genetic epistemology' of growing up has produced, in James and colleagues' view, the 'most absolute, if materially reductive image of childhood that we are likely to encounter' (1998: 18). At stake here, for Piaget, is the identification of four key developmental stages, and the processes by which children progress through them. First the sensorimotor stage (birth–2 years old) where intelligence takes the form of motor actions; second, the preoperational (intuitive) stage (ages 2–7); third, concrete (logical) operations (ages 7–11); and finally, formal (abstract) operations (11–15) conceived as the point at which the child's cognitive structures or 'mental maps' are like those of an adult, including conceptual reasoning. 'After having overcome his [sic] egocentricism', as Piaget puts it, the child receives 'the instruments necessary to extend the rational construction prepared during the first two years of life and to expand it into a system of logical relationships and adequate representations' (Piaget 1955: 386). A journey, in short, into an ordered, structured and controlled universe which is 'at once substantial and spatial, causal and temporal' (Piaget 1955: xiii). A number of criticisms can be made of this 'orthodox' viewpoint, not least concerning the (universalizing) assumptions underpinning this standardized, staged approach to human maturation with its clearly demarcated developmental pathways.[1] Parallel sociological criticisms, mutatis mutandis, may be made of Parsonian-based notions of childhood socialisation (Lee 2001: 42).

It is precisely at this point that various other sociological approaches and viewpoints arise, themselves something of a corrective, if not an outright challenge, to any such 'presociological' notions of the child. These contrasts, to be sure, should not be overdrawn. Traces or echoes of 'presociological' viewpoints, for example, remain in some latter day strands of sociological scholarship, wittingly or otherwise. Social constructionists, nevertheless, have done most perhaps to distance themselves from these former ('naturalized' or 'naturalizing') assumptions, crediting the social side of the balance sheet in a more or less thoroughgoing fashion, so to speak. It is not simply a question here, however, of stressing the shifting historical conceptions, if not the 'invention', of childhood in the dim and distant past – as witnessed for example in Aries' (1962) classic study *Centuries of Childhood* – but of the contingent constructions and the variable discursive renderings of children and childhood in the here and now, including those of children themselves (see, for example, James and Prout 1990).

Social constructionist approaches to children and childhood then, despite their differences (including 'strong' and 'weak' variants), effectively pull the rug from under the feet of those who appeal, in unthinking or unproblematic (pre- or non-sociological) terms, to universalizing notions, and/or naturalized assumptions about children and childhood, providing a powerful reminder of the contingent basis upon which any such orthodoxy-cum-ossified ways of thinking rest. It is, as such, well placed to 'prise the child free of biological determinism and thus to claim the phenomenon, epistemologically, in the realm of the social' (James *et al.* 1998: 28). Herein lies the political promise and potential of social constructionism for the sociology of childhood.

This, however, is both its strength and weakness rolled into one. What we have here, in effect, particularly in strong variants of the social constructionist message – not least the relativizing twists and turns of Foucauldian-inspired scholarship (see for example Armstrong 1983) – is a view which flips from one extreme to the other, trading biological reductionism for social reductionism; a largely reductionist version of the social, qua language and discourse, at that. The material body, let alone the biological body, largely drops out of the picture here, save for the diverse way in which these very matters are discursively constructed, including the disciplines (such as paediatrics, developmental psychology, etc.) to which they give rise. This is a viewpoint then, in keeping with its presociological counterparts, which takes us so far, but not perhaps quite far enough when it comes to childhood bodies, or the (biological) matter of childhood bodies to be more precise. Where then do we go from here?

Symbol emancipation and the 'civilized' body: bringing biology back in (or still leaving it out)?

Elias's work, for present purposes at least, provides a starting point here en route to a more satisfactory resolution to biology–society relations, in childhood as elsewhere. Not only do Elias's (1978/1939) insights into the 'civilizing process' highlight the *socialization, rationalization* and *individualization* of bodies (Shilling 1993), they also, in doing so, bring biological and social factors together in a more or less promising fashion. We see this most clearly, for example, in Elias' work on symbol emancipation (Elias 1991a) and related essays on human emotion (Elias 1991b). Despite the inescapable fact that human bodies are biological, Elias argues, evolution has nonetheless equipped them with higher-order capacities such as speech and thought which, in contrast to all other species and earlier times, release them for the necessity of further biological change. More specifically, Elias stresses, it is the biological capacity of human beings for *learning* which has emancipated them from dependence upon further biological change: something he refers to as symbol emancipation (1991a). The extraordinary capacity of human beings for learning, their unique capabilities for synthesis and their ability to transmit accumulated stock of knowledge from generation to generation via symbols, it is claimed, makes possible rapid social differentiation and adaptation to new circumstances *independently of further biological change.*

Not only have these evolutionary processes of symbol emancipation resulted in the dominance of human beings over all other species, from this Eliasian perspective, they have also facilitated the historical development of 'civilized bodies' (Elias 1978/1939): a process, as noted above, in which individuals, both historically and in the course of their own lifetimes, increasingly *learn* to control the natural rhythms and functions of bodies in various 'mannered' ways, trading external *constraint* for internal *restraint* (albeit, echoing Freud, at a price). This, in turn, throws issues of human emotion into critical relief. No human emotion, Elias (1991b) argues, is ever entirely an unlearned genetically fixed reaction pattern. Rather like language itself, human emotion results form a merger of learned and unlearned processes. Whilst a baby's smile, for instance, is more or less wholly innate, as human beings grow and develop, any such innateness is greatly weakened, becoming instead ever more *plastic, mouldable* or *malleable* in relation to antecedent as well as immediate experience. Whilst human beings therefore share certain reaction patterns such as the fight and flight response with other nonhuman species, there are also marked differences, Elias stresses, in that humans are capable of much greater *diversification* in accordance with different situations and antecedent experiences.

Clearly then, from this Eliasian viewpoint, the amount the child has to learn in terms of behavioural codes and self control – themselves a product of our 'open' or 'unfinished' bodies, including the biological capacity to learn these very self controls – has greatly increased across the long historical curve of the civilizing process. As a consequence, Elias argues, an increasing 'psychological distance' has occurred between adults and children across the span of the civilizing process. The changes taking place in codes of behaviour and conduct over many centuries, in other words, closely mirror those taking place in the lifetime of each and every one of us in the process of 'growing up', from toilet habits to table manners. This very principle indeed, constitutes what Elias terms the *sociogenetic* ground rule: namely, to repeat, that 'the individual, in his [*sic*] short history, passes once more through some of the processes that his society has traversed in its long history' (1978/1939: xii).

As with social constructionism, however, Elias's perspective is found wanting on a number of accounts, not least when it comes to children and childhood. On the one hand, it clearly does serve to bring the biological back in, problematically or otherwise, thereby representing something of an advance on strong versions of constructionist thinking. On the other hand, however, it suffers from a number of shortcomings. First and foremost, individuals in general and children in particular are portrayed as largely passive recipients of these civilizing processes: an approach, echoing other viewpoints, both inside and outside the academy, in which children are positioned as 'socialization' projects or sponges for knowledge. We also see this, for example, in the work of other writers such as Bourdieu on the transmission of (cultural) capital through the education system, and the unthinking dispositions of the habitus. Second, and related, this is a viewpoint in which children are in large part seen to be 'in transit' elsewhere, so to speak, with considerable distance to make up by current standards of adulthood and 'civilized' behaviour. There is little, or at best equivocal, recognition here, as Prout rightly comments in relation to these first two points, of the:

> possibility that children may actively appropriate and transform as well as absorb. Nor is there a sense that childhood and growing up are full of reversals, transformations and inversions rather than being a progression to an ever closer copy of adulthood. In short what is missing is a sense of childhood as a being as well as a becoming: childhood as staged and children as active, creative performers.
>
> (2000a: 116)

These problems in turn are compounded through Elias' treatment of the biological. Not only do biological factors largely drop out of the equation, post-symbol emancipation (Shilling 1993), but he also operates, as we have seen, with some questionable if not controversial distinctions between learning humans and instinctual animals (see, for example, chapters by Birke and Benton, this volume, for a corrective to such viewpoints). Add to this a general neglect or downplaying of lived, embodied experience, and one is forced to conclude that Elias's treatment of these issues, whilst at first glance holding much promise, takes us one step forward and one or more steps backwards in our quest to bring the biological back in, in childhood and beyond. The notion of the biologically and socially 'unfinished' body, nonetheless, as various commentators suggest (Prout 2000a), may be profitably built upon here, providing an important springboard to a more satisfactory resolution of these issues (see also Turner, this volume).

Embodied matters and 'hybrid' worlds: being, becoming and beyond . . .

From here it is but a short step to other more fully embodied approaches and agendas concerning children and childhood; approaches which do not so much reject these former viewpoints, particularly the notion of the 'unfinished' body, as incorporate them more thoroughly through lived themes and emotion laden issues which bring mind and body together, transcending former dualisms in the process. An existential commitment to the lived body, as Leder comments, does not so much replace the biological account, as place it in a broader perspective which 'undermines facile claims of priority' (1998: 125). It also, of course, serves to put the lived body, good and proper, back into debates on children and childhood, thereby providing an important corporeal corrective to those more 'floating' or disembodied accounts, of the social constructionist kind, considered above: approaches which, in fleeing from the biological, have tended to throw the baby out with the bathwater, if you will forgive the expression.

Mayall (1996, 1998, 2002), for instance, has been a key figure here in advancing just such a viewpoint. Adults, she notes, building critically on the work of Elias and others, *civilize* children into the social and moral order. They also *regulate* children's bodies and minds with respect to specific agendas (such as the school curriculum), and they propose 'certain bodily shapes and activities to fit socially sanctioned shapes and skills' (1998: 138). These three kinds of activities on the body (i.e. civilizing, regulating and constructing), she ventures, 'constitute interlinked themes in adult behaviour and children's experience' (1998: 138). Children, from this perspective, may well be embodied actors, negotiators and constructors of their world – a point which Mayall amongst others is at pains to stress, given previous passive viewpoints and the weight of (Parsonian) socialization theory – but these very processes and agendas are located in the context of adult structures of thought and institutionalised practices, which themselves operate powerfully on children.

Attention to issues of emotion, time and health across the public/private divide, Mayall shows, throw many of these issues into critical relief. Within the health-care arena of the home, for example, mothers' understanding of the 'interlinkages between the emotional, cognitive and the bodily', contrasts with 'school adults' separation out of these components of identity, with emphasis on the cognitive' (1998: 150). Children, therefore, are likely to feel 'more comfortable' in their bodies at home than at school. At home, moreover, children are more likely, protestations of tired parents notwithstanding, to find their bodily achievements valued, and to 'participate through embodied emotion work in constructing the social order of the home' (1998: 150). This, of course, includes embodied health-care work (Mayall 1996). School, in contrast, encourages 'high valuation of bodily skills at specified time and in relation to specified places, but generally asks children to subordinate minds to bodies' (1998: 150). Health, moreover, is not necessarily the priority it should be within such environments – see, for example, Mayall *et al.* (1996).

Civilizing children therefore from this perspective, to repeat, is the central remit of the home (encouraging and enabling children, that is to say, to manage their bodies in a fashion acceptable to participation in the social order, in the home and beyond). Regulating bodies, in contrast, falls more squarely within the domain or remit of the school, supported through various pedagogical rationales, and legitimated as a service to society in general. Civilizing, Mayall stresses, is a 'joint' enterprise, whilst regulation is a 'top-down' enterprise. Cross-cutting these themes, however, is a third countervailing or counterbalancing one pertaining to the construction of children's own bodies and the embodied identities, which in turn takes place both in child–adult negotiations, and child-to-child participation and support in various groups. The tensions between children's time and adult time is also important to stress here; issues which span both present and future-time oriented horizons and their differential expression in different social and institutional contexts. Children, in short, as this suggests:

> are positioned at the intersections of important social values: that people should take control over their emotions, and order their bodies to suit social values, but that ensuring children carry out these remits is a central adult responsibility, in two main arenas, the home and the school. For the quality of children's emotional contentment in embodied living, much depends on how far adults accept the child's personhood and contributions to the structuring of the social order.
>
> (Mayall 1998: 152)

Other recent work on the body, childhood and society, both consolidates and extends these themes in promising new directions. Prout (2000a,b), for example, raises the intriguing question as to what light the sociology of translation might shed on these debates, not least in giving the biological its due. The precise details of this perspective, indebted as it is to the likes of Latour (1993) and Actor Network Theory (ANT), need not concern us here (see Scott, for example, this volume). Suffice it to say that in stressing the heterogeneous or hybrid nature of the world, life can be understood as inescapably 'impure' (to believe otherwise is the erroneous mark of modern thinking for Latour in its search for 'purity'). Children in this respect, returning yet again to the promising notion of the 'unfinished body' raised earlier, are themselves hybrids of nature and culture, which in turn gives the lie to reductionisms of the purely biological or the purely discursive kind. It is not, moreover, from this translation viewpoint, a case of human society being constructed solely or simply through human meaning and action. The material instead is related to other elements that together, through shifting hybrid networks, go to make up society. The sociology of translation remains constructivist, in this respect, but in a radically general-ized way 'which restates a materialist sociology' (Prout 2000b: 14). This is an approach then, as Prout argues, which would place:

> childhoods and bodies in relation to not only symbolic but also material culture. What produces them is not simply biological events, not only the phenomenology of bodily experience, and not merely struc-tures of symbolic and discursive meaning – although all of these are important – but also patterns of material organization and their modes of ordering. Examining childhood bodies in this way becomes a matter of tracing through the means, the varied array of materials and prac-tices involved in their construction and maintenance – and in some circumstances their unravelling and disintegration.
>
> (2000b: 15)

Illustrating the merits of such a perspective is beyond the scope of this particular chapter (see the Prout (2000c) volume, for instance, and particu-larly Place's (2000) chapter on childhood bodies and hybrid relations in an intensive care unit (ITU)). There are nonetheless, it should be noted, certain problems here which Prout effectively glosses (or doesn't perhaps see as a problem), not least regarding the 'general symmetry' accorded many different types of 'actors' with ANT, not all of them human, organic or technological.

Perhaps the final word on these hybrid relations if not destabilizing themes, however, goes to Lee (2001), whose multiple assemblages or borrowings from Latour, Derrida, Deleuze and Guattari, and others, amount to noth-ing short of multiple *becomings*. It is not a question here, he argues, picking up on themes already touched on above, of adults seen as complete, stable and self-controlled, and children seen as incomplete, changeable and in need to control. Growing up, in an age of uncertainty, is no longer about personal completion and stability. There are no 'human beings', Lee boldly proclaims, but potentially unlimited ways of 'becoming human' (2001: 2). Social studies of childhood, we are told, should be sensitive to ambiguity and less reliant on problematic notions of human 'being'. In multiplying human becomings therefore, single human beings are allowed to 'drop from our thoughts': the 'erosion of standard adulthood', in effect, and the 'pro-liferation of childhood ambiguities' (2001: 119). This in turn paves the way for the notion of an 'immature' sociology. What this amounts to, for Lee, is not so much a call for sociologists of childhood to try and see the world through children's eyes, as the need for imagination, inspiration and creative flair in understanding and intervening in a world, which is in fact 'unfinished'. It is also, he insists, a plea not to model this fledgling field of social inquiry on the problem space defined by 'mature'-cum-'mainstream' sociology (2001: 3).

Enough has been said here, we hope, to chart the possibilities and potential of bringing the biological body back in to the sociology of childhood, with or without the likes of Latour, let alone Deleuze and Guattari, on board. It is to our own small contribution to this on-going (or unravelling?) debate, however, that we now turn in the penultimate section of this chapter, through some further realist musings on children and childhood bodies.

Realist musings: an emerging viewpoint or developing perspective?

If much of the foregoing debate has centred on the need to go beyond former reductionist pitfalls, in childhood as elsewhere, and *if* the search is still (pretty much) on for alternative viable ways of doing so, then recourse to an explicitly stated realist perspective on these matters, we venture, may well be timely. The word explicit is important to stress here, given that implicit realist themes underpin many of these debates already, acknowledged or not. Perhaps the most explicit formulation of these issues to date however, in modern day social theory at least, comes in the guise of critical realism (CR). A number of (CR) principles may be advanced in this respect, as a contribution to these debates (for fuller more detailed accounts see, for example, Archer *et al.* 1998, plus Scambler and Scambler, and Benton this volume).

First and foremost, critical realists insist, ontological and epistemological issues cannot and should not be conflated. What we know and how we know the world (epistemology), that is to say, is a very different matter from what there is to know (ontology). To collapse the two, as social constructionists are prone to do, is therefore to commit the 'epistemic fallacy'. To reduce the world to language or discourse, in similar fashion, is to commit the 'linguist fallacy'. Second, following directly on from this first point, a CR stance signs up to a stratified ontology of the world, including nature–society relations. It does so, however, through a commitment to principles of *irreducibility* and *emergence*. This in turn, echoing the aims of this volume as a whole, enables us to bring the biological back in to sociological discussion and debate, without recourse to the reductionist baggage of old and the either/or logic it implies. A both/and logic is instead substituted here, articulated in and through these very principles of irreducibility and emergence. Third, the on-going debate about the relationship between structure and agency is resolved through non-conflationary principles which involve their *mutual interplay across time*: something which can result both in *stable reproduction* or *change* through the emergence of new properties and powers. Finally, the fact that not all is revealed to consciousness because it is shaped outside our conscious awareness – not least the deep underlying structures and mind-independent generative mechanism of the natural and social world which may or may not be realised, let alone observed – makes for the 'critical' or emancipatory promise of critical realism, including the potential to challenge oppressive social practices and prevailing ideologies. In doing so, moreover, CR does not so much abandon as rethink the very notion of causation, including the possibility of reasons themselves as causes.

This, to be sure, is to grossly simplify (if not reduce) a complex set of arguments. When applied to children and childhood bodies, nonetheless, the relevance of CR becomes more or less apparent. Not only does this allow for a view of children's bodies and worlds as real, emergent, yet irreducible to any one domain or discourse, (biological or social) – itself providing a means to critically (re)examine 'developmental' processes in an 'open', non-reductionist fashion (see also Fausto-Sterling, this volume) – it enables us to explore the interplay of structure and agency in children's own embodied lives, both at home and at school, whilst simultaneously emphasising the potential for critical transformation and change, particularly in the context of oppressive social practices and injustices of various kinds which limit or deny human flourishing, health and well-being. CR, moreover, as we have seen, can readily embrace a weak form of (non-conflationary) constructionism; itself of no small importance for sociologists of childhood. This, together with CR's compatibility with a wide range of research methods, including its commitment to detailed ethnographies, means that what is on offer here is not so much an alternative viewpoint, as a more comprehensive account of the world and our place within it, in childhood as elsewhere: one which more or less readily or happily accommodates certain strands of thinking within the sociology of childhood to date, clearing up conflationary and reductionist thinking en route. On this, of course, we leave readers to judge . . .

Conclusions

What conclusions, then remain to be drawn here from the foregoing discussion and debate? First and perhaps most obviously, the sociology of childhood, as we have seen, throws the relationship between body and society into critical relief, providing in effect a litmus paper test of these broader debates. Second, in doing so, it too highlights the need to bring the biological body back in to our theorizing of these and related matters. It is not, to repeat, a question here of either/or debates, but of both/and ways of theorizing these relations, in childhood as elsewhere. This in turn, moreover, enables us to rethink a series of other problematic former divisions of the reason/emotion, mature/immature, human/animal, being/becoming kind.

Realism, we venture, in keeping with other recent perspectives considered above, provides one more or less promising way forward here in such an enterprise. It may indeed provide an important 'under-labouring' philosophy in any such undertaking: all the more so, in fact, given implicit realist themes pulsing through many of these debates already.

Perhaps the other key issue to stress here, another implicit if not explicit theme in much of the foregoing discussion in fact, concerns the role of children not simply as embodied agents and active constructors and nego-tiators of their world, but as embodied *health-care* agents within it. To stress this point, is of course to echo broader debates that seek to render the invisible visible, the private public, and so on, particularly amongst those who hitherto have enjoyed somewhat 'marginalized' status within the his-tory of western culture and society. Children to put it differently, echoing Mayall and others, are no mere socialization projects, or 'faulty'-cum-'incomplete' versions of adults, but active contributors to the social order with an intentionality of their own. Adult work by others on children's bodies, in this respect, is only part of the story, the other part of which includes their own embodied labour across the public/private divide, in sickness and in health.

Seen in this light then, a commitment to children and childhood helps us unpack or challenge a series of dualist legacies and (adult-centric) assump-tions, not least biology/society relations, which have not, it seems, served us terribly well to date. From here it is but a short step to a related series of ethical agendas, if not an explicitly rethought, restyled or refashioned *embodied ethics*. That, alas, will have to wait until Part V of this volume . . .

Note

1 It remains a moot point, of course, as to whether or not Piaget's work, sociolo-gically speaking, is beyond rescue, recovery or rehabilitation. It is nonetheless, we venture, a point or project worth pondering, particularly if/when sociological critiques become caricatures.

References

Archer, M., Bhaskar, R., Collier, A., Lawson, T. and Norrie, A. (eds) (1998) *Critical Realism: Essential Readings*, London: Routledge.
Aries, P. (1962) *Centuries of Childhood*, London: Jonathan Cape.
Armstrong, D. (1983) *Political Anatomy of the Body*, Cambridge: Cambridge University Press.
Elias, N. (1978/1939) *The Civilizing Process; Vol I: The History of Manners*, Oxford: Blackwell.
Elias, N. (1991a) *The Symbol Theory*, London: Sage.
Elias, N. (1991b) 'On human beings and their emotions: a process sociological essay', in M. Featherstone, M. Hepworth and B.S. Turner (eds) *The Body: Social Process, Cultural Theory*, London: Sage.

James, A. and Prout, A. (eds) (1990) *Constructing and Reconstructing Childhood*, Basingstoke: Falmer Press.

James, A., Jenks, C. and Prout, A. (1998) *Theorizing Childhood*, Cambridge: Polity.

Latour, B. (1993) *We Have Never Been Modern*, Hemel Hempstead: Harvester Wheatsheaf.

Leder, D. (1998) 'A tale of two bodies: the Cartesian corpse and the lived body', in D. Welton (ed.) *The Body and Flesh: A Philosophical Reader*, Oxford: Blackwell.

Lee, N. (2001) *Childhood and Society*, Buckingham: Open University Press.

Mayall, B. (1996) *Children, Health and the Social Order*, Buckingham: Open University Press.

Mayall, B. (1998) 'Children, emotions and daily life at home and at school', in G. Bendelow and S.J. Williams (eds) *Emotions in Social Life*, London: Routledge.

Mayall, B. (2002) *Towards a Sociology For Childhood*, Buckingham: Open Univeristy Press.

Mayall, B., Bendelow, G., Barkers, S., Storey, P. and Veltman, M. (1996) *Children's Health in Primary Schools*, London: Falmer Press.

Piaget, J. (1955) *The Child's Construction of Reality*. London: Routledge & Kegan Paul.

Place, B. (2000) 'Constructing the bodies of ill children in the intensive care unit', in A. Prout (ed.) *The Body, Childhood and Society*, Basingstoke: Macmillan.

Prout, A. (2000a) 'Childhood bodies', in S.J. Williams, J. Gabe and M. Calnan (eds) *Health, Medicine and Society*, London: Routledge.

Prout, A. (2000b) 'Childhood bodies: construction, agency and hybridity', in A. Prout (ed.) *The Body, Childhood and Society*, Basingstoke: Macmillan.

Prout, A. (ed.) (2000c) *The Body, Childhood and Society*, Basingstoke: Macmillan.

Shilling, C. (1993) *The Body and Social Theory*, London: Sage.

11 Hormonal bodies, civilized bodies

Incorporating the biological into the sociology of health

Lee F. Monaghan

Introduction

Hormonal narratives, similar to the genetic narratives commented upon by Birke (this volume), occupy a powerful position within our medicalised and stratified society. In the early 1990s, for example, lay, media and scientific discourses focused upon the supposed mood and behavioural effects of synthetic 'male' hormones or anabolic-androgenic steroids. While testosterone and other steroids are taken illicitly by many gym members in order to improve their physiques, it has also been claimed these drugs cause uncontrollable aggressive violence or 'Roid-Rage. This 'naturalistic' (Shilling 1993) construction of the impulsive hormonal body – as applied to a masculinist and traditionally working-class pursuit – simultaneously buttresses patriarchal notions of male dominance and female passivity while countering bourgeois notions of the consciously restrained 'civilized body' (Elias 2000/1939).

This chapter is based upon a qualitative study of bodybuilding, drugs and risk (Monaghan 2001a). Specifically, it presents an ethnoscientific reformulation of the supposed bodybuilding, steroids and violence connection. Drawing from members' accounts presented verbatim elsewhere (see Monaghan 2001a: 156–80), this chapter outlines some of the major themes and critical understandings to emerge during ethnographic research in South Wales between 1994 and 1996. Qualitative data generated among members of bodybuilding subculture challenge yet incorporate biological arguments concerning steroid mood and behavioural effects. Correspondingly, their 'lay' understandings, explored in this chapter using an embodied, non-dualist social paradigm (Williams and Bendelow 1998), provide useful materials for debating biology. Rather than 'writing out' the hormonal body, such ethnographic analysis underscores the social significance of biology and bodily health once they are conceptualised in non-reductionist terms.

Before proceeding, a brief note is required on the biological body in social theory. It should be recognized that while the (biological) body has had something of an 'absent presence' in mainstream social theory (Shilling

1993), important work is identifiable. Hence, as well as feminist concerns about the ways in which gender assumptions are read onto nature, the body and its interior (Connell 1995; also, see Birke and Fausto-Sterling in this volume), this chapter is consonant with various social scientific writings on bodily matters. For example, Elias (2000/1939) usefully explores the indeterminacy of biology in his writings on civility. Discussing the interlocking of biological and social factors during historical civilizing processes, Elias usefully draws attention to the ways in which human bodies are unfinished entities. Here people's personalities, drive economies and actual behaviour are related to changing social figurations and social learning processes which effectively free human beings from the determinacy of biology. Especially significant here is the Eliasian notion of the 'civilized body' or people's increasing ability to learn to control their emotions. However, as stated by Williams and Bendelow (1998), this 'over socialized' conception of the civilized body must be counterbalanced with Goffman's dramaturgical approach. In back-stage regions, for example, embodied social actors may engage in various uncivilized behaviours, selectively applying codes of civility according to their social audiences (Williams and Bendelow 1998: 43). Drawing from the corporeal insights of this and other work (e.g. Leder 1990), steroid assisted bodybuilding may be regarded as an exemplar of the indeterminacy of the 'naturalistic' or hormonal body (see also Griffiths and Green, this volume) and the 'socially pliable nature of human biology' (Williams and Bendelow 1998: 211). It also highlights the ways in which vibrant yet reflexive flesh and blood bodies are implicated in the successful presentation of self in a healthist, medicalized culture.

The following discussion is structured into three main sections. Brief reference is first made to the supposed steroid-violence association as described within the medical and behavioural science literature. While such writings are dominated by reductionist research that reiterates 'essentialist' definitions of masculinity (Connell 1995), some strands are cognisant of social factors. Attentive to the fact that material bodies are lived and socially embedded, the second section uses ethnography to outline bodybuilders' ethnoscientific reformulation of various versions of the 'Roid-Rage hypothesis. Critical of conventional understandings that demonized bodybuilders, many of my contacts effectively synthesized biological and social explanations when discussing possible steroid–violence associations. Members of this drug subculture, in constructing 'appropriate' bodies and identities in a larger society that sanctifies health, incorporated biology into their social understandings in a manner that both questioned and complemented the medical and behavioural science literature. Finally, the conclusion offers a summary and closing statement on scientific efforts to build 'better' bodies of knowledge; that is, less reductionist and democratic knowledge which is attentive to lived biological bodies, sociocultural meanings and understandings.

The dangerous hormonal body: scientific literature on steroids and aggressive violence

For many bodybuilders, supraphysiologic doses of synthetic 'male' sex hormones (such as testosterone and other anabolic-androgenic steroids) are used over prolonged periods without medical supervision in order to enhance bodily aesthetics. Normalized among dedicated or 'hard core' bodybuilders, illicit steroid use has been condemned by the media on the grounds that it causes uncontrollable outbursts of aggression and violence. Termed 'Roid-Rage, scientific reports support sensationalist media claims. Focusing upon the dangerous hormonal body – the aggressively masculine or testosterone-enhanced muscular body – psy-scientists have expressed concern for public safety and the safety of female partners of male steroid users (Choi and Pope 1994). Yet, despite such concerns, steroids are taken illicitly by many gym members given the representational significance and embodied pleasures of health, youth and vibrant physicality in postmodern or consumer culture (Monaghan 2001b).

In their review of the scientific literature, Riem and Hursey (1995: 236) write: 'most research assessing the affective and behavioural changes athletes encounter has taken the 'roid-rage perspective, looking for negative outcomes accompanying AAS [anabolic-androgenic steroids]'. Within this biomedical literature, the activational version of the 'Roid-Rage hypothesis is most common. According to this variant of the theory, aggression and violence are directly attributed to the immediate or slightly delayed effects of physiological processes involving neurochemical systems (Choi *et al.* 1989). Negative biological changes are claimed to be reversible upon drug cessation, though a sudden reduction in sex hormones may be associated with depression. Organizational variants of the 'Roid-Rage hypothesis claim that steroids cause long-lasting changes in brain morphology, dysfunctional reasoning and negative behaviours which are independent of subsequent hormone activity (Riem and Hursey 1995: 240). Such theories, besides conflating mood and behaviour, are underpinned by a malevolence assumption that skews perception of the body towards the negative (*cf.* Leder 1990: 153). As stated by Riem and Hursey: 'this negative pharmacological conceptualisation has biased the current literature by implicitly excluding many mediators and outcomes from consideration' (1995: 236).

Nonetheless, biomedical discourses on the dysfunctional or dys-appearing body (Leder 1990) do not constitute a master narrative; there are 'contradictory strands and fragmentary positions' (Birke 1999: 176). Some contributors to the steroids–violence literature are sceptical, if not highly critical, of extant knowledge claims. Riem and Hursey (1995: 235–6) cite several studies that question the prevalence of negative steroid effects and consider the ways such effects may be mediated by the users' expectations, changing physique and personality traits. Bjorkqvist *et al.* (1994), for example, discuss possible steroid expectancy effects. After administering steroids and a placebo to participants during a double-blind trial, these researchers empirically and conceptually challenge the popular 'Roid-Rage hypothesis. In accord with their own negative evidence (subjects receiving a placebo as opposed to steroids became more aggressive) they present a gendered argument. They suggest the immense interest in the testosterone-aggression link (including the disproportionate media coverage of the 'Roid-Rage phenomenon) reflects prevalent social attitudes, 'the cherished myth of the aggressive male, stuffed with androgens, and the submissive female' (1994: 25). They then offer some cautionary words: 'to claim . . . aggression is caused by steroids, as in the news media, is misleading and dangerous for several reasons' (Bjorkqvist *et al.* 1994: 25). Three reasons are given; namely, there is still no scientific evidence for such a relationship; even if there was a correlation this would not prove a cause–effect relationship; and finally, such a claim is dangerous because: 'Dissemination of the myth of the steroid–aggressiveness connection may lead to anticipation (a placebo effect) of aggressiveness among steroid abusers and, in turn, to actual acts of violence. It may, in fact, work as an excuse for aggression (Bjorkqvist *et al.* 1994: 25).'

As will emerge when outlining bodybuilders' subjugated subcultural knowledge, conventional understandings concerning steroid mood and behavioural effects were recognised, modified and resisted in complex and subtle ways. Undoubtedly, some concession was given to popular biomedical understandings and essentialist gender constructs; namely, aggression is a masculine trait attributable to the 'male' hormone testosterone. However, and overwhelmingly (steroid-using) bodybuilders contacted during this research rejected steroids as an exculpatory discourse for uncontrollable aggressive violence. Such talk, concordant with the rationalised and consciously restrained 'civilized body' (Elias 2000/1939), enabled responsible narrators to challenge common scientific truth claims that constructed them as socially sick as opposed to healthy, responsible people. Aside from the implications of this for ongoing social practice, these biologically infused knowledges were social in construction and consequence and therefore of sociological significance.

Reformulating the 'Roid-Rage hypothesis: synthesizing biological and social explanations

Given the tenacity of biomedicine, patriarchal ideology that naturalizes male dominance and experiential knowledge of steroid effects, many bodybuilders contacted during this research 'recognised' the 'natural' effects of the 'male' hormone testosterone. They acknowledged that synthetic testosterone, besides facilitating strength and muscular growth, *may* increase aggressiveness and propensities to violence among some current and former steroid (ab)users. Concession was thus given to 'naturalistic' (Shilling 1993) representations of the gendered, hormonal body. However, in resisting overly reductionist accounts, various versions of the 'Roid-Rage hypothesis were modified. Illustrative of the micro-level impact of historical civilizing processes (Elias 2000/1939), or, rather, the public presentation of a socially fit and morally responsible self, many emphasized the importance of rational thought and self-control over the impulsive and potentially dangerous testosterone-enhanced body. Moreover, in providing a long series of qualifications, the supposed steroids-violence (as opposed to steroids-aggression) link was considered very tenuous. Biology was incorporated into bodybuilders' subcultural stock-of-knowledge which frames steroid-taking, but biology was deemed indeterminate in its effects.

Before outlining bodybuilders' ethnoscientific reformulation of the steroid–violence link, four caveats are required. First, although my bodybuilding contacts consistently rejected claims that steroids cause uncontrollable aggressive violence, in certain interactional contexts steroid users *may* attribute their conflict-engendered transgressions to the direct consequence of neurochemical actions. In the US criminal justice system, for example, the 'steroid defence' has successfully been used as a plea of mitigation. In the larger society, steroids, similar to alcohol, have become an acceptable excuse for untoward conduct. Second, in the absence of finely spun subcultural norms ordinarily surrounding steroid use, marginal members' (or other subculturally isolated users') knowledge of steroid effects will be derived from the larger society and the mass media. This, in turn, may increase the likelihood of a self-fulfilling prophecy where the belief, rather than steroids themselves, lead to negative feelings and behaviours. Third, while historical civilizing processes underscore the significance of increased bodily control, wilful physical violence (independent of steroid use) is a form of masculine bodily deployment which may be licensed or legitimated at particular times and in particular spaces (Morgan 1993: 77). Respondents constructing 'appropriate' identities during an ethnographic interview may disavow 'uncontrollable' violence but deliberately exercise force in situations where it is hidden, accepted and/or required. Finally, steroid users have a range of views on the alleged steroids–violence link, but the views of many experienced bodybuilders and steroid users interviewed for this study clustered in the way reported below.

Individuals affiliated to the bodybuilding subculture stressed a consistent theme; namely, steroids *per se* do not cause aggressive violence. In short, they opposed crude biological determinism, claiming that a myriad of factors impact upon mood and possible behaviour. Respondents normalizing steroid use voiced many different and overlapping arguments when challenging the much-publicized 'Roid-Rage phenomenon. However, five main arguments were emphasized; namely: (1) aggression and violence are not synonymous, (2) steroid use must be distinguished from steroid abuse, (3) some people are predisposed to violence, (4) changing the body may change the attitude thus rendering aggression and violence more likely and (5) steroids are heterogeneous and thus variable in their effects.

Concerning the first point: members' accounts, in contrast to many lay, media and scientific reports on 'Roid-Rage, differentiated aggression from violence. This distinction enabled steroid users to acknowledge that some steroids (see below) have the potential when present and physiologically active in the body to cause and/or exacerbate aggressive feelings. And, while these feelings are valued if confined to the gym and directed construct-ively towards lifting weights, they *may* also manifest themselves verbally or physically through non-injurious gestures. Synthetic 'male' sex hormones may therefore have immediate or slightly delayed negative biological and social effects but physically violent behaviour was not considered inevitable. Here steroid-related mood changes, which are reportedly reversible upon drug cessation, may be consciously recognized by current users (and possibly a third party such as a partner) and deliberately controlled. In accord with the civilized body (Elias 2000/1939), bodybuilders maintained that it is possible and desirable to regulate negative emotional impulses and take strategic steps to avoid possible conflict (e.g. walk out of the room when feeling angry). Analytically, it should also be recognized that by exerting or reportedly exerting control over the potentially dangerous hormonal body, these respondents were engaged in the social construction of masculinity. Thus, while for some men 'anger is an emotional verification that they are successfully conforming to the dominant masculine stereotype [and] women are especially likely to be victimized by men's anger and violence' (Messner and Sabo 1994: 72), it is also clear that masculine 'power may lie in the manifest control over the expression of anger in physical terms rather than in the straightforward deployment of physical aggression' (Morgan 1993: 76). Without doubt, responsible narrators subscribed to this latter construc-tion of masculinity during interviewing, thereby eschewing any simplistic suggestion that steroids cause them or their peers to become uncontrollably abusive or violent towards other people.

Many bodybuilding respondents, in conceding that steroids may have real mood and behavioural effects, also made great effort to distinguish steroid use from steroid abuse. They claimed that activational steroid changes, confined to a current course of drugs (typically lasting eight to twelve weeks in duration), are far more likely to occur if steroids are taken in excessive dosages. Problems, both mental and physical, were therefore associated with steroid *abuse* rather than the planned, carefully monitored and controlled *usage* betokening the 'sensible' drug-taking bodybuilder. Significantly, total dosage was considered more important than the dura-tion of a steroid course or the simultaneous use of many steroids, overriding any possible cumulative or interactive effects between types of steroid. How-ever, and as will be discussed shortly, the type of steroid was considered relevant when explicating the supposed steroids–violence link, but again negative effects were considered dose dependent rather than interactive. Furthermore, and in accord with bodybuilding ethnopharmacological and ethnophysiological frameworks, steroid effects were claimed to vary from one person to the next. Different genetic susceptibilities and the argument that everybody is different, rendered use and abuse relative not absolute concepts. Significantly, bodybuilders taking steroids overwhelmingly presented themselves as users not abusers. Abusers were always third parties, except when the currently responsible narrator admitted to past steroid abuse as a novice (Bloor *et al.* 1998).

Being predisposed to violence was also a common theme. Again, this argument was invoked by respondents affiliated to the bodybuilding subculture in order to negate claims that steroids are intrinsically dangerous to other people's physical health. The general consensus was that if one has a propensity toward violence, either apparent or potential, then it might be exacerbated during a course of steroids. Steroids (even if taken in 'excessive' dosages) will not turn a 'reasonable person' into a violent one, and bodybuilders contacted during this research presented themselves as reasonable people. Violence was largely claimed to be an attribute or inclination that is independent of steroid assisted bodybuilding, though negative behaviours may be marginally related to these hormones. Of crucial significance in such theorizing is the perceived temperament of the person before embarking upon steroids. Individuals who are violent on steroids allegedly have violent tendencies anyway. According to several respondents, an individual's pre-existing personality characteristics and propensities to violence are so important that even if steroids are abused, violence is unlikely among those who are normally mild mannered and civilized.

Fourth, increased muscularity (with or without steroids) typically enhances feelings of self-confidence and in some cases arrogance. Here respondents claimed that changing the physique, which can be quite rapid among novice steroid users, could result in an undesirable change in attitude. Changes in the strength and size of the body, in other words, may lead to longer-lasting changes in attitude rendering aggression and violence more attractive. Certainly, some respondents claimed that physically large bodybuilders do not have to 'prove' themselves through violence – see Morgan (1993: 76), who relates a similar point to the civilizing process, rationality, power and gender. Nonetheless, it was conceded that some steroid-using bodybuilders may embrace or savour the possibility of confrontation because of their muscular build. Riem and Hursey (1995: 249) offer a similar argument. They state that aggressive behaviour might increase among steroid users not because steroids affect emotional functioning, but because a strong build and masculine appearance might facilitate the learning of physical domination as a strategy for dealing with conflict. Similar to organizational effects, this steroid related change-for-the-worse may be independent of subsequent hormone activity. However, in contrast to organizational effects, negative consequences are a function of changes in the appearance and strength of the body and the social/gendered meanings attached to these changes as opposed to structural changes in brain morphology. For the most part, these steroid users were irresponsible third parties, though some did inform me of their own feelings of invulnerability and the enactment of what one respondent called 'The Superman Syndrome'.

Finally, many bodybuilders underscored the heterogeneity of steroids. Importantly, within bodybuilding subculture there is an identifiable ethno-pharmacological stock-of-knowledge. This comprises a taxonomy of steroids which are differentiated according to their anabolic and androgenic properties, other ingredients and (side) effects (Monaghan 2001a: 95–128). Significantly, bodybuilding ethnopharmacologists maintained that some steroids are more likely than others to increase or cause aggressive feelings while active in the body. The ascription of hazardous characteristics to steroids – and thus the perceived likelihood of an adverse activational effect – therefore varies according to type of drug. *Androgenic* steroids, which are synthetic analogues of testosterone, rather than the milder and less toxic *anabolic* steroids, were considered potentially more problematic. These steroids include specific oral and injectable compounds such as Testosterone Cypionate, Halotestin, Dianabol and Anapolon 50. However, although bodybuilders claimed aggressive violence may be correlated with particular drugs, such effects were not considered inevitable. Some steroid users cited experiential knowledge as negative evidence, claiming they never became angry or violent when taking androgenics. Nonetheless, detrimental steroid changes were acknowledged as a real possibility. During interviewing, a particularly knowledgeable and reflexive respondent commented upon the possibility of a self-fulfilling prophecy where *subcultural perceptions of specific steroids*, rather than the steroids themselves, may cause aggression problems. In such a context, some users, who feared losing control of their emotions, reported modifying their steroid regimens by avoiding high dosages of androgens.

In resisting the idea that all steroids are intrinsically hazardous, respondents embodying and expressing the presuppositions of their muscle-building habitus effectively modified activational and organizational versions of the 'Roid-Rage hypothesis. Their sophisticated ethnoscientific knowledge, grounded in and acquired through the lived body, undermined conventional understandings. In short, they systematically critiqued the much publicized scientific view that past and current steroid-using bodybuilders necessarily pose a threat to other people's physical safety. Correspondingly, illicit steroid use was legitimated among respondents constructing 'appropriate' bodies and identities in a larger healthist, medicalized culture. Drawing from those arguments presented above, the steroids-violence link may be tentatively reformulated. The link is very weak and applies only to a few atypical individuals possessing pre-existing problems with aggression and violence. These 'deviant cases' are claimed to be essentially different from the bodybuilding rank-and-file who present themselves as healthy, responsible 'civilized bodies' (Elias 2000/1939). *Synthesizing biological and social explanations*, the conventional 'Roid-Rage hypothesis may be reformulated in the following ethnoscientific terms:

The molecular structure of particularly *'androgenic'* as opposed to *'anabolic'* steroids resembles the 'male' hormone testosterone. According to the taken-for-granted (sub)cultural stock-of-knowledge, concentrations of testosterone enhance 'masculine traits' such as aggression. Thus, it is expected that a course of *'androgenics' may* cause *'negative aggression'* (as opposed to violence in the form of physically injurious acts) which is reversible upon drug cessation. The likelihood of this *potentially* disruptive activational *mood-state* – which *may* manifest itself verbally or in the form of gestures rather than physically injurious violence – is heightened if *'androgenic gear'* is taken in excessive dosages, i.e. if *abused*. Individual genetic susceptibilities vary, making it impossible to state a priori what dosage constitutes steroid abuse. Nevertheless, it is expected that if individuals with an existing propensity or inclination to violence take excessive dosages then a violent tendency *may* be exacerbated. This propensity to violence is compounded among *mentally unstable androgenic steroid abusers* who are physically stronger and larger through steroids, lifting weights and diet. Given the physique-altering effects of steroids, these drugs *may* have a *mediate effect on violence* by increasing feelings of power and invulnerability as exemplified by 'The Superman Syndrome'. Possessing powerful muscles also increases an individual's ability to inflict more physical damage. Similar to steroid organisational side-effects, this ability to cause harm to others may be long-lasting and independent of subsequent hormone activity. However, this steroid-related detrimental change is indirectly related to changes in the strength and appearance of the physique as opposed to brain morphology.

This ethnoscientific theory, which is attentive to the making and doings of 'healthy' bodies in social space, could be expanded. In explaining supposed detrimental steroid changes, some bodybuilders cited contextual factors intervening between mood change and aggressively violent acts, e.g. working in potentially dangerous occupations such as the police or nightclub security work, being faced with a jealous partner following an extramarital sexual relationship, conflict with noisy neighbours or argumentative flatmates. In clarifying the dynamics of the steroids–violence relationship, and identifying intervening variables, respondents also emphasized the significance of stress (e.g. familial, work, pre-contest), the additive effects of alcohol (experienced bodybuilders warn against combining steroids and alcohol, though invariably some ignore this prescription), the combined use of recreational drugs and the physiological effects of a low carbohydrate diet on mood. Although no attempt was made to detail these additions to the conventional theory, it is worth acknowledging them. In the context of a discussion on the embodiment and social significance of biology, these sophisticated knowledge claims are instructive in constructing less reductionist understandings of the hormonal body (see also Griffiths and

Green, this volume). Indeed, to reiterate a salient point made by Birke in this volume, biological processes are important but there are many other socially embedded factors too, especially in relation to behaviour.

Conclusion: building 'better' bodies of knowledge

The social world, embodied and enacted by reflexive body-subjects, is extremely complex. Understanding and explaining this messy social reality necessarily entails categorization and simplification. All human reasoning is therefore more or less reductionist. In seeking more adequate knowledge of the social world, however, some accounts are simply too reductionist and are sociologically untenable. Biological narratives that reduce complex social phenomena to neurochemical actions and systems – where 'male' sex hormones, for example, represent the principle aetiology for aggressive violence – are too crude and distorting (see also Crossley, this volume). Nonetheless, as indicated by feminist studies of science and medicine, such stories gain widespread acceptance in a larger society that seeks to naturalize male privilege and domination. The immense interest in the supposed mood and behavioural effects of testosterone is exemplary in this respect.

Importantly, the steroids–violence literature may be dominated by highly reductionist research but there are alternative, more socially reflexive bio-medical discourses. Sociologists, who have traditionally rejected biology as non-sociological and antagonistic to their concerns, should recognize that not all biological accounts are overtly crude and distorting. Certainly, the steroids–violence literature does not tell 'a unitary story' (Birke 1999: 176). Some scientific contributors, as already noted, question the prevalence of negative steroid effects and comment upon the ways such effects may be mediated by user expectations, changing physique and personality traits (*cf*. Riem and Hursey 1995: 235–6). Other natural scientists are reflexive of the ways in which biomedicine draws from and reinforces gender stereo-types, such as the myth of the naturally dominant male and the submissive female (Bjorkqvist *et al.* 1994). For sociologists, such accounts may be taken as more satisfactory representations of biological bodies as lived, gendered accomplishments. Here some indication is given of the possibility of integrating biological and sociological concerns. Possibilities undoub-tedly exist to bridge unhelpful disciplinary divides and build better bodies of social/natural scientific knowledge.

To this end, recent social theorizing on biology discusses the possibility of more truthful accounts of 'how bodies work' (Birke 1999: 176). Taking these theoretical arguments seriously, and in contributing to a more inclusive science, bodybuilders' subcultural understandings of the 'Roid-Rage phenomenon are clearly important. Resisting scientific and media claims – where steroids reportedly cause uncontrollable aggressive violence – members of bodybuilding subculture, in this study at least, presented alternative understandings and vocabularies. Certainly, some concession was given to naturalistic representations of the gendered, hormonal body, but biology was synthesised with social explanations. Respondents endeavouring to build 'better' physical bodies offered a coherent and integrated account of the ways in which 'male' sex hormones may be implicated in the social in non-determinate ways. Importantly, this knowledge or definition of the situation is not merely of academic interest. If (steroid-using) bodybuilders define their situation as real then such definitions will be real *in their consequences*. Besides discursively presenting themselves as socially fit, 'civilized bodies' (Elias 2000/1939), these narrators gave expression to finely spun subcultural norms that ordinarily surround steroid use and which possibly militate against steroid psychosis.

Finally, it is worth noting what this means to an embodied, non-dualist sociology of health and illness. Crucially, a move to lived embodiment, echoing Williams and Bendelow (1998) and Leder (1990), facilitates the development of less reductionist, non-dualist and more integrated knowledge. Social actors may be 'mindful bodies' but they are also flesh and blood bodies. And, for reflexive body-subjects, their own and other people's bodies may become physical objects to be scrutinized and scientifically characterized. Yet, and crucially, the physical and the lived body are not two separate entities: the former is one manner in which the latter presents itself (Leder 1990: 6). Embodied meanings and understandings, even when pertaining to complex physiological processes and real reductive components such as sex hormones, are social in construction, origin and consequence. Lived material bodies, subjectively experienced and embroiled in processes of becoming and deterioration, are never unmediated or untouched by society or culture. Moreover, biological narratives, which represent the surfaces and hidden visceral depths of human physical bodies, are always expressed within and co-constitute larger social realities. An embodied, empirical sociology that explores wider social contexts, structures, interactions, meanings and gendered identities therefore needs critically to incorporate lived biological bodies in sickness and in health.

References

Birke, L. (1999) *Feminism and the Biological Body*, Edinburgh: Edinburgh University Press.

Bjorkqvist, K., Nygren, T., Bjorklund, A. and Bjorkqvist, S. (1994) 'Testosterone intake and aggressiveness: real effect or anticipation?', *Aggressive Behaviour*, 20, 1: 17–26.

Bloor, M., Monaghan, L., Dobash, R.P. and Dobash, R.E. (1998) 'The body as a chemistry experiment: steroid use among South Wales bodybuilders', in S. Nettleton and J. Watson (eds) *The Body in Everyday Life*, London: Routledge.

Choi, P. and Pope, H. (1994) 'Violence toward women and illicit androgenic-anabolic steroid use', *Annals of Clinical Psychiatry*, 6, 1: 21–5.

Choi, P., Parrott, A. and Cowan, D. (1989) 'Adverse behavioural effects of anabolic steroids in athletes: a brief review', *Clinical Sports Medicine*, 1: 183–87.

Connell, R. (1995) *Masculinities*, Cambridge: Polity.

Elias, N. (2000/1939) *The Civilizing Process: Sociogenetic and Psychogenetic Investigations*, (revised edn), edited by E. Dunning, J. Goudsblom and S. Mernel, Oxford: Blackwells.

Leder, D. (1990) *The Absent Body*, Chicago: University of Chicago Press.

Messner, M. and Sabo, D. (1994) *Sex, Violence and Power in Sports: Rethinking Masculinity*, California: The Crossing Press.

Monaghan, L. (2001a) *Bodybuilding, Drugs and Risk*, London: Routledge.

Monaghan, L. (2001b) 'Looking good, feeling good: the embodied pleasures of vibrant physicality', *Sociology of Health and Illness*, 23, 3: 330–56.

Morgan, D. (1993) 'You too can have a body like mine: reflections on the male body and masculinities', in S. Scott and D. Morgan (eds) *Body Matters*, London: Falmer Press.

Riem, K. and Hursey, K. (1995) 'Using anabolic-androgenic steroids to enhance physique and performance: effects on mood and behaviour', *Clinical Psychological Review*, 15, 3: 235–56.

Shilling, C. (1993) *The Body and Social Theory*, London: Sage.

Williams, S.J. and Bendelow, G. (1998) *The Lived Body: Sociological Themes, Embodied Issues*, London: Routledge.

12 Incorporating the biological

Chronic illness, bodies, selves, and the material world

Louise M. Millward and Michael P. Kelly

Introduction

The human body has an elusive place in the sociology of chronic illness. Different writers have noted the importance of the body for a proper understanding of the experience of illness. Yet few have successfully integrated the biology of the body into a sociological account (Kelly and Field 1996: 242). Williams has remarked,

> in the field of chronic illness ... the tendency to concentrate upon its social meaning and consequences through notions such as the 'suffering self', has led to the relative neglect of corporeal issues of embodiment and an isolation from the philosophical debates over mind and body.
>
> (1996: 41)

In part, this neglect stems from a desire to avoid biological reductionism and determinism. It also no doubt arises, as a consequence of the need to put distance between sociology and the bio-medical model. However, in common with most of the social sciences it is the sheer intellectual difficulty of integrating an analysis of biological factors within a genuinely sociological explanation that is the real problem. How is it possible to integrate something which is biological, with all its associated explanatory frameworks within another explanatory system, which in some versions at least, deny the possibility of the biological explanations a priori? How is it possible not to reduce the social to the biological? How is it possible to retain the integrity of a sociological explanation?

In this chapter an integrated material, biological and social description of chronic illness is outlined. Our purpose is to provide an holistic account of the nature of human experience embracing the material world, the biological imperatives of the human body, the social world in which human bodies reside, and the mediating role of the individual's sense of self in this.

The body in the material world

Our argument begins with a general consideration of the human body located in the material world, before proceeding to explore the implications of this for a sociological understanding of chronic illness. The physical world is the ultimate backdrop against which all human life takes place. The geology, topography, climate, ecology, geography and microbiology of the physical world, determine whether life is possible at all, and the degree to which that life is relatively pleasant or difficult. The history of the human species is one of slow and gradual adaptation to this physical external world (Megarry 1995). The recent history of the species is one of bringing the physical environment under control, or at least creating the illusion that it is under control. In the western world, technical means have been used to attempt the formidable task of deterring the impact of global forces in the form of meteorological detectors, flood barriers, microbiological quarantine quarters and such like. Yet within the physical environment the body is always potentially precarious and the physical world sets the limits of human possibilities (see also the chapters by Turner and Benton, this volume). In the western world, twenty-first century modes of technology have enabled a virtually endless supply of water and cultivated food substances for example. Modern farming prevents the natural decay and/or contamination of crops through the use of preservatives/pesticides. Government organizations monitor these, along with other hazards in the material world, such as air quality, chemicals and biotechnology, climate changes, pollution and radioactive waste (DEFRA 2001). However, periodically geological, climatic and biological forces overwhelm the best efforts of humans to control their world and casualties from flood, earthquake, famine and disease act as a reminder that the species is not omnipotent in the face of nature (Kelly 2001).

Not only does the global terrain, in which geological, climatic and organic forces operate, set limits on human conduct, the capacity of the biological body constrains the ways in which individuals can respond to this terrain. The ability to produce basic subsistence within the physical environment is itself influenced by the wider forces of nature. When Marx spelled out the principles of historical materialism, he was articulating a simple and important idea. In order to live the species has to enter into relationships with the environment to produce food and shelter (see also Benton, this volume). The species also has to engage in productive relationships with one another to do this (Marx and Engels [1932] 1970). These relationships in turn determine the social system under which humans live. In the course of constructing these relationships the forces of the material world are kept at bay to a limited extent.

The manner in which the species and individual members of it interact with the material world is mediated by the biology of the human body. What is noteworthy about the human species as against practically all other living things is that its adaptation to the physical environment has not only been a responsive and evolutionary series of changes, but also human agency has played a role in the way human society has itself developed. In this regard the human body has had an especially important role. The human body is in many ways an extraordinary thing. Its capacity to do things with hand and eye co-ordination, and the cognitive and creative aspects of the brain are extremely significant in human agency. The ability to transform the physical world, to make it productive through ingenious work using tools and machines, is an undoubted marker of the species. Tool use is critical in these processes (Berger 1964). Two tools – the body and the mind – determine the use of all other tools and govern the individual's relationship with their environment. The resource, which is the human body, is considerable, and its potential to transform the physical world is immense. We transform the world using our bodies to provide food, to make shelter and indeed all the necessities and luxuries of life.

The human body as it engages with others and the natural world generates emotional and physical experience, which are expressed through the human body. Those emotional and physical experiences are very significant aspects of human life. They stretch across the whole range of the pleasures and pains of being alive. The delights of eating, drinking, sex, laughter, sleep and intoxication, the distress of exhaustion, anxiety, pain, and childbirth, the overwhelming feelings of being in love or in mourning, are all bodily physical experiences as well as ones which are socially defined and constructed. In different ways, these experiences are defined by and self indicated by physical sensations – churning stomach, tears, sighs, taste, smell and so on. This is not to ignore the observation that similar physical sensations can be linked to different emotions, but it is to emphasize that physical sensations accompany emotions.

There are links between the body and its malfunction from a range of variables that are associated with the division of labour, including socio-economic status, income, unemployment, residential area, types of dwelling and living conditions (see, for example, Marmot and Wilkinson 1999; and Part II, this volume). In summary, modes of physical and social organization, and the species' response to both have fundamental effects on the bodies of people who inhabit them, some positive some negative. To try to conceive of the context in which human bodies are subject to illness, by focusing only on variables that are socially constructed and to leave out of the account the direct physical role of the body in response to physical and social worlds is a very limited perspective indeed. To be human is to engage with the world in a physical sense. To be human is to live in a world of physical experiences that are mediated through the body and its underlying biology. Without those experiences the nature of human society could not emerge. Culture may be thought of as the system of meanings, which render the physical and social worlds understandable. However their roots, both the social and the cultural, have a physical material reality in which the human species via its bodies must exert agency at all times to produce and reproduce and to maintain existence.

The body and the social world revealed in illness

A consideration of human physicality reveals, i) that the body has parameters of size, strength, endurance, and movement; ii) that sensory perceptions such as vision, hearing, touch and smell have limitations; iii) that the body requires constant nourishment to perform and iv), that these are related to the ageing process and change as a consequence of derangements of the body which modern cultures call illness. The body has a continuity that is irreversible. That irreversibility although usually experienced as existential continuity also allows humans to develop a more or less reliable sense of what their bodies should and should not be able to do relative to their position in the lifecourse. In other words, the human body sets both limits to the possibilities of what the human mind expects and understands as physical possibilities and facilitates the potential for human creativity. The body is also vulnerable to a range of noxious assaults from all kinds of social and environmental variables. Experiences of the body have an existence that, in their basic functional forms are somehow independent of social interaction. It is an existence that is often not brought into focus until things go wrong with the body, and that has always been one of the things which has made the study of illness sociologically so interesting. As the body stops functioning in ways that are deemed socially or culturally appropriate, the taken-for-granted assumptions about the social and the biological world are revealed for what they are – assumptions – and the relationship with, and continued safety from the material world are called into question (Schutz 1967).

In illness the body produces signs that something is wrong. These signs may well be given variable cultural meanings, but the physical nature of illness is associated with a range of physically unpleasant experiences – pain, nausea, extreme fatigue, inability to concentrate, raised temperature and so on. They might be linked to bodily movements, vision, and hearing and such like. These are self-witnessed and are not just some category of social deviance; they are real bodily sensations. In chronic illness, the body is in some kind of permanently altered state, from that which is expected, and is never completely free of the discomforts attaching to sickness (see also Turner, this volume). Whilst 'malfunctioning' bodily features are often profoundly illuminated in the social world, they are directly related to and experienced in the biological realm to differing degrees. Knowledge that something is wrong might be experienced privately or through the sharing of signs and symptoms. In any event, the physical experience of a body that ceases to function in anticipated ways has a private and a public quality. Initially, uncertainty may arise, as the individual might be unsure of whether the functional signs really are 'malfunctions' and/or whether they might recur or persist. The key point is that individuals have private access to the experiences of their bodies and that in illness, initiations of bodily change are experienced as something physical.

A feature of the relationship between the body and the social world is that the social world is where the body is scrutinized, assessed and evaluated and where meaning is reciprocated. The particular networks of meaning are socially and historically bound and subject to cultural parameters. These networks of meaning link to biological and material worlds; however, while their forms are determined by cultural parameters, the body is the self-indicated site of the experience. It is the culture that gives the biological experience meaning. Within the social world the physicality of the body is not just a functional matter, it is a feature for aesthetic assessment. Similarly, the extent to which bodies engage with the labour market is not simply determined by bodily capacity, it is determined by social norms relating to the lifecycle. The social world is where the body is defined and judged according to cultural conventions. Standards acquired from society furnish individuals with the ability to see what others might regard as a shortcoming. In chronic illness, bodies are more likely to fracture social protocols. The degree to which protocols are broken will be linked to the extent to which the physicality of the body intrudes into the social world and the degree to which that intrusion is given salience in the meanings there generated.

The social world is the place where parameters of meaning define and legitimate the chronically ill body. Networks of meaning link to the biological realm and transform bodily functions or malfunctions into the social category of illness. Meaning becomes linked to the material world through the ways in which the types of hazards influence the categorizations of illness, for example, that might be found in the environment. Social organization also stratifies modes of meaning. In advanced societies, a special group of professionals, doctors, denote and manage illness. Individuals assess professional modes of meaning about chronic illness against lay perceptions of experience. The social world is the arena where chronic illness is understood in relation to various reference points in the world. The ways in which these might be configured have important consequences.

Literature on chronic illness provides an insight into how individuals respond to the onset, duration and management of chronic illness. Illness is typically marked by bodily changes in the form of symptoms. In the face of uncertainty individuals utilize lay and professional networks in an attempt to understand what is happening to them. Aetiology, expectations about duration and/or frequency of attacks, treatments, coping and management strategies are important factors. Beyond the search for meaning are the practicalities of living with chronic illness and the impact that such practicalities might have for the individual concerned in relation to themselves, their family members and their wider social networks. Practicalities may also include socio-economic consequences, which might extend and compound the difficulties experienced in chronic illness. Bury proposes that chronic illness can be conceptualized as 'biographical disruption'; a profound disturbance of the taken-for-granted aspects of everyday life that straddles cognitive and material modes of thought and mobilizes concerns about uncertainties, resources and lay and professional modes of thought (Bury 1982). Narrative reveals the ways in which, in the face of biographical disruption, individuals interpret information in relation to various frames of reference within the social world (Williams 1984).

From physical bodies to a sense of self in chronic illness

In chronic illness the physicality of the body impinges directly on self. It does so, too, in various forms of acute illness. But the critical point about chronic illness is its permanence. So the impacts on self are permanent too. The concept of self has to be distinguished from the concept of the body, although commonsensically for many people, most of the time their body and mind together is their self, or more accurately perhaps their sense of self is inextricably bound to their physical body (Archer 2000; Kelly 1992, 2001). This is of course ordinarily speaking, because the experience of dreams or intoxication or certain other psychological states, including some induced by illness, can produce a sense of alienation of self from body. But the sense of 'me' as a person is for most people locked into a sense of bodily continuity.

From a very early age individuals have the ability to acquire a sense of self, i.e. the idea that they are a separate and unique being, different from other similar people and other objects in the environment. Post-natally, the young child very quickly learns how to invoke a response from others to meet their basic needs. A unique sense of who and what one is in relation to the environment develops, coupled by the ability to make references to oneself in relation to other individuals and objects. The frames of reference about who and what individuals are in relation to their environments, increases with wider and increasingly independent contact with the social world in which they reside. During the maturation process the developing ability to use language furnishes the capacity to mediate between types of private information that individuals have already acquired about themselves and the types of information that they continually gain through interaction with the social world. Acquisition of a sense of who and what they are is their own unique sense of self (Ball 1972).

Self is not a psychological entity. Nor is it a congenital trait. Self arises through interaction with the world and is expressed through language (Kelly and Dickinson 1997). The biological bases of the body provide scope for cognition. In turn, cognitive ability permits the development of a self; it does not direct self. The entity of self is neither static nor given. It arises as the product of continual introspective debate which hinges upon two modes of information; one stemming from the private world of the individual, the other stemming from the social environment in which the individual resides.

The only difference between the self that develops through childhood and the self that continues to develop into and throughout adulthood, is that the range of reference points that influence self are extended according to the experiences of the life course. The ingredients that furnish the continually evolving self always result from the interplay of private configurations about who an individual believes themselves to be and socially induced configurations of who others believe the individual to be. The term identity is used to describe this latter idea (Ball 1972).

Self-conceptions are reappraised and redefined in relation to illness. The extent to which self alters is contingent upon the impact of physical bodily changes, the impact of diagnostic and lay references and the impact of practical management of illness in the face of cultural standards. Bodily changes alter the sense in which individuals perceive themselves. The range of socially conferred descriptions that once defined self is extended to incorporate a new state of embodiment. Professional and lay references are called upon in an attempt to secure meaning about the onset, duration and management of bodily illness. These might introduce issues of self-regulation and morality into self-appraisal equations. The practical management of chronically ill bodies has to be offset against cultural standards, which relay information to self. Where physical bodies break societal norms and routinized codes of conduct and behaviour, individuals have the task of working at self-conceptions and self-presentations that ameliorate tensions in interaction. This is the core of the self/identity relationship. It is where socially conferred information impacts on self (Bury 1982).

The personal experience of the body becomes a social experience in relationships with others and societal responses to bodies are anticipated in relation to cultural norms (Archer 2000). The capacity to successfully align with cultural norms and maintain social roles is contingent upon the social salience of bodily illness. Social salience is mediated by impression management, which becomes a central life-organizing feature. Social salience is not simply a matter of visibility; behaviour modifications that are an inherent part of managing the body also influence degrees of social salience. Moreover, the capacity to maintain social roles, statuses and relationships, also trigger identity markers. Evaluations do not simply relate to the physicality of the body, associated contingencies such as the capacity to fulfil societal duties, are also subject to scrutiny and assessment. In this way, the social world defines the body as a master status of identity. The importance of identity markers is that they reflect back on the self. Where tensions abound, self becomes reappraised (Kelly 1992).

The concepts of self and identity evolve out of interaction with the social world (Archer 2000). However, as contemporary characteristics influence modes of social interaction and meaning, the nature of self and identity are historically and culturally bound. Self primarily concerns the *private* perceptions of who and what an individual is. Identity primarily concerns *social* perceptions of who and what an individual is (Ball 1972). Self and identity surface as the result of introspective debate about who and what an individual perceives themself to be, coupled with socially conferred information about who and what an individual is perceived to be by others. Self and identity are intrinsically bound with each other. Analytically, however, self and identity are categorically distinct.

From self to identity: the individual in the social world

Identity concerns the ways in which the individual is perceived to be by others in a social context. There is a continual oscillation between self and identity. Individuals engage in social interaction with a sense of self. Symbolically, through such things as appearance, gesture or verbal clues, the self is presented in the relationship. These provide clues as to the authenticity of who we really are. Generic anchor points include age and gender, however they might also relate to the numerous roles that individuals occupy and/or their status/es. Bodily cues help to locate those anchor points in the social and physical world. In the course of interaction a range of other reference points might be brought to bear on the interaction. These might relate to conduct, appearance, manner, or disposition, all of which could be positive or negative. The perceptions that others have of us might be conveyed overtly or covertly; the numerous modes of symbolic communication permit frank or subtle transmissions in interaction. The crux of the matter is the degree to which the outcomes of social interaction reaffirm our sense of self. Where there is a disparity between self and identity the anchors of self are called into question. The sense of self is no longer intact in the way it once was. Such disparities are tension-inducing and call into question the very essence of who we believe ourselves to be. To arrive at equilibrium, self must be reappraised. Importantly, the body has an inherent relationship in this equation.

As with self, identity is contingent upon historical and cultural modes of being and customary practices that occur in day-to-day communicative interaction with others. Such communication is symbolic in the sense that it might concern visual, written, oral or audible forms of expression. The customary nature of routinized networks of shared meaning renders much day-to-day communication and interaction as taken-for-granted. The shared sense of the ways in which individuals interact stems from the experience of intersubjectivity (Schutz 1967). Intersubjectivity is where individuals have the same proximal meanings about social life as do other individuals. Intersubjectivity is given form through a shared sense of meanings. In intersubjectivity individuals assess things in the way that others do. Consequently, evaluations about things in the world have a degree of consistency.

Body and self

What has not been adequately elucidated in the literature is the nature of the relationship between body and self. Accounts of self are repeatedly presented in formations that illustrate an affinity with identity without any reference to the body. In order to begin to understand the relationship between the body and self, three important interrelated points are of note. First, the intrinsic nature of the body has the potential to invoke introspective appraisal of self. In the same sense that successful social negotiations are unlikely to create tensions with self, 'successfully functioning' bodies are unlikely to create tensions with self. Conversely, however, in the same vein that we reappraise our sense of self in light of information induced by social relationships, we reappraise our sense of self in light of the information induced by our bodies. Second, whilst the body is integral to self, the body is qualitatively and ontologically different from self (Kelly 2001). The body is a predominantly physical entity. It is the vehicle from which numerous basic capacities are possible, such as the ability to walk, see, hear and touch. In contrast, the self is a social entity borne on language. The body permits the potential for self in the form of providing the basic capacities for cognition and language, however self is not a direct product of a bodily function. Third, the idea of 'embodiment' initiates an understanding of the self/body relationship, although in fusing the body and self together, the nature of the dynamics between the body and self might be overlooked. In embodiment the unifying relationship of the self and body are expressed. Embodiment describes the fundamental state of our human being (Williams 1996). The concept of embodiment asserts that whilst we 'feel and are embodied', our primordial sense of being is unreflexive in the sense that we conduct our day-to-day affairs without significant reference to a distinct entity that is our body (Williams 1996: 25). This is resonant to the ways in which self remains a sublime entity until it is called into question. The idea of embodiment fuses the sense of self and the physical body together. In fusing self and body together, the relational features of body and self should not be overlooked.

The ontological difference between the physical and cognitive elements of the body permit the self/body distinction. Specifically, it is the capacity to reflexively engage in appraisal of our bodies and our body's relationship to self that analytically distinguishes bodies from self. The process whereby the body is cognitively perceived in a dysfunctional sense has been termed 'dys-embodiment' (Williams 1996), however this distinction is precariously transient. Our cognitive capacities permit appraisal of our bodies in relation to who and what we are; at the same time, however, our sense of self cannot be detached from the physical realm of our bodies; self and bodies are coterminous. The biological realm is integral to our sense of self; it is largely taken for granted and unreflexive in our day-to-day affairs. Once anomalies arise however, our sense of self is fractured and reappraised.

Bodies may, in certain circumstances, be distressed by changes or disturbances in self, as in certain types of mental illness. However, of more interest are disturbances in self invoked by the experience of the body. It is precisely this point that has not been adequately elucidated in the literature on chronic illness. Analyses of self have tended to centre on the ways in which environmentally induced criteria impinge on the self, rather than the ways in which the intrinsic criteria of the body impinge on the self. Such accounts leap from the point where self is intact, to a point where self and identity are discordant. That the body has the potential to instigate this process has been largely ignored. Ignoring the biological bases of bodies and their relationship to the self renders the self/identity relationship incomplete. It is the biological substance of the body that induces changes in self and through initiation with material, social and lifeworld environments, induces changes in identity that in turn, reflect back on self.

The importance of the body in matters of identity is that the embodied self resides within material and social worlds in which it has to confront and mediate physical demands and restrictions, routines of social life and cognitive modes of subjectiveness in relation to the realms of contingencies that reside in these worlds. The importance of the embodied self in such interaction is that these worlds provide markers for identity construction, which can limit such interaction (Kelly and Field 1996). Herein lies the relationship between the body, self and identity. Biological bases of experience have very important effects on the construction of self and identity.

The importance of the material world in respect of self and identity is that self and identity are constructed with reference to a range of experiences in the material world. Robinson and Hunter (1998) note how individuals with motor neurone disease account for their condition by reference to contact with potential health hazards, which may be 'natural' or 'unnatural':

> in particular, too much contact with nature, such as with farm animals and in farming settings, or too little contact – through living in towns, working in factories and using dangerous chemicals. Sometimes the two perceptions combine – as in contacts with chemicals used in farm settings.

Similarly, in Williams' study on rheumatoid arthritis, one subject attributed their condition to toxic chemicals, extremes of heat and no fresh air in the workplace (1984). Importantly, this subject located exposure to these hazards within exploitative structural power relations and the boundaries of human agency, illustrating links with the division of labour. In terms of identity, the individual concerned compared his own onset with that of a colleague who could no longer 'make it up the stairs'. Furthermore, these links became part of the self. The respondent commented, ' "How the *hell* have I come to be like this?", you know, because it isn't me' (1984: 184). Self and identity are forged by reference to the material worlds in which embodied individuals reside. The capacities to limit the effects of illness are related to the position of individuals within the division of labour. Numerous texts chart how distributional issues and the availability of resources determine the degree to which resources can compensate for the effects of illness (e.g. Bury 1982; Pinder 1995). Notably, 'disadvantage stems from the experience of chronic illness and contributes to it' (Anderson and Bury 1988).

Conclusion

The relationship between biological, material, and social is interactive; it is not uni-directional. The biological realm provides the basic physical and cognitive capacities of the body. The body however, is understood according to the networks of meaning that embrace biological, material and social realms of experience. Stocks of knowledge about chronic illness become enmeshed within this matrix. For example, the types of illness like chronic heart disease that are related to major public health concerns, such as smoking and obesity, all have connections with biological concerns, the physical environment, the potential for economic longevity and social notions of self-regulation. The body is not peripheral to sociological debates on chronic illness, it occupies an integral position where biological, material, social and lifeworlds meet.

Using the body as an analytical device, this chapter has attempted to illuminate how the body is integral to sociological understanding of chronic illness. The body was used as an analytical tool to illustrate the ways in which illness is bound up with biological, material and social worlds of experience and the ways in which private configurations of self and publicly conferred identities become enmeshed with the stocks of knowledge that are tied to these worlds.

References

Anderson, R. and Bury, M. (1988) *Living with Chronic Illness: The Experience of Patients and Their Families*, London: Unwin Hyman.

Archer, M.S. (2000) *Being Human: The Problem of Agency*, Cambridge, UK: Cambridge University Press.

Ball, D.W. (1972) 'Self and identity in the context of deviance: the case of criminal abortion', in R.A. Scott, and J.D. Douglas, (eds) *Theoretical Perspectives on Deviance*, New York: Basic Books.

Berger, P. (1964) 'Some general observations on the problem of work', in P. Berger, (ed.) *The Human Shape of Work: Studies in the Sociology of Occupations*, New York: Macmillan.

Bury, M. (1982) 'Chronic illness as biographical disruption', *Sociology of Health and Illness*, 4: 167–82.

DEFRA (Department of the Environment, Food and Rural Affairs) (2001) *DEFRA's Aims and Objectives*, London, UK. http://www.defra.gov.uk/corporate/aims/index.htm

Kelly, M.P. (1992) 'Self, identity and radical surgery', *Sociology of Health and Illness*, 14: 390–415.

Kelly, M.P. (2001) 'Disability and community', in G.L. Albrecht, K.D. Seelman and M. Bury (eds) *Handbook of Disability Studies*, London: Sage.

Kelly, M.P. and Field, D. (1996) 'Medical sociology, chronic illness and the body', *Sociology of Health and Illness*, 18: 241–57.

Kelly, M.P. and Dickinson, H. (1997) 'The narrative self in autobiographical accounts of illness', *Sociological Review*, 45: 254–78.

Marmot, M. and Wilkinson, R.G. (eds) (1999) *Social Determinants of Health*, Oxford: Oxford University Press.

Marx, K. and Engels, F. [1932] (1970) *The German Ideology*, (ed. C. Arthur), London: Lawrence & Wishart.

Megarry, T. (1995) *Society in Prehistory: The Origins of Human Culture*, Basingstoke: Macmillan.

Pinder, R. (1995) 'Bringing back the body without the blame? The experience of ill and disabled people at work', *Sociology of Health and Illness*, 17: 605–31.

Robinson, I. and Hunter, M. (1998) *Motor Neurone Disease*, London: Routledge.

Schutz, A. (1967) *The Phenomenology of the Social World*, Evanston, Illinois: North Western University Press.

Williams, G. (1984) 'The genesis of chronic illness: narrative re-construction', *Sociology of Health and Illness*, 6: 175–99.

Williams, S.J. (1996) 'The vicissitudes of embodiment across the chronic illness trajectory', *Body and Society*, 2: 23–47.

13 'Liminal' bodies?

Sleep, death and dying

Simon J. Williams

Introduction

In this chapter I take a closer look at two aspects of embodiment which both, in their different ways, serve to delimit our conscious (waking) involvement in society. The first of these, the dormant matter of sleep, has received surprisingly little sociological attention to date. The second, in contrast, the mortal matter of death and dying, is now a thriving sub-field of sociological inquiry. Both these matters, I shall argue, not only throw corporeal issues of *liminality* – the 'in-between' (cf. Van Gennep 1960/1909) – into critical relief, they also underline the need for new (irreducible) ways of incorporating the biological into sociological discussion and debate.[1]

The chapter, in this respect, augments the themes of this volume as a whole, and this embodied section in particular, charting some new sociological territory along the way. I am not of course, in drawing these (liminal) parallels and analogies, claiming any simple or unproblematic equation of sleep with death or dying: far from it. Sleep is a reversible loss of consciousness, death is not. It is *dying* rather than death, moreover, in the modern day western world at least, which may be regarded as 'liminal': an extended phase of liminality in many cases, given protracted forms of dying. Taking this line, nonetheless, qualifications apart, has its merits, providing an instructive point of comparison and contrast between these 'liminal' states, and the biology–society relations they embody and express.

What then of sleep? What light can it shed on these liminal matters and biology/society debates? And what, in turn, does this tell us about health? It is to these very questions that we now turn, taking the preliminary question 'what is sleep (for)?' as our starting point.

The mysteries of sleep unravelled: biology and beyond

Everyone knows what sleep is. We all partake, albeit with varying degrees of success. When asked to define sleep, however, things become less clear-cut. Sleep, for example, may be defined as the closing of our eyes and/or the taking of rest. Yet neither, on closer inspection, guarantees sleep. I can lie in bed, eyes firmly closed all night long, without getting a wink of sleep. Sleep descends or 'comes over' us, as Merleau-Ponty (1962) puts it, the precise moment of which is difficult if not impossible to recall. Vital bodily processes such as heartbeat and respiration, moreover, to say nothing of brain activity, give the lie to the notion of (total) rest. We are often quite active when asleep, expending considerable amounts of energy. Not quite so simple then as things may seem.

As a 'liminal' state, somewhere between wakefulness and death, the mysteries of sleep have exercised many great minds, from Aristotle to Shakespeare. So, too, of course, have dreams: the 'royal road to the unconscious' in Freud's famous terms. For leading sleep experts such as Dement, nonetheless, the defining criteria of sleep, simply stated, are two-fold. First, the perceptual barrier it erects between our conscious selves and the world outside. Second, its more or less immediate reversibility, in contrast to death (Dement 2000: 7).

Developments in sleep science over the past forty-five years or so have done much to advance our understanding of this crucial third part of our lives. Traced through a series of recording devices, including electroencephalographs (EEGs), sleep involves a rich pattern of movements from beta to alpha waves, then on to delta waves, and from there to REM (rapid eye movement), the very point at which dreaming occurs and all voluntary muscles are temporarily paralysed given heightened brain activity (Dement 2000; Flanagan 2000). To view sleep in undifferentiated terms then, from this techno-scientific viewpoint, is itself misleading. The total sleep cycle in fact, comprises four stages of Non-REM (NREM), followed by a period of REM lasting approximately twenty to thirty minutes: a cycle, which takes between ninety and one hundred minutes to complete (Flanagan 2000: 75).

The precise mechanisms underpinning sleep need not concern us here. Suffice it to say that this, according to current scientific wisdom, involves a delicate balance between the wakefulness centre/signals of our brain (a non-continuous, light-sensitive, biological clock-dependent alerting function), and accumulating sleep debt – a process, taken as a whole, which occurs within a circadian rhythm (i.e. daily cycle) of approximately twenty-four hours. As sleep debt accumulates during periods of wakefulness, and our biological clock-dependent alerting signal becomes weaker, so our likelihood of falling asleep increases (Dement 2000). Melatonin, a hormone produced by the pineal gland and released into the bloodstream, is a key player here, resulting in drowsiness and indicating to brain and body that it is dark and time to prepare for the transition to sleep (Dement 2000: 19).

The functions of sleep too are many and varied, including a variety of *restorative*, *conservatory* and *body-building* roles (Flanagan 2000: 87). Pituitary growth hormone levels, in particular, peak during NREM sleep in both children and adults, promoting protein synthesis throughout the body, thereby facilitating processes such as new cell growth and tissue repair

(Flanagan 2000: 87). The endocrine system, in fact, readjusts all its levels during sleep (Flanagan 2000: 88). Sleep, furthermore, displays a complex relation to immune function, not to mention our moods, our sensitivity to pain, and our general sense of well-being (Dement 2000). The higher percentage of REMing in development, which declines with age – from around 50 per cent in typical newborns, through 25 per cent for adults, to 15–20 per cent in old age (Dement 2000: 106) – suggests another important role here in helping build and/or strengthen brain connections, especially the visual system, which remains 'unfinished' or 'incomplete' *in utero* (Flanagan 2000: 89) (see also Fausto-Sterling, this volume). As for the effects of long-term sleep deprivation, this includes varying degrees of impairment in analytical abilities, memory, perceptual and motor skills. These and other scientific insights, taken together, suggest a 'credible basis for thinking that sleep serves a proper biological function' (Flanagan 2000: 91). We cannot it seems, currently at least, do without sleep. Nor perhaps, would we wish to do so (a point I shall return to later).

This, however, is not the end of the story. Sleep, it is clear, is open to a variety of social and cultural influences, which take us far beyond these preliminary concerns and insights. It is to these latter sociological themes and issues therefore that we now turn, without, of course, leaving the biological out in the process.

The dormant body: sociological agendas and biological intertwinings

The key point of departure for the sociological study of sleep, expressed succinctly, runs as follows: *when, where* and *how* we sleep (let alone *what* we make of it) are all, to a considerable degree, sociocultural matters, including processes of social scheduling and management in our waking lives. This in turn is dependent on history and culture, time and place. We have, then, considerable sociocultural discretion over our sleeping patterns and arrangements, whether this serves our biological needs well or poorly; reducing, cancelling or increasing our 'sleep debt' accordingly. Sleep, to put it more formally, is irreducible to any one domain or discourse, *arising* or *emerging* through the interplay of biological and psychological processes, environmental and structural circumstances (i.e. facilitators and constraints), and socio-cultural forms of *elaboration*, conceived in temporal/spatially bounded and embodied terms. Within this (realist) formulation, principles of *irreducibility* and *emergence* are maintained, without in any way ruling out discursive, structural or biological factors in the process.

At stake here are a number of more specific sociological concerns, which I have elaborated on more fully elsewhere (Williams 2002). Let me, however, by building on the above schematic outline, spell out the implications of sleep for our understanding of biology–society relations in particular. These relations and intertwinings, I venture, can be traced through (overlapping) processes of: (i) *Socialization*; (ii) *Temporalization*; (iii) *Structuration*; (iv) *Incorporation*, and; (v) *Problematization/Colonization*.

Taking each of these themes in turn. The *socialization* of biological processes and mechanisms may be glimpsed at a number of different levels, including the 'civilizing' (cf. Elias 1978/1939) of 'natural' bodily functions, such as sleep, across the centuries and within the lifetimes of each and every one us. Sleep, one might say, or the active 'doing' of sleep (Taylor 1993) to be more precise, is yet another *learnt* body technique (cf. Mauss 1973/ 1934), experienced and expressed through the social habitus and associated (ritual) practices, and institutionalized through the sleep role (Schwartz 1970) or the socialized role of sleeper. 'The notion that sleep is something natural', Mauss proclaims, 'is totally inaccurate' (1973/1934: 80). These very practices, nonetheless, become seemingly 'naturalized' or taken-for-granted: second nature one might say. The biological dimensions of sleep, as this suggests, are themselves socially 'pliable', 'open' or 'unfinished'.

These issues, in turn, are inextricably bound up with processes of *temporalization*. Whilst night-time, biologically and environmentally speaking, may be our 'best' time to sleep, there are again considerable degrees of freedom here, aided and abetted by human interventions of many kinds, from the humble electric light-bulb to the late-night shot of caffeine. Sleep indeed, as Aubert and White (1959) appositely put it, is a temporal resource, enabling us to get more or less out of our 'day', depending on our particular circumstances. We may, for example, choose to 'sleep time away' when bored or confined. Alternatively, we may burn the midnight oil when work deadlines press. Our fast-paced lifestyles indeed, and the around the clock world of which they are a part, pose particular problems here it is claimed, denying us 'adequate' sleep time, whatever that might be (an issue to which I will return shortly).[2] Sleep then, throws issues of temporality into critical relief at a number of different levels, including (variable) relations between our biological (light-sensitive) clocks, with their intricate circadian rhythms, clock/calendar time, social time (social change), and personal/ biographical time.

As for matters of '*structuration*', the term immediately poses problems if, like certain social theorists, a conflation of structure and agency is effected. What I wish to flag instead, as noted earlier, is the degree to which sleep itself is an emergent, multidimensional, irreducible phenomenon involving the complex interplay of biological and psychological processes, structural and environmental facilitators and constraints, and agential forms of socio-cultural elaboration. Our biological need to sleep, from this viewpoint, may or may not translate into the actual partaking of sleep (though in time of course it must do), given variable structural and environmental contexts and the involvements and projects, desires and wishes of social agents themselves.

Processes of *incorporation*, quite literally, put flesh on the bones of these arguments, building on the above points in so doing. The key issue here, echoing recent debates on the body in general, is that to understand sleep adequately, we need to incorporate the biological in a more fully *embodied* fashion. The dormant body, in this respect, is itself a modality of the lived body, which incorporates yet takes us far beyond the biological body. To the degree, moreover, that the thematization or problematization of human bodies is historically and culturally contingent (cf. Foucault), and to the degree that sleep itself is part and parcel of these very processes, then we may indeed speak of the shifting corporeal significance if not *corporealization* of sleep itself, both historically and culturally.

Discussion of these latter issues beg further questions regarding the *problematization* of sleep in contemporary western society, or perhaps more correctly (echoing the temporal points above) the problematization of sleep as a neglected corporeal matter in a 24/7 global age. Posed as a sociological question, what this amounts to is the following: to what extent has our sleep (time) become problematized, if not 'colonized' in late/postmodernity, through a variety of 'dormant' expertise?

There is, according to various leading sleep experts (Coren 1996; Dement 2000), an 'epidemic' of sleep disorders in our midst – from insomnia to narcolepsy, sleep apnoea to restless leg syndrome – with people all around us trading on various levels of sleep debt or deprivation, some more chronic than others. We are indeed, Dement (2000) boldly proclaims, a 'sleep sick' society! The health and public safety implications of this, to say nothing of lost productivity, are matters of growing concern for governments, professionals and the public alike: a wake up call, one might say, in which the media play no small part. Current (US) debates surrounding the excessively 'sleepy' or 'drowsy' person, for example, are a case in point: a *liminal* state which many, we are told, now occupy in daily life, with more or less 'dangerous' consequences to self and others (Kroll-Smith 2000).

Proposed 'solutions' to this dormant conundrum, if conundrum it is, range from pharmaceutical products (such as sleep medications/prescription hypnotics) to relaxation techniques; over-the-counter remedies and alternative therapies to broader public awareness/education/safety campaigns designed to raise the profile of these sleep-related matters as a preventive measure (Dement 2000). Particularly interesting, in this respect, is the notion of 'sleep hygiene', which includes a series of behavioural and lifestyle choices designed to 'train' our sleep cycle (cf. the socialization of sleep mentioned earlier) and to promote 'healthy' sleep. Consider it 'doctor's orders' proclaims Dement (Dement 2000: 15)!

Linkages to on-going medicalization and healthicization debates may be more or less fruitful here (see Williams 2002): the former a matter of turning the moral into the medical, the latter a question of turning health into the moral (Conrad 1992). Caution is clearly needed, however, in any such claims to date. Colonization, for example, prospective or otherwise, cannot be conflated with medicalization or healthicization. Medicalization, in turn, may (or may not) occur at different levels, be it *conceptual, institutional* or *interactional*. We cannot, moreover, equate any such medicalization with intent, still less blind imperialist ambition, on the part of doctors themselves (Conrad 1992). Many doctors' indeed, it is claimed, are guilty of 'ignorance', neglect and/or the mis-diagnosis of sleep-related disorders to date (Dement 2000). This itself, nevertheless, provides a potent rallying or wake-up call, by sleep experts and the media alike (the relations of which are complex if not contested), to take sleep matters seriously within and beyond contemporary medical practice.

It may well be that sleep, at the present time, is more *healthicized* than medicalized, particularly if the above calls for basic principles of 'sleep hygiene' qua 'sleep-smart' lifestyle choices are anything to go by: the latest version of the 'you are responsible for your health' message perhaps? There are signs, moreover, that certain sleep-related states such as drowsiness behind the wheel are now becoming *criminalized* through their association with other 'irresponsible' acts such as drunk driving (Kroll-Smith 2000). The *commercialization* of sleep is another huge area, of course; itself related in complex, if not mutually reinforcing ways to issues of healthicization. A burgeoning sleep industry indeed, is busy capitalizing or cashing-in on this dormant third part of our lives, both day and night, from beds and bedding to night-wear to night-creams, not to mention best-selling books and box office hits woven around sleep-related themes and issues.

Let me, however, suggest another future trend, speculative to be sure, but instructive nonetheless. Ours is an age in which tinkering if not tampering with our biological constitution, capacities and endowments is no longer a distant dream (or nightmare) but an unfolding reality. From face-lifts to (xeno)transplants, pharmacological fixes to cloning technologies and the new genetics, past impossibilities become today's possibilities, rapidly succeeded by tomorrow's breakthroughs (see Part IV, this volume). Might sleep then, be the next target or casualty? Whether through a smart pill or a minor amendment/correction to the human blueprint, our need to sleep could well be reduced if not cancelled in the future (see Melbin 1989, for example), thereby extending our days and helping reclaiming that 'lost' third part of our lives. This, to be sure, would appeal to some – those perhaps who wish to get 'the most out of life' and/or those whose current sleep quality is poor – but not to others. What role would medicine play, moreover: guardian of sleep or future collaborator in its demise/dissolution?

Herein lies a further irony of any such development or breakthrough. Sleep itself, sociologically speaking, provides a more or less welcome release/ legitimate escape from the conscious demands of waking society. To do away with sleep, therefore, may well be self-defeating. Sleep, in other words, has many hidden benefits and pleasures, not least the corporeal opportunity it affords us to withdraw from the world, liminally or otherwise. Not an option for us all then, but a possibility for some, or perhaps more correctly for us all some of the time. Designer sleep in a designer age (Melbin 1989)? Who knows . . .

The mortal body: disintegration and sequestration

If sleep constitutes one embodied way in which the conscious demands of waking life are (temporarily) relinquished, then death and dying constitute another, this time albeit irrevocably. The links between sleep and death, in fact, can be traced back to ancient Greek mythology in which Nyx, the goddess of night, gave birth to twins, Hypnos (the god of sleep) and Thanatos (the god of death). Poets, too, such as Shelley have waxed lyrical about the 'wonders' of sleep and death, 'both so passing, strange and wonderful!' in his immortal words. Notions such as the 'Big Sleep' and 'Rest in Peace' (RIP) likewise abound in lay and popular culture; attempts perhaps to 'tame' or soften the 'finality' of death? Sleep indeed, without wishing to push these analogies too far, may be something of a dress 'rehearsal' for death: a substitution, borrowing from Bauman (1992), of 'reversible' death and temporary disappearance for the irreversible termination of life itself.[3]

As for the nature and status of death and dying in contemporary western society, these dormant connections notwithstanding, debates abound. Are we, for example, a 'death-denying' society? Has death become a medicalized and/or sequestrated experience in late/postmodernity? And is a 'revival' of death currently underway? Answers to these questions are many and varied, with advocates and critics alike. It is not my intention, however, to rehearse them again here (see Seale 1998, for example, for a useful discussion). My focus instead is on particular *types* of dying, for the clues they provide to body/self, biology/society relations, and to associated corporeal questions of liminality. 'The material end of the body', Seale comments:

> is only roughly congruent with the end of the social self. In extreme old age, or in diseases where mind and personality disintegrate, social death may precede biological death. Ghosts, memories and ancestor worship are examples of the opposite: a social presence outlasting the body. *Yet the life and death of the body sets the parameters for these and other events at the level of social relations*, so some understanding of the variable ways in which human bodies die is necessary for the sociologist wishing to understand the effects of these on social life ... *the bodily effects of particular diseases that cause death exercise considerable influence over the individual's capacity to understand themselves as 'dying' and, therefore, to choose particular cultural scripts available for the interpretation of such a role.*
>
> (1998: 34, my emphasis)

Lawton's (2000) work on the 'unbounded' body and 'dirty' dying in the hospice is particularly revealing on this count, making a significant contribution to these broader debates on death and dying in late/postmodernity in so doing. It is this therefore that I shall primarily concentrate on here, given the (liminal) matters in hand.[4] Drawing on patients' own experiences of the dying process, Lawton pays close attention to the ways in which notions of the body and self, time and space, shift from the initial diagnosis of terminal disease (advanced cancer) to eventual death.

Three issues in particular merit further discussion here. The first, alluded to above, concerns Lawton's well-made point about the problems evident in much current sociological literature in this domain, which use homogeneous categories such as the 'dying patient' and the 'dying process'. Different *types* of death and dying are therefore glossed, themselves carrying very different implications not simply for self and others, but for wider academic discussions and debates on these mortal matters. In contrast to such general categories, Lawton's findings indicate the importance of focusing on the body of the patient and the *actual disease processes* taking place *within* it and on its outer corporeal *surfaces*. Doing so it is argued – set within the broader context of pressures to cut hospice beds and the knock-on effect for admission policies – helps explain why some patients are now sequestered within hospices whilst others are not: issues linked, that is to say, to the manner in which *disease spread destroys both the ability to act and the physical boundaries of the body* (2000: 37).

One of the most common reasons for a patient's admission to the hospice, Lawton found, was for 'symptom control'. This encompassed a wide range of bodily ailments and their sequelae, such as: 'incontinence of urine and faeces; uncontrolled vomiting (including faecal vomit); fungating tumours (the rotting away of a tumour site on the surface of the skin); and weeping limbs which resulted from the development of gross oedema in a patient's legs and/or arms (the limbs would swell to such an extent that the skin burst and lymph fluid continually seeped out)' (Lawton 2000: 129). These processes, quite literally, resulted in the erosion of the patient's physical boundaries through the ravages of disease (Lawton 2000: 128).

Here we encounter the second key point stemming from Lawton's study. Once a patient's body fell 'severely and irreversibly apart' in this way, loss of self quickly followed, leaving little if anything but an 'empty body' (2000: 132). For selfhood to be realized and maintained in contemporary western contexts such as England, Lawton insists:

> certain specific bodily capacities and attributes must be possessed: the most important being a bounded, physically sealed, enclosed body (what I term the corporeal capacity for 'self-containment') and also the bodily ability to act as the agent of one's own embodied actions and intentions. Patients who lose either, or both of these bodily attributes . . . fall out of the category of personhood in both their own and other people's evaluations: they experience a diminishment of self.[5]
>
> (2000: 7)

It is at this very point that issues of biological and social death loom large: part and parcel, as Lawton puts it, of the transition from 'subject' to 'object' and the liminal issues this raises. Faced with these corporeal dilemmas, many patients 'switched off', becoming disengaged from all events and relationships around them: a 'social death', that is to say, which all too often preceded biological death. Others sought external aids, such as heavy sedation, to achieve a complete withdrawal, or made direct requests for euthanasia, thereby attempting to bring physical death back into a closer alignment with this loss of person/selfhood (Lawton 2000: 132). For some however, far fewer in fact, the problem was precisely the opposite, not of 'living too long' but of 'dying too soon', without adequate time for them or their families to come to terms with the idea of loss their death would bring about (2000: 156). The intersubjective and intercorporeal dilemmas of care are likewise thrown into critical relief here. In the process of providing a dependent patient with 'total body care', Lawton reveals, the patient's own body, to a certain extent, may become 'assimilated' or 'merged' with a carer's own sense of self – an observation which itself destabilizes the 'rhetoric's of individuality' and the very notion of 'self containment' (2000: 109).

These observations in turn feed into a broader, more general set of insights concerning the sequestration of these unbounded, uncontainable, if not 'vile' or 'grotesque' bodies, viewed symbolically as 'dirt' or 'matter out of place' (cf. Douglas 1966), within the liminal space of the hospice. The nature and types of dying considered here, Lawton argues, set against this wider cultural backdrop of beliefs about purity and danger, pollution and taboo, and on-going pressure on hospice admission policies, mean that the hospice is not simply a liminal space, but a 'no-place' which the general public, with their 'civilized' bodies and cultivated sensibilities, neither needs nor wishes to know. Understanding the hospice as a 'no place', a space within which 'the taboo processes of bodily disintegration and decay are sequestered', it is claimed, allows it to be understood, at one and the same time, as a central part of contemporary English if not western culture (Lawton 2000: 144). Setting these phenomena apart from mainstream society, from this viewpoint, 'enables certain ideas about living, personhood and the hygienic, sanitized, bounded body . . . to be symbolically enforced and maintained' (2000: 144). Lawton's work, in this respect, provides a powerful critique of the ideology of the modern-day hospices of enabling patients with advanced cancer to 'die with dignity' and to 'live until they die' – itself a key strand of broader 'revivalist' discourses and practices surrounding the mortal body in late/postmodernity (see, for example, Walter 1995). A patient's deterioration, to repeat, may have a ' "non-negotiable", debasing impact upon his or her sense of self and also upon his or her ability to sustain relationships with family and friends' (2000: 129). Dying with dignity, in such cases, proves hard if not impossible.

What we have here then, given the aims of this volume in general, is a clear illustration of the corporeal relations between the biological and the social; a situation, in this particular case, in which the integrity of the body, *qua* biological *organism*, is shown to be more or less central to the integrity of the socially constructed western self. To put it another way, what this amounts to is a corporeal reminder of the influence which 'the material life of the body has over participation in social and cultural life' (Seale 1998: 7). No mere social construction, the fleshy, material, matter of bodies, blatantly matters. This in turn sounds an important note of caution regarding the all too ready slippage from an endorsement of the leaky logos to the championing of leaky bodies. The privileging of western self-containment, to be sure, is far from unproblematic, as feminist critiques have pointed out (Grosz 1994; Shildrick 1997), but the importance and integrity of bodily boundaries, at this most basic, fundamental level (the *sine qua non* of life itself), should not be lost sight of or forgotten in any such deconstruction, postmodern or otherwise.

None of this, I hasten to add, denies the important role which social and cultural processes play in the shaping and construction of biological death and dying. Relations, of course, flow both ways, including the social patterning of mortality rates themselves and the (widening) inequalities they engender (see Part II of this volume). The aim, instead, has simply been to accord the biological its due vis-à-vis those approaches in which the body, to all intents and purposes, living or dead, is little more than a discursive entity. The realities of death and dying, in short, themselves many and varied, throw debates on biology and society into critical relief, providing yet another timely corporeal reminder why the 'return of the repressed', in this case the biological, should be given that (albeit cautious) welcome 'back in' (Benton 1991).

Conclusions

If sociology is first and foremost concerned with the conscious dimensions of (waking) social life, then this chapter, I am happy to say, is something of an exception to the rule, certainly as far as sleep is concerned. Sleep, death and dying, it has been argued, in their different ways, point not simply to those 'liminal' aspects, phases, stages or dimensions of embodiment (or *dys*-embodiment), but to the need to bring the biological (back) into our sociological theorizing, good and proper, in health as elsewhere.

Sleep, as we have seen, is a complex, multifaceted, multidimensional phenomenon, which (like the body in general) is irreducible to any one domain or discourse. *When, how, where*, and *what* we make of sleep, to repeat, are all to a large extent socio-cultural matters which *relate* and *translate*, in multiple ways, our biological need to sleep, *qua* sleep drive, serving our needs well or poorly in the process. These relations in turn, it has been suggested, may be traced or glimpsed through (overlapping) processes of *socialization, temporalization, structuration, incorporation* and *problematization/colonization*: all, in their different ways, testimony to the complex intertwining of biological and social factors. As a borderland or liminal state, moreover, sleep embodies and expresses the broader tensions and dilemmas of our age: both corporeal 'release' and corporeal 'control'; enemy and ally of the (protestant) work ethic; (potentially) medicalized 'problem' and marketable consumer 'product'; personal responsibility and public concern; 'rehearsal' of death and 'rejuvenation' of life. Any further attempts to reduce or eliminate our need to sleep, therefore, with or without the aid of the latest (bio)technological fix, must themselves contend with this dormant web of contradictions and paradoxes. The pleasures of sleep it seems, even for those who struggle to obtain them, will not be given up lightly.

As for death and dying, the particular line taken here, indebted as it is to Lawton's insightful ethnographic work, alerts us to the limits of general (undifferentiated) sociological debates on these mortal matters. It also, as we have seen, provides a stark if not grotesque corporeal reminder of the fleshy predicaments that *certain* diseases pose, in this case advanced cancer, for the socially constructed self in western society. Social death, in this respect, despite the best efforts and intentions of the hospice movement, may very well occur before biological death: the 'betwixt and between' indeed. Again, however, these corporeal relations are complex and multi-faceted, suggesting a series of relays between biology, culture and society which themselves include the social patterning of morbidity and mortality, and the (widening) gaps this entails.

The underlying perspective adopted in this chapter, it is clear, is very much in the embodied mould, itself a bulwark against various forms of reductionism, be it social or biological. It is not simply a question of sleep and dying as liminal states, however, but of embodiment in general having something of an indeterminate quality or feel to it: 'a threshold or border-line concept', as Grosz appositely puts it, which 'hovers perilously and undecidably at the pivotal point of binary pairs. The body is neither – while also being both – the private and the public, self or other, natural or cultural, physical or social, instinctive or learned, genetically or environmentally determined' (1994: 23).

Perhaps the final point to stress, or to bring out more fully here, concerns the question, which threads through this volume as a whole, as to *why* we should take the biological seriously and *what* precisely this entails. What this boils down to, I suggest, to put it bluntly, are two main cases: one more 'negative' the other more 'positive'. The first, 'negative' case, is one which states that to take the biological seriously helps guard against the twin dangers, evident or not, of sociological *hubris* and *hypocrisy*: hubris, that is to say, when the sociological temptation to dismiss other bodies of know-ledge and their subject matter proves irresistible, thereby confusing the having of *something* important to say, with *everything to say* on the matter (cf. Craib 1997); hypocrisy, when criticism of one form of (biological) reductionism is traded for another (sociological). The social construction of the biological, to repeat, within and beyond the discourses of biology and medicine, is only part of the story, however important – one or more chapters in the larger book of biology/society relations perhaps, some of which have yet to be written.

The second, 'positive' case, has an altogether more optimistic ring to it. To take the biological seriously, from this latter viewpoint, is less a rap across the knuckles and more an opportunity or invitation to think in challenging, non-reductionist, non-dualist ways which themselves open up a variety of exciting new agendas and possibilities, both now and in the future. It is also, of course, a call for new alliances, given the challenges ahead. It is not, moreover, a question of conceding ground here; principles of irreducibility and emergence see to that. No real threat at all then, but an opportunity to augment our ways of thinking and to grasp the complex reality we seek to study, shorn of former (reductionist) baggage.

Notes

1 This chapter is a substantially revised and developed set of arguments, which draw on a range of recent work by the author concerning these dormant issues and mortal matters. See, for example, Williams 2002.
2 Whilst eight hours' sleep is commonly touted as the 'recommended' number, there seems little consensus here, even amongst sleep experts themselves.
3 Relations between sleep, sexuality and death are equally fascinating.
4 The dramas and indignities of cardiopulmonary resuscitation (CPR), provide another more or less promising line of inquiry here into these liminal matters (see Meerabeau and Page (1998) for example). So too, of course, do vegetative and comatose states.
5 For feminist critiques of the 'bounded body', and the privileging of western notions of 'self-containment', see for example Shildrick (1997) and Grosz (1994).

References

Aubert, V. and White, H. (1959) 'Sleep: a sociological interpretation I', *Acta Sociologica*, **4**, 2: 46–54.
Bauman, Z. (1992) *Mortality, Immortality and Other Life Strategies*, Cambridge: Polity Press.
Benton, T. (1991) 'Biology and social science: why the return of the repressed should be given a (cautious) welcome', *Sociology*, **25**, 1: 1–29.
Conrad, P. (1992) 'Medicalization and social control', *Annual Review of Sociology*, 18: 209–32.
Coren, S. (1996) *Sleep Thieves*, London: Simon & Schuster.
Craib, I. (1997) 'Social constructionism as social psychosis', *Sociology*, **31**, 1: 1–15.
Dement, W.C. (with C. Vaughan) (2000) *The Promise of Sleep: The Scientific Connection Between Health, Happiness and a Good Night's Sleep*, New York/ London: Delacourt Press/Macmillan.
Douglas, M. (1966) *Purity and Danger: An Analysis of the Concepts of Pollution and Taboo*, London: Routledge & Kegan Paul.
Elias, N. (1978/1939) *The Civilizing Process; Vol I: The History of Manners*, Oxford: Blackwell.

Flanagan, O. (2000) *Dreaming Souls*, Oxford: Oxford University Press.

Grosz, E. (1994) *Volatile Bodies: Toward a Corporeal Feminism*, Bloomington and Indianapolis: Indiana Unversity Press.

Kroll-Smith, S. (2000) 'The social construction of the "drowsy person"', in G. Miller and J. Holstein (eds) *Perspectives on Social Problems*, Greenwich, Conn: JAI Press.

Lawton, J. (2000) *The Dying Process: Patients' Experience of Palliative Care*, London: Routledge.

Mauss, M. (1973/1934) 'Techniques of the body', *Economy and Society*, 2, 70–88.

Meerabeau, L. and Page, S. (1998) '"Getting the job done": emotion management and cardiopulmonary resuscitation in nursing', in G. Bendelow and S.J. Williams (eds) *Emotions in Social Life*, London: Routledge.

Melbin, M. (1989) *Night As Frontier: Colonizing the World After Dark*, London: Macmillan.

Merleau-Ponty, M. (1962) *The Phenomenology of Perception* (transl. by C. Smith), London: Routledge.

Schwartz, B. (1970) 'Notes on the sociology of sleep', *Sociological Quarterly*, 11, Fall: 485–99.

Seale, C. (1998) *Constructing Death: The Sociology of Dying and Bereavement*, Cambridge: Cambridge University Press.

Shildrick, M. (1997) *Leaky Bodies and Boundaries: Feminism, Postmodernism and (Bio)Ethics*, London: Routledge.

Taylor, B. (1993) 'Unconsciousness and society: the sociology of sleep', *International Journal of Politics, Culture and Society*, 6, 3: 463–71.

Van Gennep, A. (1960/1909) *Rites of Passage*, Chicago: Chicago University Press.

Walter, T. (1995) *The Revival of Death*, London: Routledge.

Williams, S.J. (2002) 'Sleep, health and society: sociological reflections on the dormant society', *Health*, 6, 2: 179–200.

Part IV

Technologizing/
medicalizing biology

A Brave New World?

14 Investing in mothering

Reproduction, sex selective technologies and biological capital in an Indian case study

Marsha Henry

Introduction

Within recent sociological writing on health and illness there has been a renewed interest in the biological body and a genuine desire to analyse biology (a discipline within which there are many different approaches) in non-reductionist ways within sociological fields (Birke 1999). However, until more recently sociological writing on reproductive technologies has only briefly touched on biological issues, with its dominant focus on criticizing cultural and social myths that posit pregnancy and motherhood as a woman's 'natural' destiny. Within this vast literature, selective reproductive technologies have been given substantial attention by feminists (e.g. Birke *et al.* 1990; Rapp 1999). In particular, there has been widespread criticism of the use of testing for the purposes of pre-sex selection and sex-selective abortions (SSAs) as well as other diagnostic processes that label embryos and foetuses as either 'defective' or 'desirable' (e.g. Arditti *et al.* 1984; Patel 1988). When reports in the 1980s traced the incidence of widespread abortions of female foetuses and the expansion of prenatal clinics to the city of Mumbai, Indian feminists, activists and scholars began contributing to the debates and challenging sex selective reproductive technologies, arguing against their detrimental effect on the immediate and long-term health and survival of women (Patel 1988; Lingam 1988, 1990; Kishwar 1987). While feminists have played an important role in exposing the differential gender impacts of reproductive technologies, they have also often problematically represented women as passive victims.

In the 1990s feminists attempted to re-write women's experiences of reproductive technologies as neither emancipatory nor oppressive, but as bound up within discursive practices (Farquhar 1996; Hartouni 1997). Much of the discussion has now shifted to focus on the gendered, social and cultural impact of the geneticization of reproductive technologies especially as prenatal technologies have 'eugenic' consequences for a number of already marginalized groups (e.g. disabled people, queer groups). Despite ongoing debates by feminists, biologists, and ethicists, in the majority of these recent responses the use of selective technologies *for the purpose of*

sex selection has been granted little attention. While sex selection technologies in the Indian context gained global attention in the late 1980s
and early 1990s in a variety of literatures, this issue has been generally
marginalized in the feminist re-engagement with reproductive technologies.
In this way, the renewed interest in reproductive technologies and biology
has remained exclusive to the West, and while Benton and Birke have
suggested that sociologists have left the work to the biologists, it might be
further argued that sociologists writing on reproductive technologies have
also let the focus remain Eurocentric.

But earlier writing on prenatal technologies and sex selection in the
Indian context also has its limitations. This body of writing has tended to
under-theorize the importance of the reproductive and biological body for
women themselves and thus warrants a reexamination. Birke has recently
argued that feminist theory needs to 'engage with multiple meanings of
"biology" and of the "biological body"' (Birke 1999: 21). She argues that
the 'biological body' needs to be theorized more fully in order to recognize
both the constraints of the material body and at the same time its openness
to transformation (Birke 1999). While much of the general re-analysis of
reproductive technologies has examined the connections between material
(sometimes biological) bodies and the representation of bodily experiences,
detailed discussions of the ways in which women view sex selective technologies and their biological and reproductive bodies has not been included in
the literature. As India was the focus of much earlier discussions around
sex selective technologies, I return to this context to re-examine how the
biological might be brought back in.

The practice of sex selective abortion in India provides an opportunity to
understand how sex selective technologies have been received and represented
in a non-western context and the ways in which they could be imagined quite
differently. In this chapter, I summarize some feminist views on sex selection
in the Indian context and outline some of the limitations of these perspectives. Then, I suggest that a theoretical approach which understands women
as agents capable of amassing capitals (especially embodied) and using these
resources in tactical bargaining might provide some different opportunities
for conceptualizing the issue of sex selection and how women come to
participate or, equally important, not participate in such practices. I draw
briefly on research from a study conducted in India in 1998 when I interviewed women who did *not* participate in using reproductive technologies
for the purposes of sex selection. In this section, I asses what investments, if
any, women make in their biology and reproductive capacity in relation to
sex selective reproductive technologies. Finally, I ask what contribution can
this discussion make to sociological reflections on biology?

Background

Amniocentesis is a surgical procedure that involves inserting a needle into
the abdomen, withdrawing fluid from the amniotic sac of a pregnant woman,

and analysing the chromosomal material and is often used in screening for sex-linked diseases, such as sickle-cell or thalassemia (Birke *et al.* 1990: 162).[1] Amniocentesis does not determine the sex of the foetus, instead, the testing provides data which trained medical staff can use to predict the sex. This procedure, which is usually conducted in the second trimester, raises a number of potential health concerns including infection from the minor surgical procedure, damage to the foetus, and, if abortion is sought, a physically painful one due to the development of the foetus (Birke *et al.* 1990: 164). The procedure is an inherently invasive one, as it requires obtaining biological material from an internal space in the body through surgical intervention – however, it is also a procedure that requires sufficient laboratory equipment and expertise at reading biological data.

In 1975, the All India Institute of Medical Sciences in Delhi experimented with amniocentesis for detecting genetic abnormalities, and, in subsequent years, studies revealed that the test was being used primarily for determining the sex of a foetus (Lingam 1988; Patel 1988; Gandhi and Shah 1992). After a testing period, scientists and doctors revealed that most of the 11,000 couples who participated in the trials were doing so for the purpose of aborting unwanted female foetuses (Gandhi and Shah 1992: 129). Based on data from a survey of clinics in Mumbai, scholars cited that, out of 8,000 abortions conducted after sex determination tests (SDTs), 7,999 involved female foetuses (Lingam 1990; Gandhi and Shah 1992). The increasing popularity and availability of SDTs became apparent after a study revealed that the number of SDT clinics in Mumbai went up from ten in 1982 to 248 in 1987 (Gandhi and Shah 1992: 130).

In 1984, a broad-based coalition in Mumbai began to lobby the government to enact legislation making sex determination tests illegal. The Forum Against Sex Determination and Sex Pre-Selection (FASDSP) strongly urged the government to ban sex testing, legislating not against abortion, but against the use of amniocentesis for sex selective purposes. In 1988, the state of Maharashtra legislated against sex determination tests and subsequently, in 1994, the Prenatal Diagnostics Techniques Act was passed for the whole of India.

Indian feminist views on sex selective technologies

Indian feminists were quick to respond to the sex selection issue and by the late 1980s and early 1990s there was a substantial body of critical writing challenging the availability and use of sex selection technologies in the Indian context (Kishwar 1987; Patel 1988; Lingam 1990; Gandhi and Shah 1992).[2] These feminist scholars have approached the issue of sex selection through a broader argument against 'patriarchy' – a system which produces conditions that are more favourable to men's survival and well-being than women's and enables violent, discriminatory practices against women and women's bodies.

Indian feminists writing on sex selection have been particularly critical of the institutions of the family and medicine. Madhu Kishwar argues that women in India are 'under tremendous pressure to produce male heirs and not burden the family by producing more than one daughter. A woman who is dependent for her very survival on men in the family is in no position to resist the pressure' (Kishwar 1987: 36). As a result of these pressures and constraints, Kishwar argues that women are forced to use sex selective technologies to obtain a son:

> Since in our [Indian] culture women are expected to subordinate their individual interests to that of the family, it is to be expected that ultimately women themselves see their own interests as indistinguishable from the family's interests, and consequently become actively involved in favouring male children at the cost of daughters, just as they ignore their own health and nutritional needs but seldom those of their husbands.
>
> (Kishwar 1995: 20)

Similarly, Lakshmi Lingam, in criticizing SDT and SSA, challenges the objectifying ideology of motherhood. She is critical of practices that reinforce women's 'procreative role', where, 'by producing a child, the credentials of the man, and more so of the woman, are established' (Lingam 1988: 2). She blames both the family and medicine as oppressive institutions, stating that 'it is the blatant unconstitutional and discriminatory attitude against women held by "technodocs" disregarding medical ethics; and using technologies which are principally meant for the detection of genetic disorders, etc. for detecting the sex of the foetus . . .' (Lingam 1988: 9). She suggests that the ideology of reproductive technologies allows the exploitation of women, for the needs not of women, but of medicine, the state and for international institutions that all have investments in population control (Lingam 1990: 20). Patel also constructs medicine and reproductive technologies as generally exploitative of women by stating that 'this perverse use of modern technology [SDT and SSA] is encouraged and boosted by money-minded private practitioners who are out to make a woman, 'a male-child producing machine' (Patel 1988: 179).

The majority of feminist writing on sex selection practices in the Indian context leaves under-scrutinized, for the most part, the body (and more so the biological body). While the focus of some of the writing is on how medical and technological interventions on women's bodies result in undesirable and fatalistic social conditions for women, some feminists have ignored the ways in which women's lives are already constituted through material, lived bodily praxis – many women actively participate in biomedical and biologically transforming projects. In doing so, feminists have failed to recognize the ways in which women's material bodies are continually written upon and fundamentally transformed by their own decisions and actions (as well as others). The underlying assumption in much of this writing on sex selection in India is that bodies are not purposeful and useful to the individual woman (at least in their biological capacities) but instead are only signifiers of social expectations and cultural 'norms'. I suggest that women's bodies, as embodying biological and reproductive possibilities, are rich sites for women's own investments. In this way, the analysis of SDT and SSA in the Indian context suggests that women's bodies, and thus their biology, are only and always used to the detriment of women themselves. While there are significant financial motives on the part of doctors who encourage SDTs,[3] women's bodies are not merely objects used by medicine and the family. Women, too, have some interest in the multiple uses of their bodies as biological, reproductive and symbolic.

Of course, decisions involving reproductive technologies and family planning are always made within the context of society – where sexual inequalities may mean that sons are seen as more 'valuable' (Patel 1988; Lingam 1990). While the arguments around choice are compelling, the feminist approach continually works on the assumption that women are always and only victims when it comes to reproductive technologies, especially sex selective ones. I suggest another conceptualization; that women make choices as agents, but that these choices are made within the context of familial, social, cultural, and economic conditions of constraint. A narrow understanding of choice excludes the possibility that women seek out technologies as aids to managing their fertility and reproductive life courses and actively using their embodied resources to increase their autonomy. Science and medicine may offer some women control over biological (bodily and reproductive) processes by allowing them to space and pace the number of children they conceive (see Gandhi and Shah 1992 for some examples). While many reproductive technologies have caused women considerable harm and distress, they have not been all detrimental – some have provided women with greater opportunities in the area of reproductive decision-making. In constructing women as passive victims, forced to use SDT, the possibility that women may invest in their biological bodies and reproductive resources and tactically choose to use selective technologies is hidden.

Towards a theory of capital

If some approaches to women's reproductive decision-making are problematic, what models can be used in the context of sex selection? The approach outlined above tends to assume that women are always coerced into participating in sex selection rather than attempt to understand how women view their own reproductive decisions and how they utilize their bodies. As a result, understanding women's own models of subjectivity and identity might provide some insight into why women use, or do not use, sex selective technologies. I suggest that attending to the content and form of women's accounts of reproductive experiences provides a more nuanced picture of what kind of investments women make and how women are able to act even while under constraint.

The concept of 'capital' can be useful for understanding how women are positioned and how they attempt to position themselves in relation to reproductive decisions and sex selection technologies. Bourdieu's notion of capital can be simply summarized as resources that provide benefits to indviduals within a given social field. According to Bourdieu's definitions, capital comes in four principal forms: economic (material and financial), cultural (scarce symbolic goods, titles and skills), social (resources accrued by social relations and membership in particular groups) and symbolic (the effects of any group of capital) (Bourdieu 1986; Skeggs 1997, 2001). I, like others, suggest that although it is most often undervalued, bodily capital is also a utilized resource, at least in some bargaining situations (Wacquant 1995; Skeggs 2001; Monaghan 2002). Both the type of capital and the amount of capital are important, as well as their trajectory in social space – and these capitals are displayed or deployed in a field, a 'structured space of positions' (Bourdieu 1986; Skeggs 2001). Those who enter fields must come with the 'right' forms of capital to be accepted as legitimate. Fields are 'sites of struggles', particularly for legitimacy in arenas where the necessary forms of capital may be shifting and fluid. Within this approach, the individual has a range of possible actions, moves, or positions that can be taken, and various consequences, benefits, losses that will result.

In Wacquant's study of male boxing, he demonstrates that many boxers invest heavily in bodily capital as a means of 'ontological transcendence whereby those who embrace it seek literally to fashion themselves into a new being so as to escape the common determinations that bear upon them and the social insignificance to which these determinations condemn them' (Wacquant 1995; p. 8 on-line version). In his study, Wacquant reaches the conclusion that boxers do not merely engage in the bodily trade of boxing as a 'vicious and debasing form of submission to external constraints and material necessity', but rather they invest in their bodies to carve out 'a margin of autonomy from their oppressive circumstances and for expressing their ability to seize their own fate and remake it in accordance with their inner wishes' (p. 9 on-line version). I propose that women who use (or do not use) sex selective technologies might be imagined in similar ways. Women might invest not just in their bodies, but in physiological capacities and processes as a means of making and fashioning a particular kind of mother-hood, femininity, etc. While many might question what exactly constitutes women's 'inner wishes' when it comes to sex selection, Wacquant's analysis of investments in the body (as transformative) suggests that embodied practices that others see as 'painful', might be understood as a form of resistance (Wacquant 1995).

Beverley Skeggs, in appropriating Bourdieu's ideas, argues that femin-inity can be a form of capital and that women's capital holdings may enable them to resist gendered and class oppression, even while they are simultaneously constrained by the forms of capital they lack (Skeggs 1997). Terry Lovell, too, utilizes the work of Bourdieu to rethink the way in which women position themselves as subjects within the social field, where she suggests that Bourdieu's approach to women is limiting (Lovell 1999: 16). According to Lovell, Bourdieu's account of women's positioning assumes that 'women are socially produced as objects, not subjects, but objects of value whose strategic circulation plays a key role in the maintenance and enhancement of the symbolic capital held by men' (Lovell 1999: 18). She takes Bourdieu to task on his theory of positioning and position-taking and counters his idea that women are primarily 'social objects, repositories of value and of capital, who circulate between the men and who serve certain important functions in the capital accumulation strategies of men, families and kinship groups' and suggests that women may strategically position themselves in an array of possible positions:

> Even if it is conceded that 'women universally have the social status of objects' it must remain questionable whether women universally and exclusively *position* themselves as objects, and indeed whether it is even possible to do so unequivocally.
>
> (Lovell 1999: 16–18)

She suggests that feminist theorists might consider how women are enabled, or not enabled, by the capital accumulation strategies of others and asks '[w]hat kinds of "investment strategies" do women follow in what circumstances? How may the existence of women as objects: as repositories of capital for someone else, be curtailing or enabling in terms of their simultaneous existence as capital-accumulating subjects?' (Lovell 1999: 23). For example, she argues that women have often tactically used notions of a 'caring self' as a means by which to accrue other forms of capital for themselves, for gaining independence, rather than for merely transferring such capitals back into the family (Lovell 1999: 28).

Bina Agarwal's work on gender relations provides a further basis for conceptualising how women may exercise agency, even under constraint, and helps to locate these ideas in an Indian context. She argues that gender relations are 'characterised by both cooperation and conflict and that their hierarchical character . . . is maintained or changed through a process of (implicit or explicit) contestation or bargaining between actors with differential access to economic, political and social power' (Agarwal 1994: 52). Agarwal challenges models where the family is not seen as an arena of bargaining and where all decisions are assumed to be made by consensus or by one member, normally the household head. In addition, she criticizes the assumption that women always act in the interest of others, such as family members, and argues that women may act in their own self-interest and therefore have a concept of well-being that is not entirely connected with others. Furthermore, she suggests that women may participate in practices that disadvantage them, but that they may not recognize these 'practices as legitimate; their perceptions are better revealed in their many covert forms of resistance to gender inequities' (Agarwal 1994: 57). For example, women who prefer sons may be strategically complying in order to gain better outcomes of bargaining in other arenas:

> [G]iven prevailing male advantage in labour markets and property rights and women's need for male mediation in the community, a woman may expend most care on her sons because she sees them as her best investment for her future, rather than because she does not perceive her own interests and has bought into the dominant male ideology, or even out of altruism: after all, would altruism be so obviously sex-selective?
>
> (Agarwal 1994: 434)

Similarly, Gail Weiss argues that women may participate in sex selective practices as a strategy for improving bargaining positions:

> A woman may possibly go along with her family's decision to pursue SSA [sex-selective abortion] in order to win concessions that will improve and strengthen her own position within the family unit on a long-term basis as well as the socioeconomic status of the family within the community.
>
> (Weiss 1995: 210)

In this way, women may actively collude with patriarchal expectations as part of a bargain and a strategy of resistance.

These models of gender relations allow women to be conceived of as actors who come to various bargaining 'tables' with different experiences and forms of capital. This approach challenges previous understandings of SSA as it encourages the conceptualizing of women as agents (rather than as passive receptors), albeit constrained in particular ways. In thinking about the different investment and accumulation strategies that may be available to women, I propose that women may also invest in the biological and reproductive potential to reproduce sons, enabled through the use of selective technologies as a way of gaining more autonomy within their families and society. However, I propose that women rely on the interface between their biological resources and available technologies, only when they have fewer forms of 'legitimate' capital to use in bargaining situations.

Mothering capitals: investing in the body, biology and reproduction

> Children may be the only or the best hope for the resources needed for medium and long term survival, in the absence of social provision for dependency . . . [e]veryone has some stake, individual or social, in

women's bodies as reproductive bodies. Babies make the world go round. They are not dispensable at present . . . [w]hether or not women 'invest' in their bodies as reproductive bodies is something that might best be explored by looking at those women who have been able to choose not to do so . . . [i]n what circumstances is it possible to refuse this form of corporeal investment?

(Lovell 1999: 24)

Based on a 'capital' approach to women's identity, subjectivity and agency, along with my research findings from a study conducted in India in 1998,[4] I suggest that women make reproductive decisions based on their accumulation of different forms of capital (Henry 2000). I take the idea of bodily capital further by suggesting that for women it consists of mothering capital of which there a number of sub-capitals including 'biological' and 'reproductive' capitals (others include health: see Blaxter, Chapter 5 in this collection). These capitals are introduced here as a way to understand how women invest in their own biological and (thus social) mothering resources – this is especially the case when all other forms of 'legitimate' capital are diminished or unavailable. Here, I suggest that women may see their bodies not only as objects for others, but also as useful and purposeful bodies for their own use and for the maximization of autonomy.

None of the women who participated in the study admitting to using amniocentesis for the purposes of sex selection, but some felt that having sons had significantly improved their lives and in many cases had increased their bargaining power with family members. Deniz Kandiyoti argues that in classic patriarchy 'women have access to the only type of labour power they can control, and to old-age security, through their married sons. Since sons are a woman's most critical resource, ensuring their life-long loyalty is an enduring preoccupation' (Kandiyoti 1997: 89/90). One woman I interviewed revealed that her grown son served as valuable resource in public spaces:

> When my husband was alive and my sons living here it was good for me. As the mother of three sons, I was the envy of many of my friends and others in the neighbourhood . . . when you have a son [sic] and even better if you have more. . . . When I was nervous that someone would take advantage of me, just the presence of my sons would prevent them from cheating me. (Romila)

(Henry 2000)

For Romila,[5] sons were a critical resource as she did not have the educational qualifications that she believed would have offered her a 'better life' and less 'dependency' (Henry 2000). Another participant, who was a Muslim woman living in a predominantly Christian and Hindu neighbourhood, suggested that she was able to amass more 'legitimate' forms of capital by giving birth to a son and therefore achieving respectability. Rishma was able to obtain a Master's, and then a Doctoral, degree after giving birth to two sons and used the fact that she had 'produced' sons in bargaining with her spouse to discontinue having children and to return to full-time study. In stating her preferences Rishma said '[e]verybody wants sons. They are much easier to take care of. That is why I was able to go back to school. A girl could not have been left on her own' (Rishma) (Henry 2000). For Rishma, without having the right form of capital to allow her to have religious respectability (she was from a minority religious group), sons proved a valuable asset. But other women in the study demonstrated that while they preferred sons, they did not necessarily rely on their sons for respectability or bargaining. For example, one participant said that she 'had a preference for sons . . . all the women secretly envy you' but that 'whether you have a son or not . . . these things are just neighbourhood gossip and in the end it is about the whole family, not just the sons' (Grace) (Henry 2000). Grace, an upper-caste, middle-class Christian woman, was able to rely on her abundance of educational and economic capital in bargaining, rather than depend upon birthing sons. She could rely less on her body as a resource and depend less on her biological potential to produce male children.

While none of the women interviewed claimed to have used amniocentesis for the purpose of sex selection, they demonstrated that, for women who have less 'legitimate' capital, sons are important in negotiating for autonomy as well as access to resources. Sons were a form of capital in the absence of educational, social or personal economic capital and proved to be integral in negotiations for a variety of resources. Sons also provided the means for women to tactically position themselves as active subjects. In this way, their accounts help to understand the processes by which some women participate in a culture of preferring sons and sex selection practices and show how women attempt to position themselves as agents even within highly constrained circumstances and in the absence of sufficient capital resources.

While the women I interviewed had not participated in using reproductive technologies to ensure the birth of sons, I propose that women who do participate in using SDT for sex selective purposes may be doing so through a conscious investment in their mothering capitals. They may be relying on their biological material (however socially constructed this is) as a means of achieving their own 'inner wish' to gain autonomy and transform their lives. When I discuss biology and motherhood here, I do not mean to reduce motherhood to a mere 'physiological function, a biologically rooted, passive . . . literally mindless . . . state of being'; 'this definition naturalises motherhood and suggests that motherhood does not depend upon a woman's consciousness for its development . . .' (Hartouni 1997: 29). Like Hartouni, I argue that motherhood is a conscious activity and the interviews led me to conclude that women's participation in using sex selective technologies may not derive from 'false consciousness' or even familial coercion, but may be because they are unable to draw on 'valid' forms of capital and thus choose to rely on their biological, reproductive and thus mothering resources.

Conclusion

Sociological reflections on biology must not only consider how the biological body is imagined and experienced differently across genders, but how women may see and use their biological bodies as a form of capital. While many feminists have shown that reproductive technologies are deeply embedded within local and national social frameworks, they have neglected to look at the ways in which women may use their bodily capital to their own benefit. If we are able to conceptualize women as agents in relation to sex selection, perhaps we can imagine that women may rely on their physical resources as a means to increasing their respectability, autonomy and bargaining power within their families and society. Based on previous research that I have conducted, I found that some women are less likely to invest in their bodily capital and biological resources to produce sons when they had a variety and abundance of 'legitimate' forms of capital (Henry 2000). The women's accounts challenge the model of female subjectivity generally relied upon in some of the literature on sex selection, which tends to suggest that some women passively accept the terms of 'patriarchy' (Patel 1988; Lingam 1990). Problematically, however, few feminists writing on sex selection have acknowledged the ways in which women may use their biological and reproductive 'capital' and available reproductive technologies to increase autonomy and agency in their lives. Furthermore, I argue that women do not necessarily take up either their prescribed biological or social role as mothers in purely conformist and 'normalized' ways. Understanding how and why women strategically invest in their biological bodies and in the social and biological role of motherhood, may provide far more insight into why women do or do not use sex selective reproductive technologies.

While I have suggested that women might use their mothering capitals in the absence of other forms of capital, I am not suggesting that this is always a good thing, especially in relation to sex selection practices. I do not believe that women's engagement with amniocentesis for the purposes of aborting female foetuses will result in any improvement in the status of women or that it has no negative biological impacts. The process of amniocentesis does produce (minimally) a significant risk to women's health and well-being – but sex selection technologies are by no means the only technologies that may have biologically hazardous consequences.[6] What I do propose is that if we imagine women's involvement with reproductive technologies in complex ways, we may begin to see opportunities for transforming the circumstances that constrain women from maximizing 'choice'. Legislation banning selective technologies will discourage some, but it will not effectively alter the circumstances of women's lives that lead them to choose investing in their biological and reproductive bodies.

Acknowledgements

Thanks to Simon Williams, Gillian Bendelow and Lynda Birke for useful feedback, patience and encouragement. In addition, many thanks to Joanna Liddle and Torry Lowell for introducing me to the work of the late Pierre Bourdieu.

Notes

1 The sex of the foetus can be determined within a week and there is a 95–97 per cent accuracy rate (Patel 1988: 179). Sex selective technologies also include aryuvedic methods, ultrasound, chorionic villi sampling and pre-implantation screening, however, in this chapter I generally refer to amniocentesis when discussing sex selective technologies (unless otherwise noted).
2 It is mostly Indian-based feminists that have written on sex selection in the Indian context and I refer to this body of writing unless otherwise indicated.
3 In India where there is no state health/welfare provision, the cost of using of selective technologies is borne by individual users.
4 In 1998, I conducted interviews with women in various states of south India on the issues of sex preferences and sex selection practices. My study consisted of 29, mostly married, middle-class, upper- or upwardly mobile caste, university-educated, Hindu women.
5 Pseudonyms have been used to protect the identity of research participants.
6 For peasant and working-class women, occupational and environmental hazards might pose just as significant a risk to women's bodies and reproductive life-courses.

References

Agarwal, Bina (1994) *A Field Of One's Own: Gender And Land Rights In South Asia*, Cambridge: Cambridge University Press.

Arditti, Rita, Renate Duelli-Klein and Shelley Minden (eds) (1984) *Test-Tube Women: What Future for Motherhood?*, London: Pandora.

Benton, T. (1991) 'Biology and social science: why the return of the repressed should be given a (cautious) welcome', *Sociology*, 25: 1–29.

Birke, L. (1999) *Feminism and the Biological Body*, Edinburgh: Edinburgh University Press.

Birke, Lynda, Sue Himmelweit and Gail Vines (1990) *Tomorrow's Child: Reproductive Technologies in the 1990s*, London: Virago Press.

Bourdieu, Pierre (1986) 'Forms of capital', in John G. Richardson (ed.) *Handbook of Theory and Research for the Sociology of Education*, New York: Greenwood Press.

Farquhar, Dion (1996) *Other Machine: Discourse and Reproductive Technologies*, London: Routledge.

Gandhi, Nandita and Shah, Nandita (1992) *The Issues at Stake: Theory and Practice in the Contemporary Women's Movement in India*, New Delhi: Kali for Women.

Hartouni, Val (1997) *Cultural Conceptions: On Reproductive Technologies and the Remaking of Life*, Minneapolis: University of Minnesota Press.

Henry, Marsha (2000) 'Gendered selections: representations of women, sex preferences and sex selective practices in India', unpublished Doctoral thesis, University of Warwick.

Kandiyoti, Deniz (1997) 'Bargaining with patriarchy', in Nalini Visvanathan, Lynn Duggan, Laurie Nisonoff and Nancy Wiegersma (eds) *The Women and Development Reader*, London: Zed Books, pp. 86–91.

Kishwar, Madhu (1987) 'The continuing deficit of women in India and the impact of amniocentesis', in Gena Corea, Jalna Hanmer and Renate Duelli-Klein (eds) *Man-made Women: How Reproductive Technologies Affect Women*, Bloomington, Indiana: Indiana University Press, pp. 30–37.

Kishwar, Madhu (1995) 'When daughters are unwanted: sex determination tests in India', *Manushi*, **86**: 15–22.

Lingam, Lakshmi (1988) *Made in India: A Dossier on the New Reproductive Technologies*, Bombay: Women's Studies Unit, Tata Institute of Social Sciences, pp. 1–9.

Lingam, Lakshmi (1990) 'New reproductive technologies in India: a print media analysis', *Issues in Reproductive and Genetic Engineering*, **3**, 1: 13–21.

Lovell, Terry (1999) '"If I was a lad, do you think I would say I'm a lass?": Bourdieu and the feminist project', unpublished paper, pp. 1–40.

Monaghan, L.F. (2002) 'Hard men, shop boys and others: embodying competence in a masculinist occupation', *The Sociological Review*, **50**, 3: 334–55.

Patel, Vibhuti (1988) 'Sex determination and sex preselection tests: abuse of advanced technologies', in Rehanna Ghadially (ed.) *Women in Indian Society*, London: Sage, pp. 178–85.

Rapp, Rayna (1999) *Testing Women, Testing the Fetus: the Social Impact of Amniocentesis in America*, London: Routledge.

Skeggs, Beverley (1997) *Formations of Class and Gender*, London: Sage.

Skeggs, Beverley (2001) 'The toilet paper: femininity, class and mis-recognition', *Women's Studies International Forum*, **24**, 3/4: 295–307.

Wacquant, L.J.D. (1995) 'The pugilistic point of view: how boxers think and feel about their trade', *Theory and Society*, **24**: 489–535; http://sociology.berkeley.edu/public_sociology/Wacquant.pdf

Weiss, Gail (1995) 'Sex-selective abortion: a relational approach', *Hypatia*, **12**, 3: 202–17.

15 Rights, risks and responsibilities

New genetics and disabled people

Tom Shakespeare

This chapter explores personal, political and sociological dimensions of biology and disability, focusing on genetics in particular. In my work with Newcastle's Policy, Ethics and Life Sciences Research Institute, I spend much of my time talking to schools and community groups about the Human Genome Project, and the social and ethical issues it raises. On these occasions I speak as a sociologist, and a science communicator, and a bioethicist, but also as a member of the disability movement, and as someone with a genetic condition. These different identities and perspectives will shape this chapter.

It is difficult, discussing these issues, to separate the personal and the intellectual. At the beginning of my career, I was drawn to sociology because it offered me ways of understanding my experience as a disabled person. I have subsequently contributed to the expansion of disability studies, an area of the social sciences and the humanities which has drawn on the work of feminist and lesbian and gay theorists, among others, to re-conceptualize disability. But as a child, I was always fascinated by biology. My father was a general practitioner, and I spent many hours reading his old textbooks of anatomy and physiology. At school I excelled in biology, but found maths, physics and chemistry tedious and difficult, and so I turned away from the sciences. Now that I work on the social and ethical aspects of biology, I am back in familiar territory. But since those early years, I have had two children, who also share my impairment. And, beginning as a student, I have developed a political consciousness as a disabled person.

This chapter explores changing ways of thinking about disability, and how genetics may turn back the clock. It looks at the question of prenatal selection, and the issues of eugenics, risk and responsibility which come into that debate. Finally, the chapter ends with a broader discussion about how genetics has the power to expand the disability category by destabilizing the non-disabled identity.

From impairment to disability

Starting with the work of the Union of the Physically Impaired Against Segregation in the 1970s, and continuing with the work of Vic Finkelstein

(1980) and Mike Oliver (1990), disabled activists and academics – who can be described in Gramsci's terms as 'organic intellectuals' – have redefined the disability experience. The traditional definition of disability centres on the biological deficit which disabled people experience – the limitation of body or mind. People with particular impairments are defined in terms of what is 'wrong' with them, and which 'normal' activities or functions they cannot perform. In this account, disability and disadvantage is a straight-forward consequence of having an impairment. This 'medical model' has dominated thinking in the health and welfare field up until recent years. But explaining the exclusion and disadvantage which disabled people experi-ence in terms of their own inadequacies seems to be like 'blaming the victim'. It is unhelpful to reduce disablement to an individual, biological attribute, when many disabled people identify collectively as members of a minority group facing oppression in society, rather than as a group of individuals deviating from the bodily 'norm'.

The political movement of disabled people has rejected the 'medical model' and substituted a 'social model' in its place. Just as early feminist writers made a distinction between sex (male and female) and gender (the social experience of being a man or woman), so disabled people distinguish impairment (a bodily difference) and disability (the way that society treats people with impairments). The problem is not having an impairment, but being disabled by society. Just as men and women have been regarded differently at different stages of history, so the status and identity of disabled people has changed in different contexts. Of course, this does not have to imply that disabled people form one unitary group: there are as many different ways of being a disabled person as there are of being a woman.

The effect of the changed definition is to relocate the issue to the social and structural level. The problem of disability might include factors such as: employment discrimination; lack of access to transport facilities or to housing or to public space; poverty; increased exposure to physical and sexual abuse; prejudiced cultural representations; interpersonal attitudes such as paternalism, intrusive curiosity and ridicule, or outright hostility. The growing numbers of researchers in the field of disability studies have found substantial empirical evidence for each of these problems.

Clearly, the problem of disability is more to do with social and cultural processes than it is to do with biology. This is further demonstrated by the way in which the experience of people with particular impairments differs depending on the country in which they find themselves: the United States, thanks to the Americans with Disabilities Act of 1990, is now a less disabling environment than, say, the United Kingdom. Equally Newcastle, with a largely accessible Metro, is less disabling for travellers with impair-ments than London, with a largely inaccessible Tube. Moreover, access to wealth and privilege reduces the difficulties of impairment: high status white males such as President F.D. Roosevelt and Professor Stephen Hawking and actor Christopher Reeve can enjoy a quality of life which paralysed people in different social situations can only dream of.

Disabled activists have flexed their 'sociological imaginations' by making private problems into public issues (Wright Mills 1959). They have used a sociological approach to redefine their experience, and identify the barriers which they want removed. But towards the end of the 1990s, some disabled feminists and others became increasingly disenchanted with the social model because of its failure to confront physical impairment and its overriding stress on structural barriers. As Liz Crow suggests:

> Sometimes it feels as if this focus is so absolute that we are in danger of assuming that impairment has no part at all in determining our experiences. Instead of tackling the contradictions and complexities of our experiences head on, we have chosen in our campaigns to present impairment as irrelevant, neutral and, sometimes, positive, but never, ever as the quandary it really is.
>
> (Crow 1996: 208)

While Liz Crow and colleagues like Jenny Morris and Liz French do not deny that society causes many problems, they also argue that bodies may cause difficulties, and they want any theory of disability to take account of the physical dimension to their lives. They suggest that in developing a social and structural analysis, the disability movement has omitted a key facet of their experience. In effect, they are recapitulating moves within the history of feminist thought, which opened up spaces to explore the concept of difference. Within the disability community the debate on the social model continues to rage. Materialist disability studies theorists refuse to dilute or revise the original social model formulation. Others attempt to develop more theoretically sophisticated theoretical bases for understanding disability (Shakespeare and Watson 2001).

Conditions such as autism, Chronic Fatigue Syndrome, and Attention Deficit Hyperactivity Disorder both challenge the polar divide between the biological and the social, and demand a richer conceptualization than the medical model versus social model debate, moving away from 'either/or' towards 'both/and' explanations (Shakespeare and Erickson 2000). Such approaches have to be able to include the role of impaired bodies, as well as the environmental and social barriers, but need to avoid 'naturalizing' disability. The work of post-structuralist and post-modernist social theorists such as Judith Butler is beginning to influence the second stage of the development of disability studies (Corker and Shakespeare 2002).

Naming and knowing disability

The Human Genome Project (HGP) and the cultural feeding frenzy which surrounds it (Nelkin and Lindee 1995) inevitably impinges onto the academic and political debate surrounding disability. The 'headline' response from disabled people has centred on accusations of eugenics and Nazi extermination plots (Shakespeare 1999), and this debate will be explored below. But, at a sociological and conceptual level, the development of new powers of genetic diagnosis has important implications for the process of naming and understanding disease. While much of the reductionism and determinism of the HGP is undoubtedly over-hyped, it is both the cultural reception of the science, as well as the biology itself, which contributes to new ways of conceptualising disability.

The HGP issues an implicit challenge to the disability movement, and the identity of many disabled individuals. As argued earlier, the social model of disability has made headway and has contributed to the removal of social barriers and the passing of anti-discrimination legislation in many countries. But the contemporary tendency to see social issues in medical terms and medical issues in genetic terms risks redefining disability as an individual pathology once again, and reducing the complexity of disability to the stark simplicity of DNA mutations. Hence the views of people such as David Colley, a disabled activist I interviewed for a radio documentary:

> Disabled people have everything to fear from the new genetics. At worst it's our very existence, that we'll be eliminated simply as genetic spelling mistakes. But even at best we will be reinforced as biological abnormalities, as defective human beings.

The re-biologization of disability is part of a wider cultural process, where genetics impacts on our understandings of difference and disadvantage in general terms. Abby Lippman (1992) has coined the term 'geneticization' to explain this: complex social and economic problems may be reduced to genetic explanations and responses, because individual medical explanations are compelling and perhaps even comforting, and because there are profits to be made in genetic manipulation, whereas there are costs involved in social investment. Similarly Erik Parens has argued that:

> Some new means that work on our bodies instead of our environments may incline us to ignore the complex social roots of the suffering of individuals. The easier it is to change our bodies to relieve our suffering, the less inclined we may be to try to change the complex social conditions that produce that suffering.
>
> (Parens 1998: 53)

However, there is a counter argument, which is that in some cases, to find organic and even genetic causes of conditions may be welcomed by people experiencing them. For example, when Dean Hamer claimed to have found a marker associated with homosexuality at Xq28, some gay groups and individuals in the United States welcomed the development, believing that it demonstrated that sexuality was not a lifestyle choice, but an innate property of individuals, perhaps even one resulting from divine creation. Similarly, if behaviours such as alcoholism and other addictions are redefined as disabilities, then some blame may be removed from those succumbing to these problems. In the case of autism, the move from blaming psychodynamic factors arising from poor parenting towards blaming organic brain dysfunction, possibly of ultimately genetic origin, has been very liberating from families, who no longer feel that they have failed their children, and may even feel that there is a hope of cures in the long term.

Within the disability community, there is no consensus on genetics. There are many genetic support groups whose members are very committed to the genetic project, for example the Cystic Fibrosis Trust and the Friedriech's Ataxia Association. Medical self-help groups like this are often founded by or dominated by medical professionals and scientists. Their conferences are an uneasy compromise between the self-empowerment agenda of people affected by conditions, and the research and therapy agenda of many scientists and doctors, not to mention the product and profit agenda of the pharmaceutical companies which often sponsor such events. The contested role of the Genetics Interest Group (GIG), Britain's alliance of genetic support groups, is an interesting example of this. While they claim to speak for all those affected by genetic conditions, their message is diametrically opposed to the generally anti-genetics campaign of the disability movement. GIG often act as cheer-leaders for the genetics profession and the genetics industry, and lobbied hard for the European Union to legislate in favour of patenting of genes.

The debate around the nature of disability and the morality of genetics have collided at the beginning of the twenty-first century, creating a situation of complexity and confusion. The project to make disability studies take on board the role of impairment is taking place in a cultural arena in which impairment and disease are being reduced to genetic conditions, and in which genetics itself is represented as being innate, unchangeable and deterministic. This sense is fuelled by media coverage, but also by the irresponsible pronouncements of scientists such as James Watson who stated many years ago, 'in the past, men thought their fate was written in the stars. Now we know, in large part, it is written in the genes.' This sort of fatalism has implications not only for many disabled people, but also for those with degenerative conditions, and those who are diagnosed with late onset disorders or a susceptibility to later disease. As psychologist Theresa Marteau has written: 'There is a strong representation in Western cultures that the term genetic in relation to health and illness is synonymous with something fixed or unchanging' (Marteau and Senior 1997).

Marteau's research shows that when a screening test for inherited risk of heart disease was seen as detecting a genetic problem, the condition was perceived as less controllable. But when the test was described in terms of raised cholesterol, participants perceived the condition as dietary in origin and hence more controllable.

New ways of mapping and understanding disability have to take into account the biological–social continuum, but also the axis ranging from 'fixed and immutable' through to 'dynamic and environmentally influenced'. In practice, everything is always entirely biological and entirely social, and neither the biological nor the environmental factors can be removed from the equation (Shakespeare and Erickson 2000).

Prevention and responsibility

Mention of those who might welcome the medicalization of their experience points to a broader question about the ways in which the redefinition of difference and disability has implications for prevention and responsibility. These issues are particularly acute in the prenatal situation. Disabled activists have reacted forcefully to the HGP, because they claim it will enable doctors to conduct a 'search and destroy mission' against disabled people on behalf of society. On this account, the HGP does not just redefine disability, it threatens to eliminate it. Moreover, transgender activists have argued that cytogenetic screening also has the effect of eliminating foetuses with sex chromosome abnormalities, who may be potential transgender people. Finally, if homosexuality is linked to particular gene alleles either in scientific evidence or the popular imagination, then those citizens who find gay and lesbian lifestyles abhorrent may have the option of screening their pregnancies to avoid birth of possibly affected foetuses. All of this adds fuel to a conspiracy theory of genetic screening as resurgent eugenics.

But as many have argued, the situation in prenatal screening is more complex than this suggests. While screening programmes need to be interrogated (Clarke 1991), the role of parents in demanding and deciding on testing and termination cannot be ignored (Rapp 2000). The rhetoric of individual choice conceals a more complex reality, in which full information, non-directive counselling and informed consent are rarely available, but nevertheless it would be wrong to maintain that parents are not exercising agency, or that the medical profession are forcing people to terminate affected pregnancies (Shakespeare 1998). Moreover, genetics will not eliminate disability: while 1 per cent of births are affected by congenital impairment, one in eight of the population are disabled. A more grounded and nuanced account of the potential impact of screening technology is needed.

Disabled people are not the only interest group in the screening scenario. The development of knowledge and technology changes the experience of pregnancy (Rothman 1988, 1998). The development of more screening and diagnostic tests means that people have the responsibility of deciding whether to use tests to discover characteristics of their foetus, and if something is discovered, the difficulty of having to decide what to do. This adds to the stress and anxiety of pregnancy for everyone, not just the tiny proportion in whom a genetic condition is diagnosed.

Table 15.1 Views of parents on prenatal tests for restricted growth

Would *want a test*	Would *not want a test*	Not *sure*
32.5%	60%	7.5%

In 1999, I surveyed members of the UK restricted growth association. I asked parents of people with restricted growth conditions whether they would have had a test in pregnancy – no genetic tests have been available until recently (*n* = 30).

A typical comment of one parent, asked whether she would have had a test was:

> Not now because we had him and we loved him immediately but had we have known via a test I honestly don't know whether we would have considered termination. All I can say is I'm glad we didn't know otherwise who knows.

Of course, it needs to be pointed out that in many cases the predictions made by technologies such as ultrasound are uncertain. Soft signs may indicate a serious abnormality, or they may be a passing problem, or an artefact of the scanning technique. Raised levels of a hormone in the blood may indicate Downs syndrome, or may be a false positive. A chromosomal abnormality may have no phenotypic effects, or may have varying phenotypic effects. In all of these situations, anxiety is inevitably raised, but there are no clear answers as to what parents should do, and of what their responsibility to do the best for their potential child consists.

Even where there is a clear diagnosis, the major difficulty is to decide what to do with that information. Does responsibility for a potential child mean in some cases deciding not to have that child? Rayna Rapp argues, in the context of amniocentesis, that 'this technology turns every user into a moral philosopher, as she engages her fears and fantasies of the limits of mothering a foetus with a disability' (2000: 128).

Contrary to the professional bioethicists (Buchanan *et al.* 2000), I argue that there are few right answers to the dilemma facing prospective parents. In most cases, it must depend on the circumstances, the characteristics, and the moral values of the prospective parents. We know that the psychological sequelae of termination of wanted pregnancies on the grounds of foetal abnormality can be traumatic and considerable. Neither outcome is free of grief or difficulty. Medical advisers should give full and balanced information, and support prospective parents to make the decision which is right for them, in the context of a society which is welcoming of disabled people and supportive of disabled people's rights. To do otherwise, is to move back towards the eugenic abuses of the past.

Yet it can be argued that one of the impacts of genetics has been to increase personal responsibility for having disabled children and to pave the way for blame being accorded to parents who exercise their choice not to use these screening technologies, or not to terminate pregnancies. As illustration of this way of thinking, Professor Bob Edwards, one of the two pioneers who enabled the birth of the first test tube baby in 1988, said at a recent embryology conference: 'In the future, it will be a sin to have a disabled baby.'

Bruce Jennings suggests that prenatal genetic testing shapes choice by making everything into a choice. Furthermore, he argues,

> There is a subtle cultural difference between, on the one hand, the kind of sympathy we give when someone receives sudden bad news that could not have been known in advance, and, on the other hand, the kind of sympathy we give when someone finds out something awful that could have been known before and could have been altered, albeit at a psychological and moral cost.
>
> (Jennings 2000: 134)

Theresa Marteau and Harriet Drake's research on 'Attribution for disability', suggests that people are inclined to blame parents who have children affected by Downs syndrome:

> both health professionals and lay groups make judgements about women's roles in the birth of children with disabilities. Women who decline the offer of testing are seen as having more control over this outcome, and are attributed more blame for it, than are women who have not been offered tests and also give birth to a child with Downs syndrome.
>
> (Marteau and Drake 1995: 1130)

Of course, an increasing number of women are now offered tests, and most people know that there are tests available, so this response is likely to spread. The condition has moved from being an unfortunate piece of bad luck, to being a blameworthy failure of surveillance and control. There are anecdotes of people facing negative or disbelieving responses from family or friends, because it is believed that Downs is an outcome which can and should be avoided. What happens to the false negative diagnosis here? What happens to the rights of parents to make up their own mind about ethical issues such as termination of pregnancy or quality control of embryos?

The negative reactions of others are only part of the social response to families having disabled children. Also to be considered are the social and economic strains which individuals may have to bear if they decide not to terminate pregnancies. In the future, having a disabled child may be seen as 'elective disability', and welfare or insurance systems may refuse to meet the additional costs of disability. This is again part of the individualization of disability which may be the consequence of genetics. Previously disability was bad luck or karma or part of God's plan. Society compensated individuals for misfortune, and took responsibility to look after its weakest members. Now it may be your fault, and you have to bear the costs because the rest of the community doesn't want to have to pay.

There is a general point that the development of the concept of 'elective disability' makes the reproductive choices of everyone less free. But there is a specific point which relates to the reproductive choices of disabled people, and perhaps also of those minority ethnic communities who have high rates of particular disorders. In the pre-war period, eugenic programmes concentrated on which people were allowed to reproduce. Post-war genetics has concentrated instead on which babies were allowed to proceed to term. If we move towards greater responsibility and blame for reproductive decisions, we might be returning to a world in which certain people are blamed for having particular children because they now have the choice not to have children affected by particular conditions. Many disabled people fear that this might lead to a eugenic backlash against disabled people, who are regarded as irresponsible if they reproduce and knowingly bring a disabled child into the world. When I was a student at King's College, Cambridge, one of the Fellows remarked, on seeing me walk through the college with my baby daughter in her buggy, that it was irresponsible of me to have had a child, knowing it would have a 50 per cent chance of having achondroplasia. Several of my friends voiced similar sentiments. Lots of disabled parents have similar stories to tell.

We are all disabled now

While genetics threatens to reduce the number of disabled people, in practice it expands the disability category, and de-stabilizes the identity of non-disabled people. There are two ways of arguing this point. First, the HGP has demonstrated what was well known to biologists all along. The idea of 'the perfect human genome' is a Platonic fallacy. Within the genetic code there is duplication, redundancy, and quirks from evolutionary history. Moreover, the DNA copying mechanisms are fallible, such that every individual has a genome full of errors – so-called 'spelling mistakes. It has been estimated that everyone, at birth, enters life with approximately 100 mutations which could cause disease. We all carry alleles for four or five recessive conditions within our genomes, which could result in diseases such as cystic fibrosis or sickle cell anaemia in our children. Moreover, the DNA in every cell of our bodies is constantly bombarded with mutagens. Manmade chemicals may be the most controversial, but life-sustaining processes such as sunlight and oxygen are also major hazards. Mutations are happening all the time, and it is DNA repair mechanisms which prevent these being debilitating or even fatal. As we age, the DNA repair mechanisms themselves fail, which is how the physical and mental signs of ageing occur, and often the reason why we ultimately die: one in four people develop cancer by the end (Kirkwood 2000). Genetics, therefore, underlines the fact that human beings are, by our very nature, frail and vulnerable creatures. The dividing line between the minority of people that society defines as disabled or impaired and the non-disabled majority is one of degree, not of kind.

Second, the growing field of predictive genetics raises a whole range of ethical, social and psychological issues relevant to those people who are born non-disabled, but are diagnosed as having late onset genetic conditions such as Huntington's Disease, or having increased susceptibility to conditions such as breast or colon cancer, Alzheimer's and so on (see for example work by Nina Hallowell, Hilary Rose, Anne Kerr and others). This presents an irony. On the one foot, genetics may enable societies to avoid the birth of disabled people, and hence have an impact on the numbers of people with impairment in society, albeit not so significant an impact as some have claimed. But on the other foot, genetics has the power to turn healthy people into disabled people, by virtue of diagnosing future illness or risk of illness in the currently asymptomatic. As soon as the genetic test has returned from the laboratory, a person's identity, future plans and psychological well-being may be completely altered. Suddenly, the population of disabled people increases many times over.

When disability studies or the disability movement use the term 'disabled people', it refers to people who face discrimination and prejudice, not people with illness or impairment. But of course, as we may increasingly see in America and other jurisdictions, people who have genetic susceptibilities may face discrimination from employers, insurance companies and others. So in that sense, as well as in their changed sense of identity, people who are diagnosed with later onset conditions may find themselves having common cause with disabled people.

This is not the place to go into the problems of discrimination in insurance and elsewhere for the new group of people with what could be called hidden or latent disabilities. But it might be worth considering how predictive genetics may change the identity and self-image of people who formerly thought of themselves as healthy and non-disabled. There is a wealth of psychological research on people diagnosed with Huntington's Disease or breast and ovarian cancer that explores the complex and difficult effects which such prediction or risk calculation has on individuals and families. No wonder one commentator has referred to predictive genetic information as 'toxic knowledge'. No wonder that only about 12 per cent of people at risk of HD choose to have a predictive test, or that another study found that only 43 per cent of people offered BRCA1 testing agreed to have it performed. When it comes to the new genetics, sometimes ignorance is bliss.

Conclusion

The impact of genetics on disability is larger than the question of prenatal screening, although that issue raises the deepest ethical dilemmas. The new knowledge generated by the HGP has the power to reconfigure our knowledge of disability in ways which will impact on non-disabled people, as well as disabled people ourselves. As well as medicine, genetics will affect health promotion and social policy. Questions of risk and responsibility, identity and definition are central to the genetics of disability. Alliances between disability studies, medical sociology, and social studies of science are important, so that biology can be understood, rather than rejected. Hearing the voices of people directly affected, and supplementing the molecular or clinical data with robust social science research is vital in order that problems are not ignored, and abuses can be avoided.

References

Buchanan, A., Brock, D., Daniels, N. and Winkler, D. (2000) *From Chance to Choice: Genetics and Justice*, Cambridge: Cambridge University Press.

Clarke, A. (1991) 'Is non-directive genetic counselling possible?', *The Lancet*, 338: 998–1000.

Corker, M. and Shakespeare, T. (2002) *Disability/Postmodernity: Embodying Disability Theory*, London: Continuum.

Crow, L. (1996) 'Including all of our lives: renewing the social model of disability', in Jenny Morris (ed.) *Encounters with Strangers*, London: Women's Press.

Finkelstein, V. (1980) *Attitudes and Disabled People*, New York: World Rehabilitation Fund.

Hallowell, N. (1999) 'Doing the right thing: genetic risk and responsibility', in P. Conrad and J. Gabe (eds) *Sociological Perspectives on the New Genetics*, Oxford: Blackwell.

Jennings, B. (2000) 'Technology and the genetic imaginary', in A. Asch and E. Parens (eds) *Prenatal Testing and Disability Rights*, Georgetown: Georgetown University Press.

Kirkwood, T. (2000) *Time of Our Lives*, London: Phoenix.

Lippman, A. (1992) 'Led (astray) by genetic maps: the cartography of the human genome and health care', *Social Science and Medicine*, 35, 12: 1469–76.

Marteau, T. and Drake, H. (1995) 'Attributions for disability: the influence of genetic screening', *Social Science and Medicine*, 40: 1127–32.

Marteau, T.M. and Senior, V. (1997) 'Illness representations after the human genome project: the perceived role of genes in causing illness', in K.J. Petrie and J.A. Weinman (eds) *Perceptions of Illness and Treatment: Current Psychological Research and Implications*, Amsterdam: Harwood Academic Press, pp. 241–66.

Nelkin, D. and Lindee, M.S. (1995) *The DNA Mystique: The Gene as a Cultural Icon*, New York: W.H. Freeman.

Oliver, M. (1990) *The Politics of Disablement*, Basingstoke: Macmillan.

Parens, E. (1998) *Enhancing Human Traits*, New York: Hastings Center.

Rapp, R. (2000) *Testing the Woman, Testing the Fetus*, New York: Routledge.

Rothman, B.K. (1988) *The Tentative Pregnancy: Amniocentesis and the Sexual Politics of Motherhood*, London: Pandora.

Rothman, B.K. (1998) *Genetic Maps and Human Imaginations: The Limits of Science in Understanding Who We Are*, New York: W.W. Norton.

Shakespeare, T. (1998) 'Choices and rights: eugenics and disability equality', *Disability and Society*, **13**, 5: 665–81.

Shakespeare, T. (1999) 'Losing the plot? Medical and activist discourses of the contemporary genetics and disability', in P. Conrad and J. Gabe (eds) *Sociological Perspectives on the New Genetics*, Oxford: Blackwell.

Shakespeare, T. and Erickson, M. (2000) 'Different strokes: beyond biological determinism and social constructionism', in H. Rose and S. Rose, *Alas Poor Darwin*, London: Jonathan Cape.

Shakespeare, T. and Watson, N. (2001) 'The social model of disability: an outdated ideology?', *Research in Social Science and Disability*, **2**: 9–28.

Wright Mills, C. (1959) *The Sociological Imagination*, Oxford: Oxford University Press.

16 A normal biological process?

Brittle bones, HRT and the patient–doctor encounter

Frances Griffiths and Eileen Green

Breaking brittle bones

> The fracture of a septuagenarian's femur has, within the world of nature, no more significance than the snapping of an autumn leaf from its twig.[1]

Before the surgical fixation of hip fractures was widely available, this 'biological' process of a brittle bone breaking was known as 'the old lady's friend', as through becoming bedridden the elderly woman became prone to bronchopneumonia and death. Where health service resources are sufficient, hip fractures are now actively managed, usually with an operation to pin the fractured bones together. Most elderly people become almost as mobile as they were before the fracture. Thus the biomedical technology used by surgeons has changed the outcome of a fractured hip beyond recognition. It has also transformed the relationship between what could be termed a 'normal biological process' and the experience and expectations of individuals and communities.

The breaking and fixing of brittle bones forms the backdrop for this chapter, anchoring it to the individual experience of a biological process: a bone snaps.[2] It is an example of what has been termed pathological medicine, which built its knowledge base from observation of individual cases, distinguished from surveillance medicine (Armstrong 1995). However, this chapter focuses on surveillance medicine using the example of the use of hormone replacement therapy (HRT) for the prevention of osteoporosis (brittle bones).

The chapter first considers the rise of surveillance medicine, with its use of what we term biostatistics. The use of HRT for the prevention of osteoporosis provides an example of a biomedical technology that is fully contained within surveillance medicine in the sense that there is no pathology present (e.g. bone fracture), but a risk of it in the future. This contrasts with biomedical technology within pathological medicine, such as the surgical fixation of a hip fracture. The chapter then uses the example of HRT used for the prevention of osteoporosis to explore the role of this biomedical technology in biology–society relations. It draws on research data exploring how individuals relate biostatistical evidence to broader health considerations and embodied experiences, within particular social contexts. Finally, the chapter considers the risks and opportunities of 'technologising biology' through biostatistics, within and beyond biomedicine, focusing on the patient–doctor encounter.

HRT, osteoporosis and the rise of biostatistics

Surveying groups or populations in relation to health status, measuring details of the individuals and aggregating the results, developed in the nineteenth century. Foucault (1988) argues that this development was a response to the pressure of population in the industrial cities and the need to regulate the population. The social sciences and medicine he claims responded to this crisis of population with the development of sociology and social medicine, both concerned with the social causes of disease (Turner 1987: 16–17). However, there is a distinction in approach as sociologists are concerned with social interactions and social pressures whereas epidemiology assesses which characteristics of individuals, in aggregate, predispose them to diseases (Nettleton 1995: 163).

Epidemiology forms one arm of what we have termed biostatistics: the use of quantifiable data and statistical methods to understand clinical/biological processes. The collection of population data allowed the development of the concept of what was 'normal' in terms of health or measures of health. Surveillance identified those who deviated from this norm, and became labelled as in need of medical or health-promoting intervention. Future health is medicalized through surveillance intended for prevention. Individuals develop a risk identity, seeing themselves as a person with an apparently measurable risk of disease (Armstrong 1995).

Surveillance and intervention for the prevention of osteoporosis has become a widespread activity in the UK health service over the last fifteen years. Osteoporosis causes no symptoms until the individual fractures a bone. Factors including family history of osteoporosis, low calcium intake in the diet, smoking, taking little weight bearing exercise and having a relatively low body mass index, are associated with an increased risk of osteoporosis, and these have become accepted 'risk factors'. In addition the technology of bone densitometry enabled the density of bone to be measured. HRT is one option for preventing a reduction in bone density. There are questions about the usefulness of bone densitometry for screening. An individual's bone density is compared with that of the normal population and if the individual's bone density is at the low end of this range then they are considered at relatively higher risk of developing osteoporosis in the future and a candidate for intervention. However, having a bone density in the low range is a poor indicator of who will have a fracture (University of Leeds *et al.* 1992).

The twentieth century saw an explosion in the number of pharmaceutical agents. Some of these drugs were clearly effective, such as penicillin for pneumonia. However, therapies for illnesses which vary between individuals and are less predictable than pneumonia needed studies of groups of patients to show overall benefit. By 1960 randomized controlled trials, a research method developed by agriculturalists, were being done on pharmaceutical products and have become the standard method for assessing effectiveness of drugs. Randomized controlled trials, and variations on this research method, form the other arm of what we term biostatistics. HRT has been subject to such trials, which have demonstrated that HRT slows down loss of bone density after the menopause, and may increase it. However, the trials raise concern about side effects, particularly an increase in breast cancer risk.[3]

Both epidemiology and randomized controlled trials collect data on individuals, then aggregate the data to provide results for a population or group of individuals. We use the term biostatistics to distinguish this from the reductionist approach of medical research where data is collected at the level of analysis of, for example, biochemistry. Both biostatistical and reductionist approaches claim prediction of outcome but neither approach is working at the level of analysis of the individual. The case study or case series that gave rise to pathological medicine was at the level of analysis of the individual.

HRT and critiques of the medical model

Critics of the medical model include feminists conducting research on midlife women's health, many of whom argue that menopause must be understood as an embodied experience, which may include 'risk factors', but is not necessarily defined by them. They are also critical of the view of women as primarily defined by their 'natural' bodies which reinforces the dominant cultural representations of women as sexed bodies and a key site for medical intervention and surveillance (e.g. Coney 1991). Feminists argue that central to such debates are images depicting women's bodies as ageing and at risk of failing.[4] However, more recent feminist writers (Harding 1997; Roberts 2002) argue that earlier feminist critics reinforced the idea of women as passive recipients of treatment when many seek technological intervention to improve their lives. Roberts argues for understanding the effects of medical technologies and practices on women's bodies, 'theorized in a way that allows for the possibility of HRT's "working" without exaggerating or underestimating the roles of either the social or the biological in such an event' (2002: 40) (see also Henry, this volume).

Popular discourses about the bodies and behaviour of women at mid-life, based on medical models which by their nature construct midlife women's bodies in universal and undifferentiated terms, suggest a uniformity which masks the impact of difference. However, bodies are historical and social constructions as well as biological entities which are mutable through time and space (Haraway 1991; Bordo 1993). The interview data with midlife women presented below, confirms the importance of contextualizing bodily experience, since their health concerns are closely interwoven with accounts of broader life changes in the middle years and frequently presented within narratives of family, work and caring. Women's accounts of an embodied sense of the menopause reveal a critical reflexivity towards the process of ageing generally and in particular, the risk of developing osteoporosis.[5]

Biostatistics, the individual and their health

Biostatistical medical evidence raises dilemmas for the individual considering their future health and for health professionals. 'Although I can say almost exactly what proportion of smokers will suffer heart attacks in a given period, that doesn't help me at all in telling the smoker sitting in front of me whether he will be one of the ones affected' (Willis 1995: 24). A study of lay attitudes to preventive health showed that people accepted illness as distributed randomly, so although a population study may show statistical risks, within these statistical tendencies 'there lies a more chaotic distribution of illness and death. Some fat smokers really do live till advanced old age, and some svelte joggers really do "fall down dead"' (Davison, Frankel and Smith 1992: 683).

We find a pertinent example of the gap between biostatistical evidence and individual risk calculations in a study of women's attitudes to HRT.[6] Here a focus group of women explored the dilemma:

Mrs G: I would have thought personally it is better to have a shorter better quality of life, it's alright prolonging life but it is quality.

Mrs L: But I think if you invest now and look at yourself rather than just a gynaecological part of you. Look at yourself in a more holistic point of view, and look on it as a good varied diet, exercise and maybe at this stage now invest a little bit in time to keep yourself mobile, and just make sure. Surely that would pay benefits in old age.

Mrs M: I am quite active in different sports and I have got friends, and as soon as they hit 50 they just drift downhill very quick . . . one friend has always been fit and her husband . . . they have just both gone downhill.

Mrs J: Is that because of the physical things? Is it the physical things, have they just rusted up?

Mrs M: . . . arthritis, osteoporosis. You are saying invest for the future, keep fit, she is strict on her diet . . . their whole outlook.

Mrs G: And it has not paid off, has it?

Mrs M: It has still gone wrong.

Mrs H: This is it. At the end of the day nobody knows.

The uncertainty explored by these women is inherent in the very nature of biostatistical evidence. There are other uncertainties for individuals and health professionals concerned with medicine (Fox 2002). Those directly relating to biostatistics include whether they are using the best biostatistical evidence available, whether the best available is robust within its own research paradigm, and whether this evidence applies to the population or group with which they are concerned. The last fifteen years has seen attention given by the medical profession to these uncertainties, particularly through the evidence-based medicine movement. This rigour has brought more certain probability, but it remains probability with its inherent uncertainty. However, certainty is something many midlife women, at least in some circumstances, say they would prefer, as the following extracts from interviews demonstrate:[6]

> I would have to have the test for osteoporosis and have very strong evidence that that was the way I was going then if somebody said HRT would prevent that then I would be prepared to have some sort of therapy to reduce that risk.

> I would (take HRT) if they could prove to me it was going to happen ... they would have to show me ... this is what your bones look like and this is what it should look like, it's starting to happen now but we can prevent it from getting worse.

Scientific medicine had been characterized as something precise and independent of context and persons (Morgan, Calnan and Manning 1991: 33), and this understanding has become incorporated into lay models of illness. Screening programmes contribute to the practices of surveillance and self-surveillance described by Foucault (1988) through which populations are observed, monitored and regulated. Foucault's work has reconceptualized the operation and process of power, viewing it as a non-centralized network that is transmitted through discourses. It is argued that medical power may be maintained through the operationalization of particular medical discourses and sustained through techniques of surveillance. Individuals may contribute to the maintenance of a dominant medical discourse through using the discourse and engaging in its surveillance practices. However, individuals also engage in resisting medicalization through the seeking and processing of information and through scepticism about the relevance of risk reduction for individuals (Williams and Calnan 1996). The women speaking in the quotes above were linking evidence about one technology to their use of another, which may reflect a resistance to a related loss of autonomy: 'Some patients recognised that, as soon as they relied on a doctor's advice, they lost part of their autonomy. One patient even talked of a sort of "dispossession of one's own body"' (Massé and Légaré 2001). This brings us to consider the embodied experience of women in relation to the biostatistics.

Biostatistics and the embodied experience

Individuals consider biostatistics in relation to their embodied experience. These experiences are in the present or past in contrast to a future possible health problem. So, for example, a woman considering HRT for prevention considers the potential for preventing osteoporosis in the future in the context of how she experiences her body at present. Side effects of the intervention may be experienced in the present, influencing women's decisions:[6] 'I'm not prepared to put up with migraine into my mid sixties' (frequency of this woman's migraines increased on HRT); 'If I start off with hormones I may get breast abscesses again'. However, other women in this study found HRT beneficial in reducing their menopausal symptoms and were very happy to continue on it for prevention of osteoporosis. Research has also found that women draw upon informal knowledge based upon the embodied experience of others:[6] 'I wouldn't like to end up with – I think Mother has – is it crushed bones or broken bones in her back?'

Knowledge about risk factors gained from surveillance technology such as bone densitometry may lead to the body being viewed as a source of continual danger to the individual. The technology identifies a weakness: 'creating an ambivalent relationship between body and self' (Kavanagh and Broom 1998: 440).

There are further dilemmas in considering a predicted risk of future health problems alongside the experience of the biological body. The notion of 'medical fallibility' developed by Gorovitz and MacIntyre (1976) as applied to pathological and surveillance medicine summarizes this. They describe the uncertainty of clinical medicine and how this uncertainty is basic to, and inevitable for, this applied science. They suggest: 'Many particulars – salt marches, hurricanes and the higher primates, for example – cannot be understood solely as the sum total of the physical and chemical mechanisms that operate on them' (ibid: 57). In the intervening twenty-six years since this was written, many disciplines including the biological sciences, have developed an understanding of the idea of 'emergent phenomena': that complex systems such as biological systems or social systems have properties that cannot be understood through reductionism, that is through understanding, for example, the biochemistry of a biological system or organism. Gorovitz and MacIntyre go on to suggest that applied scientists, such as doctors, have to understand what is distinctive about each individual, the latter being not fully knowable.

> Since the effect of a given therapeutic intervention on a given patient is always to some extent uncertain no matter how much is known about the general characteristics of interventions of that type, every therapeutic intervention is an experiment in regard to the well-being of that individual patient.
>
> (ibid: 64)

In clinical medicine where an individual seeks help for a health problem, the health professional will try to identify the problem and if possible a cause, then offer treatment. A pertinent example is the scenario sketched at the start of the chapter: an elderly woman suffers pain in her hip, a fracture is diagnosed and the fracture fixed surgically. With the assistance of X-rays fractures are relatively easy to identify. However, if the X-ray did not show a fracture, but some degree of osteoarthritis, the woman and doctor are left with an unclear diagnosis and the question: is the pain due to the arthritis (which may have been present for some time and not, until then, caused any pain) or something else? One way forward is a therapeutic trial of a drug that is usually effective for arthritis pain, and to see what happens for the woman. This is the approach discussed by Gorovitz and MacIntyre above. A therapeutic trial is for that individual. It is not a clinical trial as undertaken by biostatisticians. The latter provides an indication that a drug is safe and effective for a population, not whether it is safe and effective for an individual.

In the case of considering HRT for prevention of osteoporosis, where the woman is well and suffering no symptoms, there is no immediate problem such as pain that demands attention. A woman considering HRT has to weigh up the effect of the HRT on her body, in her own current context, with the possibility of avoiding a fracture in the future. A study on patient–doctor interactions related to the menopause showed that patients expected from their encounter both information and reassurance. 'This reassurance, they hoped would come through information adapted to their personal situation, and be based on the doctor's listening to their individual experience and performing an in-depth analysis of their personal situations' (Massé and Légaré 2001: 53). The authors add that after the encounter with their doctor, the women expressed high levels of satisfaction, suggesting that, for these women they were able to engage with the health professional in considering HRT for their own individual experience, not only in terms of biostatistics. Roberts suggests that decision-making about HRT brings 'the profound complexity of human experience to the fore' (2002: 52). In addition to the issue of the nature of medical evidence outlined above, Roberts points to other factors women include in this decision: genetic disposition, past and current illness/disability, social context and cultural influences, and that these factors may change over time.

After a woman has been screened for osteoporosis, her bone density can be rechecked after a couple of years of therapy. This is a therapeutic trial, as discussed above, but on a very much longer time-scale than trying an intervention for reducing the pain of arthritis: the former is over years, the latter over days or weeks. The longer time-scale adds to the complexity: over such a time period many other factors may influence the health, well-being and bone density of the woman. The following extract from a consultation between a woman and a doctor in a specialist 'bone clinic' after the woman has had her bone density measured,[7] alludes to this complexity.

Doctor: (the test) showed there was no change from the bone density measurements of (five years earlier). . . . So really you're sort of holding your own . . . which is really good because if you look at people as they get older over that period of time, over four years or so, you'd expect them to lose bone density.

Woman: Mmmh, so do you think that's with having the tablets then, it has certainly helped?

Doctor: I think you're sort of holding your own.

Woman: Good . . . so obviously diet's got a lot to do with that as well.

Doctor: Well that may be a part of it and of course lifestyle things as well . . .

Woman: I don't do quite as much (exercise) now, I have retired now . . . but I do try to go swimming and fair bit of walking.

Doctor: Good, that's a good thing . . .

Woman: . . . I'm still on the Didronel, should I continue with it . . .

Doctor: My view would be take a belt and braces approach. By that I mean you've changed your diet, you're doing more exercise, these two things are good for you. . . . I am a little uncertain as to which of these three strands, the diet, the exercise or the medication, is making the difference, but something is.

Biostatistics and an individual's 'social risk'

When considering whether to use bone densitometry and HRT to guard against osteoporosis, women consider social risk as well as health risk. The term social risk is used here to convey the impact of osteoporosis risk identification or use of HRT on women's social selves including how they present themselves to others. Previous research[8] has demonstrated women's concerns about the link between HRT and putting on weight: 'I don't like it . . . I was a size 12 since my early 20s and never changed . . . and suddenly . . . since I have been taking HRT . . . definitely a change . . . this is the first time in my life I have had a bigger size.' It[6,8] has also demonstrated how women discuss embodied experiences such as the return of periods and coping with 'messy' patches when using HRT in terms of social risk. With bone densitometry the women consider the social risks of finding out, or not finding out, about their risk of osteoporosis. These include being labelled as a 'medical risk', being seen as taking or not taking responsibility for their health and being a good role model for their daughters. 'There seems to be this kind of control ethic . . . where we feel as if bodies can be improved no matter what . . . your mind, body . . . anything can be improved by sheer grit and determination . . . and some things can't.'[7,8] Nettleton suggests that 'All citizens have a right and a duty to maintain, contribute to and ensure . . . their health status' (1997: 208). She suggests that 'surveillance must be examined *in relation* to citizenship, not as distinct from it, in order that the paradoxes embedded within prevention can more clearly be seen' (1997: 236).

For the health professional the notion of social risk is also pertinent. It has been suggested that general practitioners were willing to embrace screening and prevention as 'they experience a feeling of personal responsibility for the stroke patient whose hypertension has been unmeasured and uncontrolled and the woman with invasive cervical cancer who has never had a Pap smear', despite evidence questioning the usefulness of some health checks (Mant 1994: 1343). In the last decade certain screening tasks have become part of the contracted service for general practitioners, who are rewarded financially for quality of service provision. Not undertaking prevention activities incurs social risk for general practitioners.

The patient–doctor encounter and the future

The loss of bone density as individuals get older may be seen as a natural biological process. However, this process has been technologized both in 'pathological' medicine and 'surveillance' medicine. The elderly woman with a hip fracture is physically very vulnerable so the use of technology for fixing her hip is difficult to criticize. However, the assessment of risk of osteoporosis and the use of HRT to reduce the loss of bone density can be viewed as medicalization of future health with the implication that the medical enterprise is exerting power over women. A question for this book is: what risks and opportunities does 'technologizing biology' signal, within and beyond biomedicine? We consider this question with reference to the medicalization of women's future health and the role of the patient–doctor encounter in this.

When women actively engage in decisions about HRT and osteoporosis, they use information about their future risk, in biostatistical terms, and integrate it with their embodied and social experiences. These women are doing for themselves what Birke in her chapter suggests we as researchers and academics need to do: 'understanding biology as part and parcel of our socially engaged selves . . . recognising the multiple levels of "our bodies ourselves" '. Birke takes examples from a reductionist approach to understanding biology to explore this. In this chapter, with HRT and osteoporosis as examples, the integration brings a biostatistical understanding of biology to the individual biosocial being. As women engage in these decisions they are exploring and increasing their understanding of the interaction between these 'different levels of analysis' (knowledge about populations or groups, knowledge about individuals) and between the biological and the social. They are developing an understanding of the limits of prediction and the uncertainties inherent in biostatistical evidence. Through this they are rejecting a deterministic understanding of biology and are coping with the realities of uncertainty for our complex biosocial selves. This process in which the women are engaged is an opportunity for the development of understanding for biomedicine and beyond. As discussed above, doctors struggle with the same issues. The opportunity for the development of our understanding of our complex biosocial selves can be traced in our research data, with different women at different times discussing the integration and understanding described here. Any one woman may not engage with this process in full at any one time. This in itself may not limit the potential for the opportunity for the development of our understanding within society more generally, as each individual will interact with others including doctors, and so contribute to the process of developing our understanding.

We have outlined an opportunity for the development of our understanding of our biosocial selves. However, there are also risks. One risk is that health advisers, be they doctors, the media, or Internet sites, simplify the complexity of the evidence about risk and benefit of any intervention to a point where the explanations have become so divorced from the complexity of the issue that they are more myth than reality. This risk may be exacerbated by women's desire for certainty, as discussed above. The desire for certainty may be fuelled by fear such as the fear of side effects from the intervention, fear of disability in the future or fear of social stigma, as examples above have shown.

When a woman consults a doctor for advice concerning HRT and osteoporosis, the doctor attempts to provide an account of the issues which is coherent for the woman. Such an account can disguise the uncertainty inherent in it. The following is an example from our current research of a specialist doctor speaking to a patient after the patient has had bone densitometry. The doctor is explaining the implications of the result:[7]

> bone loss starts just round the very beginning that the hormones start to change, what we call the peri-menopause and then you're likely to lose bone well totally predictably to lose bone for about 10 years after the menopause so it will start to gradually come down. At the moment the results are normal, you have normal bone density but, err, after about 10 years it's going to drop into the below normal range, you can't be certain, but it's predictable, err, and it's obviously happened to your Mum.

The doctor is not completely coherent, he actually contradicts himself, but the overall tenor of the account is a simplification of the biostatistical evidence. Using simplified models for explanation is common in medical practice. It has been suggested by Willis that when a simple model is used that is not precisely true, the doctor is not lying in order to dupe the patient, but using 'controlled lying' or 'slippage' (Willis 1995: 57), in a way that hopefully will help the patient. However intended, these accounts enhance the risk of oversimplification of complex decisions.

The risk of simplifying the complex may also be exacerbated by scientific endeavour that takes a deterministic linear view of the world. As discussed above, there are areas of science where this is now changing and the non-linear nature of, and impossibility of predicting the future for, complex biological and social systems is being understood. Earlier in the chapter we discussed how the apparent precision of medicine has become at least partly incorporated into lay understanding. The use of this medical discourse along with engagement in surveillance practices by lay individuals has a positive feedback effect on the discourse and dominance of surveillance medicine. However, evidence presented above also suggests that both patients and doctors are engaging with the paradoxes and dilemmas that biostatistics and its technology presents. They are endeavouring to understand how to integrate biostatistics with the individual as a complex biosocial self. There is opportunity for the interaction between patients and doctors to result in a challenge to the discourse of medicine as 'precise and independent of context and persons' (Morgan, Calnan and Manning 1991: 33) and a challenge to the dominance of this discourse. In our current research we shall be testing whether this opportunity is being taken up through analysis of consultations between patients and doctors. We may also see whether this opportunity is being taken up through observing current developments in self-care movements and organizations within traditional medicine (so using the same evidence base as doctors), the use of 'the expert patient' which is now part of UK health service policy, and the initiation of lay involvement in health policy development, service planning and research.

Bone densitometry and use of HRT for prevention of osteoporosis has become distanced in time, life stage and experience from the biological process of breaking a brittle bone. However, individuals really do experience breaking brittle bones, with its associated pain, distress and risk of death and with its implications for the provision and distribution of health and social care. Developing an understanding of the complex biosocial self in relation to biostatistics will need to relate to the emotional experience, both of individuals, families and communities, associated with, or avoiding, the biological process, as discussed in Part III of this book. It will also need to relate to current and potential inequalities in health experience and health and social care provision, as discussed in Part II. Biostatistics, by its nature avoids engaging in debate about social experience and social values, where as sociology engages with these debates, and is able to engage more deeply when the biological is brought into sociology.

Notes

1 From Sedgwick, P. (1982) *Psycho Politics*, London: Pluto Press, discussed in Morgan, Calnan and Manning 1991: 29.
2 Whether and when a bone snaps is influenced by biological and social factors and so may not be considered a purely biological process. However, at the time the bone snaps the biological process is the immediate major concern prompting a medical technological intervention. The biological process also, of course, precipitates distress for the individual and those around them.
3 At the time of writing, a major trial of long term HRT has been halted due to concerns that the incidence of side effects including breast cancer may be much higher than expected (*Guardian*, 10 July 2002, p. 5).

4 See study presented at BSA Medical Sociology Conference 1998: Green, E. and Wadsworth, G. 'Flushed and emotional: issues of risk and control associated with women's experiences of menopause'.

5 For further discussion see: Green, E.E., Thompson, D. and Griffiths, F.E., 'Narratives of risk: women at midlife, medical "experts" and health technologies', *Health Risk and Society*, **4**: 243–86.

6 Details of the study from which this data is taken are published in Griffiths, F. (1999) 'Women's control and choice regarding HRT', *Social Science and Medicine*, **49**: 469–81, and available in Griffiths, F.E. (1997) 'Hormone replacement therapy: perspectives from women, medicine and sociology', PhD Thesis, University of Durham.

7 This data is taken from an ongoing study 'Innovative health technologies at women's midlife: theory and diversity among women and "experts"', led by the authors and funded by the ESRC programme on Innovative Health Technologies.

8 This data is taken from study in endnote 4.

References

Armstrong, D. (1995) 'The rise of surveillance medicine', *Sociology of Health and Illness*, **17**: 393–404.

Bordo, S. (1993) *Unbearable Weight: Feminism, Western Culture and the Body*, Berkley, CA: University of California Press.

Coney, S. (1991) *The Menopause Industry: A Guide to Medicine's Discovery of the Mid-life Woman*, Auckland: Penguin Books.

Davison, C., Frankel, S. and Smith, G.D. (1992) 'The limits of lifestyle: re-assessing "fatalism" in the popular culture of illness prevention', *Social Science and Medicine*, **34**: 675–85.

Foucault, M. (1988) 'The politics of health in the eighteenth century', in P. Rainbow (ed.) *The Foucault Reader*, New York: Pantheon Books.

Fox, R.C. (2002) 'Medical uncertainty revisited', in G. Bendelow, M. Carpenter, C. Vautier and S. Williams (eds) *Gender, Health and Healing: The Public/Private Divide*, London: Routledge.

Gorovitz, S. and MacIntyre, A. (1976) 'Toward a theory of medical fallibility', *The Journal of Medicine and Philosophy*, **1**: 51–71.

Haraway, D. (1991) *Simians, Cyborgs and Women: the Reinvention of Nature*, New York: Routledge.

Harding, J. (1997) 'Bodies at risk: sex, surveillance and hormone replacement therapy', in A. Peterson and R. Bunton (eds) *Foucault, Health and Medicine*, London: Routledge.

Kavanagh, A.M. and Broom, D.H. (1998) 'Embodied risk: my body, myself?', *Social Science and Medicine*, **46**: 437–44.

Mant, D. (1994) 'Prevention', *Lancet*, **344**: 1343–46.

Massé, R. and Légaré, F. (2001) 'The limitations of a negotiation model for perimenopausal women', *Sociology of Health and Illness*, **23**: 44–64.

Morgan, M., Calnan, M. and Manning, N. (1991) *Sociological Approaches to Health and Medicine*, London: Routledge.

Nettleton, S. (1995) *The Sociology of Health and Illness*, Cambridge: Polity Press.

Nettleton, S. (1997) 'Governing the risky self: how to become healthy, wealthy and wise', in A. Peterson and R. Bunton (eds) *Foucault, Health and Medicine*, London: Routledge.

Roberts, C. (2002) ' "Successful Aging" with hormone replacement therapy: it may be sexist, but what if it works?', *Science as Culture*, **11**: 39–59.

Turner, B.S. (1987) *Medical Power and Social Knowledge*, London: Sage.

University of Leeds, University of York, Royal College of Physicians and Department of Health (1992) 'Screening for osteoporosis to prevent fractures', *Effective Health Care*, **1**.

Williams, S.J. and Calnan, M. (1996) 'The "limits" of medicalisation? Modern medicine and the lay populace in "late" modernity', *Social Science and Medicine*, **42**: 1609–20.

Willis, J. (1995) *The Paradox of Progress*, Oxford: Radcliffe Medical Press.

17 Enhancing biology?

Cosmetic surgery and breast augmentation

Peter Conrad and Heather T. Jacobson

When it comes to the origins of human characteristics we often see them conceptualized as 'nature' versus 'nurture' or biology versus society. As we are increasingly learning from the social studies of genetics, it is much more accurate to see most characteristics as nature and nurture. While we are all born with a certain biological endowment, how it is manifested is a function of the social environment. This is even true about bodies. Biology may appear to set the limits on bodily development (e.g. we cannot fly), but individuals can work to improve body size and shape by working out and/or taking supplements, or through other methods of enhancement.

One avenue for body improvement is through methods of biomedical enhancement. These include drugs, surgery or other medical interventions aimed at improving body, mind or performance. Cosmetic surgery, including liposuctions, face lifts, 'nose jobs' and breast augmentation, has become a common biomedical road to bodily improvement (cf. Sullivan 2001). One observer depicts enhancements as 'interventions designed to improve the human form or functioning beyond what is needed to sustain or restore human health' (Juengst 1998: 29). While it is not always clear what is 'human form or functioning ... beyond health', since health itself is a social construction, it seems clear that a bodily enhancement is one that is additive to the 'given' biological condition. A biomedical enhancement is an intervention to improve the body (or performance) by medical means.

Clearly, what one chooses to enhance and what constitutes improvement are socially constructed and likely to vary by time and place. In a society where hitchhiking is the major mode of transportation, individuals may want to enhance their thumbs. Enhancements that modify biology and the body are a reflection of what is socially valued in a society.

This chapter examines one case of biomedical enhancement, breast augmentation in women. After exploring the cultural meanings of women's breasts, we present a brief social and medical history of breast augmentation. In particular, we examine the developments and controversies over breast implants since the mid-twentieth century. Finally, we discuss some issues concerning society's relation to biology that arise from our exploration of breast enhancement.

Breasts and bodies: the cultural meaning of breasts

The meaning of breasts and preferences about size or shape vary enormously by culture and historical moment. In some cultures breasts are seen purely as functional organs for feeding children, with no sexual connotation. Bare breasts have no particular erotic meaning here. In other societies, breasts are considered highly sexual, and are often hidden from view except in the most intimate situations. Some cultures ignore naked breasts, others fetishize them. Not all societies prefer the upright, hemispherical breasts that seem to be idealized in modern western society.

When we examine the history of the breast in western society, however, we see that the meaning and ideal size and shape of the breast has changed over time. Even a casual look at the history of the breast reveals different takes on breasts: an emblem of transition from girl to woman, a sign of femininity, a symbol and a means of nurturence (breast feeding), and an object of erotic attraction and pleasure. In western societies breasts have become very critical to women's body image, but the meanings attributed to breasts varies by time and place. Throughout most of human history breasts were certainly defined in terms of their functionality for nursing babies. Breast milk meant life or death to newborns since there was no substitute for it until the late nineteenth century. Thus it isn't surprising to find statues of multi-breasted women or bare bosomed women with large, globular breasts. By the time the Renaissance began, paintings of a nursing Virgin Mary were common and 'from the fourteenth through the sixteenth century, the nursing Madonna was the prototype of female divinity' (Yalom 1997: 48). There was a kind of holiness infused in the depiction of breast-feeding.

In the seventeenth century we begin to see depictions moving towards a more eroticized breast. The breast begins to be more connected to sexual pleasure. Bare breasts become a common feature in art. But even as breasts become eroticized, the ideal remained 'small, white, round like apples, hard, firm and wide apart' (Yalom 1997: 54).

Art did not always reflect the variety of breast preferences, however. In Renaissance society breast idealization mirrored social class and privilege. An elite 10 per cent pampered their breasts and reserved them for their intimate relations, while 90 per cent used their breasts to feed children. Lower class women often functioned as wet nurses for babies of upper class families. While the upper class ideals were compact breasts under tightly laced bodices, lower class women were revered for their large, globular and lactating breasts (Yalom 1997). Gilman (1999) points out how breasts became racialized; even into the nineteenth century large breasts were associated with Jews and blacks.

In the late seventeenth century the eroticized breast was more common, reflecting gendered power in society. As Yalom (1997: 87) notes, 'women's breasts, shorn of religious associations, became blatant emblems of male desire.' The eroticized breast has become part of western culture, only 'the ideal volume, shape and function' have changed over time (Yalom 1997: 89). Breast-feeding went out of fashion and then returned, but the sexual meaning of breasts has trumped the maternal meaning, perhaps especially in the USA.

In the twentieth century breasts became increasingly commodified, especially through the media, such as films, mass market advertising, and most recently pornography. While women in the 1920s sported a flat-chested look, preferred breast size has grown. With the rise of such stars as Jane Russell and Marilyn Monroe in the 1950s, full and large breasts became a cultural ideal. One indicator of this is measurements of Miss America contestants: in the 1920s the bust measurement averaged 32 inches, by the 1950s it had increased to 36 inches (cited in Latteier 1998). Despite an upsurge in the acceptance of smaller breasts in the wake of the feminist and fitness revolutions, large breasts appear to prevail as the American cultural preference; they are still deemed more feminine and more attractive.

The rise of breast augmentation

'The modern history of aesthetic surgery of the breast begins with breast reduction' (Gilman 1999: 219). In the nineteenth century surgeons began to offer procedures that could reshape parts of the human body. In the 1880s and 1890s they developed procedures that could reduce the size of the nose; parallel to that, 'aesthetic surgeons' began developing techniques to create a more perfect breast, which in this case focused on making large or pendulous breasts smaller. While there was a stated concern with the stress on back muscles and the strain on the body, physicians also saw the reduction of breasts as a way of reducing women's self-consciousness and boosting self-esteem. By the early twentieth century, breast reduction was a going medical concern (Gilman 1999). In the 1930s there was an active medical debate about whether breast reduction was cosmetic or reconstructive surgery. The main issue seems to be the stigma and psychological affect of 'overlarge, pendulous breasts', although both physical discomfort (e.g. excessive weight) and embarrassment were seen as rationales for treatment. These operations fundamentally reshaped breasts, allowing surgeons 'to pay more attention to the aesthetics of the breast' (Jacobson 2000: 51).

Until the 1950s, there was only limited medical interest in enlarging small breasts. There were some efforts at breast augmentation, however. Most of the early attempts could be called reconstruction rather than augmentation. Whatever work was done towards breast enhancement was done primarily as an attempt to restore surgically removed or scarred breasts. In the 1930s, Charles Willi began to experiment with 'aesthetic' breast augmentation in London. His patients wanted larger (and presumably more erotic) breasts. Willi's technique of fat transplantation ultimately failed, providing only a temporary relief from the woe of small breasts (Gilman 1999: 249–51).

While most physicians did not define small breasts as a medical problem, a few surgeons continued to look for materials for the reconstruction of injured or amputated breasts, which of course could also be used to augment small breasts. A wide range of techniques were tried including fat grafts, paraffin injections, sponge rubber prostheses, oestrogen and silicone injections. Concerns were often raised about whether the implant materials were natural or artificial and what impact this would have on the aesthetics of the breast. Eventually all these techniques failed, leaving uneven or lumpy breasts or worse, discomfort and illness.

Medical and surgical interests in breast enhancement increased after the Second World War. Before then, small breasts (rather than breasts that had been surgically removed) were not deemed a serious medical problem. But that was to change shortly. In a 1942 textbook, Max Thorek, a plastic surgeon, devoted a short chapter to the problem of small breasts, what he called 'hypomastia'. In the 1950s small breasts became more widely medicalized (cf. Conrad 1992). In an article published in *Plastic and Reconstructive Surgery* in 1950, H.O. Barnes, a cosmetic surgeon, called attention to the new disease, known equally as hypomastia or micromastia. 'Hypomastia causes psychological rather than physical distress. Its correction has been receiving increased attention only since our "cult of the body beautiful" has revealed its existence in rather large numbers' (quoted in Haiken, 1997: 236). In his article, Barnes proposed 'reshaping' the breast to create 'firmness, conical contours and fullness of the bosom directly above the breast', and a couple of years later published another article that promoted 'fat grafts' for actually enlarging the breast (quoted in Haiken 1997: 236). Robert Alan Franklyn, a somewhat disreputable physician, claimed that 'Four million women suffered from micromastia', and described 'a simple, 25 minute operation' implanting a substance called Surgifoam as a treatment (quoted in Jacobson 2000: 66). Franklyn was severely criticized by the AMA for his claims but by the 1960s there were any number of mainstream plastic surgeons offering new forms of surgical breast enhancement. The woe of small breasts, whether termed hypomastia or just unhappiness or low self-esteem, had been legitimated as a psychological syndrome that could be treated with surgical procedures. At first surgeons resisted the notion that vanity rather than discomfort underlay the demand for breast augmentation. As one surgeon wrote: 'Vanity is the desire to outdo others, while patients who seek cosmetic surgery are not trying to outdo anyone. They simply want to look normal. . . . The woman who has micromastia has a deformity that is difficult to live with' (quoted in Jacobson 2000: 119). But within a few years, vanity was no longer considered a problem, and cosmetic surgeons welcomed patients who wanted to improve their breast size and shape for any reason.

Many people seem to have bought into the cultural preference that small breasts are inferior. The 'falsies' industry became a multimillion enterprise as women sought to give the appearance of larger breasts (Gilman 1999), but surgery promised to be a better solution. One study found that 'wearing padded bras or falsies was "phony", "cheating" and made the feeling of inadequacy even worse' (Haiken 1997: 244), while women tended to be pleased (at least initially) with breast enhancements. For many women, breast augmentation is a kind of 'self improvement', enriching their distinctly female attributes, and making their bodies more like their ideal images. For others, it is an attempt to overcome the 'disability' of small breasts and to look 'normal' in their own eyes. With the help of surgeons, women could now pursue 'the body I was meant to have' (Gimlin 2000), aligning a perceived disjunction between internal identity and external body. There is considerable evidence that when successful, breast implants increase some women's self-esteem, sexual appeal, and self-fulfilment (Jacobson 2000).

Silicone breast implants since the 1960s

Silicone breast implants were introduced in the early 1960s and soon after their introduction became the most popular choice for augmentation (Jacobson 2000). The connection between silicone and breasts itself was not new, however; injectable silicone had been used to increase breast size since the Second World War. Silicone is a synthetic polymer developed for commercial use by Dow Corning Corporation in the early 1940s. Reports locate the first use of injectable silicone to increase breast size in post-war Japan (Haiken 1997; Zimmerman 1998; Jacobson 2000). Injecting silicon into breasts was introduced into the US in the late 1940s and quickly became popular among physicians, many of whom used the substance illicitly as it had not been approved for breast augmentation (Jacobson 2000). Physicians liked silicone as they believed it to be 'biologically inert and an ideal soft-tissue substitute' (Zimmerman 1998: 22).

Although silicone injections were for a time popular, with some reports estimating upwards of fifty thousand US women having had their breasts enlarged with the substance, injectable silicone presented serious complications (Zimmerman 1998; Jacobson 2000). Some women experienced pain, scarring, infections, and migrating silicone lumps in their breasts that masked breast cancer and prevented adequate screening. Breasts would often become misshapen and uncomfortable. At times, these complications resulted in amputation of the breasts. By 1971 at least four women had died due to embolisms resulting from silicone injections (Haiken 1997; Zimmerman 1998).

As a result of these complications, negative publicity about injectable silicone increased. In 1965 the Federal Drug Administration (FDA) reclassified liquid silicone as a drug, restricting its use to investigational studies

(Haiken 1997; Jacobson 2000). Despite the new monitoring, physicians continued to inject silicone, some receiving the substance through illicit means (Zimmerman 1998). In 1971 the American Medical Association (AMA) declared that 'the injection of silicon fluid to increase the size of the female breast is an unapproved surgical technique and is dangerous' (quoted in Jacobson 2000: 83).

Women 'continued to clamor for a solution [to small breasts] and surgeons continued to search for one' (Haiken 1997: 255). Despite the horror stories emerging around injectable silicon the demand for surgical breast augmentation was still high. Work on the silicone-filled implant had been well underway since the early 1960s. In 1962 the first device was implanted in a women and by 1970 Dow Corning had sold an estimated 50,000 implants. Neither the concerns nor the new regulations of injectable silicone were applied to silicone implants. At the time, the FDA still did not have the authority to regulate medical devices. Because of this, 'manufacturers were free to develop variations of the original breast implant with few studies to demonstrate their safety and efficacy' (Zimmerman 1998: 29). Analysts suggest that manufacturers and plastic surgeons often were more concerned with the 'naturalness' of the implants (i.e. the look and feel of real breasts) rather than product safety (Zimmerman 1998). It wasn't until 1988 that the jurisdiction of the FDA was expanded to require safety and effectiveness data on breast implants (Jacobson 2000).

In the meantime, from the early 1960s through to 1990 an estimated *two million women* received silicone implants (Jacobson 2000; Yalom 1997: 237). Of these, 20 per cent were for reconstructive purposes following mastectomy, while 80 per cent were for cosmetic purposes (Zimmerman 1998). While plastic surgeons reported high levels of patient satisfaction, negative publicity about silicone implants was increasing. Articles appeared in the popular press and journals questioning the safety of the devices. Women began to become vocal about various medical problems they had been experiencing since implantation of the devices. Among the main complications and risks articulated were capsular contracture (when breasts harden), silicone gel leakage and migration, carcinogenicity, interference with detection of tumours, and autoimmune disease. Some women took legal action to seek compensation for pain and suffering which they claimed was caused by silicone implants. Beginning in 1984 a number of women received multimillion dollar damage awards following rulings that silicone implants caused serious medical conditions. Throughout the 1990s, as the implant controversy exploded, tens of thousands of women joined legal suits, resulting in several global settlements against implant manufacturers.

The controversy surrounding silicone implants included the safety concerns but primarily focused on the efficacy of manufacturers and plastic surgeons in sharing and communicating the potential or known risks associated with silicone. What was at stake then, adcovates argued, was not only women's health but the right to be informed consumers. Consumer groups maintained that manufacturers had misled women about the safety of silicone implants by withholding information, including the results of manufacturing studies. A congressional hearing in 1990 found that information had indeed been withheld, in part due to a court order from an early lawsuit. In 1992 the FDA called for a voluntary moratorium on the distribution and implantation of the devices to which the manufacturers agreed. From 1992 onward silicone breast implants were only made available to women who had or will have breast reconstruction surgery, or have complications from existing implants, and only if they agree to participate in a scientific protocol or study. While many women believe that their implants caused connective tissue disease, the medical evidence is more equivocal (Haiken 1997: 232). The medical community has maintained that the scientific evidence linking breast implants and debilitating medical conditions is insufficient. Several medical associations, including the American Medical Association and the American Society of Plastic and Reconstructive Surgeons, issued position statements opposing the 1992 FDA restriction on silicone implants in which they argued the benefits of the devices outweighed the risks (Zimmerman 1998).

In view of this almost exclusive ban on silicone breast implants, manufacturers and plastic surgeons have turned to saline implants, which were marketed as a safe alternative to silicone. These newer implants are lined with silicone but filled with salt water. Directly following the peak of the controversy and the 1992 ban, breast augmentation figures plunged. In 1990 there were 120,000 implants performed, while in 1992 there were only 30,000 (Jacobson 2000). For a few years in the early 1990s, surgeons were removing silicone implants from as many women as they were implanting. However, over the course of a decade, more and more women were seeking breast enhancements. From 1990 to 2000 there was a 92.6 per cent increase in the numbers of breast augmentations. According to the American Academy of Cosmetic Surgery, in 2000 there were 203,310 breast augmentations in the US, making this procedure the third most popular cosmetic surgery following liposuction and cosmetic eyelid procedures. The widespread promotion and utilization of breast enhancements has become a concern for feminist scholars and activists.

Contextualizing breast augmentation

A main project of much feminist scholarship on cosmetic surgery is understanding beauty practices within a broader social, cultural and political context (Wolf 1991). At the forefront of these discussions is the process through which women come to choose cosmetic surgery. A traditional feminist perspective contends that oppressive beauty practices, which produce and maintain women's inferiority, propel women to seek cosmetic surgery (Bordo 1998; Zimmerman 1998). This framework argues women are influenced by cultural images of the idealized body (slenderness, eternal youth, voluptuous breasts), seeing anything outside of that vision as abnormality. Cosmetic surgery represents the extreme end of the wide spectrum of beauty practices meant to deal with 'abnormality'. Women pluck their eyebrows, wax their legs, put on make-up, colour their hair, get breast implants, tummy tucks, and face-lifts in an attempt to achieve this idealized beauty norm.

Susan Bordo points out the existence of a 'consumer system' tied to ideologies of beauty which 'depends on our perceiving ourselves as defective' (Bordo 1998: 201). Cosmetic surgery is part of this consumer system as it offers a seemingly 'quick-fix' to aesthetic 'abnormalities' such as small breasts, large 'ethnic' noses, and wrinkles. With the ability to manipulate and sculpt the body into the ideal, 'the surgically perfected body (perfect according to certain standards, of course) has become the model of "normal", [and] even the ordinary body becomes the defective body' (Bordo 1998: 212). Women therefore engage in cosmetic surgery, the traditional feminist perspective argues, for the same reasons they engage in other beauty practices: because they have internalized the cultural understanding that their value is to be found in their looks (Davis 1995; Bordo 1998). This idea is supported by a web of interlocking social, cultural and political systems. Beauty therefore becomes 'an essential ingredient of the social subordination of women – an ideal way to keep women in line by lulling them into believing that they could gain control over their lives through continued vigilance over their bodies' (Davis 1995: 24). This traditional feminist perspective therefore sees women – and increasingly men – as victims of these oppressive beauty practices.

More recent scholarship argues that while women are influenced by media norms they do not make decisions to undergo cosmetic surgery blindly (Davis 1995; Bordo 1998; Zimmerman 1998). Rather than victims of beauty standards, women negotiate various systems of meaning and actively participate in the cosmetic surgery decision-making process. Kathy Davis emphasizes the agency of women choosing cosmetic surgery. Cosmetic surgery, she argues, represents control and autonomy for women. It is something women 'do for [themselves]', something that 'takes courage' (Davis 1995: 127–8). She contends that the process can be liberating for women as they make choices perceived to increase quality of life, self-determination, and gratification despite opposition they may face from people in their lives. The women she spoke to felt pressure from husbands, lovers, family, friends, and medical professionals *not* to undergo surgery. They had to overcome this resistance in order to receive surgery they themselves felt was entirely necessary to alleviate psychological suffering or an impediment to their self-esteem. In this sense, breast augmentation is a kind of self-improvement available to women.

It is on this point of agency and empowerment that feminist philosopher Susan Bordo disagrees with Davis. While Bordo maintains that both she and Davis support the desire not to cast women as victims, as 'passive sponges', she feels Davis goes too far in the opposite direction, equating cosmetic surgery 'with a state of liberation' (Bordo 1998: 197–9). She does not disagree with Davis in that a woman can feel a perceived 'imperfection' to 'cast a shadow over her entire life, influencing how she [feels] about herself, her relationships, her sexuality, her work, and more' (Davis 1995: 72). Rather, Bordo emphasizes that the idealized body images in the media and the accompanying consumer system lead women to 'believe they are nothing (and are frequently treated as nothing) unless they are trim, tight, lineless, bulgeless, and sagless' (Bordo 1993: 45). While individual women may deny the influence of idealized images in their decisions to seek cosmetic surgery, Bordo maintains 'it's hard to account for most of the choices . . . outside the context of current cultural norms' (1998: 193). Susan Zimmerman (1998: 44) concurs: 'although women may actively and knowledgeably participate in the medicalization of femininity by choosing to alter their bodies with breast implants, their decisions are, nevertheless, rooted in a complex web of contexts that shape and perpetuate the objectification of their own bodies.'

While Davis found women had few friends and family who supported their desire to have cosmetic surgery, other scholars point to the strong influence of family members, friends, lovers, and medical professionals (Dull and West 1991; Zimmerman 1998). In her study of women who had received breast implants, Zimmerman found that the majority of her respondents (70 per cent) 'who had implants for "cosmetic" purposes perceived this decision as an action taken under specific interpersonal pressure'. Women were encouraged by spouses, intimates and friends to undergo breast augmentation. She found these women to be less than enthusiastic about breast implants but rather 'reluctantly succumbing to ideal beauty standards to please significant others in their lives' (1998: 49). At the moment, it is debatable how much the motivation for larger breasts is located in women's social network and how much breast augmentation is an act of self-expression and personal liberation.

Primary to the feminist discussions on breast augmentation and cosmetic surgery are issues of agency, control and cultural ideologies of the idealized body. Feminist perspectives on cosmetic surgery range from viewing these surgical procedures as self-determining and empowering for women to bodily alterations rooted in cultural and consumer systems that depend upon women seeing themselves as intrinsically defective. Feminists agree, however, on the influence of cultural images on the ideal body and the need to understand breast augmentation in the particular cultural, social, and historical context.

Feelings of inadequacy and inferiority over breast size do not occur in a vacuum. Nor do technological advancements in biomedical enhancement. The popularity of breast augmentation, despite the seeming failure of technology to give women what they want (safe, 'natural' looking, permanent breasts of a certain size), attests to the power of the cultural meaning of breasts in the contemporary American society.

Bodies, breasts and biomedical enhancement: where does that leave biology?

Through genetics and nutrition women are biologically endowed with a certain breast shape and size. Even casual observation suggests that breasts come in a range of sizes and shapes. Breast size and appearance have no inherent meaning and any social preference varies by culture and historical moment. Some societies have long had rituals and procedures intended to alter breasts, but with the last half-century's turn in fashion to larger breasts and the emergence of cosmetic surgery implant techniques there has been a significant rise in breast augmentation. Physicians did not create the desire for breast enhancement, but they reinforced, facilitated, and profited from it. 'There is no question that women's desire for breasts of the right size and shape existed. But the transformation of that desire into a medicalized need was something that followed the introduction of implant surgery' (Jacobson 2000: 141). The popularity of breast augmentation was facilitated by several factors, including an increase in the number of plastic surgeons, a decrease in the stigma associated with cosmetic surgery, and a decrease in the cost of the procedure (Sullivan 2001). For example, a full-page advertisement in the mainstream *Cosmopolitan* magazine offered breast enlargement for $2,799 plus a $600 operating fee (December 2001, p. 229). As surgeons have improved their ability to mimic the natural, the call for their services has increased. What we see here is that under the conditions of a cultural demand (larger breasts), a legitimated enabling medical technology at an affordable cost can expedite biological bodily alterations. This results in what might be deemed a commodification of the body, putting a monetary value on and profiting from body alterations.

Lest we see breast size manipulation as an American affectation, it is worth noting that in Brazil breast reduction is common among middle-class families to distinguish their bodies from lower-class black women and in Argentina breast augmentation is so popular that 'a million operations have been performed since 1970, one for every thirty Argentines' (Gilman 1999: 226).

It is also worth noting that it was technologies originally developed for breast restoration and repair (after amputation) that were adapted by plastic surgeons for breast enhancement. The frequently proposed distinction between treatment and enhancement (Daniels 1994) – where treatment is deemed for disease or debility while enhancement improves the normal – breaks down with medicalization. When a technology is available and a demand is extant, then the medicalization of a problem (e.g. as hypomastia) is the likely justification for biomedical enhancement.

With the potentials of bodily enhancement, it seems clear that biology is no longer destiny. Today it is breasts (and noses and fat), what might it be in the future? Given the available medical technology, people can buy characteristics they desire and literally reshape their bodies. This exacerbates existing social inequities, enabling enhancements to those who can afford them. While breast augmentation is largely a cosmetic alteration, it is possible that other enhancements may affect more fundamental sources of self.

Beyond modifying appearance, enhancements can improve the body's performance. Athletes have long used drugs such as steroids or human growth hormone to improve performance (see also Monaghan, this volume). But athletes are not alone in the drug enhancement quest. Some people use Prozac and similar medications to augment their pursuit of happiness (see Crossley, this volume), beta blockers for 'stage fright', or Paxil for shyness. A widening array of people see prescription drugs as a legitimate manner of altering the body's performance capacity. In addition to raising questions of equity and fairness, this broadens the issue of what is body authenticity and integrity.

The potentials of genetic enhancement may create a whole new set of issues that make breast augmentation appear mundane and primitive. While genetic enhancements are yet to be developed, some experts believe that they are likely to be available in some form in the not-so-distant future (Silver 1997). Mehlman (2000: 523) defines a genetic intervention as an enhancement '(1) when it is undertaken for the purposes of improving a characteristic or capability that, but for the enhancement, would lie within what is generally accepted as a normal range for humans; or (2) when it installs a characteristic of capability that is not normally present in human beings'. The first would include greater cognitive abilities, improved physical performance, or augmented body size or function (including breasts). The second might include the ability to see clearly at night, glow in the dark, or grow wings. While these latter types currently reside in the realm of science fiction, possibilities of radical genetic bodily orientation remain.

It seems clear that when we consider genetic interventions, the potential for bodily modification and enhancement expands well beyond current capabilities. This would move our interventions from body manipulation to genetic manipulation – from designer bodies to designer babies – which may affect not only an individual's biology but also the biological basis of future generations.

References

Bordo, Susan (1993) *Unbearable Weight: Feminism, Western Culture and the Body*, Berkeley, CA: University of California Press.

Bordo, Susan (1998) 'Braveheart, babe, and the contemporary Body', in Erik Parens (ed.) *Enhancing Human Traits: Ethical and Social Implications*, Washington: Georgetown University Press, pp. 189–221.

Conrad, Peter (1992) 'Medicalization and Social Control', *Annual Review of Sociology*: 209–32.

Daniels, Norman (1994) 'The Genome Project, individual differences, and just health care', in Timothy F. Murphy and Marc A. Lappe (eds) *Justice and the Genome Project*, Berkeley: University of California Press, pp. 110–32.

Davis, Kathy (1995) *Reshaping the Female Body: The Dilemma of Cosmetic Surgery*, New York, NY: Routledge.

Dull, Diana and West, Candace (1991) 'Accounting for cosmetic surgery: the accomplishment of gender', *Social Problems*, **38**: 54–70.

Gilman, Sander L. (1999) *Making the Body Beautiful: A Cultural History of Aesthetic Surgery*, Princeton, NJ: Princeton University Press.

Gimlin, Debra (2000) 'Cosmetic surgery: beauty as a commodity', *Qualitative Sociology*, **23**: 77–98.

Haiken, Elizabeth (1997) *Venus Envy: A History of Cosmetic Surgery*, Baltimore, MD: The Johns Hopkins University Press.

Haiken, Elizabeth (2000) 'The making of the modern face: cosmetic surgery', *Social Research*, **67**: 81–97.

Jacobson, Nora (2000) *Cleavage: Technology, Controversy, and the Ironies of the Man-Made Breast*, New Brunswick, NJ: Rutgers University Press.

Juengst, Eric T. (1998) 'What does enhancement mean?', in Erik Parens (ed.) *Enhancing Human Traits: Ethical and Social Implications*. Washington DC: Georgetown University Press, pp. 29–48.

Latteier, Carolyn (1998) *Breasts: The Women's Perspective on an American Obsession*, New York: Haworth Press.

Mehlman, Maxwell J. (2000) 'The law of above averages: leveling the new genetic enhancement playing field', *Iowa Law Review*, **85**: 517–93.

Silver, Lee M. (1997) *Remaking Eden: Cloning and Beyond in a Brave New World*, New York: Avon Books.

Sullivan, Deborah H. (2001) *Cosmetic Surgery: The Cutting Edge of Medicine in America*, New Brunswick, NJ: Rutgers University Press.

Wolf, Naomi (1991) *The Beauty Myth: How Images of Beauty are Used Against Women*, New York: Morrow.

Yalom, Marilyn (1997) *A History of the Breast*, New York: Knopf.

Zimmerman, Susan (1998) *Silicone Survivors: Women's Experiences with Breast Implants*, Philadelphia, PA: Temple University Press.

18 Through the lenses of biology and sociology

Organ replacement

Renée C. Fox

This chapter identifies and explores some of the interconnections between the biological and technological attributes of organ replacement and its social and cultural concomitants. It draws on the more than four decades of first-hand field research that I have conducted in a variety of settings where organ transplants and/or artificial heart implants have been performed. It is offered as a set of case materials that illustrate the complexity of the interplay between biological, social, and cultural factors, and that suggest the fruitfulness and the fascination of probing these important interrelationships further.

Organ replacement – the excision of human organs critically damaged by end-stage disease, and their replacement, either by organ transplantation or by the implantation of an artificial organ – is experienced by all those who are involved in these surgical and medical interventions as more than bold, potentially life-saving and life-sustaining biological and technological acts. The removal, giving, receiving, and transposing of live and cadaveric organs, and the substitution of manufactured mechanical organs for 'natural' ones are fraught with psychological, social and cultural meaning for donors, recipients, families and medical professionals. Corporeally, psychically and interpersonally, participants in the replacement of organs are confronted with phenomena associated with the more-than-biological significance of human organs, and with the relationship of the human body (its integrity, manipulation, and the events that transpire within it) to individual and collective identity, the nexus between self and other, humanness and personhood, and to the existential as well as the physical borders between life and death.

Neither a biological orientation that is tightly contained within a deterministic, logico-rational, positivist system of thought, and that maintains a Cartesian split between body and mind, and a mechanistic view of bodily organs, nor a sociological outlook which attaches overweening importance to social structure, minimizes the role of culture, and which is strongly sceptical about the influence of biological factors on social sentiments and experiences, is optimally equipped to take serious note of these aspects of organ replacement, or to make interpretive sense of them. What is called for is a framework of analysis that draws upon and integrates biological, social and cultural knowledge and insights in a way that gives special consideration to the implicit as well as explicit symbolism and meaning of organ replacement for its intricately entwined participants, within the context of the society to which they belong.

The language of immunology

Such an approach, for example, draws attention to the distinctive vocabulary of immunology – the basic medical science fundamental to understanding the biological processes underlying organ transplantation – and raises sociological questions about how the perspective on transplantation that is coded into its terminology is related to the meaning that transplanters attribute to this procedure, or how they feel about it.

To a striking degree, the language of immunology is pervaded by vivid, teleological concepts, terms, and images. Incorporated and assimilated into its scientific lexicon are notions of the 'tolerance', 'acceptance', and 'rejection' of transplanted tissues and organs; the capacity of the body of a recipient to 'recognize' tissues and organs that are 'foreign' to it, and to distinguish 'self' from 'nonself', and 'tolerating self' from 'attacking nonself'; 'natural killer', 'target', and 'helper' cells, portrayed as protagonists in the warlike conflict between two immune systems that 'acceptance/rejection' involves; the 'migration' and 'colonization' of cells between transplanted organs and their recipients; and the 'chimeras' of genetically different groups of donor and recipient cells that are formed – a term derived from the name given in Greek mythology to a fire-breathing monster with a lion's head, goat's body and serpent's tail. It is unclear to what extent the medical scientists who coined these concepts deliberately intended them to have the animistic connotations and philosophical outlook that they contain, whether what they express is consciously recognized by members of the medical transplantation community who use them, or what relationship they have to the mind-set with which transplanters approach the transposition of human organs from donors to recipients.

The transplantation of human organs

What is intriguing, however, is how closely some of the psychosocial experiences that organ recipients undergo parallel what happens inside their bodies upon receiving an organ transplant. In 1972 and 1973, transplant surgeon Thomas E. Starzl and colleagues published their discovery that not only do special white cells (leucocytes) move from the recipient's immune system into the transplant, but a flux of leucocytes from the donor graft into the recipient's organs also takes place. Starzl has proposed that this two-way 'exchange of migratory leucocytes between the transplant and the recipient with long-term cellular chimerism' (the development of genetic composites) in both is the key to what has long been an 'immunological enigma': the questions of 'the mechanism by which antirejection treatment with immunosuppressive drugs permits a transplanted organ to be "accepted" by the recipient's body' (Starzl *et al.* 1992; Starzl *et al.* 1993: 1127). In a special study that he made of some of the longest surviving kidney and liver recipients in the world, Starzl found that donor cells had distributed themselves throughout the body of the recipients (Starzl 1993: 343–6). 'If the organ survives,' he stated in a personal interview,

> that means that the recipient of an organ is physically more intimately connected with that . . . donor of unknown ethnicity [and] unknown sex . . . than any other person in their entire life, with the possible exception of their mother – and probably more intimately connected with the donor than the mother.

Does this mean, one organ recipient asked him, 'when I put on my lipstick in the morning that I'm touching the cells of . . . ?' 'That's exactly what it does mean,' he replied, 'because if you biopsied a piece of cheek or lip skin or anything like that, you are going to find donor cells' (Fox 2003).

Only some recipients are cognizant of these microbiological processes that are integral to the successful transplantation of an organ; and yet there is a striking correspondence between the pervasion of recipients' bodies with donor cells, and the feelings that recipients have about the organ that has come to reside within them. In the research on organ replacement that medical historian Judith Swazey and I have done together, we have found that many recipients of cadaveric organ transplants grapple with the haunting sense that along with the organ they have received, some of the psychic and social, as well as the physical qualities of their unknown donor have been transferred into their body, personhood, and life. Richard McCann, a writer and teacher of literature who received a liver transplant, vividly expressed such feelings in the essay entitled 'The Resurrectionist' that he wrote about what he called the 'shadow side' of transplantation. McCann depicted the donor organ as 'a bearer of its own cellular memories'; and he described the long nights when he thought of the donor – always 'with great tenderness' – sometimes perceiving him as a male, and sometimes her as a female (McCann 1999: 135–47). 'My blood has adopted a child who shuffles through my chest carrying a doll,' wrote J.F. Reed in a poem about the 'girl's heart' that a cardiac transplant recipient had received (Reed 1970: 126). Some recipients say that the individual who they surmise was their organ donor recurrently appears in their dreams. Others report that they have noted changes in the activities and foods they enjoy, in their daily habits, and in their personality traits, which they attribute to characteristics of the donor that have somehow been infused into their being along with the organ he/she has contributed. In one case about which I have written, two unrelated recipients, each of whom received a kidney from the same cadaveric donor, testified that they felt they had 'become brother and sister', because their transplanted organs had created 'brotherly love' between them (Fox 1978: 1166).

The sense which recipients have that the spirit of the donor lives on in a personified and transforming way within them is augmented by the magnitude of the 'gift of life' they have received, which is of such surpassing significance that it is inherently unreciprocal, and in the case of cadaver transplants, by the recipient's realization that an unknown, unseen human benefactor had to die in order for them to survive and flourish. Perhaps because they intimately know their donors and do not have to wonder and imagine who they were, what they were like, and what kinds of lives they led, the recipients of live organ transplants from family members, or from what is referred to in the vernacular of the transplant community as 'emotionally related' donors, seem to be less prone than those who receive cadaver organs to anthropomorphize them, or to feel that they have been mysteriously altered by them. However, recipients of live organs are especially subject to what Judith Swazey and I have termed the 'tyranny of the gift': to the way in which the great indebtedness they feel to the person whose life-saving organ has become a part of their body may make it difficult for them to maintain psychic distance and independence from the donor, and to reassert their own separate identity and being. In some instances, their struggle to do so may cause a serious rupture in the relationship of the recipient to the live donor (Fox and Swazey 1974: 382–3; Fox and Swazey 1992: 39–42).

Can it be said that recipients are biologically 'imprinted' with the indwelling presence and some of the traits of donors through the intermediary of their transplanted cells, tissues and organs? Such an allegation would seem to be pushing biological causality too far, and in too occult a direction. And yet there are intriguing analogies between the biological processes involved in graft acceptance, and the responses of recipients to the organs implanted in them, and to the persons from whose bodies they came. What is unambiguously clear is that for both donors and recipients, the organs they exchange and that link them to each other, are more than anatomical and physiological entities.

Xenotransplantation

The prospect of xenotransplantation – the grafting of animal organs (and also cells and tissues) into human beings – presents another array of questions and issues concerning the relationship between the body, self, and other, between animality and humanness, and between medical interventions and individual and collective well-being. Because they cross species boundaries, animal-to-human organ transplants trigger what the medical literature describes as 'formidable' and 'deadly' immune responses, known as hyperacute and vascular rejection. The outcome of the few chimpanzee and baboon xenografts that have been performed since the early 1960s has been ill-fated, resulting in the immediate, post-operative deaths of all but one of the patients on whom the procedure has been tried. As a consequence, an informal moratorium has been called on whole-organ xenotransplants in North America and in Europe.

Nevertheless, since the 1990s, a surge of renewed interest in xenotransplantation has become manifest, propelled by optimism about experiments being conducted with the transplantation of insulin-producing pancreatic islet cells from pigs into persons with diabetes; by what is felt to be the promise of developing genetically engineered, 'transgenically modified' animals, especially pigs, whose organs and tissues might be made less immunogenic and susceptible to rejection when grafted into human beings; and by the urgently felt lack of a sufficient number of donated human organs for the long waiting lists of persons with end-stage diseases hoping to become recipients.

At present, it is only possible to speculate about what the psychological and social meaning, as well as the biological and evolutionary consequences of crossing the barriers between animals and humans via xenotransplantation might be. If and when it becomes feasible, how will the recipients of pig organs, for example, feel about having these living porcine parts inside them, and permeating their bodies through the process of cell migration? Will they think of themselves, and be seen by others, as strange hybrids, who are partly human and partly not – akin to mythological chimerical monsters? And should the reactions of fright, repugnance, or stigma that such combined beings might evoke be taken into account in deciding about the advisability of eventually moving xenotransplantation from the laboratory into the clinic?

These questions are not being debated at this time. However, there is a considerable amount of ongoing discussion centred on the existence of an uncertain, but 'greater than zero' risk that xenotransplantation could transmit known and unknown infectious agents from animals to humans, that might spread from individual organ recipients to members of their families and other intimates, to the health professionals who care for them and, beyond that, to the general human population, thereby threatening national and international public health. In an era when the so-called 'emergence' of as many as twenty-seven new infectious diseases (most devastatingly HIV/AIDS) and the 'reemergence' of numerous 'old' infectious diseases (such as tuberculosis, malaria and sleeping sickness) have reached epidemic and pandemic proportions, this is an eventuality, however incalculable, that cannot be facilely dismissed. It brings medical scientists and physicians face to face with the dilemma-ridden tension that exists between an 'individual ethic' and a 'distributive ethic' – in this case, between their committed desire to find ways of making more organs available to gravely ill individuals who might benefit from a transplant, and their obligation to safeguard and promote the health of larger collectivities of persons by protecting them against the onset of additional infectious diseases.

Organ transplantation and 'brain death'

Since early in its clinical history, organ transplantation has been associated with the concept of 'brain death' – the determination and declaration of an individual's death on the basis of medical tests that show irreversible cessation of all functions of the entire brain, including the brain stem. The use of cadaver organs for transplants, and the development of intensive care medicine, especially cardiopulmonary life-support systems, were the chief precipitants of this 'whole brain' notion of death. It was proposed in response to three sets of problems that these medical technological advances have brought in their wake: ascertaining when a mechanically assisted patient is dead; deciding when it is acceptable to terminate life-sustaining treatment; and finding ways that organs of potential cadaver donors can be kept viable without causing the death of such patients by removing their organs before their demise. Although 'brain death' has come to be viewed as the 'new definition of death', it has not superseded the 'older' cardiopulmonary method for pronouncing death on the basis of the irreversible cessation of circulatory and respiratory functions, which continues to co-exist alongside it.

More than the 'updating' of a biological understanding of death and the increasing of the technical precision of its determination have been involved in the institutionalization of brain death. It has required societal sanctioning in the form of special legislation that legally establishes these new means for determining and declaring death. Paradoxically, the process of legitimizing brain death has uncovered disquieting ambiguities and uncertainties about what death is and precisely when it occurs, even in a society like the United States where the concept of brain death was first set forth. There is structured irresoluteness, for example, in the fact that the new, legalized criteria for pronouncing death have not displaced the older ones, and diffuse uneasiness among physicians and nurses, as well as members of the lay public, regarding how to think about a patient in whose brain-dead body the heart still beats and respiration continues, maintained by life-support machinery. Despite the dictum about death as 'the one great certainty', the introduction of brain death and the discussion it has catalysed have made it more societally apparent that death is not a clear-cut, instantaneous event; that it involves a complex, life-to-death trajectory; and that the exact borderline between life and death is difficult to discern. Deeper questions about the meaning of death, its relationship to life, to our humanity, and to our inevitable mortality have hovered just below, and occasionally pierced the surface of the medical, legal, and public pondering of brain death that have taken place in the United States.

These questions have been more paramount and vociferously expressed in Japan, where the concept of brain death, and its interconnection with cadaveric organ transplants has been acutely problematic. In the ongoing Japanese debates about the ethics of organ transplantation, the idea of brain death has been a focus of profound apprehension, not only because of the pragmatic fear that it could lead to 'defining individuals out of existence' (Kass 2001) for the sake of obtaining and using their still-living organs, but because of existential concern that manipulating and changing conceptions of life and death in this way, could alter and distort 'the nature of the human being' (Awaya Tsuyoshi, cited in LaFleur 2002). In 1999, two years after brain death was finally made legal in Japan, the first legalized cadaveric organ transplant from a person declared brain dead was performed there. Nonetheless, such transplants are still rare occurrences. The legitimization of brain death by law does not seem to have offset the fears that conceiving of death in this way have evoked in Japanese milieux, or the trepidations that the idea of transplanting live organs from a dead person brings forth.

The quest for an artificial heart

The development of organ transplantation has been accompanied by a bioengineering vision of designing off-the-shelf parts for the human body that can replace those that have been severely damaged by disease. The discrepancy between the number of organs that are donated and the number of persons awaiting a transplant – the so-called 'organ shortage' – has intensified the ardour with which this goal has been pursued. The most daring attempt to realize this 'spare parts', bionic dream is the dauntless quest to fashion a totally implantable artificial heart that, in the words of cardiovascular surgeon O.H. Frazier, is 'unobtrusive in the patient's daily activities, and essentially forgettable by the patient and his or her family and friends' (Texas Heart Institute Online News Release 2001).

The clinical trials of artificial hearts that have been conducted, however, have been far from 'unobtrusive'. At its most flamboyant height, the 1982 to 1988 media coverage of the implantation of 'permanent' Jarvik-7 artificial hearts in five men with end-stage cardiovascular disease was comparable to the kind of attention that was accorded to the Apollo astronauts who made the first manned trip to the moon. In fact, in the US media, explicit analogies were drawn between the cosmic voyages of the American astronauts, and the pioneering journeys into the unknown and the humanly unprecedented, on which the artificial heart recipients had embarked. This was the same imagery that had been invoked in 1968, the year when the world's first human heart transplants were performed. These recipients, too, were compared to astronauts soaring through unexplored space, and walking on the moon. And conversely, when in March 2002 a team of American astronauts travelled into space to repair and upgrade components of the Hubble Space Telescope, the media used a mixture of artificial heart and heart transplant metaphors to describe what they portrayed as the 'heart-stopping' replacement of the telescope's central power controller:

> The Hubble Space Telescope is alive and in stable condition, with electricity surging through its instruments today. . . . With Hubble secured to a workbench across the cargo bay of the space shuttle Columbia, two astronauts replaced the malfunctioning power control unit in a risky procedure that has been likened to a heart transplant. Switching the unit, which channels the electricity from Hubble's solar panels to its instruments and batteries, required turning off all the power for the first time since the observatory went into space in 1990 and putting the telescope into a coma from which some feared it might not awaken. But after a shutdown of 4 hours 25 minutes, during which Dr John M. Grunsfeld and Dr Richard M. Linnehan pulled out the old power unit and connected a new one, ground controllers signaled the telescope to power up, and it responded with an initial stream of information. 'A postoperative report,' Mario Runco Jr, another astronaut radioed the shuttle from mission control. 'We have a heart beat.'
>
> (Leary 2002)

The implantation of the Jarvik-7 artificial heart in human subjects also called forth allusions to the mythic Oz stories written by the American author Frank Baum – especially to the tale of the Tin Woodman, and his pilgrimage to the Emerald City to implore the Wizard of Oz to replace his metal heart with a human one. References to the inverse correspondence between the Tin Man's search for a human heart, and the substitution of plastic and titanium Jarvik-7 hearts for human ones not only appeared in the media, but in medical and scientific journals as well.

Astronaut metaphors have not been used in the media reporting of the most recent (2001–2003) clinical trials of a self-contained, battery-powered artificial heart: the implantation of an experimental device called the AbiCor Replacement Heart in nine men on the brink of death from end-stage heart failure. And the manufacturer of this mechanical heart, Abiomed, Inc., has attempted to restrain 'media frenzy' about these trials by establishing a policy of withholding news of an implant for up to thirty days after it takes place, followed by 'a quiet period' during a recipient's recovery, unless there is a significant change in his condition. Nevertheless, news of each of these implants, biographical and human interest stories about the recipients, reports on their clinical course, and announcements of the recipient deaths that have occurred have been prominently and continually covered by the print and electronic media, and carried on the Internet, in great, and often colourful detail. The Tin Man of Oz has made an occasional reappearance in these accounts. And some of them have contained poignant statements about the implications of 'losing' a human heart, even if receiving an artificial one can '[bring] a man back from the brink of death and onto the brink of a new definition of life':

> This medical development is miraculous but, to the romantically inclined, it is also . . . disturbing. We consider the human heart to be more than a mechanical pump. In literature and sociology, after all, it is the center and source of emotion and personality. . . . In the mechanical sense, doctors can now mend a broken heart. But, when a human being is asked to reveal what is in his heart, the answer still should never be 'plastic.'
>
> (Venocchi 2001)

Such affirmations about the significance of the human heart were more abundant in what was written about the Jarvik-7 trials. Our analysis of these texts revealed, as Judith Swazey and I have stated, that 'older, more vitalistic sentiments and beliefs about the heart . . . lie below the surface of the scientific and technological view of it that modern-day Americans overtly espouse':

> The heart, it seems, is still regarded and experienced as the locus of the inner self, the home of the soul and the seat of emotions, the center of knowledgeable wisdom and understanding, the source and repository of love, desire, and courage – a cosmic space where the body, mind, and spirit coexist and penetrate each other.
>
> (Fox and Swazey 1992: 161)

It is because the human heart is not only biologically perceived as a vital organ that functions as a muscular pump within our bodies, but is culturally imbued with profound emotional, moral, and spiritual meaning, that removing it from the chests of a small group of men and substituting a machine for it has received such public notice and awed attention.

Conclusion

As this chapter has attempted to show, looking at organ replacement sociologically, through the lenses of biology and medicine, brings to the surface some of the deepest, most serious things about its import – nothing less than matters that concern the human heart and brain, and their relation to our humanness; the somatic, psychic, and moral implications of receiving a 'gift of life' from an unknown, sacrificial other; our self-transcending communal responsibilities; the mysteries of death; and our ultimate mortality.

I do not have simple formulaic recommendations to make about how to forge an analytic framework that not only identifies, but illuminates these dimensions of organ replacement. But at the very least, what is required, as

I hope these reflections have suggested, is a sensitive and supple mode of non-reductionistic thought that uncovers and interconnects their biological, social, and cultural symbolism and meaning for the participants in these forms of organ-exchange, and for the societies in which they are enacted.

References

Fox, R. (1978) 'Organ transplantation: sociocultural aspects', in W.T. Reich (ed.) *The Encyclopedia of Bioethics*; Vol. 3, New York: The Macmillan Company and the Free Press, pp. 166–9.

Fox, R. (2003) 'The transplant surgeon, the sociologist, and the historian', in C. Messikomer, J.P. Swazey, and A. Glicksman (eds) *Society and Medicine: Essays in Honour of Renée C. Fox*, New Brunswick (USA) and London (UK): Transaction Publishers, pp. 245–59.

Fox, R. and Swazey, J.P. (1974) *The Courage to Fail: A Social View of Organ Transplants and Dialysis*, Chicago: University of Chicago Press. A revised, second edition of this book was published by the University of Chicago Press in 1978; and in 2002, it was republished, with a new introduction by the authors, by Transaction Publishers (New Brunswick, USA) and London (UK).

Fox, R. and Swazey, J.P. (1992) *Spare Parts: Organ Replacement in American Society*, New York: Oxford University Press.

Kass, L.R. (2001) Personal communication (11 December).

LaFleur, W. (2002) 'Philosophy and fear: Hans Jonas and the Japanese debate about the ethics of organ transplantation,' in Rolf Eberfeld and Günter Wolfhart (eds) *Komparative Ethik: Das 'gute Leben' zwischenostichen und westlichen Denkwegen*, Köln: Edition Chora.

Leary, W.E. (2002) 'Hubble power controller replaced with soft touch', *New York Times* (7 March): A27.

McCann, R. (1999) 'The resurrectionist', in S.S. Fiffer (ed.) *Body*, New York: Avon, pp. 135–4.

Reed, J.D. (1970) 'Organ transplant', *New Yorker* (26 September): 126.

Starzl, T.E. (1993) *The Puzzle People: Memoirs of a Transplant Surgeon* (with a new Epilogue), Pittsburgh: University of Pittsburgh Press.

Starzl, T.E., Demetris, A.J., Murase, N., Ildstad, S., Ricordi, C. and Trucco, M. (1992) 'Cell migration, chimerism, and graft acceptance', *The Lancet*, **339** (27 June): 1579–82.

Starzl, T.E., Demetris A.J., Trucco, M., *et al.* (1993) 'Cell migration and chimerism after whole-organ transplantation: the basis of graft acceptance, *Hepatology*, **16**, 6: 1127–52.

Texas Heart Institute Online News Release (28 September 2001), 'Texas Heart Institute and St Luke's Episcopal Hospital Physicians Discuss AbioCor Artificial Heart Procedure'.

Vennochi, J. (2001) 'From the heart, disturbing questions', *Boston Globe* (6 July): A23.

19 Prozac nation and the biochemical self

A critique

Nick Crossley

In this chapter I outline the basic framework for three interrelated arguments. First, I argue that biochemical models of the mind are achieving increased prominence in contemporary western societies, particularly in relation to interpretations of emotional difficulties. I briefly discuss Oliver James' (1998) *Britain on the Couch*, in this context, both as a way of illustrating the popular profile of the biochemical model and of highlighting the fact that rates of emotional problems in the UK are increasing. Second, I argue that the prominence of the bio-medical model is a combined effect of this increase in emotional problems, the practical constraints upon doctors in dealing with these problems and the power of the pharmaceutical industry. Finally, I argue that the biomedical model is a highly problematic way of thinking about emotion. My arguments are schematic. They are in need of refinement, embellishment and qualification; both empirically and theoretically. I hope, however, that the bare framework is sufficiently interesting and persuasive to provide an incentive for such further work.

Categories of mind

In his important essay, 'A category of the human mind', Marcel Mauss (1979) explores the cultural variability and history of the schemas which human beings use to render their own 'selves' intelligible. What we 'are', he shows, is by no means self-evident to us. Rather, our self-understanding is shaped by the collective representations of our society or social group. In modern western societies these representations are manifold and often conflicting. They emerge in competing social fields and represent the logic of 'the game' of those fields and the interests and powers therein. Furthermore, some schemas, including the much-discussed Cartesian model, are compromises forged at the interstice between fields. Descartes' ([1641] 1968) dualistic model of the person, comprising a mind attached to a body, as many critics have suggested, expresses his divided loyalties between the authority of the emerging materialist science of his day, specifically his reverence for Galileo's conception of 'matter', and the longer standing and still dominant (at the time) authority of the church, with its conception of an immaterial soul (Husserl 1970; Crossley 2001).

If we remain drawn between these and other competing fields in the West today, however, there can be little doubt that physiological or bio-medical conceptions of the self, closer to Descartes' body than to his mind, have gained considerable ground in recent years. And they have done so in a way which is both 'technological' and closely tied to the various emotional problems which western individuals seem increasingly to be experiencing (see below). Indeed, one might argue that these models have gained ground precisely by seeming to offer technical illumination of, and solutions to, these problems (see also Lyon 1996).

We are all familiar, for example, with the new scanning technologies which allow neuroscientists both to see and demonstrate to the wider public, through various media outlets, that (and how) the brains of such 'residual deviants' (Scheff 1984) as 'Attention Deficit Disorder' children differ from our own. We may not understand what we see but it is difficult for us to argue with this visible evidence. These presentations, which invite us to identify with the image on the screen, self as brain, often draw the inference that the biological states illuminated on the screen are the effective causes of whatever deviance is being discussed. These inferences are unwarranted. Deviant brain states themselves must be caused by something and this cause is not necessarily going to be biological in nature. Even in instances where social and psychological causes are admitted, however, there remains a strong tendency to centralize and thematize the bio-chemical description of distress.

Low serotonin society?

Oliver James's (1998) important and interesting popular book, *Britain on the Couch*, sub-titled '*Treating a low serotonin society*', is an example of this. In this book James makes a number of important arguments. First, he argues that levels of depression and other emotional problems are much higher in the UK now than fifty years ago, in spite of greatly improved material prosperity. In addition to depression there are increases in addiction, suicide, compulsions, anxiety disorders, problems of aggression and many other forms of emotional difficulty. Second, he argues that these increases are due, primarily, to changes in society. New expectations have been generated which fail to match with the realities of our lives; sweeping changes have left us increasingly uncertain of our roles and status; the things which matter to us, such as relationships, have become more difficult to achieve, etc. There is a Durkheimian logic to this argument. Variations in rates of emotional problems cannot be explained by reference to constants, such as our biological constitution, *ceteris paribus*, is assumed to be. They must be explained by reference to variables, such as we find in our social environment, and are therefore 'social facts'. However, the way in which James develops his argument, as 'low serotonin societies' suggests, trades heavily upon biochemical descriptions and categories. His questions and arguments are routinely framed by 'low serotonin' adjectives: e.g. 'why are there more low serotonin people compared with 1950?' (James 1998: 42). Indeed, his whole thesis regarding society and the emotional problems it engenders is diverted along a bio-chemical detour: '. . . we are unhappier . . . people who are unhappier tend to have lower levels of serotonin and . . . levels thereof are largely caused by our social psychological environment' (James 1998: 29).

I use the term 'detour' advisedly. James is clear about the effect he is describing. It is unhappiness. He is also clear about its causes. They are changes in society. Both of these referents are intelligible and self-sufficient. We know what 'unhappiness' is and we know what 'society' is, or at least whatever vagueness attaches to these concepts is not clarified by reference to serotonin. And the same applies to the causal relationship between 'unhappiness' and 'society'. Everyday experience informs us that we are affected, emotionally, by meaningful events and relationships: e.g. failures, successes, friendships, conflicts, etc. It also informs us that each of these factors may be affected by social change. We can understand, for example, that a demand for greater geographical mobility in the workforce will draw many people away from friendships that otherwise enrich their emotional lives. Therefore, we can understand why social changes will generate changes in our emotional lives. So why make reference to serotonin?

The claim appears to be that serotonin mediates between social conditions and emotional states. Social conditions affect serotonin, which in turn affects emotion. The plausibility of this claim derives from the fact that we can, to a degree, technically manipulate mood by manipulating levels of such neurotransmitters as serotonin with drugs. However, the claim entails a category error. Insofar as one can establish an association between 'unhappiness' and 'low serotonin', this is not an association between two different 'things' or 'states' which could interact or enjoy causal relations. As I will discuss in more detail later, it is a relationship between two different levels of description of the same thing. To say that one affects emotions by manipulating serotonin levels is akin to saying that one broke a window by first breaking the glass; as if breaking the glass were a distinct act from breaking the window and could 'cause' the latter to happen. 'Glass' and 'windows' can't enjoy causal relations because they are not distinct things. They are the same thing described from a different perspective. So it is with bio-chemical accounts of brains or neurotransmitters and psychological or commonsense accounts of 'unhappiness' – although the complexity of the 'things' in question is obviously much greater and, in a longer essay, would require some qualification. One might legitimately argue that specific social situations cause changes in serotonin levels, or that they cause changes in happiness levels, but there is something odd, and problematic, in claiming that they cause changes in serotonin levels which, in turn, cause changes in levels of happiness. Furthermore, the jump between levels of description decreases rather than increases the clarity of the causal account as it requires us to switch frames of reference, twice. It is not obvious, for example, why 'divorce' would increase serotonin levels, because 'divorce' and 'serotonin' belong to two quite distinct levels of description; one 'social', the other 'biochemical'. Similarly it is not obvious that or why low serotonin would be associated with unhappiness, for the same reason. To put 'serotonin' into the account, to reiterate, is a detour.

I am not suggesting that James is wrong to make some reference to serotonin in his account. However, the high profile he affords it, given that it is not required to make his argument intelligible and introduces category errors into it, illustrates the symbolic power which the biochemical model commands in our society and the ritual deference which is afforded to it. We are increasingly attuned to hear references to 'brains', 'neurotransmitters', etc. as more real, truer and deeper accounts of what and who we are. We are less trustful of our own everyday language of self-hood and personal life, more enamoured of the 'hard' facts of the 'hard sciences' of the brain. 'Misery' is not enough, we believe only in 'low serotonin'. In this chapter I want to consider some of the implications of this. Before I do, however, one further and important aspect of bio-medical dominance should be identified.

Or prozac nation?

James's remedy for the increasingly unhappy state of the nation entails a three-pronged strategy. Since society is the cause of the problem, he believes that social changes are necessary. He is very vague about the nature of these changes, however, and doesn't appear particularly convinced that much will happen at this level. Social change, after all, is immensely complex and cannot be steered or managed with any degree of exactitude or guarantee of success. This leaves the option of treating the 'low serotonin individual', rather than society as a whole, by way of both psychotherapy and drugs. Psychotherapy can help by adjusting our expectations and lifestyles, so that they are not so likely lead us to unhappiness. And drugs treat the serotonin.

He concedes that this latter option will appear preposterous to some. First, because drugs do not treat the causes of the problem, only its biological mechanism. Second, because the causes of the problem, when more closely analysed, appear to be specifically related to the nature of 'capitalist' societies, and yet capitalists, in the form of large pharmaceutical companies, stand to profit from drug-based solutions. Yet, he argues, we must be pragmatic. For some people, some of the time, drugs work. Why deny them this choice?

It is difficult to argue with this, except to say that James' pragmatism, like his 'low serotonin' descriptions, is symptomatic and illustrative of a broader social trend. Busy GPs and psychiatrists with tight budgets and limited time, like the desperate individuals whom they treat, have little option but to be pragmatic. Meanwhile, large pharmaceutical companies,

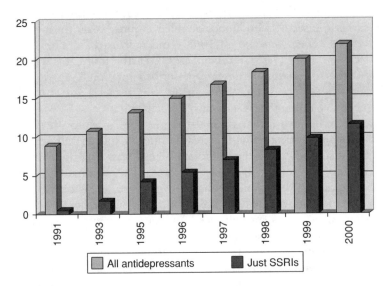

Figure 19.1 Prescriptions for all anti-depressants and selective serotonin reuptake inhibitors (SSRIs) specifically in England (millions)

Source: Prescription Cost Analysis (England), Department of Health Statistics Division, 1991–2001

in a highly competitive industry, with an economic interest in 'biological solutions' and sufficient economic power to both court clinicians and set research agendas, have a considerable and growing influence in shaping how the pragmatist will respond. With fierce battles over patents in the latter half of the 1990s, for example, the number of active drug company reps in the USA, with generous expense accounts and innumerable 'freebies', nearly doubled (*The Observer* 18/6/00). Not that much influence is necessarily required. Drugs appear to 'work' in many instances, at least if 'work' means reducing symptoms. They are relatively cheap, not least because their administration is not very time consuming. Indeed, they may be the only practical solution that can be administered in a brief consultation, sandwiched between many others. And for these reasons they are the easy and pragmatic solution. Consequently, rates of prescription for anti-depressant drugs, particularly the new 'Selective Serotonin Reuptake Inhibitors' (SSRIs), such as Prozac, have risen dramatically in the last decade (see Figure 19.1).

Prozac and related products have become household names; ready-made solutions for easily identified and only too common problems. Indeed, they have become part of our culture. As a recent Social Audit report indicated, for example, over twenty recent popular books have 'Prozac' in the title (www.socialaudit.org.uk/24treati.htm). Elizabeth Wurtzel's (1996) *Prozac Nation* is one very obvious example of this. Young people and children are not exempt from this trend. Prescriptions of Ritalin, the drug of choice for the various 'attention deficit' and 'hyperactivity' disorders usually identified with (ever earlier phases of) childhood, doubled in most years during the mid-to-late 1990s (*The Guardian* 31/10/00) and increased by 270%, to 90,000, in 1996–97 alone (*The Guardian* 3/3/99). Furthermore, it is widely acknowledged that the 'adult' drugs are prescribed for 'mild', as well as more serious forms of depression, with some psychiatrists arguing that this extends to 'ordinary unhappiness' (see also Lyon 1996).

Individuals may be aware that these drugs are controversial – e.g. allegedly addictive and associated with increased rates of suicide and aggression – but they also know their 'good' points. They know that these drugs are powerful and potentially available to them. This affords the bio-medical model practical dominance. Whatever 'new age' maps of the soul we are attracted to in our moments of reflection, we are increasingly drawn to bio-medicine in our moments of need. And our moments of need, as James (1998) persuasively argues, are increasing.

This practical dominance should also lead us to be cautious of claims regarding the apparent growth in prominence of so-called bio-psychosocial models within medicine and psychiatry. I do not have the space to discuss these models here or the evidence regarding their increased prominence. It is important to note, however, that the evidence for this increase must be considered against the background of the massive growth in chemical interventions for emotional problems and the increased range of problems now treated in this way. As James's arguments illustrate only too clearly, even those who prioritize social factors in their diagnosis of a problem can find themselves constrained by practicalities into prioritizing biochemistry in their solutions. This could only count as 'holistic' in the most hollow of academic senses. Whatever claims we may make to viewing ourselves in a more holistic manner, the rapid growth of chemical interventions suggests that we are increasingly inclined to *treat* ourselves (in the double sense of the term) as biochemical objects.

But what are the consequences of this 'practical dominance'? In the second part of this chapter I will spell out what I believe they are. My point of departure is a more detailed reflection upon the nature of the 'bio-medical gaze' and the ways in which it differs from our everyday ways of reasoning and perceiving.

From the natural attitude to the bio-medical gaze

The bio-medical perspective is partial. It is constituted, in part, by a process of bracketing out certain features of human existence and abstracting and focusing upon others. It consists in a particular way of looking at human beings, qua 'bodies', quite far removed from our everyday ways of perceiving 'bodies' and 'persons'. In our 'natural attitude', as many phenomenologists have argued, the bodies of others are simultaneously expressive, moral and aesthetic (Husserl 1970). Or rather, we do not really experience them as 'bodies' at all. As when we read words on the pages of a book, the physicality of others is submerged beneath the meanings and intentions which their actions communicate to us, by the moral implications of these actions and by their beauty or ugliness. Some of this is acquired. We learn to 'read' and judge others as we learn to read texts. As Merleau-Ponty (1965) has noted, however, the behaviour of very young infants suggests that they, too, experience the behaviour of others as 'significant', albeit perhaps in a more basic way (see also Crossley 1996). The actions of others are meaningful events for them rather than physical facts.

In the case of our own bodies things are more complex. At one level I am my body and my primary experience is not of myself, my body, but rather an embodied experience of the world to which I belong (Crossley 1996, 2001). Of course my perception of the world entails a tacit sense of myself as a perceiving, embodied being. This is why objects strike me as 'close' or 'high'. It is why the sight of approaching projectiles is coloured with fear and motivates me to duck. However, this self-perception is a tacit background structure of an experience that is otherwise 'of the world'. Even my more intense feelings of pleasure or pain are 'intentional' experiences, in the phenomenological sense of 'intentionality'; experiences 'of' a world beyond my own 'body' which brings me pleasure (ibid.). This tacit self-experience of embodiment can become more thematic, as when I feel weary or tired, when my muscles ache or when I need to sleep. Furthermore, by internalizing the perspective that others take towards my body I can learn to experience it more reflexively still (ibid.). I can experience it as beautiful or ugly, too big or too small. Always, however, as with my perception of the other, my perception is moral, aesthetic and existential.

The bio-medical gaze shifts this gestalt, effecting an 'epistemological break' with the natural attitude and constituting the person, qua body, as a mechanical object. It strips away the aesthetic aura of the body, brackets its moral status and refuses the intercorporeal dialogue, the exchange of meanings, which a meeting of bodies, seer and seen, ordinarily effects (ibid.). These 'natural' features of the perceived body are pushed into the background in order to draw its physical substrate to the foreground, where it can be dissected. The 'words' of the text are refused their meaning in order that they can be decomposed into physical objects, defined only in terms of their physical properties of size, weight, colour, density, etc. The body becomes a site of mere physical, causal processes. 'This' secretes 'that', sending an impulse 'there', causing 'that' to contract. Another way of putting this might be to say that the bio-medical perspective focuses upon the 'parts', where the natural attitude focuses upon the 'whole', a whole which is so much more than the sum of its parts, in a multitude of dimensions.

This is perhaps one amongst the many reasons why medicine has such strong historical associations with death (Foucault 1973; Leder 1998). The dead body effects a practical shift of the gestalt. Even if it retains something of the beauty of the person it once embodied, even if it commands respect and carries a final characteristic expression, it has ceased to partake in the lived time of an intersubjective, social world, such that its 'all too human' characteristics have slipped into the background, foregrounding the physical elements, the 'corpse', that is the proper object of the bio-medical gaze.

In the clinic

This is not to say that the natural attitude and the bio-medical gaze never meet or merge. They do, specifically in the clinic. It is here, however, that some of the problems emerge. The bio-medical perspective, at least insofar as it is applied to 'psychological problems', is very much dependent upon the perspective of the natural attitude as such problems are only visible from within this attitude. One cannot see 'depression' or 'anxiety', less still 'challenging behaviour', in the brain or the nervous system. These are terms that have developed, albeit with some help from psychologists, in the contexts of everyday life. Insofar as they have a referent it is human activity and expression as a whole, judged in terms of the context in which it occurs. But they are more than mere descriptive labels. They arise out of everyday ways of negotiating, influencing and co-ordinating social interaction; that is, language games. This is why we do not immediately recognize 'depression' when the TV psychologist shows us 'enlarged pink areas' on a brain scan photograph. The brain cannot be depressed because it does not belong to the language games from which the concept of depression derives its meaning. To seek out 'depression' in the brain is akin to seeking out 'off-side' in snooker. It mixes up (language) games. The clinician can only bring 'brains' and 'depression' together by mapping the bio-medical gaze over that of the natural attitude; that is, by taking an individual who, from the point of view of the natural attitude, is recognizably depressed, and ascertaining what is happening in the brain during their periods of depression. They must shift the gestalt back and forth, checking the biological description against the everyday description.

This may be helpful. If we understand what is 'going on' physiologically when we are in a particular 'state' then we are in a position to develop drugs to manipulate these 'goings on' and, by implication, the emotional states to which they belong. However, there is a danger here that, for practical purposes at least, the biological description takes precedence over the description from the 'natural attitude', and a human problem is transformed into a technical, physical problem. 'Low serotonin' effectively becomes both the problem and its cause. The depression of the individual is assumed to be caused by low serotonin, if only because time restraints prevent medical practitioners from considering the wider possibilities. And 'low serotonin' is substituted for 'depression' as the problem to be solved. Lift the patient's serotonin levels and the problem is solved. This is problematic in itself as it diverts attention and resources away from what might be the real cause of the depression. It also generates a range of dangerous social side-effects.

First, it alienates the 'patient' from their emotional life and puts them in a relationship of dependency upon the doctor. I do not mean to suggest by this that individuals ordinarily enjoy perfect self-possession with respect to their psychological lives. It is a mistake, attributable to Descartes ([1641] 1968), to believe that our own mental life is immediately and perfectly transparent to us. In certain respects we are more obscure to ourselves than to others. Furthermore, we learn how to attribute mental states to both self and other within the context of specific language games, and these judgements are defeasible and open to argument (Crossley 2001). However, we do have an interest in the process whereby our states of mind are defined and we ordinarily play a central and active role in these processes. As I have suggested elsewhere, for example, our emotional and psychological lives can be argued over with others at numerous levels (Crossley 1998, 2000). We can argue over the nature of the emotions we are expressing. Am I justifiably annoyed with you, for example, or simply jealous? We might also argue over the normative standing of our emotions. Are we right to feel as we do? Are we being fair? Are we overreacting? Should we hide our feelings? Finally, we can argue over the causes, or perhaps rather the reasons for our emotions. We might explain to a friend, for example, that there is no reason to feel jealous because things are not as they seem. Or again, we might explain why 'things aren't that bad', why there is a 'bright side', etc. Through such interactions we shape not only the ways in which emotions are defined and expressed but also the very emotions that we have; anger, for example, might quite genuinely be transformed into joviality by way of a conciliatory dialogue. The bio-medical approach short-circuits this process, reframing emotional life at a level which is at once alien and esoteric. Serotonin levels aren't the sort of thing many people are able to discuss or argue over. I don't know what my serotonin levels are, wouldn't know if they are appropriate and couldn't say for sure if I have any. I don't know what causes their ups and downs (at least in biological terms) nor what relationship they have to such wonder-drugs as Prozac. If the doctor says that they are a problem then they must be. Insofar as I accept a bio-medical definition of myself, therefore, I am alienated from my own self-understanding and dependent upon the doctor. Indeed, I may even lose confidence in those areas of self-ascription about which I once felt confident. Am I happy or have my serotonin levels risen?

This is problematic in its own right but is also related to a further problem, concerning the 'functions' and meanings of emotion. To say, as I have, that emotions are intimately bound up within the languages games of everyday life requires that we recognize that they have an active and meaningful role therein. They bind us into social 'games' and variously constitute or occasion our activities therein. A 'fear reaction' to a situation, for example, may, qua behaviour, function to draw an individual out of a dangerous situation or, qua 'pang', occasion reflection by the individual on the possible safety of the situation. Furthermore, much of the moral fabric of the everyday world is constituted through emotions: e.g. guilt, shame, pride, affection, indignation and outrage. The more we embrace the bio-medical model, allowing it to colonize our self-understandings, and the more we submit our emotional lives to the technical interference of drugs, the further these important aspects of human existence slip out of our hands. Our sociality is dampened and dulled.

This relates to a second problem. The advance of the bio-medical gaze into areas once regulated by the common sense of the natural attitude is corrosive of forms of understanding and practical reason which are both existentially and socially necessary. As I noted above, the bio-medical gaze is constructed by a process which brackets out the expressivity of 'the body' and its moral and aesthetic qualities. It abstracts only certain features of the body which are amenable both to its narrowly physicalist conception of life and to its positivistic methods of analysis. The body is reduced to those of its dimensions which can be measured, weighed, etc. This is undoubtedly necessary for an effective bio-medical science. However, everyday human life cannot afford to bracket out the expressive, moral or aesthetic dimensions, and thus cannot afford to concede too much to the bio-medical model. 'Fact-minded sciences', to quote Husserl (1970), 'make fact-minded people'; but as he recognized, many of the problems facing human beings are not factual or technical in nature. They are precisely moral, existential and aesthetic. As such they require from us a capacity to reason about such matters. Consider Oliver James again:

> This book is about the angst of normal people. . . . It offers an explanation of why we are so much more likely to be miserable than our grandparents, why we are so discontented and self-attacking (I'm fat, I'm stupid, I'm ugly, when you are not), why we feel our lives are not under our control, why the moments of emotional richness and freedom of our childhood are less frequent, why so many of us feel there is 'something missing' from our lives.
>
> (James 1998, xi)

The language which James uses here, which he assumedly believes will allow his readers to recognize themselves in his account, is an unashamedly existential, aesthetic and moral language. It is a language which speaks of our paralysis in the face of the world, our lack of meaning and recognition, and the discrepancy between the lives we want to lead or people we want to be and the lives we do lead and people we are. These are existential, moral and aesthetic problems. They are problems which individuals and societies have always struggled with; how to live, individually and together; who to be; what it all means and what the point is. However we interpret the psychiatric statistics they seem to indicate that we are losing this battle.

The bio-medical gaze purports to offer a solution but one is forced to wonder if it is not, in fact, part of the problem. As a 'fact-minded science' it undoubtedly contributes to the production of 'fact-minded people'; that is to say, people less capable of engaging with the existential, moral and aesthetic problems that a human life necessarily throws up. It offers technical solutions to existential problems; which is to say, no solutions at all but rather further exacerbation of the problem.

I do not mean to suggest here that bio-medical interventions are always inappropriate. The problem, rather, is that the scope of the bio-medical model has been over-extended. We have lost sight of its proper place. In a world where 'technology' so often seems the solution to our problems, we have allowed technology, in the form of the bio-medical gaze and psychoactive drugs, to replace ways of thinking which it is incapable of replacing.

The critic may respond that the bio-medical gaze and drug technologies are only used in cases where 'reasonable' emotional behaviour is breached. My concern, however, is precisely that our capacity to see emotions as reasonable or meaningful human responses to situations is threatened by the bio-medical gaze, for which all emotions are a matter of levels of this or that neurotransmitter. We need to preserve our sense of the moral and rational meanings of emotion, but to do this we must shield our conception of emotion and self-hood from the bio-medical gaze. Furthermore, there is a danger that our conception of 'reasonable emotion' itself is affected, and narrowed, by the effect of technical interventions.

This brings me to my final point: we tend to become dependent upon technical solutions, such as prescription drugs, and our behaviours and thresholds of tolerance alter and become moulded around them. We are used to hearing this argument in relationship to such things as cars and television. How did people live without these things? How have our ways of living changed, such that we now presuppose the existence of these things at a very basic and mundane level? Andrew Scull (1993) makes a very similar argument with respect to psychiatry and the lunatic asylum in the nineteenth century. There is good evidence that those who could afford to be were rather hesitant about using the first 'madhouses' when they began to emerge in Britain in the eighteenth century (Busfield 1986). The idea that others, motivated by profit, might take care of one's unfortunates went against the grain and madhouse keepers made great efforts to convince potential clients of the value of their service. As Scull indicates, however, once the idea took off it began to spread very rapidly. More importantly, the numbers of the insane began to increase rapidly, suggesting that the definition of insanity was becoming broader. A wider range of behaviours and experiences were now being deemed 'unreasonable'. In other words, psychiatry did not simply remove from everyday life individuals whose behaviours and experiences had always been deemed intolerable. Its capacity to intervene changed people's levels of tolerance and their definitions of reasonable behaviour, such that once acceptable behaviours and experiences ceased to be so. Furthermore, these shifts necessarily made people more dependent upon the technologies (psychiatry) that were able to deal with these decreasingly tolerable individuals.

That our levels of toleration and definitions of what is reasonable have continued to reduce is, I suggest, evident. Craib (1994), for example, has argued that individuals are increasingly looking for quick-fix solutions to personal problems. People no longer expect to have to tolerate unhappiness, loss and disappointment, he argues. He blames this state of affairs on the therapy industry. To this, however, we must add the pharmaceutical industry. Prescription drugs are the stereotypical 'quick fix' solution to emotional problems, including 'mild depression' and simple unhappiness. And like nineteenth-century asylums, they change our definition of 'problems', lowering our thresholds for coping with and tolerating a range of experiences and behaviours. More to the point, as our tolerance decreases our dependency upon the pharmaceutical companies increases, granting them greater power over our lives.

Conclusion

This chapter has laid out a few basic arguments for suggesting that and why bio-chemical models of the self are gaining a stronger foothold in our society, and has sought to identify some of the potential consequences of this. I hope that this is not read as a diatribe against biological approaches. It is not intended in this way. In many respects my criticisms are focused more generally upon the problems posed by increased levels of 'technical' intervention into our everyday lifeworlds and the colonization of those lifeworlds, to paraphrase Habermas (1987), by a variety of 'experts'. The problem here is that technical forms of knowledge cannot address and therefore tend to undermine ethical, existential and aesthetic issues. This might apply as much to social or psychological interventions as to bio-medicine and to any of the most sophisticated bio-psycho-social models. Medicine tends to take the rap here, however, because whatever the good intentions and bright ideas of both researchers and practitioners in the medical field, the power of pharmaceutical companies and the pragmatics of health service delivery conspire to afford chemical solutions a practical dominance. And if bio-chemistry dominates at the level of solutions and treatments then it dominates to all practical purposes.

The challenge which my chapter throws out, therefore, is not simply a call for better ways of connecting biochemical understandings with sociological and psychological understandings, but equally of connecting each of these (unquestionably useful and important) scientific forms of understanding with the existential, aesthetic and ethical textures of everyday life. In this chapter I hope that I have made some headway towards addressing that question by way of the concept of 'the gaze'. Mind, (biological) body and society are not separate 'things', each joined in ways which scientists might 'discover'. They derive from different ways of looking at the same 'thing'. Each necessarily foregrounds and 'constructs' certain objects, concerns, etc., pushing other potential objects and concerns into the background. So it is with the existential, aesthetic and moral concerns of everyday agents in their lifeworlds. They, too, are a product of a particular (and necessary) way of looking at the world.

The necessarily exclusive nature of these 'gazes' precludes the possibility of any one of them making a legitimate claim to the territory of the others. Biologists (qua biologists) cannot determine morally appropriate ways to act any more than a moral discourse could determine the facts of such processes as serotonin uptake. Furthermore, this puts a question mark over attempts to combine them in a 'jumbo' model (e.g. a bio-psycho-socio-existential, etc. model). A more appropriate response, in my view, is for us to recognize the vices and virtues of each perspective or gaze, and to seek out ways in which representatives of each, including the everyday representatives of the lifeworld, can work together, appreciating the point of view of the other without reducing it back to the same. Sometimes the issues foregrounded by one perspective will have more importance, other times it may be another perspective, but it is unlikely, in any situation, that only one of these perspectives will have something of value to say, and it is unlikely that the biological perspective(s) will always be the most pertinent or appropriate – even if economic and political pressures conspire to bring them to the fore. What is needed is a genuinely 'dialogical' perspective which admits of the value of different perspectives and refuses to prejudge which, or which combination, will be of most relevance in any given instance.

References

Busfield, J. (1986) *Managing Madness*, London: Hutchinson.

Craib, I. (1994) *The Importance of Disappointment*, London: Routldge.

Crossley, N. (1996) *Intersubjectivity*, London: Sage.

Crossley, N. (1998) 'Emotion and communicative action', in G. Bendelow and S. Williams (1998) *Emotions in Social Life*, London: Routledge, pp. 16–38.

Crossley, N. (2000) 'Emotions, psychiatry and social order', in S. Williams, J. Gabe and M. Calnan (2000) *Health, Medicine and Society*, London: Routledge, pp. 277–95.

Crossley, N. (2001) *The Social Body: Habit, Identity and Desire*, London: Sage.

Descartes, R. ([1641] 1968) *The Meditations*, Harmondsworth: Penguin.

Foucault, M. (1973) *The Birth of the Clinic*, London: Tavistock.

Habermas, J. (1987) *The Theory of Communicative Action*, Cambridge: Polity.

Husserl, E. (1970) *The Crisis of the European Sciences and Transcendental Phenomenology*, Evanston: Northwestern University Press.

James, O. (1998) *Britain on the Couch: Treating a Low Serotonin Society*, London: Arrow.

Leder, D. (1998) 'A tale of two bodies', in D. Welton (1998) *Body and Flesh*, Oxford: Blackwell, pp. 117–30.

Lyon, M. (1996) 'C. Wright Mills meets Prozac', in V. James and J. Gabe (1996) *Health and the Sociology of Emotion*, Oxford: Blackwell.

Mauss, M. (1979) 'A category of the human mind: the notion of person, the notion of self', in *Sociology and Psychology*, London: Routledge & Kegan Paul, pp. 57–94.

Merleau-Ponty, M. (1965) *The Structure of Behaviour*, London: Methuen.

Scull, A. (1993) *The Most Solitary of Afflictions*, Yale: Harvard University Press.

Scheff, T. (1984) *Being Mentally Ill*, New York: Aldine.

Wurtzel, E. (1996) *Prozac Nation*, London: Quartet.

Part V
Reclaiming biology

(Bio)ethics and beyond

20 The bioethics of biotechnology

Alternative claims of posthuman futures

Arthur W. Frank

In 1904 the Greek poet C.P. Cavafy wrote 'Waiting for the Barbarians', a poem that imagines a group of Romans gathering each day in the forum to wait for invaders, fearful yet fascinated by what will happen. At the end of this particular day, no barbarians arrive. The Romans wonder what will happen, without the barbarians. 'They were, those people, a kind of solution' (Cavafy 1975: 18). In journalistic and scholarly analyses of the present and future 'revolution' in biotechnology, I hear us waiting for Cavafy's barbarians. One day, real barbarians did arrive in Rome, and history changed. But Cavafy reminds us that the real change was immanent in the fantasy of the barbarians' future arrival. The Romans needed the barbarians to show them what they could not recognize about who they already had become.

* * *

Biology used to refer to what bodies irrevocably are; it marked the boundary at which interpretive construction seemed to end. Increasingly biology refers to what might be. Biotechnology is an umbrella term covering present realities and future possibilities for altering living things: plants, animals, and people. Human modifications range from pharmacology to change bodies and minds, to genetic screening and gene modification (which can embed changes in future generations), cloning, implanting computer chips in bodies, and other possibilities best described as 'fiction science' (Baldi 2001). The scope of this topic is massive, so I restrict this chapter to two recent, articulate, well-informed, and distinctly different visions of humanity's biotechnological future. My point is not to critique these books but to explore the alternative views they represent. Each view is ethical, though each projects a different form of ethics. Each view describes the future as 'posthuman', though neither is very clear on what this provocative term means.

Our Posthuman Future: Consequences of the Biotechnology Revolution was recently published (2002), to considerable journalistic attention, by Francis Fukuyama, professor of political economy at Johns Hopkins University, recent appointee to the US President's Council on Bioethics, and author of the scholarly best-seller, *The End of History and the Last Man*. Fukuyama's book seems to have been in press when Pierre Baldi published *The Shattered Self: The End of Natural Evolution* (2001). Baldi lacks Fukuyama's best-seller aura, but has impressive academic credentials. His full academic title is significant, if only because it concatenates words that would not have made up an intelligible sequence in earlier academic configurations. Baldi is Professor of Information and Computer Science and of Biological Chemistry in the College of Medicine at the University of California, Irvine, where he is Director of the Institute for Genomics and Bioinformatics.

Both Fukuyama and Baldi see the future dominated by biotechnology. Each emphasizes different technologies and foresees a different future, and while their respective visions hardly exhaust the possibilities, they provide a representative contrast. I will present their differences in three sections. First, what's possible in the coming 'posthuman future'; second, what the distinct benefits and dangers of this future may be; and third, what ethics are appropriate to guide humanity into this future.

The posthuman possibility

Although Fukuyama, or his editor, chose to place 'posthuman' in his title, he says even less about what this term means than Baldi does. Fukuyama's vision of posthumanity is characterized by threat. In a chapter titled 'A Tale of Two Dystopias' (those presented by Aldous Huxley and George Orwell), Fukuyama writes: 'the most significant threat posed by contemporary biotechnology is the possibility that it will alter human nature and thereby move us into a "posthuman" stage of history' (2002: 7). The threat is that biotechnology will alter human nature, and something constitutive about who humans are will be lost; more of this argument below.

Baldi sees not threat but promise in posthumanity. In a chapter titled 'The Last Frontier', he writes: 'In time, we could progressively create new beings – not necessarily *Homo sapiens* – with higher forms of intelligence. Perhaps from *Homo sapiens* we could derive beings with bigger brains, or even multiple brains' (2001: 108). Baldi does not specify that the beings we will 'derive' will be all that humanity is by then; thus we 'derive' ourselves. The page facing these words has a photo of a two-headed Pacific gopher snake. It becomes strangely beautiful, the longer one looks at it.

The quotations above stake out a provocative difference, but they do not specify what's meant by posthuman, which remains defined by the fright or allure it elicits. For more content I turn to an influential statement by the literary scholar Katherine Hayles. Hayles is clear that 'posthuman' does not admit strict definition. She describes posthuman as 'a point of view' characterized by certain assumptions, which she presents as 'suggestive rather than prescriptive' (1999: 2). These assumptions are:

First, the posthuman view privileges informational pattern over material instantiation, so that embodiment in a biological substrate is seen as an accident of history rather than an inevitability of life. Second, the posthuman view considers consciousness, regarded as the seat of human identity in the Western tradition long before Descartes thought he was a mind thinking, as an epiphenomenon, as an evolutionary upstart trying to claim that it is the whole show when in actuality it is only a minor sideshow. Third, the posthuman view thinks of the body as the original prosthesis we all learn to manipulate, so that extending or replacing the body with other prostheses becomes a continuation of a process that began before we were born. Fourth, and most important, by these and other means, the posthuman view configures human being so that it can be seamlessly articulated with intelligent machines. In the posthuman, there are no essential differences or absolute demarcations between bodily existence and computer simulation, cybernetic mechanism and biological organism, robot technology and human goals.

(Hayles 1999: 2–3)

By 'informational pattern' I understand Hayles to mean a code from which different things can be generated: one digital code, read by a CD player, generates music; DNA, as a potentially digital code, gestated in a womb, generates a human being. Thus music, buildings, weather patterns, and life itself have a common denominator in that each can be reduced to some informational pattern. As an informational pattern, each can be stored, manipulated, and – given the right equipment – reproduced either exactly or in some variant form. I quote Hayles at length because she provides a clearer and more comprehensive statement of what Baldi looks forward to, and what Fukuyama fears, than either of those authors provides.

Baldi's posthuman is the evolutionary stage that follows what he calls the 'bootstrap phase' (2001: 46) of human history. The posthuman stage begins when 'the frontier between biological computing and silicon computing' blurs even further than it already has (2001: 91). The definitive event in the shift to posthuman is the mapping of the human genome, which Baldi calls 'the most significant event in our history, and perhaps in the 3.5 billion-year history of life on Earth' (2001: 1). This discovery, coupled with the implications of Moore's law on the increase in 'the number of operations that can be carried on a given piece of silicon real estate' (2001: 91), presents 'the ability to treat genomes as programs, and to be able to perform all the standard operations one performs on computer files: read, write, execute, copy, edit, cut-and-paste, insert, delete, replace, transfer, and so forth' (2001: 35). This ability, implemented through technologies like cloning, makes possible 'genetically smart brains' that can be put together 'in ways that far exceed anything we have ever seen' (2001: 61). My brief quotations from Baldi lose the lucid detail with which he renders plausible such 'gee whiz' sounding statements. His book is a model of accessible scientific explanation, and his vision of the posthuman future is all the more compelling for that lucidity.

Fukuyama breaks down the posthuman future into three areas, which do not include the body/machine interface that is definitive for Hayles and Baldi. Fukuyama concentrates, first, on the implications of new genetic knowledge on the increasing tilt towards the importance of nature, now understood as genetic heredity, over nurture. He then discusses neuropharmacology, specifically Ritalin and Prozac, because he believes: 'Virtually everything we can anticipate being able to do through genetic engineering we will most likely be able to do much sooner through neuropharmacology' (2002: 173). Fukuyama's 'everything' does not, on my reading, include the smart brains that fascinate Baldi; again, his posthuman future includes less machine/body interface. Fukuyama's third area is the prolongation of life, something that also intrigues Baldi, but with a different emphasis. 'A genome is immortal,' Baldi writes, 'regardless of whether or not it has physical incarnation' (2001: 120), a statement that recalls Hayles's posthuman criterion that informational pattern gains privilege over material substrate. But the immortality that Fukuyama sees people wanting to prolong is decidedly linked to their biological substrate, thus creating problems such as 'havoc with most existing age-graded hierarchies' (2002: 64). This issue moves us to the second area of comparison between Baldi and Fukuyama, their respective evaluations of possibility and danger.

Posthuman risk society

Baldi grounds his sense of posthuman possibility in his carefully argued belief that humans' sense of who we are and our place in the world is 'scientifically wrong' and 'the result of evolutionary accidents' (2001: 3). Traditional views arose during what he calls 'our evolutionary bootstrapping: a world without molecular biotechnology, human cloning, and the Internet' (2001: 3). In the posthuman future when we 'can raise our clones and have multiple brains', a new vision of humanity is needed: 'The boundary between the self and the other, the self and the world, the inside and outside has begun to blur, and ultimately may evaporate entirely' (2001: 4). This latter statement is illustrated by the Internet, which for Baldi is not a handy place to shop, do research, or even send person-directed messages. Rather the Internet represents the possibility of merging smart machines into a common intelligence, just as what we now think of as individual brains might someday merge in common capacity. Baldi writes that he finds such possibilities 'as disturbing as anyone else does' (2001: 5), but he is far more fascinated than repelled.

Baldi acknowledges risk. Writing of ectogenesis (fetal gestation outside the human womb), he acknowledges that 'we are bound to make a few tragic mistakes along the way' (2001: 41), but these mistakes will fade into a generally improved future. 'Science,' as Baldi interprets its history, 'has been one of the greatest forces driving the evolution of human societies over the centuries. In spite of a few hiccups along the way, the majority of effects have been, overall, positive' (2001: 158). Thus it is 'high time to get rid of our defensive reactions based on an old "magic" view of the world and take a closer scientific look at the reality' (2001: 72).

One such defensive reaction is to judge practices to be unnatural. Baldi rejects such arguments. One reason is the variety already inherent in how nature accomplishes things like birth: 'The in vitro development of a variety of organisms is very common in nature and in biological laboratories; hence it is not an unnatural notion' (2001: 37). Since 'embryonic development outside of a maternal body is the norm' (2001: 37) for many living species, why should humans be distressed by the prospect of producing a full-term infant entirely in vitro? More significant to Baldi's evaluation of risk is his belief that evolution means constant change without any governing essentialist benchmark. 'Things do not stop where we are, or where we think we are, but extend continuously' (Baldi 2001: 137). Because things do not stop, 'preserving our humanity is not a good reason' (2001: 136) to fail to explore as biotechnology allows.

Fukuyama's evaluations of risk are more immediate and political. His three categories of biotechnological change – different perceptions of how personal abilities and traits are inherited, increased use of neuropharmacology, and prolongation of life – all point towards a new eugenics and to changes in the composition and solidity of social hierarchies and inequalities. Early in his argument he quotes Thomas Jefferson's Enlightenment realization that 'the mass of mankind has not been born with saddles on their backs, nor a favored few booted and spurred, ready to ride them legitimately, by the grace of God' (quoted in Fukuyama 2002: 9). For Fukuyama, 'the ultimate question [and risk] raised by biotechnology is, What will happen to political rights once we are able to, in effect, breed some people with saddles on their backs, and others with boots and spurs?' (2002: 10).

Fukuyama finds new eugenics dangerous, whether it is accomplished by genetic manipulation or through use of pharmaceuticals (of which Ritalin and Prozac are only the beginning), and even though (or perhaps because) it presents itself as a 'kinder, gentler eugenics' (2002: 86, 87), used by individual choice, not coerced by the state. Ostensible choice only conceals a new form of coercion. 'This kind of genetic arms race,' Fukuyama writes,

> will impose special burdens on people who for religious or other reasons do not want their children genetically modified [or subjected to pharmaceutical improvement]; if everyone around them is doing it, it will be much harder to abstain, for fear of holding their children back.
> (2002: 97)

The same can be said of national bioethics standards and the biotech industries they risk holding back.

Baldi would wonder why people would want to hold back either their own children or humanity as a whole. To reduce the differences between Baldi and Fukuyama to the latter's more considered attention to the immediate generation of political and economic inequalities – breeding some with saddles on their backs, in Jefferson's metaphor that Fukuyama likes – risks unfair political labelling of Baldi and the position he represents. More fundamental differences involve their opposing views of evolutionary change. Baldi, as I understand his argument, could share Fukuyama's commitment to human equality but dismiss many of his arguments as mistakes resulting from extrapolating present political and economic realities into a future when the material parameters will have changed. The core difference between Baldi and Fukuyama is not their politics but their divergent understandings of the emergent properties of complex systems.

Fukuyama provides a useful example of a complex system and how its behaviour emerges.

> The distinctive and easily recognizable behavior of a flock of birds or a swarm of bees, for example, is the product of the interaction of individual birds or bees following relatively simple behavioral rules (fly next to a partner, avoid obstacles, and so on), none of which encompasses or defines the behavior of the flock or swarm as a whole. Rather, the group behavior 'emerges' as a result of the interaction of the individuals that make it up. In many cases, the relationship between parts and wholes is nonlinear: that is, increasing input A increases output B up to a certain point, whereupon it creates a qualitatively different and unexpected output C.
>
> (2002: 163)

Output C, then, is the emergent property of a complex system. Earlier in Fukuyama's argument he describes the brain just as I have quoted him describing a flock of birds: 'The brain is the archetype of a so-called complex adaptive system – that is, a system made up of numerous agents (in this case, neurons and other brain cells) following relatively simple rules that produce highly complex emergent behavior at a system level' (2002: 79). Another example is 'the interaction of genes' (2002: 79).

Fukuyama understands emergent properties as representing uncontrollable risks. 'Any attempt to model the brain using brute-force computational methods,' he argues, 'is almost certainly bound to fail' (2002: 79), and Baldi would, I believe, agree. Baldi, however, puts far greater faith in our imminent ability to compute the very large numbers that are involved in modelling complex emergent behaviour and thus to progress beyond such 'brute force' methods. Baldi is especially lucid arguing why very large numbers, although mind boggling at first, are still subject to computation and manipulation. He attributes such importance to Moore's law of increasing computational power because that makes possible the modelling of 'system-level complexity as an emergent property' that Fukuyama says is necessary, while avoiding the reductionist fallacies that Fukuyama fears (Fukuyama 2002: 163). But their respectively different appraisals of computational ability depend on a more fundamental difference in their beliefs about what humanity is.

Fukuyama believes in what he calls 'Factor X', the indefinable something that 'gives [humans] dignity and a moral status higher than that of other living creatures' (2002: 171). Factor X will always remain outside any modelling and is endangered by biotechnical manipulation, regardless of human ability to compute large numbers. Fukuyama's core argument is: 'We do not want to disrupt either the unity or the continuity of human nature' (2002: 172). This emphasis on continuity distinguishes him from Baldi, for whom there is no unity or continuity of human nature, because the whole idea of a human nature is a mistaken product of an evolutionary phase that humanity is now prepared to move beyond. Fukuyama thus rejects the posthuman privileging of informational pattern over – not Hayles's material instantiation – but over Factor X. Baldi believes we will only realize Factor X, representing posthuman potential, when we do privilege the informational pattern. Thus we reach the difference of what ethical framework is necessary to guide posthuman society.

Posthuman ethics

Baldi counsels being careful, but he sees no reason not to proceed with care (and with tolerance for some of those 'few hiccups' that mark scientific progress). He describes his position as more '*ontological* rather than ethical' (2001: 136; original emphasis). This ontological view:

> contends that our common notion of who we are is erroneous in the same way that the notion of a flat Earth is wrong, regardless of our personal feelings, desires, and ethical positions. The way we see ourselves is in part the result of historical and evolutionary accidents. It does *not* correspond to the broader reality that is rapidly emerging with the explosion of the Internet, computers, and biotechnologies.
>
> (2001: 136; original emphasis)

Thus Baldi confidently sweeps aside previous philosophy – 'the supreme goal of ethics . . . to establish universal principles of right and wrong, and what constitutes moral behavior' (2001: 136) – as 'a mirage and sometimes the source of mistakes' (2001: 137). Earlier ethics depends on concepts that 'were introduced [when] our ancestors did not know anything about the real atomic structure of matter, about DNA, about proteins, about neurons, and about computers' (2001: 105). Baldi is sympathetic to ideas like humanity and dignity, but

> their vague definitions are bound to be problematic and inefficient when the time comes to apply them with legislative precision to situations raised by modern biotechnology: from gene patents [one of Baldi's foremost ethical issues], to abortion, to IVF, to artificial twinning, to cloning, to name the mildest ones.
>
> (2001: 137)

To address these issues ethics must be 'flexible' (2001: 141) and precise. Baldi finds both qualities in utilitarianism, which is 'mathematical; it is an optimization problem' (2001: 142). What is to be optimized is happiness; alternatively, suffering is to be reduced. Thus Baldi's utilitarianism produces statements like: 'This kind of gene therapy [to remove the mutation that causes sickle-cell anaemia, among other conditions] is useful, reduces total human suffering, and hence is ethical' (2001: 152). Flexible utilitarianism reverses Fukuyama's Jeffersonian fear of biotechnology's eugenic potential to increase and rigidify inequalities. Baldi argues that the initially restrictive expense of cloning would be a benefit, since it minimizes risk to the entire gene pool by limiting the procedure: 'Initially, its diffusion is likely to be slow, which will provide us with additional time for reflection' (2001: 145).

Yet Baldi's utilitarianism resists being trivialized. He too has a metaphysics, harkening back to Plato's cave but without any Platonic essentialism:

> We do not know who we are, but we know enough to know that we are not who we think we are. Who we think we are is the result of an illusion produced by our evolutionary odyssey. As we begin to enter the realm of very large computational systems, a thick fog sets in. Qualia and the psychology of large numbers, strangely far from our daily experience but at the same time close to our technological limits, begin to take their toll. We do not yet fully understand the laws of computation for such large systems.
>
> (Baldi 2001: 165)

For Baldi we will only understand – not only large systems but also who we are – when we enter what he calls 'the information space' (2001: 166–7), in which the self will increasingly disappear; hence his title, *The Shattered Self*. With specific reference to Plato, Baldi imagines that in the information space, an object, whether a genome or a self, 'does not depend on . . . a specific material realization' (2001: 166), and this end of the material is the core of Baldi's posthuman vision.

Fukuyama's book may be most important as a refutation of the utilitarianism that Baldi embraces. The ultimate realization of that utilitarianism leads right where Baldi goes: to a disembodiment of humanity, or as Hayles calls it, the privilege of informational pattern over material instantiation. Fukuyama's rejection of this future, and his self-conscious reliance on the old philosophy that Baldi rejects as grounded in wrong, inadequate knowledge, depends on the place that Fukuyama affords to suffering in human experience. Here is the core of Fukuyama's refutation of utilitarianism's goal to make the reduction of suffering the measure of all things:

> No one can make a brief in favor of pain and suffering, but the fact of the matter is that what we consider to be the highest and most admirable human qualities, both in ourselves and in others, are often related to the way that we react to, confront, overcome, and frequently succumb to pain, suffering, and death. In the absence of these human evils, there would be no sympathy, compassion, courage, heroism, solidarity, or strength of character. A person who has not confronted suffering or death has no depth. Our ability to experience these emotions is what connects us potentially to all other human beings, both living and dead.
>
> (Fukuyama 2002: 173)

Both Fukuyama and Baldi privilege human connection, but they differ radically on what makes connection possible. I imagine Baldi replying that Fukuyama is trapped in the defence of virtues that were only necessary at an earlier stage of evolution: because suffering was inevitable, sympathy, compassion, and solidarity were privileged. But in Baldi's vision of post-human potential, it makes no sense to hold back the evolutionary advances that will eliminate suffering, because such advances might jeopardize virtues that were only required because suffering was believed to be inevitable. Compassion is necessarily a virtue as long as the genome remains tied to its material instantiation. In the previously unimaginable information space, far more intimate connections will be possible: 'the self may progressively disappear in the ocean of the information space' (Baldi 2001: 167).

Fukuyama's response to Baldi could be that human connection on these informational terms is no longer either human or connected. What are then called humans lack what Fukuyama calls 'depth', the very quality that makes them human. Then we enter the circularity of their respective arguments, with Baldi replying that Fukuyama's version of 'depth' is another product of the necessities of the 'bootstrapping' stage of human evolution.

An unconcluding narrative

I cannot conceive any theoretical synthesis of Baldi's and Fukuyama's alternative visions of our posthuman future. What each counts as potentials and risks, the assumptions that ground their ethics, and what they imagine humanity aspiring to, do not admit reconciliation. Meanwhile, as we await the posthuman future, our too human lives continue to require immediate, practical choices and reconciliations. A parent, Bill Keller (2002), writes about the death of his child. Charlie, whom Bill and his wife Emma came to know so well through extensive ultrasound images that they named him, was aborted at the limit of New York's legal deadline. Medical advice, based on weeks of extensive testing, was that Charlie would be born dead or in a vegetative state, and his birth would be significant danger to the health of his mother. 'Facing the prospect of a greater heartbreak, watching a child die or suffer inconsolably, or exhausting the emotional resources needed for two other children, we decided to end it', Keller (2002) writes. 'The last thing Emma was aware of before surrendering to the anesthetic was Charlie kicking madly.'

Keller writes that Emma 'is convinced that if we had just let nature take its course, without sonograms and amniocentesis, "we would have lost that baby, but we would not have killed that baby." All the same, the next time around we tested' (Keller 2002). Keller evokes the difficulty of parents exercising viable choice in the face of medical and social pressures to know, and he imagines that 'in a world of market-driven health care', the decision whether to test 'will slip more and more from our hands'.

Keller's story ends with the birth of their next child. In that affirmation of life, and in the tone of Keller's prose, we witness the virtues that Fukuyama enumerates as resulting from encounters with suffering and morality. We also find a situation that Baldi would identify as calling for more science: if in vitro fertilization techniques were routine, preimplantation screening might have fixed Charlie's problems and prevented the parents' suffering.

Keller (2002) writes that Charlie's life and death 'has deepened my suspicion of moral clarity, and also of disembodied rationalism, both of which seem to offer a kind of ethics without human beings'. Baldi and Fukuyama could each take this statement as affirming his respective position. In that duality of interpretation lies the difficulty of posthuman ethics.

References

Baldi, P. (2001) *The Shattered Self: The End of Natural Evolution*, Cambridge, MA: MIT Press.

Cavafy, C.P. (1975) *Collected Poems*, trans. by E. Keeley and P. Sherrard, Princeton, NJ: Princeton University Press.

Fukuyama, F. (2002) *Our Posthuman Future: Consequences of the Biotechnology Revolution*, New York: Farrar, Strauss & Giroux.

Hayles, N.K. (1999) *How We Became Posthuman: Virtual Bodies in Cybernetics, Literature, and Informatics*, Chicago: The University of Chicago Press.

Keller, B. (2002) 'Charlie's Ghost', *The New York Times*, 29 June.

21 Biology, vulnerability and politics

Bryan Turner

Introduction

In the history of social thought, 'nature', and more recently 'biology' and 'genetics' have been contrasted with 'society' in a moral discourse, the aim of which is to discipline people. In this moral paradigm, self-discipline is necessary, if society is to achieve its civilising effects. Individuals cannot achieve selfhood without the civilising process. For example, Malthusian population theory was an attempt to regulate human sexuality through an argument about natural scarcity that condemned human beings either to regulate their sexuality or starve to death. Contemporary genetic counselling attempts to improve the quality of the product of human sexual relations by, in effect, regulating reproductive rights in the interests of social production. The relationship between knowledge and (human) nature was the principal theme of Michel Foucault's history of the social sciences, in which he sought 'to sketch out a history of the different ways in our culture that humans develop knowledge about themselves: economics, biology, psychiatry, medicine and penology' (Foucault 1997: 224).

It does not follow, however, from any history of the social sciences that natural constraints (for example of food and space) are merely rhetorical restraints. There is a demographic discourse of scarcity, but there are actual population characteristics of societies that have real effects. Contemporary China would be an obvious example, where the one-child family policy has brought about major changes in human behaviour and has had profound consequences for the social structure. An analysis of discourses is quite separate from a study of their social effects, and a sociology that takes nature seriously is concerned to see how institutions actually connect with human needs and biology. In a more systematic treatment of these issues, it would be necessary to distinguish more carefully between nature, biology and genetics (Soper 1994). In this chapter, my intention is threefold: to make the analytical distinction between discourses (ideology) and their effects (social consequences), to examine the relationship between embodiment and institutions, and to develop a theory of rights on the basis of human vulnerability.

In sociology, I have been interested in three institutions – medicine, religion and law (or social and human rights) – and their relationship to the human body. These three orders are institutions of normative coercion and as such are fundamental to the organization of society. Adapting Foucault to sociological inquiry means paying attention to discourses, institutions and their social effects. Unfortunately, too much critical and investigative effort has been given to discourse thereby neglecting institutional practices and their intended and unintended consequences. Discourse analysis, for example of 'the body' cannot tell us about the social effects of discourse.

Resurrecting the body

In order to give an account of why I think sociology cannot and should not neglect a biological account of human nature, I start somewhat immodestly with a brief intellectual history. My interest in medical sociology emerged in the 1970s at the University of Aberdeen where I was intellectually influenced by the work of a number of key sociologists in the Aberdeen MRC unit. These figures were numerous and important – Gordon Horobin, Raymond Illsley, David Oldman, Sally MacIntyre and Phil Strong. In that period, two traditions of sociological analysis, symbolic interactionism and the sociology of knowledge, heavily influenced the Aberdeen sociology department. From symbolic interactionism, the approach to medical sociology was in terms of the interactional settings of health and illness. The attractions of medical sociology were fairly obvious. It appeared to have a practical focus; it generated interesting research questions; it raised very important issues about suffering and ethics; and it produced a profound challenge to sociological theory in the form of a question – what is the place of the body in theories of social action and social structure? I began to combine the sociology of religion and medical sociology to make the body a central topic of social theory. When Mike Hepworth joined the department, we developed an undergraduate course on the body, self and society that reflected a growing interest in the body and social interaction, and this emerging interest began to produce a sociology of ageing, that went well beyond the narrow concerns of conventional gerontology.

In the 1960s, *The Social Construction of Reality* (Berger and Luckmann 1967) was one of the most influential books in British sociology. Integrating the legacies of Marx, Weber and Durkheim, it produced a general theory of how subjective meanings and objective institutions combine to construct social reality. Given the political *Zeitgeist* of the 1960s, it is perhaps not surprising that the book was read by radical students as a critical assault on the establishment, because the theory suggested that institutions were socially and politically precarious. In fact, Berger and Luckmann's message was conservative, because the argument was that human beings require secure institutions if they are to protect themselves from anomie. The socially constructed nature of institutions needs to be ideologically obscured if they are to function at all. In retrospect, the paradox of Berger's alleged radicalism was its dependence on the conservative theories of Arnold Gehlen.

Following Nietzsche, Gehlen (1988) argued that human beings are not yet finished animals. By this notion, he meant that human beings are poorly equipped in biological terms to deal with the natural world into which they are involuntarily thrown; they have no finite instinctual structure that is specific to a given environment, and depend upon a long period of socialization in order to adapt themselves to this world. The core of Gehlen's contribution was a theory of institutions. Human beings are characterized by their 'instinctual deprivation' (*Instinktarmut*) and they do not have a stable structure within which to operate. Institutions are the social bridges between humans and their physical environment, and it is through institutions that human life becomes coherent, meaningful and continuous. To protect themselves from anomic conditions, humans create culture that provides an over-arching guarantee for the everyday world. Institutions offer relief (*Entlastung*) from the tensions generated by their undirected instinctual drives, and habit is a central feature of relief, because it reduces expenditure on motivation and control in everyday life. Gehlen's philosophical anthropology indicates that human societies must ensure the stability of the cultural world in order to protect individuals from the imminent threat of anomie. In particular, individuals depend on stable narratives and institutions in order to manage the trauma of chronic illness and to protect their identities from the tribulations of ageing.

One of the most influential contributions to the debate about social constructionism was based upon a specific interpretation of the instinctual structure of human life, namely instinctual deprivation. In modern sociology, this aspect of Berger and Luckmann's sociology has been lost or obscured, and contemporary theories of social construction are almost invariably relativistic and cultural. Within the 'cultural turn', 'biology' is typically regarded as merely a rhetorical device to justify existing social arrangements. Constructionism is critical of concepts such as need, instinct or human nature that formed the basis of social theory from classical political economy onwards. Current criticism of social constructionism is in part an intellectual movement to restore aspects of political economy, critical theory and a realist epistemology. Taking human nature seriously is necessary in order to develop a critique of society as false, or inauthentic or alienated. In the Paris Manuscripts, Marx had a conception of the natural condition of human beings in order to produce a theory of alienation in the capitalist division of labour. While Marx criticized the utilitarian perspective of human beings as rhetorical, he had to embrace a view of the actual conditions of nature in order to understand what human labour entailed. The point of this argument is to claim that a critical assessment of the function of 'nature' in public argument does not preclude a realist epistemology of natural processes. A social constructionist argument that denies these assumptions about embodiment and its effects is a modern version of idealism.

My approach to the body as a specific topic in sociology developed out of this initial encounter with symbolic interactionism and the sociology of knowledge, and with the substantive fields of religion and medicine. From an engagement with Goffman, it became obvious that any sociological account of social interaction would require, however minimal, an understanding of the human body, or better still of embodiment. If sociology, like economics and politics, is a science of social action, then it requires a set of assumptions about 'the social actor'. We assume as sociologists that human beings are agents, or at least that they have a capacity for agency. While sociology has been preoccupied with the question of agency (for example in the structuration debate), it has been less interested in developing a systematic and explicit understanding of the agent. Because it has taken for granted the question (what is a social agent?), sociology often assumes by default an outmoded form of Cartesianism. The principal characteristic of the social actor in conventional social theory is, not that they are embodied, but that they have choice. In the social sciences, the social actor is a rational agent making choices between alternative courses of action by reference to a scarcity of means, but their embodiment remains implicit.

Reading Goffman confirmed my notion that symbolic interactionism had important insights into the embodiment of the self, but social theory generally had a primitive understanding of the body, emotions and choice. Many of Goffman's key contributions involved a perspective on the body as a symbolic system in face-work (Goffman 1959, 1967) and stigma (Goffman 1963), but his analysis of total institutions also required assumptions about real bodies and social process (Goffman 1961). Furthermore, I had come to the view in *Religion and Social Theory* (1983) that religion is that which we take most seriously, and what we define seriously is in fact closely connected with basic bodily issues including sexuality, birth, suffering, ageing and death. Religion speaks to our vulnerability, and our vulnerability is a consequence of our embodiment. In particular, religion is constitutive of the civilizing process, because it is a set of practices that achieves a regulation of the body in order to discipline the soul.

In the 1980s Foucault began to have an important impact in Britain on the development of the sociology of the body. In retrospect the influence of Foucault has been diverse and there are many competing interpretations of his work, but more recently there has been a theoretical convergence around the idea of governmentality as the master concept (Foucault 1991). My own approach to Foucault was in terms of a theory of the regulation of the body through the historical study of diet in 'the government of the body' (Turner 1982). Foucault's understanding of the history of knowledge and power has been enormously productive and creative, but in many respects his impact on sociology has had specific limitations, if not negative consequences.

Foucault's perspective raises particular problems for the sociology of health and illness. First, because he adheres to the anti-humanist philosophy of

Martin Heidegger, his framework rigidly precludes any analysis of the phenomenology of sickness. Research on the experience of pain can, within a Foucauldian paradigm, only mean an investigation of how the discourse of pain emerges in medical systems of knowledge. 'Pain' becomes a matter of 'noso-politics' (Foucault 1980: 168). For example, Foucault's analysis of the human body was an attempt to show that the 'body' was a contingent effect of power rather than a fact of nature. In his *Technologies of the Self*, there is the claim that '[a]ll of my analyses are against the idea of universal necessities in human existence. They show the arbitrariness of institutions' (Foucault 1988: 11). The legacy of Foucault thus stands firmly in the way of any notion of natural necessities or a shared biological fate. Second, the notion of 'the social' disappears in Foucauldian philosophy, because the realm of social interaction is not an object of scientific interest. Foucault dismissed the whole area of 'doctor–patient interaction' as simply subject-ivism. In short, the legacy of symbolic interaction – the study of the meaning of health and illness in the natural settings of everyday life – cannot be accommodated in Foucault's historical analyses of medical knowledge and institutional power, and the legacy of phenomenological sociology – the experience of the lived body in the traumatic context of disease and illness – is disallowed by the Heideggerian anti-humanist notion of *Dasein* (Being). Although there are theoretical incompatibilities between Foucault and Goffman, there are nevertheless obvious parallels between the carceral and total institution.

We might argue that Foucault merely developed an alternative, if pro-ductive and sophisticated, notion of 'medicalization' that had its origins in the 1970s when sociologists began to examine the penetration of medical categories into the social fields of institutional regulation. The medicalization thesis explored the impact of medical discourse and practice, and their social effects in the regulation of social behaviour. Colin Gordon (1980: 246) provided a useful summary of Foucault's theoretical contribution in terms of 'certain forms of explicit, rational, reflected *discourses*; that of certain non-discursive social and institutional *practices*; and that of certain *effects* produced within the social field'. In sociological terms, we might summarize these 'general orders of events' as ideologies, institutions (or institutional practices) and their unintended consequences. The problem with much of the Foucauldian legacy is that it has directed attention to how social practices are inscribed on the human body as merely a passive object. This question of the passive as opposed to the lived body was a problem in *The Body and Society* (Turner 1984) and hence Arthur Frank's analytical review of the field was a useful attempt to 'bring the body back in' by shifting attention from the body as a problem for society to a problem for itself (Frank 1991: 47). Frank's work is important because, against the sick role concept, it explores the body out of control in a condition of permanent rather than temporary sickness, and the problem of suffering is central to any account of embodiment that wants to take ethics seriously (Frank 1995). It is only through a departure from or supplement to the theme of governmentality that one can begin to engage with ethics, pain and illness narratives. It is only by recognizing the ontological vulnerability of the human body that the social sciences can understand and contribute to the study of social suffering. It is in terms of what we might call a secular theodicy (explanations of the problem of suffering and injustice in society) that biology can usefully enter or rather re-enter, the social sciences.

The problem with relativism in political theory is that it cannot simultaneously develop an ethic of care and satisfy questions about justice. The recognition of difference does not easily feed into a theory that can give a convincing account of the general conditions of justice. There is therefore an ongoing question about justice, namely the universality of the treatment of human beings as human beings. The conviction that embodiment is a fruitful platform for an argument in favour of the generality of human rights via the notions of frailty and vulnerability is partly grounded in the notion of the ubiquity of human misery.

Embodiment, vulnerability and precariousness

Human beings are ontologically frail and their natural environment, precarious. In order to protect themselves from these vagaries, they must build social institutions (especially political, familial and ecclesiastical institutions) that constitute what we call 'society'. We need social reciprocity, which, through the com(pan)ionship of bread (*pan*), provides us with means of mutual support and cooperation. In Durkheimian terms, we depend upon the creative force of ritual and the emotional effervescence of common festivals to renew social bonds and to build effective institutions, and we need the comforts of social institutions as means of fortifying our lives. These institutions are, however, themselves precarious and cannot provide an enduring, secure and reliable social environment. Institutions typically go wrong and break down, because they cannot easily adapt to social change, and over time they become mere fossils of their original purpose. Because human beings are biologically vulnerable and are dependent during socialization, these conditions generate inter-societal patterns of dependency and social interconnectedness that, in their more psychological manifestations, produce sympathy and empathy, which are necessary for trust.

Social existence is characterized by the contradictory social processes of scarcity and solidarity. Human beings are both confronted by the brute facts of economic life, namely scarcity of means to ends, and also by the endless renewal of intimacy and sociality in the midst of hardship. In modern societies, we typically experience these processes of trust and solidarity in patterns of friendship. These are social facts in Durkheimian terms rather than merely rhetorical devices. This characterization of society as the endless struggle between two contradictory principles of scarcity and solidarity is obviously Hobbesian, because its premise is that life is nasty, brutish and short, but it rejects Hobbesian notions of individualism and social contract. Instead, human and social rights are treated as juridical expressions of basic patterns of solidarity whose foundations are in the common experiences of vulnerability and precariousness, and social dependency and reciprocity (Turner and Rojek 2001). My intention in this chapter is to sketch out a general sociology of everyday life, based on embodiment, institutions and social networks, that establishes the sociological paradigm for the study of human rights that are institutional manifestations of our global vulnerability and dependency. This discussion of vulnerability and rights has to be located within a global social system, where the growing hybridity and fragmentation of culture bring into question our ability to sustain solidarity.

The term 'vulnerability' is derived from the Latin *vulnus* or 'wound'. It is particularly important for the sociology of the body that 'vulnerability' should have such an obviously corporeal reference. In the seventeenth century, vulnerability had both a passive and active significance, namely to be wounded and to wound. The verb 'to vulnerate' is thus to wound, but in its modern usage this corporeal dimension has been hidden, because vulnerability now refers more frequently to the human capacity to be exposed to psychological or moral damage. It refers increasingly to psychological suffering rather than to physical wounding. To be vulnerable as a human being is to possess a structure of sentiments, feelings and emotions by which we can steer a passage through the uncertainties of the social world.

In order to provide some conceptual depth to this model of vulnerability and precariousness, it is necessary to develop a notion of embodiment as a framework for a theory of social action. Adopting the notion of the social as process, it is important not to reify 'the body', but to treat embodiment as a social process, namely the social processes of embodying that disciplines our biological foundations. Embodiment is the consequence of ongoing practices of corporalization. In this respect, embodiment is a life process that requires education in 'body techniques' – walking, sitting, dancing, and eating (Mauss 1973). Embodiment is the ensemble of such corporeal practices that produce and give a body its place in everyday life. Embodiment places particular bodies within a social habitus and requires the production of a sensuous and practical presence in the life world. Embodiment is the lived experience of the sensual or subjective body and it is, in this sense, consistent with the general idea of social practice.

Practice involves the sensual, lived body and its effects on social relations, and is the active shaping of the lived world by embodied activities. But embodiment is also a collective project, because it takes place in a life world that is already social. Embodiment cannot be the isolated project of the individual, because it is located within a social world of interconnected social actors. Finally, while it is the process of making and becoming a body, it is also the project of making a self. Embodiment and enselfment are mutually dependent and reinforcing social processes. The social self involves a corporeal project within a specific social nexus where the continuous self depends on successful embodiment, a social habitus and memory. Following both Marx and Bourdieu, embodiment and enselfment always take place in specific spatial contexts, and the habitus is a set of practices in a particular location; it must, we might say, secure emplacement. Thus, the sociological notion of a 'body' involves three related processes: embodiment, enselfment and emplacement.

Relativism and human rights

Cultural sociology has become decorative, because it provides little basis for political action or ethical analysis and the cultural turn has reinforced the anthropological legacy of relativism. While relativism often breeds a sensitivity to cultural differences and social variation, it neglects or underplays the importance of social solidarity that connects people across cultural divisions. The importance of this argument for a sociological understanding of the rule of law and human rights has been cogently expressed by Philip Selznick (2002: 78) in *The Communitarian Persuasion*, where he observes that, while the anthropologists of the 1930s advanced the arguments of cultural relativism, they also endorsed the notion of 'the psychic unity of mankind'. The anthropological tradition, while urging us to recognize the significance of cultural difference, wanted 'humanity to be understood as biologically One and culturally Many' (Selznick 2002: 78). The growth of human rights legislation, institutions and culture in the twentieth century was based on a common recognition of human vulnerability, and if human rights are grounded in a common vulnerability, then the humanitarian response is to foster empowerment through development strategies. My argument is not a defence of the universality of rights, but of their generality and in particular their effective imbedding in local political struggles (Ignatieff 2001: 7).

The point of this formulation of ontology is to provide a foundation for a sociological and normative defence of human rights as protective institutions. First, there is the argument that the biological nature of human vulnerability requires human rights as a protective canopy, and second, social institutions are necessary but precarious. Given vulnerability and precariousness, human beings need juridical institutions in which to secure legal protection, specifically the rule of law. As I have already indicated, both arguments (vulnerability and precariousness) constitute an alternative version of Hobbes's theory of the state without the limitations of a utilitarian notion of social contract. Hobbes argued in *Leviathan* that rational human beings with conflicting interests in a state of nature would be in a condition of perpetual war. In order to protect themselves from mutual, endless slaughter, they create a state through a social contract, which organizes social space in the collective interests of rational but antagonistic human beings. Furthermore, the institutions, which humans create as protective mechanisms, have to be sufficiently powerful to regulate social space and as a consequence come unintentionally to present a threat to the human beings that instituted the state through a social contract. For example, the state, which holds a monopoly of legitimate violence, is a guarantor of social security but also an instrument necessarily of violence.

Human beings are rational, but they are also embodied and their dependency creates capacities of sympathy towards their fellow human beings. The capacity for suffering (another feature of vulnerability) is an important prerequisite of membership of a moral community. The notion that sympathy is the social glue of a society characterized by precariousness can also be seen as a contemporary restatement of the theory of sentiments in classical political economy. The point of this sociology of the body is to provide a theoretical structure which will connect individual human rights as protective arrangements, the organization of the state as an institution which both guarantees and threatens rights, and the notion that sympathy and trust are requirements of all social connectedness. The body provides a platform for the defence of a social theory of human rights, and permits sociology to transcend the limitations of complacent cultural relativism. Because a comprehensive justification of this claim is beyond the scope of this chapter, my aim is to indicate the contours of such a defence rather than its substantive content. There are of course powerful anthropological arguments in favour of a relativist stand on rights discourse and thus a sociological defence of rights against a relativist consensus will need to be robust. I shall concentrate on basic criticisms, namely that the body is socially constructed and as such could not act as a general foundation for human rights. The objection would be that the body and embodiment are too variable and unstable to provide a foundational argument for the generality of human rights claims.

Let us consider four possible objections to this argument that derives human rights from biological vulnerability. First, it can be reasonably objected that some are more frail than others, and that social inequalities mean that many do not experience suffering and despair. Social Darwinists might argue that in the struggle for survival, the weak go to the wall. The counter argument is that, in the context of the life course, all human beings will end their lives in a state of disability, frailty and enfeeblement. Both Freud and Darwin saw that suffering was inevitable, given the vulnerability of our bodies. Second, it may be argued that medical technology has reduced our vulnerability, as demonstrated, for example, by rising life expectancy. The counter argument is that medical advances often make us more dependent and vulnerable, because increasing longevity has inevitably resulted in greater impairment and disability. The third criticism is that, if we define humanity in terms of vulnerability, we could not distinguish easily between human and animal rights. I do not see this criticism as problematic, since to protect human beings we will also need to protect our environment and the animal life that it sustains. Finally, while the capacity to suffer may define humanity, it is extremely variable. It is self-evidently true that, as Barrington Moore Jr (1970: 11) argues in *Reflections on the Causes of Human Misery*:

> suffering is not a value in its own right.
> In this sense any form of suffering becomes a cost,
> and unnecessary suffering an odious cost.
> Similarly, a general opposition to human suffering
> constitutes a stand-point that both transcends
> and unites different cultures and historical epochs.

It is possible to distinguish two forms of suffering. This first defines a negative condition to which certain organisms are susceptible because of their biological constitution, and suffering is associated with the actual bodily pain and the moments of consciousness that accompany and anticipate that pain. The second type involves existential or psychological suffering when a person feels desolated or in despair. One could accept the argument that social suffering involves essentially the devaluation of a person as a consequence of accident, affliction or torture, but pain is less culturally variable. Whereas bankruptcy involves some variable degree of psychological suffering, a toothache is a toothache. If we claim that disability is a social condition (the loss of social rights) and thus relative, we might argue that impairment is the underlying condition about which there is less cultural variation and political dispute. In short, some conditions or states of affairs are less socially constructed than others. The fundamental proposition is the commonality of pain as a basis for community.

Conclusion: taking the body seriously

Ontological vulnerability includes the notion that human beings of necessity have a propensity to disease and sickness, that they are beings unto death, and that their ageing bodies set up a tension between the body as lived experience, the objective body and the body image which through the life cycle involves us routinely in existential discomfort. This Nietzschean quality of 'unfinished' human life is not simply a rhetorical device, but is an empirically verifiable claim about human biology. As sociologists, we can measure this vulnerability through indices of disease, disability, chronic illness, morbidity, life expectancy, low birth weight, and through a range of modern conditions such as HIV/AIDS. In fact public health measures now provide a wealth of vulnerability indices such as DALY (disability adjusted life years). One can argue about their methodological validity as measures of vulnerability, but it is difficult to regard ageing, chronic illness and impairment as simply socially constructed phenomena. As a result of these disabling conditions, human beings are involuntarily implicated in various relationships of dependency through their life course.

Because embodiment has in fact many dimensions, one can talk about having a body in which the body has the characteristics of a thing, being a body in which we are subjectively engaged with our body as a project, and doing a body in the sense of producing a body through time. These distinctions are more felicitously expressed in German where there is a ready-made distinction between the body as an object (*Körper*) and the body as lived experience (*Leib*). The body is simultaneously an object that I can observe and the mode of being that makes that observation possible. However, the relationship of individuals to their own bodies is never an external, objective or neutral relationship, because identity is inextricably bound up with subjective being in the material world. It is in relation to the traumatic consequences of chronicity, impairment and disease for identity that medical sociology finds a compelling scientific and ethical rationale.

References

Berger, P.L. and Luckmann, T. (1967) *The Social Construction of Reality*, London: Allen Lane.

Foucault, M. (1980) 'The politics of health in the eighteenth century', in C. Gordon (ed.) *Michel Foucault: Power/Knowledge*, Brighton: Harvester Press, pp. 166–82.

Foucault, M. (1988) 'Truth, power, self: an interview with Michel Foucault', in L.M. Martin, H. Gutman and P.H. Hutton (eds) *Technologies of the Self*, London: Tavistock, pp. 9–15.

Foucault, M. (1991) 'Governmentality', in G. Burchell, C. Gordon and P. Miller (eds) *The Foucault Effect*, London: Harvester/Wheatsheaf, pp. 87–104.

Foucault, M. (1997) 'Technologies of the self', in *Michel Foucault: Ethics. The Essential Works 1*, London: Allen Lane, pp. 223–51.

Frank, A. (1991) 'For a sociology of the body: an analytical review', in M. Featherstone, M. Hepworth and B.S. Turner (eds) *The Body: Social Process and Cultural Theory*, London: Sage, pp. 36–102.

Frank, A. (1995) *The Wounded Storyteller: Body, Illness and Ethics*, Chicago: University of Chicago Press.

Gehlen, A. (1988) *Man, His Nature and Place in the World*, New York: Columbia University Press.

Goffman, E. (1959) *The Presentation of Self in Everyday Life*, New York: Doubleday Anchor Books.

Goffman, E. (1961) *Asylums: Essays on the Social Situation of Mental Patients and Other Inmates*, Harmondsworth: Penguin.

Goffman, E. (1963) *Stigma: Notes on the Management of Spoiled Identity*, Harmondsworth: Penguin.

Goffman, E. (1967) *Interaction Ritual: Essays on Face-to-Face Behaviour*, New York: Doubleday Anchor Books.

Gordon, C. (1980) 'Afterword', in C. Gordon (ed.) *Michel Foucault: Power/Knowledge*, Brighton: Harvester Press, pp. 229–59.

Ignatieff, M. (2001) *Human Rights as Politics and Idolatry*, Princeton: Princeton University Press.

Mauss, M. (1973) 'Techniques of the body', *Economy & Society*, 2: 70–88.

Moore, B. (1970) *Reflections on the Causes of Human Misery and upon Certain Proposals to Eliminate Them*, London: Allen Lane.

Selznick, P. (2002) *The Communitarian Persuasion*, Washington: Woodrow Wilson Center Press.

Soper, K. (1994) *What is Nature?*, Oxford: Blackwell.

Turner, B.S. (1982) 'The government of the body, medical regimens and the rationalisation of diet', *British Journal of Sociology*, 33: 254–69.

Turner, B.S. (1983) *Religion and Social Theory*, London: Heinemann Educational Books.

Turner, B.S. (1984) *The Body and Society*, Oxford: Basil Blackwell.

Turner, B.S. and Rojek, C. (2001) *Society and Culture: Principles of Scarcity and Solidarity*, London: Sage.

22 Ecology, health and society

A red–green perspective

Ted Benton

During the 1980s a pervasive new intellectual tide ran through the humanities and social science disciplines. Closely related linguistic and cultural 'turns' drawing inspiration from trends in European and analytical philosophy as well as literary criticism called into question basic assumptions of the prevailing materialist and realist traditions in sociology and political science in particular. Where these traditions researched large-scale and long-term social processes, critically exploring relations of power and inequality, the implications of the new discursive approaches were at their most challenging. Radical critiques of the existing order of things appeared to claim objectivity, both for their research findings and for their underlying ethical standpoint. How could this 'privileging' be justified? Where was the Archimedean point from which to decide between rival accounts of a supposed 'reality' external to discourse. Were not all accounts simply that – accounts, narratives, discursive constructs? Lacking direct or authoritative access to 'the real', analysis of discursive constructs must take its place. The world, including the social world, is relegated to the status of an unknowable noumenal realm, or, in more provocative rhetorics, disappears entirely into its discursive 'representations'.

Threadbare as the philosophical underpinnings of these approaches often were, the critical challenges they posed enlivened and enriched the social science disciplines in important ways. Easy and settled assumptions about the material basis of 'interests' and collective identities were unsettled by new emphases on the complexity and fluidity of personal and social identities. Unquestioned assumptions about distributive justice and historical 'progress' encountered sceptical dismissals from the newer versions of cultural and moral relativism. New fields of study emerged and new angles on old topics came to notice. But there was also a cost. Unsettling comfortable assumptions is one thing. Displacing a whole disciplinary matrix quite another. Showing that much of the sociological research of the past worked with unjustifiably simple views of the relationships between, for example, class position, class interests and social consciousness did not entail (though it often lead to) abandoning the task of analysing relationships between structure, consciousness and agency. Why not take on the challenge of creating more sophisticated accounts, deploying the more sophisticated cultural theory now available? Earlier work had established robust linkages between class division, poverty, and ill-health and reduced life-expectancy, had exposed the forms of social exclusion, bodily abuse and job discrimination connected with gender divisions and racial ideologies, and had investigated the role of power and economic coercion in maintaining unequal life-chances and impoverished lives. Under the influence of the discursive turn, these topics became unfashionable. But this was not inevitable. Each of these fields of enquiry would be enriched and strengthened through an encounter with the newer cultural theory. Equally, however, they would have tested the limits of the more radical discourse-reductionisms. In each case relations and processes are lived and understood in and through their discursive construction. But no case is reducible to the play of discourse alone. Embodied existence and its involuntary and pre-discursive experience, the materiality of social and physical environments are inescapable presences. They are the producers, bearers, the media and the referents of discourses, the very conditions of possibility of discourse itself. Perhaps to explain the coincidence of the discursive turn and the abandonment of so much of the agenda of earlier sociology we have to look outside the discipline itself, to the severing of links between that agenda and a wider social democratic and socialist political context.

But the severing of those links, and the rise to dominance of a neo-liberal consensus across the mainstream political institutions, has not abolished the states of affairs addressed and criticized by the materialist traditions. In many respects the processes they exposed to view have become more clearly evident, and more ethically demanding, precisely because of the intellectual and political defeats of the left.

If sociologists are to regain their capacity to gain a serious hearing in the wider public sphere (and many, of course, will not wish to), then the big challenge is to re-work the realist and materialist heritage in the light of the insights on offer from the newer cultural theory.

During the 1980s it seemed to me that one way of doing this, paying due regard to the cultural turn, was to take as a starting point for social theorizing the cognitive work of a range of so-called 'new' social movements. Taking seriously popular and lay discourses, re-valuing them in relation to authorized scientific and 'expert' knowledges involved recognizing social movements themselves as 'cognitive innovators' (Eyerman and Jamison 1991) implied treating them not simply as sociological subject-matter, but looking to the forms of understanding developed by them as a key source of sociological insights. I identified the feminist movement, animal rights, political ecology and the new politics of health as four such sources (Benton 1991). In their different ways, each movement radically problematized the way the sociological traditions had hitherto hermetically sealed off the human, social and cultural world from its 'other': the world of 'nature'. This latter was the acknowledged domain of the natural sciences – until, that is, radical constructionists in the sociology of science and post-modern social theorists 'deconstructed' the category of nature itself and rendered it amenable to the ontological blow-torch of discourse-reductionism. Now that 'nature' no longer existed, ecological social movements (for example) could be represented as self-deluded advocates of an impossible return to an imagined arcadian past. For example:

> Nature is not nature, but rather a concept, norm, memory, utopia, counter-image. Today, more than ever, now that it no longer exists, nature is being rediscovered, pampered. The ecology movement has fallen prey to a naturalistic misapprehension of itself. . . .' Nature' is a kind of anchor by whose means the ship of civilisation . . . conjures up, cultivates its contrary: dry land, the harbour, the approaching reef.
>
> (Beck 1994, quoted approvingly in Giddens 1994: 206)

But this argument could be turned on its head. What if we social scientists took the cognitive work of the social movements seriously, refused analytical strategies which a priori denied the authenticity of their own self-understanding, and sought to open up social scientific assumptions themselves to the critical scrutiny of social movement knowledge? Ecological politics in its many forms exposed the extent to which patterns of social, economic and political life were dependent on the resourcing, conditioning and recycling activities of 'nature', and how the modes of interaction between human society and these naturally-given conditions acted back upon both nature itself and social life. Feminists, having emphasized the *irreducibility* of social and cultural dimensions of gender-divisions to mere 'biological' sex-divisions, were increasingly seeking to theorize the *interconnections* between sex-differences and their sociocultural transformation into patterns of oppression and social exclusion. The *possibility* of a feminist politics depended on the first, but its *specificity* depended on the second (Hartsock 1983; Rose 1983; Birke 1986).

Meanwhile, a 'new' politics of health was actively challenging a dualist 'biomedical model', deeply implicated in the contemporary institutionalization of medical knowledge and health-care. On the one hand, there was an 'alternative' emphasis on holistic approaches which recognized both the importance of emotional and psychological dimensions of the whole person to health and the social and environmental context of life for the health of whole communities. On the other was a powerful set of arguments emphasising the causal role of class division, poverty, unemployment and powerlessness in generating statistically very persistent and robust inequalities in health and life expectancy, both within the rich countries of the West, and between 'First' and 'Third' worlds. None of this could be understood without bringing into a single analytical scheme the relationships between social structure, ecological conditions of life, bodily constitution and activity, social and cultural processes, and mental and emotional dispositions, skills and experiences.

The politics of animal welfare and rights exposed to public consciousness the immensity of contemporary consumer-culture's dependence on abusive treatments of nonhuman animals in scientific research and development, and on cruelly distorting and confining intensive regimes in meat production and live transportation. Not only was this a dimension of social and economic life hitherto virtually excluded from social scientific attention, but the cultural phenomenon of its contemporary emergence as an urgent moral issue called into question the most fundamental assumption of the sociological traditions: their categorial division between the human and the animal. If nonhuman animals can acquire moral standing in their own right, what does this imply for our view of the relationship between humans and animals? Of course, the owners of pets (or 'companion animals' as some prefer), afficionados of TV wildlife shows, shepherds, and initiates of Darwinian evolutionism were all well aware that nonhuman animals are capable of sophisticated learning, participation in human social practices, a wide range of emotional responses, and varying degrees of self-identity. What the animal rights and welfare movements achieved was an articulation of the moral and political implications of these forms of commonality between humans and animals, in virtue of their shared liability to be benefited or harmed by their positioning in social life. What the Darwinian understanding of our evolutionary kinship with other species, the underlying explanation for these commonalities, called into question was the theoretical sequestration of sociological views of human nature from the rest of science.

This, of course, was no accident (as we used to say). During the period of formation of autonomous social science disciplines such as sociology and anthropology, the dominance of reductive appropriations of Darwinism to legitimate gender and racial hierarchy, imperial conquest and ruthless market competition provided good and powerful reasons for rejecting any simple subsumption of the human social sciences under Darwinian categories. In our own time these reasons are as powerfully persuasive as they ever were. Overtly racist movements are on the march again in many countries, and sophisticated moves to rehabilitate the imperial project are discernible. At the same time, new forms of reductive Darwinism have achieved considerable authority as rivals to both religious and secular–humanist traditions in providing popular understandings of human nature and prospects. 'Popular science' sections of our increasingly monopolist bookshops are stacked with ultra-Darwinian claims to explain as 'natural' our propensity for warfare and aggression, the inevitability of patriarchy, hierarchy and kin-selfishness, the male preference for young women and the alleged universal aesthetic preference for open landscape paintings! Finally, the immense and rapid advances in molecular biology underpin a major cultural onslaught against the achievements of the new politics of health. The biotech companies and their advocates promise us a utopia of 'technical fix' health care, with the prospect even of the ultimate conquest of death itself.

Cloning, the storage of umbilical stem cells, eugenic 'designer' babies, gene therapy, xenotransplantation, each of us shadowed by a specially engineered 'self-pig', and new, more individually tailored drug-therapies are the routes to this wonderland (see Part IV, this volume). But who has asked for this future? What sort of social and economic relationships are presupposed by it, and which will it produce? With current public health-care systems in crisis for lack of funding, the pre-eminence of neo-liberal hostility to increased taxation, and moral panic at the prospect of the future 'burden' of an elderly, economically inactive population, these are rather serious questions. Perhaps we should be reassured by the recruitment of a growing army of 'experts' in medical ethics who will resolve these issues on our behalf. Hmm. Maybe . . .

So, with resurgent biological determinisms again in the ascendancy, our challenge is to assign to the life-sciences and their subject matter their proper place in our understanding of social processes, but to do so in ways which obstruct uncritical and reductive solutions. The example of evolutionary psychology will be useful here. This successfully promoted bid for an evolutionist take-over of the social sciences works with a version of evolutionary theory sometimes called 'neo' or 'ultra' Darwinism. The molecular gene is regarded as the basic unit upon which natural selection operates, organisms being regarded, in Dawkins's metaphor, as mere 'vehicles' for their genes. Generally, the evolutionary psychologists distance themselves from the racism of earlier forms of social Darwinism, and also recognize that not all traits of organisms are to be explained as genetically determined outcomes of selective pressures. Rather, they deploy a metaphor of 'reverse engineering', according to which current complex and improbable traits are explained as inherited 'solutions to engineering problems' encountered in ancestral environments – in the human case, the African savannah up to some 100,000 years ago. Leading popularizer of evolutionary psychology, Stephen Pinker, combines this version of evolutionary theory with an account of the human mind as a 'neural computer', with specialized modular functions each of which inherits its 'hardware' from the selective pressures at work on the ancestral human population. Our genetic constitution, then, determines the 'basic logics' by which the mental modules function, but not directly, as in the case of the cruder, earlier forms of sociobiology, our behavioural patterns themselves. However, it is through the shaping of behaviour by mental functioning that cultures are formed, so that culture is the outcome of a reductive one-way causal chain from genes to mental organization to culture:

> The geneticist Theodosius Dobzhansky famously wrote that nothing in biology makes sense except in the light of evolution. We can add that nothing in culture makes sense except in the light of psychology. Evolution created psychology, and that is how it explains culture.
>
> (Pinker 1997: 210)

This is not the place for a detailed critical encounter with evolutionary psychology (see Benton 1999; Rose and Rose (eds) 2000; and Higgs and Jones in this volume), but we can already see that its particular way of grounding an understanding of human social life in evolutionary biology is only one of a wide range of actual and possible alternative ways of making links between the human and the life sciences. The available options do not amount to either reluctant acquiescence in evolutionary psychology's victory over what it calls the 'standard social science model' (for an explanation of this, see Higgs and Jones, *op. cit.*), or a defensive retreat into what Catton and Dunlap call 'human exemptionalism' (Catton and Dunlap 1978, 1980). The key to opening up this wider space for alternative theorizing across the divide between nature and culture, or biology and society is to focus not, initially, on resisting the reduction of the social and cultural to the 'biological', but, rather, on the reductionism within the life sciences which assigns all significant causality to the molecular gene. Despite the enormous concentration of resources in genetics-related biotechnology research, and the powerful media promotion of advances in these fields, there remain relatively autonomous fields within the life sciences which retain their own specificity, as well as thoroughgoing alternatives to the ultra-Darwinian approach to evolution itself (Gould 1990; Goodwin 1994; Eldredge 1995; Rose 1997; Rose and Rose (eds) 2000 and many more). Physiology, developmental biology, pathology, gerontology, taxonomy, ethological studies of the behaviour of animals in their habitats, and ecological studies of the interactions and interdependencies between populations of organisms and their physical conditions of life may, indeed, draw upon molecular biological knowledge, but they still define their own research problems and deploy conceptual vocabularies appropriate to the level or kind of subject-matter with which they deal.

If, then, we seek to re-work social theory in ways which overcome its isolation from the rest of the life sciences there are numerous 'bridgeheads' across which communication (two-way communication, at that) can be established. I have argued for a broadly naturalistic but anti-reductionist philosophical framing for such communication. This acknowledges the overwhelming case for an evolutionary view of humans as a primate species, sharing many attributes with our close kin among the surviving 'great apes'. More widely shared are the psychological attributes of consciousness, sensory perception and learning. Still more widely shared with other living species are the processes and phases of the individual life-course, birth, development, reproduction, vulnerability to disease and predation, senescence and death, as well as the 'maintenance' functions of respiration, nutrition and excretion of wastes. These maintenance functions are a further reminder of the ever-present necessity of what Marx called the human 'metabolism' with nature – our immensely complex web of ecological interdependencies with both living and non-living beings, forces and processes.

Given the powerful discursive nexus of ethical and ontological connotations which attaches to the conceptual opposition between the human and the animal, there is a necessary struggle to find an appropriate language to carry such an anti-reductive naturalism: simply to assert our commonality with other species by including us within the category 'animal' is to invite reductionist misrepresentation. Marx's own term 'active natural being' serves very well as a means of designating the commonality of humans and nonhuman animals. But a non-reductive approach is required to address both the commonality of active natural beings and the particularity of each – in the case of our theme here, the particularity of the human. How is this to be done? One very pervasive strategy has been to acknowledge the 'biological' commonality of humans with other animals, whilst asserting psychological, linguistic, social, cultural or spiritual uniqueness. One problem with this strategy is that it tends to reproduce the Cartesian view of humans as a heterogeneous compound of mind and matter, the connection between them remaining mysterious and unintelligible. Another is that it fails to acknowledge the psychological and social attributes of nonhuman animals, whilst simultaneously failing to register the 'biological' diversity and particularities among them.

An alternative strategy for thinking about human specificity (as of any other species) is to think of Darwinian evolutionary theory not as a 'grand narrative' of life on earth, but, rather, as a heuristic device for constructing the particular narratives of specific lineages. Each presently existing species is a population of organisms whose genetic constitution has been acquired as the contingent outcome of countless past generations of its ancestors' interactions with one another and their ecological conditions of life. In each case the immensely complex and ever-shifting constellation of factors shaping survival and reproduction from generation to generation constitutes a unique narrative of formation. What we now refer to as 'biodiversity' is but a time-slice of the unimaginable diversity of unique solutions thrown up by evolutionary processes to the problems of organic survival. This is an image which effectively counters the reductionist tendency to generalize about evolutionary outcomes, and, in particular, to subsume the human species a priori under the laws of 'parental investment', 'the territorial imperative', male dominance, social hierarchy, or genetic 'selfishness'. At the same time, this view also disrupts the dualist strategy of counterposing human uniqueness to an undifferentiated 'animal' nature. Humans are, indeed, unique: the unique outcome of a unique sequence of historical interactions undergone by their ancestor populations: but no less and no more could be said of other surviving animal species. Given how little we know about the particular sequence of social, ecological and organic conditions, interactions and transformations which shaped our ancestral populations, there are as yet no good reasons for allowing speculative attempts at 'reverse engineering' to override the painstakingly established empirical knowledge of human social life provided by anthropology, comparative sociology, history, human geography and the other human sciences.

Viewed from this perspective, human specificity 'goes all the way down': a skeletal structure adapted to an upright posture, associated differentiation of hands and feet, distinctive developments in the brain and central nervous system, vocal organs, unique reproductive biology, with continuous sexual receptivity, prolonged infantile dependency and post-birth brain development, very limited sexual dimorphism and so on. Of course, any one of these characters may be shared with other species, but as a combined, inter-linked 'syndrome', or constellation, they are peculiar to us. These organic differences between humans and even our closest relatives are strongly suggestive of complex and relatively pacific sociality, symbolic coordination of activity by means of language, freeing of sexuality from narrowly reproductive functions, cooperation of the sexes in the nurturing of offspring, and so on as 'written into' our evolutionary ancestry. In other words, our distinctive pattern of organic attributes can be understood as acquired in the course of the evolution of a distinctively human social, cultural and psychological mode of life. It is hard to understand how, for example, the selective pressures leading to the combination of vocal organs and the appropriate adaptations of brain and nervous system necessary for language use could have arisen other than in the context of an already highly social ancestor population.

Whatever narrative is eventually constructed to account for the emergence of this distinctive constellation of attributes and capacities in the course of hominid evolution, there is little doubt that the outcome was not a species characterized by increasingly specialized adaptation to a particular ecological 'niche'. Instead, what evolved was a species with emergent powers enabling an unprecedented adaptability to any and every ecological niche – in the long-run, also one with an unprecedented capacity to collectively transform its own ecological conditions of existence. It is this latter capacity which exposes the limitations of reductionist, 'neo-Malthusian' approaches to environmental politics, with their assumption of fixed, ecologically determined limits to human population. The notion of a fixed 'economy of nature', providing 'niches' with limited 'carrying capacities' and to which populations become adapted through selective pressures is very much open to criticism as a way of thinking about the ecological relationships of other species, since they, too, alter their environments and also adapt to new ones. However, in the human case it is manifestly inappropriate. As Jonathan Kingdon puts it:

> Here for the first time, was an animal that was learning a multiplicity of roles via the invention of technology. An increasing number of animals now had a new competitor that would encroach on at least a part of their former niche. In some cases – perhaps some of the scavengers – the overlap may have been so great that the hominids took over.
>
> (Kingdon, quoted in Stringer and McKie 1997, p. 25)

Of course, 'technology' here should be understood in a very wide sense. The flexible adaptability acquired through symbolic coordination and emotional bonding of social groups, and the cumulative acquisition of environmental knowledge through learning and linguistic communication would have been highly significant independently of the manufacture of artefacts. From here on, the selective pressures would have favoured the flexibility-enhancing dependence on learning and social cooperation as against the 'hard-wiring' favoured by the evolutionary psychologists.

However, a species with unprecedented capacities for social and cultural learning and adaptation, capable of devising modes of engagement with its ecological conditions of life which vastly increase its geographical and ecological range does not thereby float off into ecological outer space, or entirely detach itself from its status as an 'active natural being'. Too much of the social scientific heritage proceeds as if this were the case. It remains a reasonable expectation that human individuals inherit some 'hard-wired' learning-dispositions, a complement of basic emotional capacities and needs, some emotional and psychological developmental rhythms to complement their organic ones, and, consequent on all this, social and environmental necessary conditions for their flourishing, and outer limits to their capacities for successful adaptation to their given social or physical conditions of life. Given the range of known human sociocultural forms past and present, it seems that the conditions under which humans may flourish are diverse, and the limits to their adaptive capacities are wide. *How* diverse and *how* wide are questions which are open to research, and sociocultural variations in patterns of health and ill-health are an obvious and important source of evidence. This is especially so if we conceptualize health in terms of a positive notion of personal and social fulfilment, rather than in terms of mere absence of pathology (though, of course not discounting the great importance of the latter).

But we can make interesting links across the divisions between life and human/social sciences also at the level of organized populations. An implication of the view of humans as 'active natural beings' is their necessary dependence on external material reality for their survival and well-being:

> *Man* is directly a *natural being*. As a natural being and as a living natural being he is on the one hand endowed with *natural powers, vital powers*. . . . On the other hand, as a natural, corporeal, sensuous objective being he is a *suffering*, conditioned and limited creature, like animals and plants. That is to say, the *objects* of his instincts exist outside him . . . yet these *objects* are objects that he *needs* – essential objects, indispensable to the manifestation and confirmation of his essential powers. . . . *Hunger* is a natural *need*; it therefore needs a *nature* outside itself, an *object* outside itself, in order to satisfy itself, to be stilled.
>
> (Marx, in Marx and Engels 1975: 336)

Again:

> Just as plants, animals, stones, air, light, etc. constitute theoretically a part of human consciousness, partly as objects of natural science, partly as objects of art – his spiritual inorganic nature, spiritual nourishment which he must first prepare and make palatable and digestible – so also in the realm of practice they constitute a part of human life and human activity. . . . Man *lives* on nature – means that nature is his *body*, with which he must remain in continuous interchange if he is not to die. That man's physical and spiritual life is linked to nature means simply that nature is linked to itself, for man is a part of nature.
>
> (Marx, in Marx and Engels 1975: 275–6)

Our dependence on continuous exchange with external nature is, on this view, a universal feature of the human condition, something necessary for the meeting of a range of needs which flow not merely from our status as an active natural being (e.g. hunger and food), but from our status as a social and cultural being: one who has need of nature as an object of curiosity and aesthetic meaning.

But the peculiarity of our evolved social and cultural character is that our exchanges with nature are conducted through historically and geographically variable forms of coordination, mediated by a variety of artefacts: weapons, tools, machines and so on, and variously shaped by practices of modification of both living organisms and ecosystems. I have found the historical materialist concept of 'modes of production' a helpful starting point for getting some conceptual grasp on this diversity of socially organized modes of appropriation of nature (see Benton 2000). However, in the work of Marx, the dynamics of human social interaction with natural forces and processes are relatively under-theorized by comparison with the emphasis on the dynamics of social division and conflict proper to each mode (recent Marx-scholarship disputes this: see Foster 2000). One outcome of rethinking these concepts in the light of contemporary ecological ideas is to theorize social relations not simply as relations between social actors, nor yet between human actors as occupants of social positions, but also as relations between human social actors and elements or aspects of nonhuman nature: physical objects and forces, artefacts, chemical substances, populations of cultivated, domesticated and wild varieties and species of nonhuman animals and plants, spatial envelopes, land and ecosystems, both modified and unmodified by past human social activity, and so on. Thinking like this is one way to dissolve the dualistic opposition between 'society' and 'nature' without giving in to either a social constructionist reduction of nature to culture, or the reverse reduction of social life to a mediated epiphenomenon of the human genome.

Such a perspective enables us to think about health and ill-health in terms of conditions of flourishing, or limits to adaptability offered or imposed by the complex web of interdependencies within which the individual and collective life of humans is located. The requirements of individual humans in virtue of their embodiment, their distinctive psychological endowments, developmental, emotional, social and cultural needs and capacities can be understood in relation to the variable conditions for their autonomous satisfaction supplied (or not) by a complexly structured environment – comprising intimate relationships, wider socioeconomic, political and cultural structures and material/ecological dimensions. For individuals, vulnerability to ill-health and opportunities for fulfilment will be determined by a complex interweaving of their own bodily constitution, including their genetic endowment, the socioecological relations characteristic of their society, and their own position within that society, as lived out through the life-course (see, for example, Hertzman *et al.* 2001 and chapters by Blaxter and by Bury and Wadsworth in this volume). This avoids the simplistic opposition of 'nature' versus 'nurture' in relation to health. It can readily be acknowledged that some diseases have a direct and deterministic relationship to genetic constitution, and that addressing such conditions through gene-therapy is entirely appropriate. There is also good reason to think that individuals are variably vulnerable to some conditions in virtue of their genetic constitution, but in more complex and mediated ways. So, for example, vulnerability to chronic lung disease through exposure to air pollution may well be very variable as between different individuals in ways which are gene-linked. Whether a society tackles the problem by way of gene-therapy, medical treatment of disease-sufferers, or reducing air pollution is not simply a scientific question, but a political one – settled ultimately by political struggles in whatever institutional structures are available. However, an appropriate knowledge-base from which policy alternatives could be developed will depend crucially upon research informed by sophisticated models of the interactions between gene-expression, developmental, emotional, life-course and socioecological processes and relations (see also Davey, this volume). Neither bio-tech reductionism nor the undifferentiated and unanalytical 'holism' of some exponents of 'alternative' health are equipped to sustain such research.

Using the above approach, we can re-visit some of the established social scientific work on the social distribution of health and ill-health. Class differences in morbidity and mortality, and statistical relationships between poverty and unemployment and ill-health are well-established. To move beyond statistical analysis towards theoretical explanation of such associations requires an effort of critical integration of ecological, bio-medical and socioeconomic knowledges. A pioneering study of this sort was Engels's *Condition of the Working Class in England*, which achieved a remarkable synthesis of socioeconomic and ecological class analysis, linking class divisions in working life with patterns of residential segregation, cleavages in food consumption, access to clean water, sanitary conditions, air pollution and associated health risks:

All putrefying vegetable and animal substances give off gases decidedly injurious to health, and if these gases have no free way of escape, they inevitably poison the atmosphere. The filth and stagnant pools of the working people's quarters in the great cities have, therefore, the worst effect on the public health, because they produce precisely those gases which engender disease; so, too, the exhalations from contaminated streams.

(Engels [1845] 1969: 128)

There is strong evidence that much of the increased longevity and greatly improved health status (though with persistent class inequality in health) of the populations of the industrial democracies since Engels wrote owes more to public health measures in the shape of sewage and water infrastructures, town planning and building regulations, health and safety at work, regulation of industrial emissions and discharges and imposition of food standards than to the development of medical technologies and health-care services (see McKeown 1979; Szreter 1995). However, neither of these historic achievements may be taken for granted. Conditions akin to those described by Engels remain widespread in Third World cities, and persist in some districts even in the richest countries of western Europe and the USA. At the same time, health-care systems are under increasing pressure, in part as a result of advances in medical technology themselves.

Meanwhile, new threats to health and well-being have emerged. Ulrich Beck's (1992) insightful analysis of a new order of high-consequence risks associated with new, large scale industrial technologies is relevant here. The nuclear and chemical industries, as well as the new bio-technologies, impose risks which are unprecedented, and thus unpredictable and in some cases uninsurable. They are potentially unlimited in their spatial and temporal scope and consequently indiscriminate in their social incidence in ways that earlier generations of industrial hazard were not. Whilst regulation may minimize the risk of things going wrong, risk cannot be entirely eliminated: the improbable can still happen, and, if it does, the effects are catastrophic (Bhopal, Chernobyl). However, what Beck's analysis fails to fully acknowledge is the extent to which health-threatening hazards and risks have to do not simply with new technologies but with the commercial dynamic governing the development and deployment of them, political policies and failures of governance. The case of BSE (Bovine Spongiform Encephalopathy) is instructive here: a high-consequence risk of exactly the sort identified by Beck, but not brought about by technological innovation. Subsequent analyses suggest the causal importance of a complex intertwining of a distinctive biological infective agent, new animal feeding regimes introduced to enhance profitability, narrow and reductive advisory science, a deregulatory political ideology, and elementary failures of monitoring and enforcement of safety standards at successive stages of food processing. Similarly, Beck's analysis, dispensing as it does with class as an analytical category, over-states the extent to which the new hazards are socially indiscriminate in their incidence: the environmental justice movement, a significant phenomenon in the USA, has brought to public attention the extent to which hazardous industrial facilities, exposure to toxic leakages from chemical dumps, contaminated soil and water and polluted air are all concentrated on socially disadvantaged districts, often associated with racial and ethnic discrimination (Faber 1998).

Less clearly connected to the hazards associated with particular industries are the health risks associated with large scale ecological transformations brought about by whole patterns of social and economic development. Most often recognized here are the global issues of climate change and ozone depletion. The former is already associated with extreme weather events, and seems set to further increase liability to flooding and storm damage in some areas, increase rates of desertification and disruption of patterns of food production elsewhere. Ozone depletion, often cited as an example of successful international environmental action, continues to cause concern and is already responsible for large increases in skin cancer rates. So far, public health improvements in the industrialized democracies associated with higher standards of environmental regulation have been won by social movement pressure on national governments. Often, however, these achievements have been won at the cost of off-loading environmentally damaging activities onto poorer and less regulated societies: re-location of polluting industrial processes, toxic-waste dumping, ecologically damaging mineral ore and fossil fuel extraction and logging operations are well-known examples. Whilst neo-liberal trading and investment regimes have made this possible, they may also undermine the capacity of rich-nation governments to sustain existing regulatory standards in the face of market pressures. This, together with other 'boomerang' effects in the shape of increased pressures for asylum, economic migration, political instability and international terrorism suggest that the optimistic project of 'ecological modernization' may not be generalizable beyond a small number of industrialized democracies, and may, indeed, soon unravel even here.

As well as a new swathe of material industrial hazards, we should not neglect a growing body of evidence of the emotional and psychological costs of new class relations and occupational divisions (see, for example, Wilkinson 1996; and Blaxter this volume). In the UK both employers' and trade union organizations have produced disturbing evidence of bullying and stress at work. It seems likely that much of this has to do with increased international competitive pressures on productivity and performance, with the associated individualization of working conditions, loss of job security and weakening of trade union power. Another dimension is the growth of service occupations in which workers are required not simply to expend physical effort, but to subject their forms of emotional expression and personal styles of social interaction to the commercial demands of the job – a dimension of alienation more radically subversive of the human self than even Marx envisaged (a pioneering sociological analysis of this was Hochschild's (1983) study of airline cabin crew). There is a growing body of evidence of the extent to which long-term stress and anxiety connected to powerlessness and vulnerability at work is a causal factor in the epidemic illnesses of the industrialized countries: heart disease and cancer. More directly, however, the massive extent of dependency on drug therapies for depression and anxiety is an unmistakable symptom of the scale of psychological suffering induced by the newer forms of social and economic life (see, for example, DeGrandpre 2002; and Crossley, this volume).

Viewed in this light, current concerns about escalating demand and funding crises in the health care system can be put in context. A massively powerful pharmaceutical/biomedical complex increasingly shapes public discourse and policy-making, favouring a profitable 'technological fix' policy agenda (see DeGrandpre 2002; Martorell 2002). Deep-rooted ecological and socioeconomic processes at work in generating new orders of ill-health and human distress remain unaddressed, whilst highly profitable but often ineffective palliatives place increasingly unsustainable burdens on the social provision of health-care. The clear threat is that radical inequalities in vulnerability to the causes of ill-health will be compounded by new inequalities in access to increasingly privatized health-care. A new politics of health was never more urgently needed, one which advocates deep-level transformations in our living and working environments and the power relations implicated in them, alongside, and integrated with, an accessible, fully socialized and accountable health-care system.

References

Beck, U. (1992) *Risk Society*, London: Sage.

Beck, U. (1995) *Ecological Politics in an Age of Risk*, Cambridge: Polity.

Benton, T. (1991) 'Biology and social science: why the return of the repressed should be given a (cautious) welcome', *Sociology*, 25: 1–29.

Benton, T. (1999) 'Evolutionary psychology and social science: a new paradigm or just the same old reductionism?', *Advances in Human Ecology*, 8: 65–98.

Benton, T. (2000) 'An ecological historical materialism', in F.P. Gale and R.M. M'Gonigle (eds) *Nature, Production, Power*, Cheltenham and Massachusetts: Edward Elgar, pp. 83–104.

Birke, L. (1986) *Women, Feminism and Biology*, Brighton: Harvester Wheatsheaf.

Catton, W.R. and Dunlap, R.E. (1978) 'Environmental sociology: a new paradigm', *The American Sociologist*, 13: 41–9.

Catton, W.R. and Dunlap, R.E. (1980) 'A new ecological paradigm for post-exuberant sociology', *American Behavioural Scientist*, 24: 15–47.

DeGrandpre, R. (2002) 'Constructing the pharmacological: a century in review', *Capitalism, Nature, Socialism*, 13, 1: 75–104.

Eldredge, N. (1995) *Reinventing Darwin: The Great Evolutionary Debate*, London: Orion.

Engels, F. [1845] (1969) *The Condition of the Working Class in England*, London: Panther.

Eyerman, R. and Jamison, A. (1991) *Social Movements: A Cognitive Approach*, Cambridge: Polity.

Faber, D. (ed.) (1998) *The Struggle for Ecological Democracy: Environmental Justice Movements in the United States*, New York: Guilford.

Foster, J.B. (2000) *Marx's Ecology*, New York: Monthly Review.

Giddens, A. (1994) *Beyond Left and Right*, Cambridge: Polity.

Goodwin, B. (1994) *How the Leopard Changed its Spots*, London: Weidenfeld & Nicolson.

Gould, S.J. (1990) *Wonderful Life*, London: Hutchinson Radius.

Hartsock, N. (1983) *Money, Sex and Power: Towards a Feminist Historical Materialism*, London: Longman.

Hertzman, C., Power, C., Matthews, S. and Manor, O. (2001) 'Using and interactive framework of society and lifecourse to explain self-rated health in early adulthood', *Social Science and Medicine*, 53, 12: 1575–85.

Hochschild, A. (1983) *The Managed Heart: Commercialization of Human Feeling*, Berkeley, CA: University of California.

McKeown, T. (1979) *The Role of Medicine*, Oxford: Blackwell.

Martorell, J. (2002) 'How drug companies subordinate human life to profit', *Capitalism, Nature, Socialism*, 13, 1: 105–13.

Marx, K. and Engels, F. (1975) *Collected Works*, Vol. 3, London: Lawrence & Wishart.

Pinker, S. (1997) *How the Mind Works*, Harmondsworth: Allen Lane/Penguin.

Rose, H. (1983) 'Hand, brain and heart: a feminist epistemology for the natural sciences', *Signs*, 9, 1: 73–90.

Rose, S. and Rose, H. (eds) (2000) *Alas, Poor Darwin*, London and New York: Harmony, Jonathan Cape.

Stringer, C. and McKie, R. (1997) *African Exodus: The Origin of Modern Humanity*, London: Random House.

Szreter, S. (1995) 'The importance of social intervention in Britain's mortality decline, c. 1850–1914: a reinterpretation of the role of public health', in B. Davey, A. Gray and C. Seale (eds) *Health and Disease: A Reader*, Buckingham: Open University.

Wilkinson, R.G. (1996) *Unhealthy Societies: the Afflictions of Inequality*, London: Routledge.

23 A metaphysics for alternative medicine

'Translating' the social and biological worlds

Anne Scott

Introduction

The split between naturalistic and social conceptualizations of the body has long proved problematic in health practice. The problem seems to be that the body sits within a crossroads – a 'borderland':

> A border is a dividing line, a narrow strip along a steep edge. A border-land is a vague and undetermined place created by the emotional residue of an unnatural boundary. It is in a constant state of transition. The prohibited and forbidden are its inhabitants.
>
> (Anzaldúa 1987: 3)

The living body sits along the line drawn by western culture to divide agent and object, to separate knowing subject from naturalized mechanism. The problem faced by biology is that it must deal with entities which are simultaneously natural and social; they are suffused with intentionality and desire, yet subject to natural causation. As Latour argues, modernity arose with the simultaneous birth of humanity, of a 'crossed out God', and of non-humanity – of things, objects, beasts and bodies (1993: 13). While conjoined at birth and throughout their development, these three types of entity have been treated in the modern era as separate and as entirely separable. The human body, somewhat paradoxically, is generally treated within biomedicine as 'non-humanity' – as a thing. The problems which result are all too familiar to sociologists of health and illness; biomedical discourse has difficulty in adequately conceptualising emotion, pain, reproductive health, risk and many other phenomena.

Linda Birke argues convincingly, in this volume and her previous work (1999), that belief in the body's fixity generates both biological and sociological reductionisms. The regulated body of physiology undergirds accounts of willed, human agency. Equally, it sits as a backdrop to the malleable body-surfaces of post-structuralist theory. At the level of health practice, belief in the body-as-object has generated a dualism between biomedical treatment of individual bodies and attention to the social, cultural, psychological and spiritual life-worlds these bodies inhabit. This dualistic separation of 'natural' and 'cultural' has been challenged within the new social movements of the past thirty years. Alternative, 'holistic', therapies developed in popularity as members of the health and women's movements struggled to produce practical theories of the body which could cut across dualistic boundaries.

A critique of dualism is central to discourses of alternative medicine.[1] Within diverse therapies, an avowed holism plays a prominent role. Although alternative therapies differ dramatically in the way they interpret 'holism', a common theme exists in their varied attempts to integrate emotion, life history, spirituality, and/or environmental influences into the diagnosis and treatment of physical ailments (Power 1991). It is rare, however, for alternative therapies to succeed in integrating all of the above. Richard Grossinger argues, in fact, the impossibility of *any* one therapy doing this. Noting that the human organism is a fragmented entity, he argues it must be treated '. . . level by level, persona by persona' (1990: xxvi). Surgery and drugs work at one level, chiropractic works at another, and Bach flowers at still another level. In practice, many alternative therapies give diagnostic primacy to emotional, mental and spiritual considerations. The challenge for alternative medicine, then, is to find practical ways to work with a body understood simultaneously as material and sociocultural.

Despite statements of adherence to holism, this is no easy task. Reductionism and dualism re-emerge, in various guises, within alternative medicine. Some therapies, (e.g. Ayurvedic medicine, rebirthing, some TCM practices) aim to develop patients' mental/spiritual mastery of their body and emotions. Termed 'cybernetic holism' by Morris Berman (1990), they reinstate a dualistic division between form and matter. These practices may prioritize the pure form of the 'subtle body' over the patient's life-world (Scott 1999). Moreover, some therapies rely on practitioners to symbolically interpret patients' symptoms. This produces epistemological dualisms as thoroughgoing as any found within biomedicine (Scott 1998). Thus, there are a variety of ways of failing to sustain a 'holistic' therapeutic practice.

Nevertheless, the diverse alternative therapies may be taken as a wide-ranging set of experiments for refiguring the terms of our embodiment. With long histories, the more traditional therapies can ground empirically tested, alternative, understandings of the relationship between agency and object, vis-à-vis the body. In this chapter, I will explore some ways in which nonreductionist ontologies are being modelled within the world of alternative medicine. Conceptualizing these therapies as communication technologies brings surprising connections to bioscience to the fore. Suggesting that Bruno Latour's concept of 'translation' may be a key trope for understanding the body/society relationship within alternative medicine, I will argue that homoeopaths are working towards a model which can avoid the pitfalls of both reductionism and dualism.

The informational paradigm in biology

Practitioners of alternative medicine often define themselves in opposition to the mechanical model, as practiced within biomedicine. These therapies, however, have much in common with a second, less obvious, biomedical model. Donna Haraway (1991; 1999) describes emerging biological practices as communications engineering. In the last forty years, biologists have increasingly turned the focus of their attention from organisms to systems – while medical discourse has devoted increasing attention to the network pathologies which lead to immune diseases, hormonal disruptions and stress-related disorders. Emily Martin notes that, in modern immunology, the body is conceptualized as a communications network, 'a whole, interconnected system complete unto itself' (1992: 123). Suggesting that the biomedical body is now a complex, meaning-producing, semiotic system, Donna Haraway argues that any account of the biomedical body 'must start from the multiple molecular interfacings of genetic, nervous, endocrine and immune systems' (1999: 211). She argues that stress – defined as communications breakdown between and within systems – is the privileged disorder of our era (1991: 163).

'At the origin of things', Haraway argues, 'life is constituted and connected by recursive, repeating streams of information' (1997: 134). Many emerging biological sciences – of which molecular biology and immunology are two of the more prominent – now conceptualize their objects of study as networks, in relation to information flows. Developing the capacity to translate biological processes into forms of code which can be digitalized, manipulated, engineered and commodified has been key to a new phase in the enculturation of life. To use Haraway's phrase, life has been 'enterprised up' (1997: 12). While this approach abandons the crude mechanical metaphor of older biomedical models, it sits rather comfortably with the new reductionisms of genetic engineering and biotechnology. It also has parallels with the 'cybernetic holisms' found within some forms of alternative medicine. The information metaphor can certainly work reductionistically, but I would like to suggest it may also generate new, non-reductionistic, ways to conceptualize the body.

These new tropes for conceptualizing 'nature' find a comfortable home within the models of reality opened up by actor network theory (ANT). Bruno Latour has argued that the nature/society divide is an ideological construct, energetically maintained in the face of strong evidence that our world is actually composed of networks encompassing both humans and nonhumans. The idea of networks, he says, is: 'more supple than the notion of system, more historical than the notion of structure, more empirical than the notion of complexity' (Latour 1993: 3). ANT action is a property of associated entities which form 'hybrids', or networks, with distributed agency (Latour 1999).

If organisms are natural objects, it is crucial to remember that organisms are not born; they are made in world-changing technoscientific practices by particular collective actors in particular times and places. . . . The actors are not all 'us'. If the world exists for us as 'nature', this designates a kind of relationship, an achievement among many actors, not all of them human, not all of them organic, not all of them technological. In its scientific embodiments, as well as in other forms, nature is made, but not entirely by humans; it is a co-construction among humans and non-humans.

(Haraway 1992: 297)

Translation is a key concept within actor network theory. As a new actor or actant is enrolled into a network, its original goals may be displaced; its nature may be modified. There may also be a modification in the goals or functions of the newly associated entity. Translation involves the creation of a link that did not exist before, and this modifies all the partners to the new connection (Latour 1999: 179). Translation is thus inescapably historical in nature. It involves 'social' relations between network actants; it is not restricted to individual, human actors.[2]

Rather than struggling to conceptualize biology as sociocultural, or to explain the social basis of biological traits, biocultural entities such as the human body can become exemplars of the world's organization as networks. Human bodies are rooted in history and immersed in social relations – they are ever-engaged in internal and external communication. It seems that there is a great deal of common ground here with new frameworks being developed by the theorists of alternative medicine.

Alternative medical therapies as communication technologies

While alternative medicine may seem, on the face of things, to be enormously different from bioscience, notions of information and translation are often employed in ways which are rather similar. Some theorists (Manning and Vanrenen 1988; Grossinger 1990) have begun using the term 'bioenergetic therapies' in reference to certain alternative medical practices (e.g. shiatsu, bodywork, Ayurvedic medicine, homoeopathy and acupuncture). These therapies work with 'energy' flows within the organism. Within bioenergetic therapies, the term 'energy' does not refer to the biochemical energy generated by mitochondria, but to something more akin to an information flow. The terms 'qi' in traditional Chinese medicine, 'vital force' in homoeopathy, and 'prana' in Ayurvedic medicine all connote an 'intelligent' energy which translates information between different systems within the body, providing a 'subtle' framework for the organization of physical, mental and life-world systems. As in ANT, translation involves more than communication between diverse systems; it also involves the creation and maintenance of enduring connections between them. In the process, each system is modified, and a cohesive, organized, healthy body is the result. As one homoeopath put it:

> I see the remedy as being a spiritual instrument. Because it's entirely an energy. The way I can imagine it is the remedy is the energetic representation of the whole, and we are . . . a distorted piece of that whole. The energetic power of the remedy is drawing us toward our wholeness, if you like.
>
> (Homoeopath A: 1994)[3]

Parallels between vital energy and coded information can be drawn in very concrete terms. Alluding to Jacque Benveniste's claim that information may be imprinted on water in the process of homoeopathic remedy preparation,[4] Peter Fisher, the director of research at the Royal London Homoeopathic Hospital, argued:

> If you take homoeopathic medicine to be analysed, a pharmacologist would say it's water and ethanol and sugar, and that's true. But if you take a floppy disc to a chemist he will say it is ferric oxide and vinyl. The information is stored in physical form.
>
> (Seymour 2001: 48)

Deepak Chopra, an Ayurvedic practitioner, argues that endocrinological accounts of neuro-peptide movements, the concept of 'prana', and the movement of consciousness describe different aspects of the same process; the intelligent body organizes itself through the creation of chemical patterns. 'It is these patterns that jump in and out of existence', he argues, 'paralleling what happened in Benveniste's test tubes' (1989: 130).

If we define 'technologies' as 'human-made artefacts or processes which, within particular social contexts, are expected to enhance human capabilities', it seems that many alternative medical therapies can be seen as communications technologies. They translate information in a variety of ways. Some, such as acupuncture and homoeopathy, facilitate the movement of 'vital energy' between different levels, or systems, within the patient's body. Others use the intersubjective space shared by practitioner and patient to facilitate movement of bodily knowledge into consciousness. Helle Johannessen, for example, describes the muscle test within kinesiology as a way of both creating dialogue between the practitioner and patient's bodymind, and as an interview guide for exploring psychological, social and environmental issues in the life of the patient (Johannessen 1996: 123). Lucy Goodison (1992) uses intuitive massage therapy to establish dialogue with patients' bodies, which she sees as communicative agents using pain or disablement to express psychosocial conflict. Images and symbols evoked within the massage become foci for more traditional forms of psychotherapy.

Thomas Csordas has described the alternative therapies as 'somatic modes of attention' – culturally elaborated ways of attending, both to and with the body, within a socially constituted environment (Csordas 1993: 138). They are means, in other words, of facilitating the translation of bodily information across different domains and levels of being. After having noted that different therapies work at varying levels within organisms, Richard Grossinger goes on to argue:

> Because these levels are actually interpenetrating fields – oscillating flows of biomorphic and psychic 'energy' – medicines and meanings introduced into one will be transmitted to all. That is the optimism and legitimate promise of holism. However, a medicine will be directly curative only in the level at which it is introduced. What it translates to other levels may be curative insofar as those levels shift within mind–body awareness and cry out for their own treatments.
>
> (Grossinger 1990: xxvi)

Grossinger's allusion to 'translation' points towards problems of communication across different systems which have also been, as noted above, a central theme in the emerging biosciences. It also points to a second issue, which I alluded to in my earlier discussion of the problems raised by cybernetic holism. How can we sustain, within an informational model, the integrity of each organism and, indeed, of each level of activity within an organism?

'Translating' the social and biological worlds

In both the new biosciences and alternative medicine, the need to find a means of translation across different domains of being – of communication across difference – has emerged as a central problem. Biology has become a kind of cryptography, in which solutions to key problems rest on theories of language and control (Haraway 1991: 164–5). The world is subdivided into boundaries which are differentially permeable to information, while information takes different forms within different systems. The achievement of 'universal translation', Haraway argues, is thus seen as crucial to 'unhindered instrumental power' (1991: 164).

> [C]ommunications sciences and modern biologies are constructed by a common move – *the translation of the world into a problem of coding,* a search for a common language in which all resistance to instrumental control disappears and all heterogeneity can be submitted to disassembly, reassembly, investment and exchange.
>
> (1991: 164)

This quest for a means of perfect translation is directed towards the achievement of unity through the incorporation of difference. This is, in very essence, a reductionistic project. As Lynda Birke has argued, 'Denying or downplaying the integrity of the organism – as the genetic/information model does – permits us literally to dismember it' (1999: 146). There are high stakes attached to these politics of bodily meaning. The effective control of matter by disembodied flows of information depends on transparent communication between different systems. The search for uncomplicated unity, it would seem, cannot be confined to the more naïve discourses of 'holistic' medicine.

By drawing on Haraway's figure of the cyborg, however, a less reductionistic process of translation may become possible. Cyborgs exist by linking different systems and entities into a cohesive, functioning whole (1991). They thus depend on communication – on the translation of information across deeply different systems (1991: 176). The cyborg's existence, however, is equally dependent on sustaining its differences; one aspect of its being *cannot* – indeed, *must not* – be subsumed into another. 'Cyborg politics' Haraway argues, 'is the struggle for language and the struggle against perfect communication' (1991: 176). The challenge is to facilitate communication between systems, while maintaining the integrity and identity of each individual organism, each biological subsystem and each natural system. Nature is – and *should* be – a high tension zone.

A rejection of reductionism is, of course, core to 'holistic' medicine's critique of biomedicine. Yet, as noted above, reductionism can also be found within alternative medical practices. Some therapies work with a series of levels of increasing 'subtlety'; physical and emotional phenomena are considered to be derivative of the non-material levels.

> I think that spirituality has been hijacked, in a way. It's been hijacked by religions, and turned into some kind of control number. It's been hijacked by the New Age movement as well.
>
> (Homoeopath 'B': 1994)

Less reductionistic ways to translate across difference are needed – means of creating associations between different substances, systems and processes without reducing one partner to a sub-system, in relation to another.

Some homoeopathic practitioners are exploring new ways to conceptualize the activity of the vital force without subsuming matter to form. These approaches tend to draw on complex networks of identity and difference, in which grounded metaphor can facilitate a stating of 'imagined connections' with empirically demonstrable healing effects.[5]

> I've always had a real love for nature. And I think that's where homoeopathy connects up again. I just find it so amazing. . . . That you take something from the world, be it from the animal kingdom, the mineral world, whatever. Say, gold. As a substance, gold is fairly inert. And you potentise it in a homoeopathic remedy, and it has this *whole*

different energy. But you can still see the connection between that energy and the substance gold. And then somebody comes along, who is *that*. And giving them a little bit of that allows them to move on, or for their auras to resolve.... It's just that incredible connection between all things. It really gives you an amazing sense of your place within it all.

(Homoeopath C: 1994)

In this homoeopath's statement: 'somebody comes along, who is *that*', identification turns on a form of natural metaphor. In clinical terms, the patient *is* the gold, while also remaining fully herself. The materiality of the world has not been transcended, and there is no attempt at cybernetic control. Instead, a translation between the properties of gold, and this patient's symptoms, creates a new set of links. The gold, the remedy Aurum Metallicum, the practitioner and the patient are enrolled into a healing network which has some similarities with the healing networks discussed within ANT, but which emphasizes the symbolic level.

Remedy networks may extend beyond a single patient to encompass other remedies, natural substances, and social or environmental histories. Homoeopathic practice[6] is based on the belief that each of the 2,000 to 3,000 remedies within the homoeopathic materia medica is associated with a set of physical symptoms and ailments. It has characteristic emotional states, dream images, food preferences, climatic responses and belief structures. It belongs to a remedy 'family', with positive and negative relationships with other remedies. It is associated with a keynote – or a 'way of being' in the world. It is, in itself, a material substance of some sort, and these substances play their own part in the natural and social world. Ursula Sharma argues, in fact, that one cannot speak of 'the body' within homoeopathic practice at all – there are as many bodies as there are 'remedy pictures' (Sharma 1995).

This complexity provides a rich space for 'translations' of biological, emotional, environmental and social phenomena. For example, Melissa Assilem published an analysis of the remedy Thea which explored the symptoms it created within provings (tests) on healthy people. These ranged from 'dryness and swelling of mucous membrane' (1994: 27) to dreams involving the murder of children (1994: 21). She connected these, and other, disparate conditions by retelling the story of the Mad Hatter's (everyday) tea party. Drawing links between the cultural ritual of the tea party, the biochemical action of tannic acid, the focus on purity and hygiene which characterised a particular episode in the history of western feminism, the colonial and industrial structuring of plantation-based tea agriculture, the dreams and images which emerged in provings of the remedy, and the throat and mouth ailments treated by Thea, Assislem concluded that this remedy's keynote relates to the 'civilized' repression of sexuality and creativity in modern western culture – to its killing of the inner child (Assilem 1994). Not only are many aspects of our bodied and social worlds interrelated within this account, but they are interrelated within a 'storied' ontology of nature (Haraway 1997).

Rajan Sankaran takes the concept of the remedy network one step further, with his concept of a 'situational materia medica' (1994). He argues that each remedy picture represents the best possible response to some set of social or environmental circumstances. A closer look at a single homoeopathic remedy – staphysagria – may clarify this idea. Although associated with tumours and other major illnesses, staphysagria is more commonly associated with minor complaints; its primary physical symptom is extreme sensitivity and touchiness. Every small wound or injury stings or smarts, particularly if it is touched. The remedy is also associated with a numb and heavy feeling in the head, with a tickling cough, with colicky, cramping stomach pains, with diarrhoea, cystitis and sharp genital pains, and with a trembling, nervous exhaustion. It has a number of emotional symptoms, including irritability, forgetfulness, and an extreme sensitivity to reprimand. This wide range of symptoms is connected by staphysagria's keynote – suppressed anger or indignation.

People in a staphysagria state cannot allow themselves to lose their self-control. They do not respond outwardly to insults, abuse or other humiliations. They feel violated, and feel angry about this violation, but do not express their indignation directly. Their feelings of anger and indignation find physical expression instead – in extreme touchiness, cramping stomach pains, nervous exhaustion, sensitivity to reprimand, and the other symptoms associated with the remedy. They also find occasional expression in, seemingly unprovoked, violent outbursts. Castro tells us that the staphysagria patient is both apathetic and capricious (1990: 154).

Classically, staphysagria has been firmly associated with men of high social status. Kent (1988), the nineteenth-century homoeopath who produced the standard account of the remedy, tells the story of a gentleman who gets into an altercation with one beneath him in social station. He is insulted, but feels that losing self-control would be beneath his dignity. So he goes home, broods over the incident, and enters a staphysagria state. Sankaran tells a similar story and, furthermore, speculates that the remedy picture would fit Mahatma Gandhi (1994: 233).

Contemporary feminist practitioners, however, have noted that this feeling of suppressed anger may be generated within situations of abuse or humiliation suffered in ongoing relationships. In order to survive, the victim suppresses his/her feelings of anger and indignation, maintaining perfect self-control. In her short account of the remedy, Miranda Castro notes that staphysagria is indicated for children who are being bullied, or for adults who have suffered at the hands of 'an angry boss or spouse, or are in any situation where they feel violated while seething inside' (1990: 154). Castro's account describes the physical and emotional feelings, and the personality structure, which can be generated by the experience of domestic violence or other ongoing forms of harassment.

Elizabeth Spelman (1992) argues that anger is a very political emotion. While subordinate groups are traditionally expected to be emotional, their anger is not tolerated. The expression of anger by members of subordinate groups is often actively and violently suppressed. To openly direct anger at one's oppressor is to risk provoking dangerous retaliation. Staphysagria can thus be seen as a remedy which describes aspects of the experience of oppression. It represents the body/mind posture adopted by a person whose survival depends on the maintenance of perfect self-control in the face of continued violation and humiliation.

Since homoeopaths believe that remedies which represent a particular posture can, when used in treatment, enable a patient to break out of that posture, treatment with staphysagria has political implications; some feminist homoeopaths have claimed that this remedy can bring a patient to openly express her anger and to challenge her oppression. Several of my participants mentioned using staphysagria in the treatment of women who had been involved in abusive relationships.

> When people come to me who've experienced abuse, or unhappy relationships, they often make excuses for their abusive partners. Then after the remedy, they stand up to their partner and deal with the situation. What a change! They suddenly have the gumption to tell someone off, and say 'Look, I've had enough of this. I don't want any more of this.' That's something that very much happens with staphysagria.
>
> (Homoeopath D: 1994)

A homoeopath who had been deeply involved in Women's Aid regretted that the women's refuge at which she had worked had not been able to do more to help women move on, emotionally, in their lives. 'Wouldn't it be great,' she joked, 'if we could just put staphysagria in the water supply?' (Homoeopath B: 1994).

With the remedy reinterpreted in this way, it seems that the non-feminist homoeopaths have missed the situation where staphysagria is *most* applicable. In both discourse and in clinical practice, feminist homoeopaths have enrolled staphysagria into a network which encompasses new family forms, socio-political action against domestic violence, and new discourses relating to sexual abuse. In doing so, they have modified its 'nature', thus extending the processes of translation and enrolment from the clinical action of the remedy to the construction of the remedy picture itself. If 'nature' is indeed a co-construction between humans and nonhumans (Haraway 1992; Latour 1999), remedy actions *should* change as the historical processes of translation and enrolment create new connections and modify old ones. The feminist reconceptualization of staphysagria may thus be understood as translating a material resource, enrolling it for use by people living in oppressive relationships.

Conclusion

In this chapter I started with the problem of reductionism. How can we develop a medical practice which is appropriate to the complex interrelationships between our biological and social worlds? How can we develop a medicine for the borderlands in which the human body sits – that place where clear divisions between agent and object cannot be sustained? How can we develop a way of 'doing health' that acknowledges shared space, connections, and information flow, while sustaining the integrity of each individual organism? Emerging from feminism and the politics of health, some practitioners of homoeopathy and other alternative medical practices are taking up this challenge. Conceptualizing the body as whole in itself, as a network of systems and personae, and simultaneously as one node within wider networks linking the social, physical, cultural and environmental worlds, they are practising a 'cyborg' medicine. The ANT concept of 'translation' describes a crucial aspect of this approach. Communication across differing systems and domains creates enduring associations between them.

This concept of translation can be put to work within a paradigm of cybernetic control, with information flows intended to bring about universal translation between systems and thus effectively to control 'subordinate' material systems. Practices of cybernetic control can be found within both biomedical *and* alternative medical practices. An alternative paradigm starts with the trope of the cyborg. The challenge here is to achieve partial, rather than perfect, translation. Networks of identity and difference can then be created – associations rather than unities. As Richard Grossinger argues (1990), the promise of 'holism' can be fulfilled with recognition that therapies should be curative *only* for the systems and levels at which they have been introduced. Further healing will then depend on a translation between levels and systems, on enrolments and modifications – creating resources which will work appropriately for those systems. In short, medical agency is distributed around bodily and biocultural networks, and this is as it should be. Within the model of homoeopathy as partial translation, remedies are conceptualized as acting through the development of associations with the actants in bodily/social networks:

> They open a door. Or they can just turn you that way, because you're always looking this way. They do that, but it's up to you to take the next step . . . it's up to the person to actually walk that road.
>
> (Homoeopath E: 1994)

Notes

1 A sector including practices as diverse as TCM, voodoo, yoga, iridology, biofeedback, osteopathy, herbalism, faith healing, and massage. I have used the

term 'alternative medicine' within this chapter, instead of the more commonly used 'complementary medicine', to emphasize the fact that many of these therapies define their 'holistic' approach as *alternative* to biomedical ontology.

2 Great debate accompanies ANT's controversial claim that a symmetrical relationship, particularly as regards intentionality and agency, can be maintained between different kind of entities – such as self-reflective humans and microbes, or tools – within networks.

3 Homoeopath quotes come from research carried out with feminist homoeopaths working in the North of England during 1994 and 1995. My thanks to the participants for their contributions.

4 Benveniste was head of a scientific team in Paris testing the homoeopathic claim that intense dilution of biological reagents, combined with sucession (vigorous shaking), produces remedies with potent healing action. His team found that, even when diluted beyond the levels at which a single molecule of the original substance might remain, anti-IgE effectively catalysed antibody reactions. They suggested this might be due to the 'imprinting' of information on the molecular structure of the water during sucession. *Nature* published the article, but also organized an investigation; the investigatory team included James Randi, a fraud-busting magician. *Nature*'s team repudiated Benveniste's experiments as 'delusion', and his hypothesis that water can be imprinted with information as 'fanciful' (Maddox *et al.* 1988). This unprecedented treatment of a peer-reviewed author generated intense controversy.

5 There has long been strong anecdotal evidence for the clinical effectiveness of homoeopathy. More recently, clinical trials using biomedical protocols have produced some, albeit strongly contested, positive results beyond placebo. See Linde, *et al.* (1997) and Kleijnen, *et al.* (1991).

6 Homoeopathy works on the principle that 'like treats like'. Substances which have instigated a particular set of physical, mental and emotional symptoms in 'provings' on healthy people are used to treat unhealthy people exhibiting similar characteristics.

References

Anzaldúa, G. (1987) *Borderlands/La Frontera: The New Mestiza*, San Francisco: Aunt Lute Books.

Assilem, M. (1994) *The Mad Hatter's Tea Party*, Tunbridge Wells: Helios Homoeopathic Pharmacy.

Berman, M. (1990) 'The cybernetic dream of the 21st century', in J. Clark (ed.) *Renewing the Earth*, London: Greenprint.

Birke, L. (1999) *Feminism and the Biological Body*, Edinburgh: Edinburgh University Press.

Castro, M. (1990) *The Complete Homoeopathy Handbook: A Guide to Everyday Health Care*, London: Macmillan.

Chopra, D. (1989) *Quantum Healing: Exploring the Frontiers of Mind/Body Medicine*, New York: Bantam.

Csordas, T. (1993) 'Somatic modes of attention', *Cultural Anthropology*, 8, 2: 135–56.

Goodison, L. (1992) *Moving Heaven and Earth: Sexuality, Spirituality and Social Change*, London: Pandora.

Grossinger, R. (1990) *Planet Medicine: From Stone Age Shamanism to Post-Industrial Healing*, 5th edition, Berkeley: North Atlantic Books.

Haraway, D. (1991) 'A cyborg manifesto: science, technology and socialist-feminism in the late twentieth century' (1985), reprinted in D. Haraway, *Simians, Cyborgs, and Women: The Reinvention of Nature*, London: Free Association Books.

Haraway, D. (1992) 'The promises of monsters: a regenerative politics for inappropriate/d others', in L. Grossberg, C. Nelson and P. Treichler (eds) *Cultural Studies*, London: Routledge.

Haraway, D. (1997) *Modest_Witness@Second_Millenium. FemaleMan©_Meets_ OncoMouse™*, London: Routledge.

Haraway, D. (1999) 'The biopolitics of postmodern bodies: determinations of self in immune system discourse', in Janet Price and Margrit Shildrick (eds) *Feminist Theory and the Body: A Reader*, Edinburgh: Edinburgh University Press.

Johannessen, H. (1996) 'Individualized knowledge: reflexologists, biopaths and kinesiologists in Denmark', in S. Cant and U. Sharma (eds), *Complementary and Alternative Medicines: Knowledge in Practice*, London: Free Association.

Kent, J.T. (1988) *Lectures on Homoeopathic Materia Medica* (1905), New Delhi: B. Jain Publishers.

Kleijnen, J., Knipschild, P. and ter Riet, P. (1991) 'Clinical trials of homoeopathy', *British Medical Journal*, **302**, 6772: 316–23.

Latour, B. (1993) *We Have Never Been Modern*, Cambridge: Harvard University Press.

Latour, B. (1999) *Pandora's Hope: Essays on the Reality of Science Studies*, Cambridge: Harvard University Press.

Linde, K., Clausius, N., Ramirez, G. and Melchart, D. (1997) 'Are the clinical effects of homeopathy placebo effects? A meta-analysis of placebo-controlled trials', *Lancet*, **350**, 9081: 834–43.

Maddox, J., Randi, J. and Stewart, W. (1988) '"High-dilution" experiments a delusion', *Nature*, **334**, 6180: 287–90.

Manning, C. and Vanrenen, C. (1988) *Bioenergetic Medicines East and West: Acupuncture and Homeopathy*, Berkeley: North Atlantic.

Martin, E. (1992) 'The end of the body?', *American Ethnologist*, **19**, 1: 121–40.

Power, R. (1991) 'Ideologies of holism in health care', *Complementary Medical Research*, **5**, 3: 151–9.

Sankaran, R. (1994) *The Substance of Homoeopathy*, Bombay: Homoeopathic Medical Publishers.

Scott, A. (1998) 'Homoeopathy as a feminist form of medicine', *Sociology of Health and Illness*, **20**, 2: 191–214.

Scott, A. (1999) 'Paradoxes of holism: some problems in developing an anti-oppressive medical practice', *Health*, **3**, 2: 121–49.

Seymour, J. (2001) 'As if by magic', *New Scientist* 292: 46–8.

Sharma, U. (1995) 'The homoeopathic body: "reification" and the homoeopathic "gaze"', in H. Johannessen, S. Gosvig Olesen and J. Østergård Anderson (eds) *Studies in Alternative Therapy 2: Body and Nature*, Odense: Odense University Press.

Spelman, E. (1992) 'Anger and insubordination', in A. Garry and M. Pearsall (eds) *Women, Knowledge and Reason: Explorations in Feminist Philosophy*, London: Routledge.

Index